A

A HISTORICAL COMMENTARY
ON ST. PAUL'S EPISTLE
TO THE GALATIANS

by
Wm. M. Ramsay

BAKER BOOK HOUSE
Grand Rapids, Michigan

Reprinted 1979 by
Baker Book House Company
from the 1900 edition published by
G. P. Putnam's Sons, New York

ISBN: 0-8010-7680-3

This volume is part of the ten-volume
William M. Ramsay Library
ISBN: 0-8010-7685-4

PHOTOLITHOPRINTED BY CUSHING - MALLOY, INC.
ANN ARBOR, MICHIGAN, UNITED STATES OF AMERICA
1 9 7 9

PREFACE.

THE attempt is made in this book to show how much light the Epistle to the Galatians throws on contemporary history in the widest sense—the history of religion, society, thought, manners, education—in the Eastern Provinces of the Empire. The introductory study of society and religion in Central Asia Minor may seem perhaps too elaborate ; but it could not be put more briefly if any adequate conception were to be given of the forces acting on the minds of Paul's Galatian hearers.

The Commentary is intended to be complete in itself, able to be read and fully understood without continually looking back to the Introduction. The Commentary was written first, and published in the *Expositor*, June, 1898—September, 1899. Many passages have now been completely rewritten (after the Introduction had been composed), three chapters have been suppressed and eleven added.

My first intention was tacitly to carry out the South Galatian Theory, leaving the reader to contrast the flood of light thrown on South Galatia by the Epistle with its barrenness as regards North Galatia. But it might be stigmatised as unscholarly if no reference were made to the view still widely assumed as true in Germany and wherever fashionable German views (yet see p. 316) are taken as final. Hence I am, as Lightfoot says, "distracted between the fear of saying too much and the fear of saying too little". Probably I say too little; but the cause (an accident preventing work) is stated on p. 478. The same cause prevented the proper final revision of proofs, which may perhaps have left some errors unremoved.

In former works I applied simply the principles of Imperial history learned from Prof. Mommsen. On this book Prof. Mitteis's *Imperial Law and National Law* (*Reichsrecht und Volksrecht*) has left a strong impression. His title emphasises the opposition between Roman and National, which I have been for years entreating the North Galatian champions to notice. As to my novel theory of Seleucid law in Galatians, ignoring Halmel, those who want German authority for everything may find it in Prof. Mitteis's words : *jedenfalls wird auch durch Ihre Ausführungen dasjenige was Halmel "das röm. Recht im Galaterbrief" sagt, aus dem Feld geschlagen.*

We must all study German method, and practise it day and night; but the first principle in German method is to disregard authority (even German) and follow after truth.

I have not seen Mr. Askwith's recent work on the Galatian Question (see p. 478).

CONTENTS.

HISTORICAL INTRODUCTION:

b

Contents

HISTORICAL INTRODUCTION.

Society and Religion in Central Asia Minor in the time of St. Paul.

SECTION 1.

PRELIMINARY.

THE Epistle to the Galatians is a document of the highest importance for students of history. Not merely is it a peculiarly important authority for all who study the early stages in the Christianisation of the Roman Empire: it also throws much light on the condition and society of one of the Eastern Roman Provinces during the first century of the Empire—a difficult subject and an almost unknown land.

The study of this document is encumbered with a great preliminary difficulty. It is not certain who were the persons addressed. While some scholars maintain that the "Churches of Galatia," to whom the Epistle is addressed, were planted in the four cities of Southern Galatia, Derbe, Lystra, Iconium, and Pisidian Antioch, others assert that those Churches were situated in North Galatia. These two opposite opinions are conveniently designated as the South-Galatian and the North-Galatian Theory.

This doubt as to the destination of the Epistle hardly

affects the study of its dogmatic or doctrinal value, with which we are not concerned.

Even as regards its historical value, small importance might seem on a first superficial view to attach to the question whether the Churches addressed were situated in the south of the province or in the north. The distance of Pessinus, the nearest in the northern group, from Iconium in the southern is only about 120 miles. From Pessinus to Antioch is about 30 miles less as the crow flies, but almost as much as the traveller goes.

Similarly, the question has been discussed whether the so-called " Epistle to the Ephesians " was addressed to the Church of Ephesus or of Laodicea, or is a general Asian letter. The distance by road from Ephesus to Laodicea was 91½ Roman miles. But it makes no very serious difference even to the historical student whether the letter was addressed to the one or the other city : no question as regards the time of composition, or the order of Paul's travels, or the history of the Church as a whole, is affected by the doubt.

But the doubt as regards the Galatian Churches stands on a quite different footing. The date when the letter was composed, the order and facts of Paul's travels, several important questions of general Church history, are all affected by the doubt. To the student of Roman history and society there are also serious differences between the two theories. The North-Galatian cities belong to quite a different line of development from the South-Galatian. See Sections 15, 17.

In this case, as in all other historical questions, the doubt is due to insufficiency of knowledge. The countries both of North and of South Galatia are most obscure. A good

deal has been done by modern scholars to illuminate the
history of North Galatia in the pre-Roman period by collecting and comparing the references in literature ; but little
has been done for the Roman period. South Galatia was
no more than a name, and hardly even a name, until within
the last few years.

It might have been expected that, in a question so important and so obscure, all investigators who approached
the subject would have begun by carefully studying the
condition of both districts, North and South Galatia ;
and thereafter would have reached a conclusion based on
adequate knowledge.

That method, however, has not been practised. The
commentators on the Epistle, with the single exception of
Lightfoot, have had little inclination to the historical side
of their subject. The dogmatic and doctrinal overpowered
every other aspect in their view. Where they touched
on the historical questions that are involved, they did so
unwillingly and as briefly as possible. As a rule, having
made up their minds beforehand that Paul wrote to the
Churches of North Galatia, they took a hasty glance
into the history of the country and people, and selected a
few facts that seemed to suit their foregone conclusion,
when taken apart from the surroundings. In their prepossession any facts that were unfavourable to their view
remained unnoticed. They did not even observe that
Juliopolis, which many of them pitched upon as the site
of one of Paul's Churches, was a city of Bithynia, not of
Galatia.[1]

---

[1] It was attached to Galatia about A.D. 295 ; and most of our
authorities for the northern limits of Galatia are later than that
date. Hence the error.

Even as regards Lightfoot, his historical faculty is not shown at its highest level in his Galatian commentary. He began his great series of Pauline commentaries with perhaps the most difficult Epistle, certainly the one that is most widely decisive as regards Pauline history. It might have been a more fortunate choice if he had first practised his method on one or two Epistles which determine fewer questions beyond their own scope, and then applied his perfectly trained powers to *Galatians.* Comparing his introductions to *Galatians* and *Colossians*, one sees how much more thorough and well-balanced the latter is. In his *Galatians* he devotes a quite disproportionate space to the question whether the European invaders of Asia Minor belonged to a Germanic or a Celtic stock: the answer to that question makes practically no difference to the right understanding of the Epistle.

It is remarkable, considering how delicate the balance of evidence seemed to him and how much he was able to say on the opposite side in several places, that he seems never to have re-opened the case. The reason doubtless was that no new evidence became available until the last years of his life. The study of Asia Minor is, pre-eminently, one in which the scholar at present must never consider his opinion final, and must be prepared to modify and change it as new evidence is discovered.[1]

It is a duty here at the outset to make clear my attitude towards that great scholar, who necessarily will be so often mentioned in the following pages.[2] I have been charged with " holding up to ignominy " as " intellectually or morally

[1] See below, note on p. 10.

[2] This paragraph is adapted from *Expositor*, May, 1896, p. 344, in answer to a charge made in the preceding number, p. 254.

discreditable " his opinion on points on which we differ. The charge is peculiarly painful to me. For Lightfoot's work I have felt and often expressed to friends the highest admiration since my undergraduate days ; for his personal kindness to me as a beginner in the path of learning I feel gratitude that grows stronger and warmer as the years pass by. But his immense and well-deserved influence is now supporting an error, which could only have arisen in his mind about an unknown land. An example from another topic will make clear my relations to him on this subject. In the traditional epitaph of Avircius Marcellus, Lightfoot rightly caught the ring of genuineness amid all the corruptions that defaced it. Rightly maintaining its authenticity, he attempted to disprove the arguments which seemed to older scholars, like Tillemont and Garrucci, to be conclusive proof of its spuriousness ; but his discussion of the evidence was wrong throughout.[1] Fortunately he lived to recognise the complete change which better knowledge of the country necessitated ; and in the latest edition he cut out the whole of his erroneous discussion, and substituted a brief reference to the real facts ; yet, had he died a few years earlier, I should have had to struggle long against the almost universal belief in England that his discussion of that subject must be correct. So now, had his life been prolonged a few years more, he would have been the first to see (long before I saw) the bearing of the new information about Phrygia, Lycaonia, and Galatia, on the foundation of the early Church in Asia Minor ; he would have himself corrected the errors about the history and geography of these countries that were inevitable, when his earlier

[1] See his edition of *Colossians*, p. 54 ff.

works were written; and I should never have been compelled to assume the position of criticising him, but have been free to be in external appearance, as I always have been in reality, his humble admirer.

For a number of years the present writer has maintained that the North-Galatian Theory is seen to be impossible, as soon as one makes oneself properly acquainted with the history and character of the people, and the geography of the country. That theory seemed to be possible only so long as no clear conception of the facts existed ; but when the facts were collected and looked at in their entirety, it lost any appearance of justification. To collect the historical and antiquarian evidence bearing on the question, to try to show Galatia as it really was about A.D. 50, is the proper method of treating this subject.

In these circumstances, the necessity is entailed of prefixing to this commentary on the Epistle a careful study of a district where the Apostle Paul never set foot, and to which he never wrote. The process may seem strange ; but in the progress towards truth the first step is often the elimination of errors.

Further, it may appear that the introductory study is too elaborate, even if it had been devoted solely to the country where St. Paul travelled and to whose people he wrote. But it is much more difficult to dispose of an inveterate error than it would be simply to illustrate the Epistle, if the task were encumbered by no erroneous prejudice. An illustration of this may here be quoted :—

"In every department of historical investigation," says Professor R. Engelmann, the distinguished archæologist, "examples may be quoted to show how long errors that have once established themselves in the ordinary teaching

may last, and how even the noblest and best scholars give
themselves the toil of championing them and demonstrating
that they are the only truths."[1] He goes on to exemplify
from the department of Greek architecture this remarkable
tendency to cling to an error that one has been taught from
childhood. He shows how the view that Greek temples as
a rule were open above to the sky, founded on a mistranslation of a passage of Vitruvius[2] and supported by misinterpretation of several other passages—though vigorously combated by one or two investigators on grounds
that are now seen to be correct—established itself in
general opinion, was taught in every school, and dominated
archæological research for fifty years. Only recently has
it been successfully attacked ; and some time must pass
before it disappears from the lecture-room and the ordinary
manuals. So blinded were some excellent investigators
by the prejudice created in their minds, that they found in
the modern discoveries of the last twenty years conclusive
demonstration of the accepted theory, and on the result
of modern excavations they exultingly declared that their
few opponents were demonstrated to be strangers to the
realities of Greek Art.

Similarly, the North-Galatian Theory, which was possible
only because of the obscurity of the subject and the general
misapprehension of historical facts, established itself in
current opinion and was taught in every school and in all
ordinary text-books. Though always denied and contested
by a few, yet it was practically master of the field of
instruction ; and thus it could create a presumption in its

---

[1] Quoted from his admirable *résumé* in *Vossische Zeitung, Beilage,*
26th March, 2nd April, 1899.

[2] III 1.

favour in almost every mind. The vast majority of readers never heard of any other theory ; and it became known to individuals usually through some contemptuous reference made by some revered teacher, who glanced at it only to dismiss it. Finally, distinguished and deservedly respected scholars deduced from the epigraphic results of modern research conclusive proof of the accepted theory, and declared that the opposite view was now finally ejected from educated minds.

These facts and the analogy just quoted, show how carefully and deeply laid the foundation must be on which the South-Galatian Theory is to rest. It is not enough to state in a brief summary the general bearing of the facts, geographical, political, historical, legal, which disprove the current North-Galatian view. That has been done, and the North-Galatian champions meet some one statement with a flat denial, and treat the rest with silent contempt : then, dislodged from their first defence, they deny some other statement, and again necessitate a laborious demonstration.

It is therefore best to attempt to picture the state of Central Asia Minor, at the time when Paul and Barnabas crossed the great belt of the Taurus mountains, and to show how the racial, political, geographical and religious facts of previous history had contributed to produce it. Some of the historical facts mentioned in the following sections may seem at first sight remote from the Epistle ; but all have a real bearing on the argument. Our aim is to make the student judge for himself on the " Galatian Question ".

Instead of describing the character of the Galatians—a method which always is liable to seem too subjective, over-coloured to suit the argument—we attempt to exhibit the

Galatians in action and in history, so that the reader can judge of their character for himself.

The account of the Galatian wars and raids (which occupy most part of the existing treatises on Galatia) has been cut down as much as possible, but may even yet be considered too long. It was however necessary to bring out the fact, which has not been noticed previously, that the mixed Galatic State was much stronger than the unmixed Gaulish armies ; and that Galatia increased in influence over the surrounding countries, and reached its highest importance as a power in Asia Minor during the Roman period. Commonly, the history of the Gauls in Asia Minor is painted as a process of steady decay from initial power. Really, the Gaulish element ruled an immensely wider tract of country in the first century B.C. than it had ever done before. In the third century the Gauls were fighting for existence : in the first century Gauls ruled Galatia proper with parts of Lycaonia, Paphlagonia, Pontus, and Armenia.

The " Galatian Question " should not be taken in too narrow a sense. It is not merely a question of Pauline interpretation and chronology. Under it is concealed the great subject of the Christianisation of the entire inner Asia Minor, and the relation of the new religion to the older religion, society and education of those many regions and countries, Phrygia, Upper Lydia, Upper Caria, Lycaonia and Isauria, Cappadocia, North Galatia, Pontus. He that desires to understand the " Galatian Question " thoroughly will not be content with dipping into books on the history and antiquities of Asia Minor, in order to pick out, with least trouble and in the shortest time, illustrations of the Epistle and arguments to support a foregone conclusion as to its meaning and scope. He will first acquire as good a

conception as possible of life, religion and society in inner
Asia Minor before Paul entered the country ; and he will
then proceed to study the history of the country under
the new influence.   The subject is very obscure, and the
authorities deplorably scanty.   At present we must be
content with tentative and inadequate results.   But we
can at least make a foundation, on which exploration and
discovery will build, and we can lay down principles by
which both present study and future exploration may be
guided.

In this preliminary study of pre-Pauline society and life
in inner Asia Minor, the settlement of the Gauls in the
country is a critical epoch.   As Monsieur Theodore Reinàch
says, the Gauls were *un élément destiné pendant trois siècles
à jouer un rôle prépondérant dans l'histoire de la péninsule.*[1]
To study even South Galatia one must study the relations
of that warlike and proud Gaulish people, "the noblest of
barbarians," as Plutarch calls them, to the oriental peoples
around them.   From every point of view the student of
central Asia Minor must make North Galatia his starting
point.

Note.—DR. HORT ON THE GALATIAN QUESTION.   In
Dr. Hort's posthumously published works (taken from his
university lectures), there are some indications pointing to
a development in his views on this question.   In his
Lectures on 1 Peter, delivered in 1882 and the following
years, he takes one view: in those on Ephesians, 1891,
he expresses a different opinion.

In the former he points out that St. Peter included as
Churches of Galatia "the Churches founded by St. Paul in

[1] *Rois de Bithynie,* p. 8.

Galatia proper, in Lycaonia and in Phrygia"; but he declines to admit that St. Paul reckoned the latter as Churches of Galatia, on the sole ground that Lightfoot has proved the contrary.[1]

But in the later series of lectures he says that, in the journey described in Acts XVIII 23, St. Paul "visited . . . Antioch, where he stayed some time, and then followed his old course through southern Asia Minor, and this time was allowed to follow it right on to its natural goal, Ephesus ". That sentence contrasts Paul's uninterrupted route through Cilicia, Derbe, Lystra, etc., to Ephesus in XVIII 23 with his previous attempt, XVI 1-5, to reach the same goal, which was interrupted in the middle.[2] No one could speak thus who held the North-Galatian Theory, for that theory inexorably implies that, in Acts XVIII 23, Paul did not traverse southern Asia Minor, but took a new route from Cilicia northwards to Tavium, Ancyra, and Pessinus.

Hort had evidently become a " South-Galatian " between 1882 and 1891, already seeing the bearing of recent discoveries in Asia Minor. Death prevented him, as it had prevented Lightfoot, from being the pioneer of the South-Galatian Theory in England.

[1] See pp. 17, 158, etc. The views on the Provinces were probably left unrevised after 1882, see *Expositor*, Jan., 1899, p. 46.

[2] See the preceding part of the paragraph.

SECTION 2.

NORTH GALATIA: LAND AND PEOPLES.

THE peninsula of Asia Minor, stretching out like a bridge from Asia to Europe, consists of a great central plateau, from 2000 to 4000 feet above sea level, with a fringe of low-lying coast around it. A rim of mountains, called on the south side Taurus, separates the plateau from the coast-lands.

The country that was called Galatia included a broad zone in the northern part of the central plateau. It was an irregular oblong, which may be roughly estimated as about 200 miles long from east to west, and 60 to 80 miles broad from north to south. If we leave out of notice the extreme northern parts which border on Paphlagonia (as these are historically quite unimportant and practically almost unknown to modern travellers), the country as a whole is of uniform character. It consists of a vast series of bare, bleak up-lands and sloping hill-sides. It is almost devoid of trees, except, perhaps, in some places on the north frontiers; and the want of shade makes the heat of summer more trying, while the climate in winter is severe. The hills often reach a considerable altitude, but have never the character of mountains. They are commonly clad with a slight growth of grass to the summit on at least one side. The scenery is uninteresting. There are hardly any striking features; and one part is singularly like another. The cities are far from one another, separated by long stretches of the same fatiguing country, dusty and hot and arid in summer, covered with snow in winter.

In the description which is given on p. 35 of the geographical character of the plateau as a whole, almost the only trait that is not true of Galatia is the " certain charm ". Galatia is the least interesting, the most devoid of charm of all the Asia Minor lands, the only one that the writer found wearisome. The great plains in the centre of the plateau are far more interesting, because being more absolutely level, they permit a wide view; and the eye sweeps over a vast extent of country to the distant lofty mountains, Taurus, Hassan-Dagh, etc., which rim the plateau or rise like steep volcanic islets from its bosom. But Galatia is just undulating enough to make the view almost everywhere contracted and confined : rarely, if ever, does the traveller get the impression of width, of greatness, of long lines, or of the contrast between level plain and sharp mountain peak, needed to give a standard by which one can realise the immensity of the eye's range.

To show the impression that North Galatia makes on a competent observer, one may quote a description of the central and western parts from Major Law's *Report on the Railways of Asiatic Turkey* (Blue Book : Turkey, No. 4, May, 1896): " The aspect of the country is exceedingly monotonous—a series of larger or smaller plains, surrounded by bare, desolate-looking hills, with streams or small rivers flowing in the centre, but little cultivation and few villages. The average high elevation is maintained, and the climate is trying both in winter and in summer ; there is a terrible

absence of trees, and the soil, which is fairly productive
under the influence of seasonable rains, is too frequently
burnt up by the prolonged droughts which in unfavourable
years are the cause of distressing famines. There is extensive pasturage, but the country is exposed and the grass
poor, and the cattle look generally in poor condition ;
sheep, goats and camels are, however, reared with success
in large numbers, and the Angora mohair and wool have
long been famous. Where there is water and cultivation,
cereals grow well, and there is a considerable production of
cotton, besides tobacco, opium and hemp. The town of
Angora (*Ancyra*) itself is exceptionally favourably situated
in a sheltered, fertile plain."

Owing to difficulty of transport (which the recently
opened railway from the Bosphorus to Dorylaion, *i.e.*,
Eski-Sheher, and Angora will in time obviate), the only
products of Galatia which play any important part in
modern commerce are wool and mohair (the product of
the fleece of the beautiful Angora goat). In ancient times
wool and slaves formed the only important Galatian articles
of trade,[1] so far as our authorities go ; but much more
wheat and other cereals were grown then than now.

A country of this character can never have nourished a
dense population. In ancient times the aspect of most of
the land away from the few great cities was much the same
as it is at the present day—bleak stretches of pastoral
country, few villages, sparse population, little evidence of
civilisation. There would, however, be much larger flocks
of sheep in ancient than in modern times. But in the
occasional districts where arable land abounds, the scene
would be very different then and now : the soil would be

---

[1] Also perhaps mohair, *Impressions of Turkey*, p. 273.

thoroughly cultivated, houses and villages numerous, the activity and education of man apparent everywhere. Such districts, however, are not many, and are found chiefly beside the cities which were fostered by them.

The description given of one of these fertile spots, given by Mr. J. G. C. Anderson in the *Journal of Hellenic Studies*, 1899, p. 91, may be quoted here : " The little village at the foot of the mound is pleasantly situated near the head of a plain which runs down to the railway and contains some fairly fertile arable land—a rare thing in this neighbourhood. The country through which the road passes between the Sangarios and Angora is, as Hamilton says, ' perfectly uncultivated ; no traces of vegetation were visible except in the dried-up stems of a few thorny plants and flowers, which cover the ground instead of grass '. The description may be extended to the whole Haïmane-country : ' there are no gardens here, it is all desert,' as a Turk of Balikkoyundji wearily said to us."

Bithynia and Paphlagonia bordered on Galatia to the north, Pontus to the east, Cappadocia and Lycaonia to the south, Phrygia in the narrower and later sense to the west. The exact bounds are best studied on the map.

The country afterwards called Galatia was in primitive time divided ethnographically and politically into two parts, eastern and western : the division was made by the river Halys, which in this part of its course runs in a northerly direction towards the Black Sea. Galatia east of the Halys seems to have been originally reckoned to Cappadocia, though part of it was probably sometimes described as included in Paphlagonia ; but the bounds of those countries were so indeterminate, and the ancient writers themselves were so ignorant of the geography of those lands, that it is quite impossible to say anything positive and certain on the subject.

The enigmatic race called White-Syrians (*Λευκόσυροι*) certainly inhabited part at least of Eastern Galatia. But it is useless to speculate whether the population of Eastern Galatia, at the time when the Galatae first entered the country, was mainly Cappadocian, or White-Syrian, or of any other race.

Eastern Galatia lies mostly in the basin of the Halys (Kizil-Irmak, the "Red River"). The Halys itself has very few and quite insignificant tributaries. In Eastern Galatia the Delije-Irmak (whose ancient name is unknown) is the only tributary of any consequence; and most of the country lies in its basin; but the river, though it looks large on the map, carries very little water except in flood, when it becomes a broad and raging torrent, exactly as its name indicates, the "Mad River".

The eastern frontier-lands of Galatia lay in the valley of the Iris (Yeshil-Irmak, the "Green River"). Tavium, the Galatian and Roman capital of the district, and Pteria, the pre-Galatian capital, once the imperial city of Asia Minor, were situated on affluents of the Iris.

The Halys at the crossing of the road between the capitals Tavium and Ancyra is 2350 feet above sea level. The altitude of Eastern Galatia averages between 2300 and 3000 feet.

Galatia west of the Halys, which was much larger than the eastern country, was the most important and the most typical part of the country; most of our scanty information relates to it; and in general, when any statement is made about North Galatia, the writer has the western part of it in his mind. This western region was originally part of the vast land called Phrygia ; and, clearly, the population of the country in the early part of the fourth century were known to the Greeks as Phrygians (Φρύγες).

This Phrygian population of Western Galatia was not a homogeneous, but a mixed race. On its character see Section 3.

Almost the whole of Western Galatia is included in the basin of the Sangarios, the great river of Phrygia, still called Sakaría (implying an ancient form Sagaris, of which Sangarios is a Grecised variety). The Halys, as was stated above, drains a very narrow basin, and about twelve miles west of that river, on the direct road from Tavium to Ancyra, one finds oneself on the watershed of the Sangarios, 4000 feet above sea level. Thus the Sangarios, though it has a very much shorter course than the Halys, drains a far greater area than that river.

Ancyra, still called Angora (Enguri in Turkish), the capital of Western Galatia, is situated on a tributary of the Sangarios in a picturesque and very strong position, commanding a fertile district, about 3100 feet above sea level. The rest of the country varies in altitude from the banks of the Sangarios, 1600-2200 feet, to parts of the Haïmane (the hilly country south and south-west from Angora), 3600 feet : the hills near Ancyra are still higher.

In this country, with its already existing population, were settled large numbers of Gaulish immigrants about B.C. 232. The settlement was not brought about simply by Gaulish conquest. It was caused by agreement of the Greek kings, who made an arrangement by which this country was recognised as the property of the Gauls, on the condition that they confined themselves to it.

The changes that were produced thereby, and the

2

character of the resulting people, must be studied in more detail.   The method usual among New Testament scholars, treating Galatia as if it were simply a country peopled by the Gaulish tribes, is an erroneous one and leads to much misapprehension.

Note.—Descriptions of the fertile and beautiful plain of Ancyra are quoted by some writers as if they gave a true picture of Galatia generally.

SECTION 3.

PRE-GALATIC HISTORY OF NORTH GALATIA.

Pre-Phrygian state (probably subject to Pteria) . before tenth century.
Independent Phrygian chiefs and kings .   .   tenth century-674.
Cimmerians for a short time   .   .   .   .   .   . after 675.
Phrygian kings under Lydian suzerains .   .   .   .   . -546.
Persian Empire   .   .   .   . -333.
Alexander the Great and his successors .   .   .   . 333-232.
The Gauls recognised as owners of Galatia   .   .   . about 232.

At an early date, probably not far from B.C. 900,[1] a European race from Macedonia or Thrace, which crossed the Hellespont, had overrun great part of Western Asia Minor, and formed several distinct states. The Trojan city and the dynasty of Priam belonged to this people; and the Trojan legend, as it has come down to us in the *Iliad*, preserved the recollection of the struggles that were waged on the banks of the Sangarios between the invading Phryges and the native population of the inner lands. The native population is described in legend as the Amazons (see Section 5). The Phryges gave their name and their language to the land which they conquered.

---

[1] Professor A. Körte, a distinguished explorer of Phrygia, would assign B.C. 1500 or 2000 as the date (*Athen. Mittheilungen Inst.*, 1897), but his reason seems inadequate. He has proved, not that the conquering Phryges were so old, but that they adopted some arts from the older race whom they conquered.

(19)

The name Phrygia at an early time seems to have included
not merely Galatia and the Sangarios valley generally (except in its maritime parts), but also the whole of the lands
lying immediately south of the Hellespont and Propontis.[1]
The characteristic Phrygian names and legends, Askanios,
Askania, Otreus, Otroia, Mygdon, etc., are found in the
extreme south and the extreme north of that vast region :
e.g., Lake Askania is a name on the Pisidian frontier and
in Bithynia a few miles south-east from the Propontis (with
a town Otroiai beside it, like Otroos far south in the
Phrygian Pentapolis).   And not Phrygia alone, even in the
widest sense, was overrun by that European race, but also
part or the whole of Lydia, termed Maionia, and Caria.
Hence arises the close association of Maionia and Phrygia
in the *Iliad*,[2] hence the application of the name Phrygia to
the country and the heroes connected with Mount Sipylos
near Smyrna.

In all those lands, doubtless, the conquering race became a military aristocracy, of varying strength in the
different countries, while the older inhabitants formed a
subject population.   It may be assumed that in Phrygia
the conquering race was more numerous in proportion to
the subject race than in Lydia or Caria, and imposed its
language and name on the country, while in Lydia and in
Caria there were probably only a certain number of immigrants, who became chiefs and nobles in those lands.   But
probably, even in Phrygia, the old native population was
more numerous than the conquerors ; and in course of time
the victorious race gradually lost its individuality and original character, and became merged in the native race.   The

---

[1] καὶ Φρυγίη καθύπερθε καὶ Ἑλλήσποντος ἀπείρων, *Iliad*, xxiv, 545.

[2] *Iliad*, III 401, X 431, XVIII 291.

joint race, however, continued to bear the Phrygian name and probably to use the Phrygian language.

The old Phryges were a sea-people as well as land-conquerors. A people who cross from Macedonia to Phrygia must have learned to subdue the sea to their will; and Greek historical tradition mentions a Phrygian Thalassocracy lasting twenty-five years from B.C. 905.[1] No value can be laid on the exact years; but probably they are not remote from the truth as to the period when the Phrygian power was at its height.

At that time there can hardly be any doubt that the Phrygian people and power were continuous from the Hellespont and the coast of the Troad through Mysia (to use a name of later origin), and up to the banks of the Halys. The references to easy intercourse between the Troad and inner Phrygia furnish sufficient proof of this : see below, p. 27.

The Phrygian sea-power very soon passed into other hands; and tradition assigns to it a duration of only twenty-five years. The land-power failed also to maintain its continuity. Tribes from Thrace, Mysoi, Thynoi, Bithynoi, crossing the Bosphorus, forced their way south-west, south and east; and the Mysians formed a new population which split the Phrygian people into two fragments. Henceforward we hear of two Phrygian countries—Hellespontine or Little Phrygia, a vague undefined region, which was little more than a name, and in which no distinct political constitution is discernible—and Great Phrygia, Phrygia Magna, a vast region extending from the borders of Lydia and Caria to the Halys on the north-east, and to the Pisidian and Lycaonian frontiers on the south and south-east.

[1] Diodorus, VII 11.

The centre of power in Great Phrygia lay to the north
in the Sangarios valley. Scanty tradition is confirmed in
this respect by archæological evidence. Partly this was due
to the greater strength of the conquering people in the
north : it grew more scanty and more scattered as it pene-
trated farther from its origin. Partly also the predominant importance of Northern Phrygia was due to the fact
that the great line along which civilisation and political
development moved led across the Sangarios valley. That
line was the "Royal Road," which connected Pteria the
great capital among the White Syrians with Sardis in Lydia
—a road which had been older than the Phrygian immigration and belonged to a pre-Phrygian order and unity
extending from one to the other of those two great cities.
The "Royal Road" ran through the entire length of Galatia
(to use the later name), and over the North Phrygian
mountains, crossed from the headwaters of the Tembrogios
(a tributary of the Sangarios) to the upper reaches of the
Mæander basin past the important trading centre, Keramon
Agora, and thence passed on to the Hermos valley and
Sardis.

The course of the "Royal Road" was marked by a series
of great Phrygian cities, Ancyra of Galatia, Gordium of
Galatia, Pessinus of Galatia, and the Phrygian metropolis,
whose very name is now unknown,[1] but whose remains are
so imposing. Not far from its course lay other cities,
whose names attest their old Phrygian connection, Gordou-

---

[1] I think, however, that it was known to the Greeks as Metropolis
(as will be shown in *Cities and Bishoprics of Phrygia*, Part III).
Perhaps the name may be only a Grecised form of the original
Phrygian ; but more probably it is a Greek epithet that took the
place of the native name. The city lies over the "Tomb of Midas".

kome in Bithynia, Midaion, Kotyaion, Aizanoi, Kadoi, in Phrygia, Gordos in north-eastern Lydia—associated with heroes of Phrygian mythological history, Gordios, Midas, Kadys or Kotys.   But the only Phrygian town of the south that plays any important part in early history and semi-historical myth—Kelainai—owed its importance to quite different conditions, *viz.*, to trade with the Greeks at the mouth of the Mæander.[1]

The powerful kingdom of Great Phrygia (with Galatia) fell before a new swarm of invaders from the north.   These were the Kimmerioi, a people from the Crimea and the South-Russian coasts, who swept in devastating hordes (like the Huns and Mongols of later days) over the fairer lands of the south : their conquest of Sardis (all but the citadel), Antandros, and Magnesia on the Mæander was remembered in Greek history, and their unsuccessful attack on Ephesos (when the temple of Artemis outside the city was burned) is mentioned by the contemporary poets Callinus and Archilochus.[2]   With approximate exactitude, the year when the Cimmerians captured the Phrygian metropolis, and the Phrygian king Midas killed himself in despair, has been fixed as B.C. 674 by Assyriologists (whose sphere of study begins to touch central and western Asia Minor about that time, and thus imparts much greater exactitude to it).

The Lydian kings, Ardys 652-615, Sadyattes 615-610,

---

[1] See *Cities and Bishoprics of Phrygia*, Ch. XI, p. 412 ff.

[2] The destruction of the Ephesian temple and of Magnesia is often attributed in Greek accounts to the Amazons, a confusion of the primitive native population with the later invaders.   What remained in memory was that a people of barbarous, non-Greek type had attacked the Ionian cities.

and Alyattes 610-561,[1] resisted and finally drove back the Cimmerian hordes ; and in doing so extended their empire over Great Phrygia.   There still continued to rule in Phrygia Phrygian kings, for Adrastus, son of the Phrygian king, lived as a refugee (for the crime of homicide) at the court of Crœsus (561-546) in Sardis.   But these Phrygian kings were no longer independent sovereigns, but were subject to some kind of Lydian suzerainty, for the treaty concluded in 585 between Alyattes and the Median king Kyaxares fixed the Halys as the boundary between the Lydian and Median Empires.

About 546 Galatia with the rest of Great Phrygia passed under Persian rule, and remained so until Alexander the Great marched to Gordium and the Galatic Ancyra in B.C. 333.   After his death in 320 his successors struggled and fought with one another with varying success during great part of a century.

The fate of Galatia during this disturbed period is far from certain.   When the pretensions of Antigonus and his son Demetrius to succeed to the realm of Alexander were shattered at the battle of Ipsos in 301, Lysimachus was recognised as lord of Phrygia and the north-western countries, and of course Phrygia is to be taken as including Galatia. When Lysimachus fell at Korupedion in 281, the victorious Seleucus of Syria, who had previously ruled the south-eastern regions, became master of all Asia Minor.   But Mithradates of Pontus (B.C. 302-266) allied himself with

---

[1] I follow the dates preferred by Gelzer *das Zeitalter des Gyges* in *Rhein. Museum,* 1875, vol. xxx, not as certain, but as best attested. The ancient authorities vary considerably, and the moderns still more.   The careful and accurate historical investigators of recent years vary as regards the date of the conquest of Lydia by Cyrus between 554 and 534.

some Greek cities on the north coast against him, and in 281 Seleucus was murdered, and his son Antiochus I (281-262) found himself surrounded by enemies. The opinion of E. Meyer is that Galatia passed under Pontic power at this time ; but he makes the curious mistake of distinguishing Galatia from Phrygia, whereas, of course, any statement made by historians about Phrygia at that time must be taken as true of Western Galatia, while Eastern Galatia belonged either to the Pontic or the Cappadocian kings. It seems more probable that Antiochus remained nominal king of Great Phrygia (including Galatia) ; but in his difficult position his authority would hardly have any real power in the remote north-eastern parts of Phrygia (the future Galatia). During these wars the Gauls entered Asia Minor, B.C. 278-277 ; and a new period begins. They found in Galatia the people whose history we have been describing. This non-Gaulish people formed the substructure on which the Galatian aristocracy rested.

We must therefore try to gain some conception of the non-Gaulish people of North Galatia—the mass, it must be remembered, of the population.

SECTION 4.

THE PRE-GAULISH INHABITANTS OF GALATIA.

THIS outline enables us to estimate the character of the conquering Phryges. In comparison with the native peoples, they were a race of warriors, fiercer, probably better armed, and certainly more apt in the use of weapons. We may suppose that they brought with them something of the spirit of the later Teutonic and Germanic races, to whom they were probably akin, a love of war and a love of freedom, an energy and pertinacity and self-assertiveness, which always seem to be stronger and more deep-rooted in the north and the west than in the south and the east. Hence the memory that the old Phryges have left in history is that of warriors and rulers, by sea and by land, whereas the character of the later Phrygians in history is that of slaves, effeminate and cowardly.

As the name "Phrygians" may denote equally the European conquering tribe and the mixed race formed from the amalgamation of the conquerors and the conquered, we shall use the term "Phryges" to designate the immigrant tribe, and "Phrygians" for the united people resident in Phrygia.

The impression made by that ancient Phrygian power was strong in the Greek mind in the age when the *Iliad* was composed. Priam tells how "erewhile fared I to

(26)

Phrygia, the land of vines, and there saw I that the men of Phrygia, they of the fleet steeds, were very many, even the hosts of Otreus and gallant Mygdon, which were then encamped along the banks of Sangarios. For I, too, being their ally was numbered among them on the day that the Amazons came, the peers of men " (*Iliad*, III 187 ; Philost. *Her.* 20, 41). In return for this, when Priam was in danger, "Phorkys and god-like Askanios led the Phrygians from far Askania, and these were eager to fight in the battle-throng" before Troy's walls (*Iliad*, II 862).

Helen, when she recognised the guileful and dangerous goddess Aphrodite, said to her : " Verily thou wilt lead me further on to some one of the well-peopled cities of Phrygia [1] or lovely Maionia, if there too thou hast perchance some other darling among mortal men " (*Iliad*, III 401). Helen knew Aphrodite as the goddess whose haunts are most in Phrygia : this remarkable fact is explained by the Homeric *Hymn to Aphrodite*, and especially by the following lines, which the goddess speaks to Anchises, her favourite, concealing her real nature and personality, but telling of her own land :—

" No goddess am I, . . . but a mortal, born of woman. My father is Otreus, of famous name, belike thou hast heard of him, who is king over all Phrygia, land of walled cities ".[2]

In truth, she who in those passages was expressed in Greek religious forms as Aphrodite was in her essence the Mother-Goddess of the Phrygian land : she was found there by the immigrant Phrygians, and reverenced by them as the great divinity of the country.

We cannot trace the steps in this alteration of the Phrygian type ; but analogy shows its general character. The Phryges

---

[1] πόλεις εὖ ναιόμεναι.   [2] Φρυγίης εὐτειχήτοιο, l. 112.

had settled among a peaceful and unenterprising people. For some centuries they maintained their power by strong fortified cities or citadels on the summits of rocky hills. Such is the situation of Ancyra and of Giaour-Kalessi in Galatia, of the city by the Midas-Tomb, and of the little fort beside the Lion-Tombs.[1]

When their power was destroyed by the Kimmerioi, there was no longer the stimulus of pride to maintain their national spirit; and they sank to that placid level of character which belonged to the older subject population and is produced by the genius of the land in which they dwelt (see Section 5, p. 35)—the character of "an agricultural and cattle-breeding population of rustics, peaceful and good-humoured".[2] Apart from the *Iliad,* that is the character of the Phrygian people and their heroes in Greek popular estimation : Gordios is a farmer, Midas a well-to-do rough old "country gentleman". The warrior stock has melted into the older stock, and disappeared at least from the surface. We must, therefore, beware of attributing to the warrior Phryges every myth and every legendary or religious name that we find in local legend : many of those personages, even if they did originate in the conquering race, have softened into the traits of the conquered rustic people.

It is generally said that Ashkenaz, which seems to denote the mass of Asia Minor (distinguished from the western coasts, Javan, and the eastern parts, Togarma, etc.) in Genesis X 4, is the name of the Phrygian people; but this name certainly belongs, not to the warrior race, but to the

---

[1] Ancyra is marked as a Phrygian city by its name (also that of a city in the north-west corner of Phrygia), and by tradition associating it with Midas (see Steph. Byz. *s.v.*).

[2] E. Meyer, *Gesch. des Alterthums*, I, p. 300.

older agricultural stock. It is evidently the religious and personal name Ἀσκαηνὸς or Ἀσκάνιος, in Phrygia, Lydia, and the Troad. But Genesis X 4 can hardly be younger than the tenth century B.C., and is therefore probably older than the conquest of Phrygia by the Phryges. The family of Anchises, Aeneas, and Askanios, is professedly of a different stock from the family of Tros and Priamos in the Trojan legends; and we take it to represent the pre-Phrygian element in the population, closely connected with the worship and mythology of the native goddess.

Thus we have in Phrygia and Galatia a warrior-race ruling a powerful kingdom for over two centuries[1] before 676, and in the course of the centuries that followed melting into the type of the Anatolian peasant class, which both preceded and followed it. Before the end of the fifth century the change was complete. The old warrior Phryges had disappeared under Lydian and Persian domination; and the Greeks had forgotten about them, and thought only of the Phrygian slaves, with whom they were familiar. The Phrygian was the slave *par excellence;* by nature he possessed only the unheroic qualities.

The most important points in the transformation are these: (1) The degeneration of the conquerors probably did not begin until they had ceased to be a dominant people. (2) The process of amalgamation between the Phryges and the older population seems connected with the adoption by the former of their subjects' religion. Cybele was indubitably the ancient native goddess: the Phrygian name Askanios was modified from a pre-Phrygian divine and national name.

[1] Prof. A. Körte would extend the period to 900 or 1400 years, see note, p. 19.

The conquering race adopted the native religion ; but
in adopting it they contributed elements which modified
it.   Zeus Benneus, the god of the car, and Zeus Bronton,
the thundering god, whose worship remained in later time
characteristic of the cities nearest the old Phrygian metropolis, have all the appearance of gods of the immigrant
Phrygians.   They represent the male element, which gave
strength to the conquerors.   In the religion of Cybele the
female element is dominant : p. 40 f.

Probably, if the Phrygian power had not been so suddenly
destroyed, the warrior race would have affected the amalga-
mated people much more than was actually the case.   But
a warrior race cannot keep its fighting instinct in defeat
and subjection ; and thus hardly a trace of the earlier
Phryges can be discerned in the later record of the race.
Even in an Asiatic army the Phrygians ranked, not among
the martial races, but along with Ethiopians and Egyptians,
in B.C. 480.[1]   They are rarely mentioned as an element in
the armies of later Persian or Greek kings, and only among
the unimportant light-armed troops.   In the first Mithridatic war, Cassius tried to make a Phrygian army, but
abandoned as useless the attempt to train " men unsuited
for war ".[2]

To bear a name that seemed Phrygian was a disgrace.[3]
" To slave in mid Phrygia " was proverbial for the lowest
kind of life.[4]   Phrygians and Thracians were mentioned
together by Greeks as the least honoured of mankind.
They were accustomed to sell their own children into

[1] Herod. IX 32, *cp.* VII 73, VIII 113.
[2] ἀνδράσιν ἀπολέμοις, Appian *Mithr.* 19.
[3] αἰσχρὸν γὰρ ὄνομα Φρυγιακὸν γυναῖκ' ἔχειν.
[4] Dio Chrys. XXXI 113, *cp.* 158, X 4.

foreign slavery,[1] which they seemed to accept as their natural lot. They wore ear-rings like women.[2] The only Phrygian who attained any celebrity in Greek story was Aesop the slave. They are described as slaves by nature, and of small value as slaves; but this last point probably refers only to their simple character and slowness of wit, for Socrates said that the Phrygians, being industrious, were for that very reason suited for slavery:[3] he was, of course, judging from those Phrygians whom he saw slaves in Attica.

But in these qualities we may see rather the effect of their situation than an index of their real character. They were far from the sea and the opportunities of travel and intercourse; they had few products except slaves in their country that would reward and stimulate trade; the opportunity of getting education from contact with other races was denied them, and their religious system, so far from favouring education, tended to keep them on a lower social plane than their Greek neighbours; Greek coast colonies surrounded them on three sides, and the keen, enterprising, quick-witted, highly-trained colonists regarded with extreme contempt the slow, apathetic, contented, and unutterably ignorant Phrygians, incapable of being roused or excited by any cause except their vulgar and degrading superstitious rites.

This contrast between Greek and Phrygian, and the inevitable victory of intellect in the conflict between them,

---

[1] Philostr. *Apoll.* VIII.

[2] Dio Chrys. XXXII 3 (so Lydians Xen. *Anab.* III 1, 31).

[3] Aelian *Var. Hist.* X 18 : people who were naturally idle, like the Persians, had a more independent spirit, said Socrates.

gave form to many legends — Marsyas conquered and tortured by Apollo, Lityerses slain by Herakles.[1]

Almost the only inventions attributed to the Phrygians were in music: various kinds of cymbals and similar instruments, the flute, the trigonon, perhaps the syrinx, were considered Phrygian : a musical mode, said to be of melancholy yet emotional and exciting character was called the Phrygian : certain tunes, the Lityerses or harvest song, the harmateion or carriage song,[2] etc., were of Phrygian origin. There was also a Phrygian dance. These are all creations and accompaniments of the Phrygian religion.

Associations connected with the Phrygian worship, passing under various names in different parts of Asia Minor, such as the *Herdsmen*, the *Korybants*, the *Hymn-Singers*, the *Satyroi*, survived even in Roman time and have thus become known to us.[3] They are still represented by the Mevlevi or dancing dervishes of modern Turkey, with their strange yet most impressive music and dance, which have probably been preserved in essential characteristics from the worship of Cybele.

Further, the art of embroidery was said to be derived from Phrygia ; and the Romans gave the name Phrygiones to those that practised the art. The occupation is of a feminine, and therefore Phrygian, type.

In literature, only the fable, the least cultured of literary

---

[1] Not that this contrast is the only element in those tales. Each is a growth, to which only the final form was given by this idea of contest between Greek and Phrygian. Another form of the Lityerses legend is that he was slain in the field by the sickles of the reapers, evidently the older form (see p. 35).

[2] Many conflicting accounts of the ἁρμάτειον μέλος are given, as war-song, etc.

[3] *Cities and Bishoprics of Phrygia*, Part II, pp. 359, 630.

forms, the simple expression of rustic wisdom and wit under the guise of anecdotes about beasts and birds, was attributed to Phrygia. Even this came probably from much further east ; but the Greeks heard it from Phrygia and thought it characteristic of that country.

In this picture of Phrygia, as Greeks and Romans have handed it down, the living characteristics of a real people are clear. Scanty and vague as is the picture, it is at least true and convincing in the general effect. The people stands before us in its general type. Every traveller will recognise in it the modern, so-called " Turkish," peasantry of the same country ; and he sees before him every day in the country the same old conflict between the quick-witted, subtle, enterprising Greek, and the slow, dull, contented Turk. The modern peasantry has reverted under the pressure of similar external conditions, and through the influence of the same natural surrounding, to the primeval Phrygian type. Whatever pride of religion and stock was for a time imparted to the landsmen by the Turkish intermixture has now almost disappeared, since the Turks ceased to be a dominant warrior caste.

What we may call the " Phrygian " race, then, is the fundamental stock into which by degrees all immigrant races tend to melt, as soon as circumstances cease to support the favoured and dominant position of the " outlander " aristocracy. It was not without reason that the Phrygians called themselves the autochthonous people, the original and oldest race in the world. But that old stock was not the European immigrant *Phryges*, it was the older Ashkenaz, the people of the Amazones.

In North Galatia and in South Galatia we meet this ground-stock in two totally different stages. In North

Galatia it was mastered and overlaid and ruled by an
immigrant aristocracy, which gave tone and colour and
variety and power of development to the inert mass, so
that the latter, with its plastic nature, took on it for the time
the character of the dominant race ; and the Galatians were
severed by a broad and deep chasm from all the surrounding
peoples.

In South Galatia the same stock appears as trained to
a certain extent in the cities by some centuries of Greek
municipal institutions and law and a smattering of Greek
literature and education.   With their marked receptivity
and plasticity, the Phrygians took on themselves with
perfect readiness a certain element of Hellenism : "without
any observable resistance and with great facility they
adopted Greek myths, fashions, education and language".[1]
The result was not true Greek—the Phrygians could never
become Greeks even on the surface—but it was at least a
new product, which showed something of the qualities of
both Phrygian and Greek—Phrygian sincerity and simplicity
and readiness to sink their own individuality in what they
accepted as a higher training—Greek desire for learning
and education.

He that would appreciate rightly the "Galatian Question"
must begin by rightly conceiving the historical development
of North and South Galatia ; and he will not neglect to
acquire some conception of the Phrygian ground-stock, as
it can best be seen either in actual contact with the modern
peasantry or in the picture of them drawn by sympathetic
travellers.   Equally necessary is it to appreciate the general
type of Phrygian religion, on which see next Section.

[1] Haase in Ersch und Gruber *Realencyc. s.v. Phrygien*, p. 292.

SECTION 5.

THE RELIGION OF ASIA MINOR.

THE tone and spirit of the Anatolian land have been described in the following words, which I quote from the *Historical Geogr. of Asia Min.*, p. 23:—

"The plateau from the Anti-Taurus westwards consists chiefly of great, gently undulating plains. The scenery, as a rule, is monotonous and subdued; even the mountains of Phrygia seem not to have the spirit of freedom about them. The tone everywhere is melancholy, but not devoid of a certain charm, which, after a time, takes an even stronger hold of the mind than the bright and varied scenery of the Greek world. Strong contrasts of climate between the long severe winter and the short but hot summer, a fertile soil dependent entirely on the chances of an uncertain rainfall, impressed on the mind of the inhabitants the insignificance of man and his dependence on the power of nature. The tone can be traced through the legends and the religion of the plateau. The legends are always sad—Lityerses slain by the sickles of the reapers in the field, Marsyas flayed by the god Apollo, Hylas drowned in the fountain—all end in death during the prime of life and the pride of art."

The influence of these climatic surroundings on the mind of the people that dwell among them may be illustrated from an author who has observed human nature with the

(35)

eye at once of a physician and of a man of letters.   Narrating his experience in a ship, shut in the ice and waiting the single chance of a favourable wind to open a passage through the impassable barrier, he says: "At present we can do nothing but . . . wait and hope for the best.   I am rapidly becoming a fatalist.   When dealing with such uncertain factors as wind and ice, a man can be nothing else."[1]

In the course of generations the influence of those surroundings on the race that dwells among them must be deep and powerful.   Even on the individual who lives and works among them, they exercise a very perceptible influence.

In the preceding section it has been shown clearly that the one strong feature in the Phrygian character lay in their religion.   Only through their religion and the accompaniments which it created—music, musical instruments, religious dances, religious societies—did the Phrygians impress or affect other races.

In 205 the Phrygian religion was solemnly welcomed into the Roman State from its old seat in Galatia.   It was brought into Attica in the fourth and even in the fifth century B.C., and continued to be an influence there in spite of the ridicule of the comic poets, the scorn of philosophers, and the hatred of patriots.

How is it possible to recover any knowledge of the Phrygian religion at that early time?

We can do so, because that religion was so permanent and unchangeable over great part of Asia Minor.   When Paul traversed the region of Phrygia, the religion was the same as that which prevailed when the Gauls entered

---

[1] Conan Doyle, *Captain of the Pole-star*, p. 23.

Galatia. A cult of fundamentally the same character—the native Anatolian religion—prevailed over the whole vast peninsula before Gauls, or Phryges, or Greeks had entered the country. Those three immigrant peoples produced considerable effect on it within their own sphere ; but the effect was more in the way of limiting its power than of changing its character. The brief allusions made to its rites by Demosthenes, Aristophanes, and many other Greeks who satirised it in the fourth and fifth centuries, show beyond question that it was fundamentally always the same.

Hence, with proper discretion, we can use the memorials of the Roman time for the illustration of the ancient period. The evidence is gathered slowly, point by point, from the monuments scattered over the country, illustrated by the references of ancient writers. The scattered fragments are all collected and studied individually in the *Cities and Bishoprics of Phrygia.* Here we can only give a brief outline of the facts needed (1) for the study of the Epistle to the Galatians, and (2) for the comprehension of the " Galatian Question ".

The accounts which have been transmitted to us of the Phrygian religion are most unfavourable. Demosthenes describes with the keenest contempt and sarcasm the Phrygian rites of which his great rival Aeschines, as he says, had been a celebrant.[1] Certainly, with their loud cries or howls, and their grotesque ceremony of purifying the nude *mystes* with potter's clay and bran, they lent themselves readily and deservedly to caricature as the irrational and degrading ritual of unwashed savages.

The Christian writers, and especially Clement of Alexandria,[2] give a terrible picture of the repulsive and immoral

---

[1] *De Corona*, 259-260.   [2] *Protrept.* 2, p. 76.

drama of divine life that was acted before the initiated in
the Phrygian Mysteries. The details cannot be quoted.
The drama that was acted was the drama of humanity, as
it was apprehended by a rude and primitive people, who
regarded the mystery of life, changing from parents to
children, yet remaining unchanged through its variations,
as the great fact in which the divine nature was manifested.
The divine parents give birth to the divine children ; and
the children are only the parents in another form. The
daughter is the mother : Leto melts into Artemis, and
Artemis into Leto : they are only two slightly differentiated
forms of the ultimate divine personality in its feminine
aspect : the continuity of life is unbroken : the child re-
places the parent, different and yet the same.[1] The feminine
element is regarded as the fundamental one : the male god
is its accompaniment to complete the cycle of life, but he
is almost always regarded as the inferior, the servant, or
the companion of the Mother-Goddess. From their union,
which is represented as an act of violence and deceit, springs
the daughter, Kora or Artemis in Greek names. Again
from another act of violence and deceit the daughter bears
the young god ; and he is simply "the god" once more,
different and yet the same : "the bull is the father of the
serpent, and the serpent of the bull ".

The punishment for these horrors is the mutilation which
the god perpetrates on himself, and which the celebrants
often in religious ecstasy performed upon themselves.

To understand the relation in which the Epistle stands
to this religion, we must observe the following points :—

I. The Anatolian religion was carried out in an elaborate

---

[1] Taken nearly verbatim from *Cities and Bish. of Phrygia*, pt. I,
p. 91.

and minute ritual. Demosthenes' satirical description of the ceremony of purification in preparation for the celebration of the Mysteries,[1] would be enough to show this. Also there was a separate kind of purification for bloodshed,[2] and there were regulations about sacred animals, distinction of prohibited and permitted food, and many other rules implying a highly artificial system of life.[3]

II. In the oldest Anatolian system, the divine power exercised through the priests was the chief, almost the only, ruling influence acting permanently upon the people.

There was no municipal system, nothing corresponding to the Greek city with its thinking citizens, acting on their own initiative, and interesting themselves directly in the fortunes of their state. The evils of the Greek city system, with its weakness in the central government and the law, and its over-stimulation of the half-educated individual, are apt to blind us at the present time to the immense gain that has accrued to the world from the healthy freedom that inspired the Greek citizen-states.[4] We can imagine the contempt with which the free, thinking, acting Greek looked down on the enslaved, mindless, priest-guided Phrygian or Lycaonian.

The Anatolian social system was the village organisation. The villagers lived side by side, but apparently had no administrative rights. They looked solely to the religious centre for direction and for orders. The prophets and priests interpreted the divine will to the people ; and "the

---

[1] See above, p. 37.   [2] Herod. I 35.
[3] *Cities and Bish. of Phrygia,* I, p. 134 ff.
[4] To have recognised properly this glory of the Greek system is Grote's merit. Some more recent historians abroad have neglected it too much,

command of the God (or Goddess) " is very often mentioned in the inscriptions as the motive for the villagers' actions. Beyond this there was no education, and no state, and probably little or no formal law.[1]

There was probably in the earliest time a central rule of a king; but this was exercised, undoubtedly, in alliance with, and through the agency of, the priests at the great religious centres.

III. The Phrygian religion was the perpetuation of a primitive social condition, which the people in 'their ordinary life had long risen above. There was in that religion no marriage, but merely secret and fraudulent union of goddess and god. Hence there arose this dangerous situation that the religion of the country was on a lower moral standard than the ordinary life of society. In their religion the people learned that the divine life was the unrestrained existence of the wild animals, and that those who were serving the god, possessed by the divine ecstasy, or acting under the divine command, were bound to act contrary to the social customs recognised in ordinary life.[2]

IV. The Anatolian religion was a glorification of the female element in human life. As has appeared in the preceding section, the national character is receptive and passive, not self-assertive and active. The character of the people was created and nourished by the genius of the land in which they lived; and their religion represented to them the female element as the nobler development of humanity, while the male is secondary and on a lower plane. The Goddess-Mother was represented in the mystic ritual

[1] On the village system see *Cities and Bish. of Phrygia,* I, pp. 124, 129; Anderson in *Journ. Hell. St.,* 1897, p. 412.

[2] Compare the *Church in the Rom. Emp.,* p. 397 f.

as the prominent figure ; the God comes in only to cause the crises in her life, and of his life we hear nothing more : the life of the Goddess is the fulness and the permanence of nature.

Among the peoples of the west it was very different.

The most complete and characteristic development of Hellenism—in Athens and in the great colonising cities of Ionia—was accompanied by a depreciation and subordination of the female element. The true glory of woman among them was to be as much as possible unheard of and unknown. She was, if honourable, to live a life of seclusion and repression : she could be educated and active only through dishonour and shame.

A race which, like the Phryges, forced its way into Asia Minor by violence and war, necessarily trusted to the qualities that are most easily developed and maintained in the male sex. A conquering race in a foreign land usually brings with it more men than women : it takes wives from the daughters of the conquered land, and the power of the male in the family is inevitably strengthened in such a condition of the nation.

It is natural, therefore, to find in the neighbourhood of the old Metropolis of the Phryges that the worship of Zeus the Charioteer and Zeus the Thunderer was predominant in the Roman period (p. 30). Beyond this, there was a considerable change produced throughout Phrygia (1) in the outward forms of religion, and (2) in social institutions.

(1) There were several personages in the divine family, whose interaction makes the drama of nature and life. One of these personages was commonly selected in each district as the most prominent in ordinary life; and, according to the qualities of the people and the influence of the

natural surroundings, characteristics and powers, titles and epithets, were bestowed upon this divine personage. In the mysteries the entire divine drama of life was revealed ; but in common life some one deity was usually appealed to. The power of the Phryges tended to give popular pre-eminence to the God, and to make the Goddess less conspicuous than she had formerly been.

(2) As we have seen, the Anatolian religion stereotyped a primitive phase in the social system of the country. It had taken form as the consecration and divine authorisation of that primitive system ; and in its inner character it preserved the original features. The immigrant Greeks and Phryges and Gauls powerfully affected the whole fabric of society and law ; Greeks and Phryges certainly modified the external aspect of the ritual ; they made the inner mysteries of the Anatolian religion more secret, more mysterious, further removed from the light of day, and of course prevented it from being the universal guide and director of the people ; they raised up alongside of it new motives to action ; the Greeks, especially, circumscribed its power by imparting education, philosophic thought, political interests, and municipal ambition to part of the people.

V. The practical performance of the ritual was much connected with the grave ; but the grave was regarded not as concerned with death, but as the opening of life : it is expressly stated on many gravestones, that the stone is "the Door," and this was made clear by its shape or by the name "Door" engraved upon it.[1] Every grave was a

[1] On the Phrygian customs of burial, see *Cities and Bish. of Phrygia,* pt. I, p. 99, pt. II, p. 367, no. 226, p. 384, and J. G. C. Anderson in *Journal of Hellenic Studies,* 1899, p. 127. Noack has described the "door-stones" in *Mittheil. Instit. Athen.,* 1894, p. 326. Illustrations also in *Cities and Bish.,* pt. II, pp. 628, 661, 791.

sanctuary, and the dead man was living in and with the divine nature ; the making of the grave was regarded as the discharge of a vow to the God; the deceased is described on some stones as the " God "; common forms of dedication are " to the Gods beneath the earth and the deceased," " to the deceased and to the God a vow " ; a man often prepares his own tomb as " a vow to the God (or the Goddess)," " on behalf of his own salvation a vow to the God," or even, " by (divine) command a vow to the God, and for himself while still living ".

Further, as the tomb was a sanctuary, so every sanctuary was closely connected with a tomb. The ancient Phrygian hero went back to the mother that bore him, for all sprang from the Mother-Goddess in some one of her various manifestations, whether she is the divine lake Koloe beside Sardis and the Naiad Nymph of the Troad,[1] or appears in human form to her favoured Anchises. She is the Earth, the universal Mother, called Ma by all men. She is the life of Nature, the spirit of the lakes and forests and rivers and crops, the patroness of all wild animals, of everything that is free and strong and joyous. Beside her sanctuary is the burial-place of her sons. Wherever there was a shrine marking some holy place, it took the form of a great mound covering a grave, or a rock-sculpture forming the front of a grave, or rising high beside a grave. The same custom lives on to the present day under the Mohammedan veneer that is spread over it. Wherever the divine presence is indicated by any outward sign, such as hot springs, or even simply by the haunting presence of ancient life and civilisation amid their ruins, there is a shrine—always in the form of the grave of some hero, who now bears a

[1] *Iliad*, II 865, XIV 444, XX 384.

Moh'ammedan name such as Black-Akhmet, or Uryan Baba, or Omar Baba, or so on. But of old the shrine and the hero were there ; only they bore Phrygian, instead of Arabic or Turkish names.

Further, if the custom has continued to the present day, must it not have lasted unbroken through the Christian period? Paul expostulated with the Phrygians of Colossae about their devotion to the "worship of angels," Col. III 12 ; this is usually represented by commentators as a Judaistic or Essene idea, but may it not be the Christianising form given to the worship of the dead heroes? In later time, if we knew more about the worship of martyrs in the country, we should probably find that it retained much of the ancient connection with the grave. That is certainly the case with the legend of Saint Abercius ; but few *Acta* of the Phrygian Saints are preserved.

How easy and natural it was for any one brought up in the Jewish theology to identify the worship of the deified dead with the worship of angels is shown by the following comment on the remarkable passage of Luke XX 36, *they are equal to angels, for they are sons of God, since they are sons of the resurrection.* "The Jews shared in the common notion that the dead lived in the underworld. They also believed that some persons could escape from the dead and be taken directly to the abode of God, like Elijah. This was interpreted to mean that they became angelic members of the heavenly host (Ethiopic *Enoch* 12, 3, 4). Further, in Gen. VI 4, angels are called sons of God. Luke XX 36, means, therefore, that when the resurrection occurs, all who participate in it are heavenly beings." [1]

[1] Professor Shailer Matthews in a notice of Professor G. E. Barton on the "Spiritual Development of Paul," *Biblical World*, April, 1899, p. 279.

SECTION 6.

SETTLEMENT OF THE GAULS IN GALATIA.

IN the year B.C. 278-7 a large body of Gauls, who had
been ravaging the south-eastern parts of Europe, Greece,
Macedonia and Thrace, crossed into Asia Minor at the
invitation of Nicomedes, king of Bithynia (278-250). They
came as a migrating nation, with wives and children, not
as a mere body of mercenary soldiers engaged by a king
to help in his wars. This national character gave permanence to their settlement, and made their migration an
epoch in the history of Asia Minor.[1] Bodies of Gauls often
in the following century engaged as mercenaries for a time
with some king ; but the nation remained a body to which
the mercenaries returned. Had the Gauls consisted only
or mainly of men, they would probably have soon been
scattered in military colonies and rapidly have been merged
in the native population. But it is recorded that of the
20,000 who came under Leonnorius and Lutarius in 278-7,
only half were armed men.

But, owing to this national character of the immigration,
the Gauls required to have something in the way of a home
and a centre. However hardy and courageous their women
were, families cannot live a life of raiding, as a body of
mercenaries could. Naturally they would gradually drift

[1] See above, p. 10.

(45)

to the point of least resistance; and the account which has just been given of the Phrygian people explains why this point was found in Phrygia.

Further, it was found in north-eastern Phrygia, for the south and west were strengthened against the Gauls by the armies of the Seleucid kings of Syria and of the Pergamenian rulers. The fate of the western and southern two-thirds of Asia Minor hung on the rivalry between those two dynasties. The Seleucid dominion over Lycaonia, Phrygia, Caria, Lydia, etc., was contested with varying success by the Pergamenian kings, until at last, in B.C. 189, the Seleucid armies were finally expelled. But while they held to their Lydian rule, the Seleucid kings had to maintain the open road through Lycaonia and southern Phrygia against the Gauls. Similarly in north-western Phrygia the Pergamenian kings were always striving to establish their authority, and thus kept pushing the Gauls eastward.

Thus, after fifty years of promiscuous raiding over great part of western Asia Minor, during which the Gauls, "alternately the scourge and the allies of each Asiatic prince in succession, as passion or interest dictated, indulged their predatory instincts," [1] they were at last fixed in a country which was recognised as their permanent possession.

The conditions, as thus described, explain why the final settlement of the Gauls is attributed variously by ancient authorities. Their settlement was the result of the long-continued pressure of circumstances; and some single event in the fifty years' fighting is selected by one historian as the most critical and decisive, while others mention other events as more important. The Gauls, or according to the

[1] Lightfoot, *Galatians*, p. 6.

Greek name, Galatae,[1] were during this period struggling for life and a home : they were powerful rather through alliance or mercenary service with some of the warring kingdoms in Asia Minor than through their own strength. It is practically certain that they could not have stood unaided against either of the two great Hellenistic powers, the rising Pergamenian kingdom, or the huge Seleucid Empire (which stretched from Smyrna on the Aegean Sea to some vague limit far in the heart of the Asian continent) ; but they never were unaided. The principal events in that fifty years of raids and wars may be described as follows.

According to Apollonius, the Carian historian,[2] the Galatae were in alliance with Mithridates I, King of Pontus (B.C. 302-266), and were by him settled round Ancyra; and E. Meyer infers that that country must have belonged to the Pontic kings at the time. But the inference is wrong. The facts merely prove that Antiochus's authority over north-eastern Phrygia was weak at the time. Kings prefer to give away their neighbour's dominions rather than their own ; and so Mithridatcs did to the Gauls.

According to Livy [3] the Gauls at this early period of their ravages were in three divisions : the Trocmi wasted the lands towards the Hellespont, the Tolistobogii plundered Aeolis, and the Tectosages took the inner country as their sphere of operations. It was, therefore, the Tecto-

---

[1] *Galli*, warriors : *Galatae*, nobles. The latter name probably spread from the Greeks of Marseilles. There is some tendency to use Κέλτοι or Κέλται as the generic name of all cognate tribes. The general name for the speech is Κελτική, Κελτιστί.

[2] Apollonius, of unknown date, is often said to belong to the Cilician Aphrodisias; but obviously he was of the Carian city. Suidas says only Ἀφροδισιεύς.

[3] XXXVIII 16, 12 (on the authority doubtless of Polybius).

sages, doubtless, who were aided by Mithridates to settle
about Ancyra ; and the understanding between the Gauls
and the Pontic kings lasted for a considerable time. The
Seleucid Antiochus I was at this time the chief enemy of
both. He is said to have gained a great victory over the
Gauls ; but it cannot have been a very decisive one ; and
in 281 he was slain by a Gaul, probably in a battle against
either Philetaerus of Pergamus or Ariobarzanes of Pontus
(266-246).

The reign of Antiochus II was very disturbed ; and he
could not regain the lost Seleucid authority over the region
of Ancyra, seized by the Tectosages. His son Seleucus II
(247-226) gave his youngest sister (perhaps named Laodike)
in marriage to Mithridates II (246-190) ; and as dowry
she brought with her Great Phrygia to the Pontic king.[1]
This fact means that Seleucus in his difficulties was trying
to secure the Pontic alliance, or at least neutrality ; and
relinquished his claims to a country, in the remoter parts
of which his predecessors had ceased to possess any authority. It also implies, as E. Meyer recognises rightly, that
the Gauls round Ancyra were regarded as more or less
dependents, and not exactly as equal allies of Mithridates.

At this period so dangerous were the Gaulish raids over
the western regions of Asia Minor (in which they are said
to have ravaged as far south as even Themisonion[2] and
Apameia[3]), that Eumenes I of Pergamos (263-241) bought
safety by paying tribute to the Tolistoagii.[4] His successor

[1] Justin, XXXVIII 6.
[2] *Cities and Bish. of Phrygia*, I, p. 264.　　　[3] *Ibid.*, II, p. 422.
[4] Tolistoagii is the name in the early inscriptions. The form
Tolistobogii is also found in early authorities, and is universal in
inscriptions and coins of the Roman period. The relation between
the names is obscure.

Attalos I (241-197) refused to continue this tribute; and when the Tolistoagii invaded his country, he defeated them in a great battle at the sources of the Caicos, 240, or possibly a little later.

Soon after began the "Brothers' War" between Seleucus and Antiochus Hierax, the prize being the Seleucid dominions in Asia Minor. The Gauls were hired as mercenaries by Antiochus, and Mithridates also preferred this alliance to that of his father-in-law, Seleucus, who was defeated in a battle beside Ancyra[1] about 235. Then followed a quarrel between Hierax and his Gaulish mercenaries; and Hierax escaped by flight. Thereafter the Gauls appear as equal allies of Hierax, who became lord of Seleucid Asia Minor; and war broke out with Attalos I. In this war Attalos gained four great victories. The first, or second, was fought at the sanctuary of Aphrodite close to Pergamos (implying a raid by the allies up to the city) against the Tolistoagii and Tectosages and Hierax. In the other three battles (in Hellespontine Phrygia,[2] at Koloe, and on the Harpasos in Caria) only Antiochus is mentioned; hence probably the Gauls were decisively defeated at the Aphrodision, and the limits of their country were definitely drawn about 232, and a peace concluded with them, so that they took no further part in the war, whose issue was that Attalos I became lord of all Asia up to Taurus.

At this point, the Gaulish tribes were compelled to concentrate themselves in the country which henceforth bore

[1] So Polyaenus; Eusebius says in Cappadocia. Cappadocia here means, doubtless, the territory of the Pontic king (the name Pontus for the kingdom had hardly yet come into use), and therefore may include Ancyra. The Gauls are named as the victors by Trogus and Polyaenus; Mithridates by Eusebius.

[2] This may possibly have been the first battle.

4

their name. The Tectosages remained about Ancyra ; the
other two were forced into the same neighbourhood. There
was a kind of bargain struck. On the one hand Attalos
recognised the right of the Gauls to that land ; they were
no longer to be regarded as interlopers and outlaws; they
now had their acknowledged home as one of the peoples
of Asia Minor. On the other hand, the Gauls evidently
agreed to observe their fixed boundaries on the side towards
Attalos, and to refrain from raiding his territory.

Clearly, their bounds on the west were now drawn more
narrowly. A region west from Pessinus bore in later times
the name of the Gaulish tribe Troknades ; and yet it was
part of Asia (*i.e.*, the Pergamenian kingdom), and not
included in Galatia. There seems no other occasion except
this when such a region is likely to have been taken from
the Gauls by the Pergamenian kings. At the same time
Pessinus was relieved from the pressure of the Gauls.
Whether they had ever succeeded in capturing that great
religious centre, or had only mastered the open country
round it while the strong and populous city maintained
itself against them, certain it is that for the following fifty
years Pessinus was in close alliance with Pergamos and at
variance with the Gauls.

If the Gauls were thus shut in on the west, how were
they to find room? Probably they found it by spreading
in other directions. They did not spread north, because
we find them henceforth allied with their northern neighbour Paphlagonia ; and Bithynia seems not to have lost
any territory to them, as Juliopolis remained Bithynian for
centuries. South, they bordered on territory disputed
between Attalos and the Seleucids, from which therefore
they were debarred. But on the east they had more scope ;

and the friends of Pergamos, which represented the Hellenising and civilising power in Asia Minor, must be foes of
Pontus, the oriental and barbarian power. This makes it
probable that now they crossed the Halys, and occupied
part of the Pontic territory. Some years afterwards, too,
we find them in the later stages of a quarrel with Cappadocia about territory claimed by both, evidently east of
the Halys. For a time, then, the face of the new nation,
the Galatae, was turned towards the east.

Here originates the name Galatia. The use of that name
implies more than mere occupancy of the land by roving,
unsettled bands of Gauls. It implies a political reality, a
form of government, a recognised " land of the Galatae ".
Henceforth, we speak of this people by the name which
they bore among the Greek-speaking races—Γαλάται.

But what was the sense in which this term, Galatae, was
used? Did it indicate simply the Gaulish conquerors? or
did it include the entire population of the country Galatia?
At first, of course, the Galatae were only the Gaulish conquerors, who were as sharply marked off from the Phrygian
subject-people, as Normans were from English about A.D.
1066-1100. But, obviously, not a thought of separation
between two sections of the population remains in the minds
of those writers who in late-Roman or Byzantine times
speak of the Galatian people. After the lapse of several
centuries, the Gauls had become as undistinguishable from
their subjects as Normans now are in England: a few old
families might trace their Gaulish descent,[1] but it was not a
practical factor in the life of the country.

[1] That families in Galatia boasted of their ancient lineage, Gaulish
or otherwise, is proved by several inscriptions: C.I.G. no. 4030 and
Cities and Bish. of Phrygia, pt. II, p. 649.

When and how this change was produced will be shown
in Section 8.

Note.—PRINCIPAL MODERN AUTHORITIES (apart from
Commentators) :—

Holder, *Alt-Celtischer Sprachschatz* (A-M).

Van Gelder, *De Gallis in Graecia et Asia ante an.* 150 (1888).

Staehelin, *Geschichte der Kleinasiatischen Galater* (1897).

Körte in *Mittheilungen des Instituts Athen. Abth.* (1897).

Zwintcher, *de Galatarum Tetrarchis.*

Anderson in *Journal of Hellenic Studies* (1899).

Crowfoot in *Journal of Hellenic Studies* (1899).

Perrot, *Explor. Archéol. de la Galatie* (1862).

Perrot, *de Galatia Provincia Romana* (1867).

Perrot, *Mémoires d'Archéologie,* p. 229 ff.

Meyer, *Geschichte des Koenigreichs Pontos* (1879).

Th. Reinach, *Rois de Bithynie, de Pont, de Cappadoce* (1888 and 1887).

Hennig, *Symbolae ad As. Min. Reges Sacerdotes* (1893).

Wroth, *Catalogue of Brit. Mus. Coins, Galatia,* etc. (1899).

Radet in *Revue des Universités du Midi* (1896).

Ramsay, *Histor. Geography of Asia Minor,* Ch. H, K.

Pauly-Wissowa, *Real. Encyclop. s.vv.* Attalos, Antiochos, etc.

The General Histories of the period.

See also p. 102.

SECTION 7.

THE HISTORY OF GALATIA, B.C. 232-64.

DURING this period only isolated glimpses are afforded us into the fate and fortunes of Galatia, as the Gaulish tribes came into relations with the western peoples, whose history is better known.

Before describing the scattered facts, we may summarise the general result as follows. The Galatian power on the whole declined; and finally the skilful and vigorous Pergamenian policy, by gradually introducing Greek civilisation into the country and forming a philo-Greek party, was on the point of destroying the Galatic isolation, and bringing the tribes under Pergamenian and Hellenistic influence, when Rome interfered to preserve the Galatian independence. The result was a strong reaction against Hellenism and a recrudescence of the old barbaric and Celtic character: the philo-Greek party in Galatia seems to have been annihilated, and Galatian isolation and dissimilarity from the surrounding Graeco-Asiatic peoples was maintained.

The amalgamation of the immigrant Celtic and the old Phrygian population in Galatia seems to have proceeded rapidly after 189 B.C.; and there ensued a decided growth in Galatic strength, unity and vigour, and this reinvigorated nation began to press outwards on its weaker neighbours and to enlarge its bounds, no longer by mere raid, but by

(53)

occupation. Finally it was able with Roman help to maintain itself against the united Asiatic and Greek reaction under Mithridates, and to emerge from that terrible struggle stronger and greater than before.

As we saw, the Gauls played no part in the later wars of Attalos. The cis-Tauran dominion of the Pergamenian king lasted only for a few years. Seleucus Keraunos (226-223) started personally for a campaign in Asia Minor, when he was poisoned by a Gaul named Apatourios, doubtless a leader of mercenaries in his service.[1] Under his successor Antiochus the Great, Achaios recovered the Seleucid dominion in Lydia, Phrygia, etc. Thereafter he rebelled against his cousin, King Antiochus, once more endangering the Seleucid realm in Asia Minor. Attalos now began to recover his power ; and, in order to strengthen himself, brought over from Europe a Gallic tribe, the Aigosages, with whose aid he made a raid in B.C. 218 into Aeolis and then eastward across Lydia into north Phrygia as far as Apia. Thereafter he settled the Gauls in the Hellespontine Phrygia, where, however, they were destroyed by Prusias, King of Bithynia, in 217-16.

The northern part of Phrygia seems henceforth to have remained subject to Attalos, probably by arrangement with Antiochus the Great. The latter had Attalos as his ally, while besieging Achaios in Sardis, which he captured in 214. During the following years Attalos became possessed also of Phrygia Epiktetos, the region of Kotiaion

[1] Galatic mercenaries regularly served in the Seleucid armies and were courted by rebellious satraps : compare Polybius, V 53, 3 and 8 ; 79, 11 ; XXI 20 ; Livy, XXXVII 8 and 38 ; Appian *Syr.* 6 and 32. Galatic mercenaries in the Egyptian armies, Polybius, V 65, 10 ; 82, 5.

and Dorylaion, which previously belonged to the kings of Bithynia. Perhaps this acquisition was the result of the war with Prusias in 207-6. That Attalos's dominion reached to the neighbourhood of Pessinus, and that he cultivated friendly relations with the great sanctuary there, is proved by the following events.

In B.C. 205 the Sibylline Books were found to promise victory in the Carthaginian War to the Romans, if they brought the Great Idaean Mother from Pessinus to Rome. This pointed to an active Eastern policy in Rome; it implied that the state must come into closer relations with the eastern Mediterranean peoples; and in view of Hannibal's settled plan of uniting those peoples in an anti-Roman league, the new Roman policy was prudent.

Five ambassadors with five quinqueremes were sent to Delphi, and the Oracle referred them to Attalos. Attalos seized the opportunity of linking his fortunes to the great republic of the west, welcomed the ambassadors, and in person conducted them to Pessinus. Through his influence the sacred stone, the symbol of the goddess, was delivered to the Romans, and brought in state to Rome. Along with the sacred stone, the whole Phrygian ritual, with its eunuch priests, was established in Rome.

In this transaction it is obvious that the Gauls had no part. The power of Attalos extended close up to Pessinus, and he was in direct relations with the governing priestly hierarchy. The Gauls did not need to be consulted, and therefore cannot have had any footing in Pessinus. As we shall see, it was not till between 189 and 164 that they succeeded in establishing themselves in that city.

In the period 232-200 the Gauls of Galatia were not active in western Asia Minor. Whatever was the reason, the agreement concluded with Attalos when they were settled in Galatia, was strictly observed by them for a time. Apparently they turned their attention northwards, and their unsuccessful siege of Herakleia on the Euxine may be referred to this period.[1]

The alliance with Morzeos, King of Paphlagonia, which we find existing in 189, apparently as an old-standing connection, would be useful in this siege.

Shortly after 200 they were turning their attention westwards once more. In 196, the year after Attalos died, they were threatening Lampsakos on the Hellespont, and that city procured from Massalia in Gaul a letter of recommendation to the Tolistoagii.[2] All the chiefs of the Gauls had renounced their friendship with Pergamos before 189, with the single exception of Eposognatus,[3] one of the Tolistoagii. This formal renunciation of friendship implies that the Galatian tribes had begun to observe international courtesies, and wage regular war in place of raids.

Probably the Galatian tribes were on bad terms with Pontus during this time. In 189 the Trocmi must have dreaded attack from the east, for they sent their wives and children for safe keeping among the Tektosages.

In 189 the consul, Cn. Manlius Vulso, in order to strike terror once for all into the nations west of the Halys, led an army against the Gauls, who had fought for Antiochus against Rome at the battle of Magnesia.

---

[1] Memnon 28, the only authority, says that the siege occurred " before the Romans entered Asia," *i.e.*, before 190.

[2] Lolling and Mommsen, *Mitth. Instit. Athen.*, VI, p. 96 ff, 212 ; Mommsen, *Rom. Gesch.*, Ed. 8, I, pp. 724, 742, (transl. II, pp. 447, 469).

[3] Livy, XXXVIII 18, 1.

The Tolistobogii with their families and the warriors of the Trocmi occupied Mount Olympus, evidently a hill of no great height,[1] probably part of the low range on the right hand as one goes from Pessinus to Ancyra.[2] Manlius defeated them with immense slaughter,[3] and captured 40,000 prisoners to be sold as slaves. Then he proceeded to occupy Ancyra, and thereafter defeated the Tectosages, who had concentrated on Mount Magaba (probably south-east from Ancyra); the slain Gauls are estimated at not more than 8000, and of the captives no estimate is given.[4]

Content with these severe blows, Manlius finally made peace, stipulating only that the Gauls should no longer make those armed raids in western Asia Minor, which had been the terror of all the cities for about eighty years.[5]

The stipulation is significant. It shows that the danger of a Gallic raid was still ever present to the peoples of western Asia Minor: the victories of Pergamenian and Seleucid armies over the Gauls had not been so decisive as to tame the unruly Galatian barbarians. According to Roman ideas, the consul was fully justified, now that Rome had interfered decidedly in Asian affairs, in ensuring peace by making the Roman power felt all round the limits which the republic for the present set to itself, *viz.*, the Taurus mountains and the Halys river. That he carried out this policy with a spirit of greed and rapine is true; but it is a mistake to regard the expedition as a mere plundering

---

[1] The operations, as described by Livy, prove this.

[2] It is the watershed between the Ancyra stream and the Ilidja-Su.

[3] Estimates of slain vary from 10,000 to 40,000.

[4] Livy, XXXVIII 27.   [5] *Ibid.*, 40.

raid. The blow against the Gauls was inevitably demanded by Roman policy.[1]

Taken in connection with the Paphlagonian alliance, the Heracleian siege, and the threatening of Lampsakos, the terms concluded by Manlius show how powerful and menacing was this Galatic state in the heart of the Græco-Asiatic world as late as 189. The Roman allies were more gladdened by the defeat of the Gauls than of Antiochus himself, such was their hatred of those terrible barbarians[2] and their never-ceasing terror of a possible attack at any moment. The relief which was felt all through Asia carried the fame of the Romans even to Syria and Palestine, and a confused recollection of the results of the Galatian war was part of the foundations of their reputation in the eyes of Judas Maccabaeus, and induced him to seek alliance with them against his Seleucid foes in B.C. 161.[3]

In this war we observe that the chiefs of the Galatae were divided. One of the tetrarchs, Eposognatus, sided with Eumenes and the Romans. A small party among the Galatae was now inclined to prefer the alliance with the west, the side of civilisation, though the vast majority rallied to the standard of barbarian independence. In the following years the former party grew stronger.

But, while ready to strike down the Galatic pretensions to terrorise Asia, the Romans were not disposed to encourage Eumenes too much ; and their subsequent policy shows a settled intention of discouraging his schemes and

---

[1] Such is Mommsen's view, as against the superficial opinion that Manlius was a mere piratical raider.

[2] *Immanium barbarorum*, says Livy, XXXVIII 37.

[3] 1 Macc., VIII 2 : the passage illustrates the vague and inaccurate conceptions of the Jews as to the Roman exploits.

preventing his acquiring a decided supremacy in Asia. The aim of Rome was to keep the various interests in Asia balanced uneasily against one another, and draw the hopes of all towards herself. As usual, she governed by dividing and by preventing the concentration of power in any hands but her own ; and the immediate necessity was to keep Eumenes weak by encouraging the Galatian tribes.

Manlius had charged the Galatians to keep peace with Eumenes ;[1] but very soon a war broke out, in which they, along with Pharnaces of Pontus and Prusias of Bithynia, fought against the Pergamenian king.[2] Ortiagon, a chief of the Tolistobogii,[3] aimed at supreme power among the Gauls ;[4] but in 181 several chiefs are mentioned, implying that the ordinary tetrarchic or cantonal system[5] continued. As Polybius conversed with Ortiagon's wife at Sardis, while other chiefs are mentioned as the regular allies of Pharnaces,[6] it is probable that two factions existed after 189 in Galatia : one headed by Ortiagon favoured a Per-gamenian alliance and consolidation of the country after the analogy of a Greek kingdom ; the other favoured the Pontic alliance, and the old Gaulish tribal system. The latter party proved stronger, and Ortiagon had to retire with his family into Pergamenian territory.

But it soon became evident to the Galatians that a Pontic alliance meant a Pontic tyranny. Pontic armies domineered in Galatia. In these circumstances the same

---

[1] Livy, XXXVIII 40.   [2] Trogus, XXXII *prolog.*

[3] He fought at Mt. Olympus, where no Tectosages were engaged ; and his wife was with him, while the women of the Trocmi had been sent to Mt. Magaba.

[4] Polyb., XXII 21.   [5] See section 8, p. 72.   [6] Polybius, XXIV 8, 6.

chiefs, Carsignatus and Gaizatorix,[1] that had previously
led the Pontic faction, now joined Eumenes in B.C. 181 ;
and the Pergamenian king marched through Galatia into
Cappadocia to join his ally Ariarathes ; but, when they
were about to attack Pharnaces in his own land, the
Roman ambassadors ordered both sides to cease hostilities.
At last in 179 peace was concluded, one condition being
that Pharnaces should abandon all attempt to interfere in
Galatia, and that his agreements with Galatian chiefs should
be invalid.

Thus the Pergamenian faction apparently gained the
upper hand in Galatia for a time after B.C. 179; and
Galatian auxiliaries are mentioned in the Pergamenian
armies 171 and 169.[2]   Among them Carsignatus, the
former ally of Pharnaces, is mentioned, showing how completely the friendship of Eumenes was adopted in Galatia,
and making it probable that Ortiagon's policy of unifying
Galatia was at an end.   Eumenes had learned, with his
usual tact, that a Greek system of monarchic government
could not be forced on the Gauls.   It is, however, highly
probable, as Van Gelder has rightly recognised, that at
this time the amelioration of Galatian manners and the
introduction of more civilised ways into the country, was
gradually and cautiously fostered by the patient skill and
administrative ability of Eumenes.

The magnificent temple at Pessinus, whose construction
Strabo assigns to the Attalid dynasty, was probably built
or at least begun during this period.

But Roman jealousy of Eumenes's success stopped the
pacification of western Asia, which Eumenes was carrying

---

[1] Gaizotorios in Polyb., XXV 4.   [2] Livy, XLII 55, XLIV 13.

out so skilfully. True and loyal as the king had been to Rome, he was accused falsely of favouring the Macedonians, though he had actively assisted Rome against them. In 167 the Galatians, instigated by Prusias, invaded his country, under a chief named Advertas, and nearly succeeded in destroying his monarchy,[1] and the Romans would not permit him to punish the nation. In the following years they lent ready ear to Bithynian and Galatian ambassadors complaining of Eumenes.

In spite of the Roman covert opposition, Eumenes again proved victor. A peace was concluded in 165 with the help of the Romans, guaranteeing the freedom of Galatia, but binding the Gauls to abstain from raids like those of 167 and 166. Thus Eumenes's Galatian ascendancy was ended, and the reactionary Galatian party was triumphant.

This war had evidently been carried out by the reactionary party in Galatia, and was marked by a recrudescence of the old barbarous custom. The handsomest captives were sacrificed to the Gods ; the rest were speared ; and even those whose hospitality the Gauls had previously enjoyed were not spared.[2]

About 164-160 there was a long dispute between the Galatians and Ariarathes of Cappadocia as to certain border country, which the Trocmi had tried vainly to seize.[3] At first the Roman favour inclined to the Galatians, but Ariarathes bought the favour of all ambassadors, and finally of the senate ; and the dispute was probably decided

[1] Livy, XLV 19.

[2] Diodor, *excerpt. de Virt. et Vit.* 31, 2, p. 582, referred to this period by Van Gelder, p. 265, rightly.

[3] Polyb., XXXI 13.

in his favour (which Polybius evidently considered to be just).

To the years immediately following belongs a correspondence between Eumenes or his successor Attalos II (158-138) and the high priest of Pessinus.[1] The high priest who had assumed the priestly sacred name Attis, was a Gaul,[2] but an adherent of the Pergamenian faction; and the correspondence shows that there was a good deal of dissension among the Gauls and intriguing for and against the Pergamenian influence, which had its chief centre at the great *hieron* of the Pessinuntine Goddess. Pessinus, then, had by this time come under Galatian power, and a Gaul was high priest. Now, an inscription of the Roman period shows that half of the college of priests who ministered at the hieron of Pessinus were of Gaulish birth, so that the priest who ranked tenth in the college was fifth among the Galatian priests; and this seems to prove that an arrangement must have been made dividing the priesthoods between the old priestly families and the Gaulish conquerors[3] (doubtless all of the Tolistobogian tribe, to whom Pessinus belonged).

The acquisition of Pessinus by the Tolistobogii must be assigned to the period between 189 and 164.

In these long wars it is evident that the Trocmi occupied the most unfavourable, and the Tectosages the most favourable situation. The Trocmi were close to Pontus; the Pontic kings were always trying to assert their authority over

[1] Best published by Domaszewski in *Arch. Epigr. Mittheil. Oesterreich*, 1884, p. 95 ff.

[2] His brother bore the Gaulish name Aiorix.

[3] Professor A. Körte found and published the inscription *Mittheil. Inst. Athen.*, 1897, pp. 16, 39; and accepts the above interpretation, *Philolog. Wochenschrift*, 1898, p. 1 f.

Galatia; and in every war the Trocmi would suffer most. They were evidently cramped for room, for they had made many attempts to seize parts of Cappadocia;[1] but ultimately failed, at least in part. They then probably turned their efforts in another direction. They could not go north, for the allied Paphlagonia prevented them. Bithynia was too strong on the north-west; Pergamos pressed them on the west and south-west.

On the south alone was Galatic expansion comparatively easy during this period. Here lay the open, defenceless country of Lycaonia. Under the Seleucid kings Lycaonia was shut against them, for it was the gate to the Seleucid Phrygian and Lydian territory, and must be kept open and safe at all costs. But when the Seleucid power was driven out, and confined to the country south and east of Taurus, then Lycaonia was the most distant and defenceless part of the Pergamenian territory. Moreover, as Pisidian Antioch was made a free state, Lycaonia was nearly cut off from the Pergamenian realm ; and a glance at the map will show how difficult it must have been to maintain Pergamenian power in Lycaonia when thus separated. What, then, was the lot of Lycaonia in the century following the constitution of the Pergamenian kingdom in 189?

The authorities, Polybius and Livy, are both agreed that Lycaonia was assigned to Eumenes in 189. On the other hand, it is certain that Lycaonia was not part of the Pergamenian kingdom in 133, for the whole kingdom passed to Rome and became the Roman Province Asia. The assured

---

[1] Incidentally, we note that this implies a very scattered system of habitation among the Gauls. For their numbers their territory was not really narrow. But evidently their system consisted in a parcelling out of the territory in lots to the tribal aristocracy.

fact then is that, if Livy and Polybius are right,[1] Lycaonia dropped out of the Pergamenian realm between 189 and 133.

Now, Ptolemy mentions a country called the " Added Land,"[2] which was at some period tacked on to Galatia. It lay on the west side of Lake Tatta, and therefore must have originally belonged to Lycaonia, and been taken and added to Galatia, just as the " Acquired Phrygia "[3] had been taken from Bithynia and added to Phrygia about 206.

Further, Pliny[4] mentions that a part of Lycaonia was given as a tetrarchy to Galatia—making one of the twelve tetrarchies into which Galatia was divided.

Evidently these facts must be taken together, the tetrarchy taken from Lycaonia was "added" to Galatia; and the time when this occurred was when Lycaonia was protected neither by the Pergamenian nor by the Seleucid kings, between 189 and 133. We may go further, and say that the time was probably about 160, when the Galatae had failed to get the accession of territory from Cappadocia which they desired, and when the Roman influence protected the Cappadocian bounds as settled by the Imperial State; and the Galatae, pressed in on all other sides, found expansion easiest on the Lycaonian frontier.

It is not a real objection to this identification that Ptolemy excludes Iconium from the " Added Land," while Pliny says that Iconium was the capital of the Lycaonian

---

[1] Here one need not estimate the value of the conjecture advanced in *Cities and Bish. of Phrygia*, pt. I, p. 285. It must either remain uncertain, or be absolutely set aside, unless new evidence should be found. Livy, XXXVIII 39, had before him Polybius, XXII 27, as the MSS. have it now.

[2] Προσειλημμένη, V 4, 10. The word has been corrupted in many MSS.

[3] Ἐπίκτητος.   [4] *Nat. Hist.*, V 95.

tetrarchy added to Galatia. As we shall see, p. 105 ff, the double division of Lycaonia into the Tetrarchy or Added Land and Lycaonia Proper [1] gave place later to a triple division into the Added Land, the Lycaonian Diocese, and Cappadocian Lycaonia ; and that is the system which Ptolemy tries to describe, though as usual he makes mistakes.

Thus about B.C. 160 Galatia was greatly extended, having taken in Pessinus and probably Lycaonia as far as Iconium and Lystra.[2] This expansion must have taken place with the consent of the sovereign Rome, and is doubtless connected with their anti-Pergamenian bias at this time. The Galatians were encouraged in order to counterbalance the strength of Pergamos.

Trogus mentions [3] that Lycaonia and Cilicia were given in 129 to the sons of Ariarathes, King of Cappadocia, in reward for the help their father had given to Rome in the Asian revolt. It is fairly certain that the expression *Lycaonia et Cilicia*, used by Trogus, describes the same stretch of country in Lycaonia and Cilicia which is mentioned by Strabo, pp. 535, 537, as having been given to the kings of Cappadocia by the Romans : [4] this territory stretched from Derbe on the west by Kybistra to Kastabala on the skirts of Mount Amanus, and was called the Eleventh Strategia of Cappadocia, so that it includes all that part of Lycaonia which was not in the Galatic tetrarchy.

The testimony of Trogus, when rightly understood, thus

[1] Called *Lycaonia ipsa* by Pliny, V 95 (using an old authority).

[2] There were fourteen cities in the tetrarchy, and it seems impossible to make up that number without going as far south as Lystra, which moreover was closely connected with Iconium, being only eighteen miles from it.

[3] Justin, XXXVII 1, 2.

[4] So rightly Bergmann, *de Prov. Asia*, pp. 16, 17.

corroborates our conclusion as to the tetrarchy.   Lycaonia
now consisted of two parts: one was attached to Galatia
as an "added tetrarchy," and one to Cappadocia as an
"eleventh Strategia".

Thus, for some years the history of Galatia shows the
Gaul̦s fluctuating between the Pergamenian and the Pontic
alliance.   The former represents the tendency to civilisation and order; and had it triumphed, Galatia might have
adopted Greek manners and law.   But the party which
favoured the Gaulish manners and the old barbarian methods
gained the upper hand, thanks chiefly to the moral support
that Rome, jealous of Pergamenian power, gave them.

In the following century, when the Pontic kings roused
the Greeks of Asia Minor against Rome, the Galatian tribes,
as the faithful allies of the Italian state, were thrown into
still more violent antagonism to the Greek element in Asia.

Thus the Galatians were kept free from Greek civilisation.
Against it they allied themselves first with the Asiatic
barbarism of Pontus and thereafter with Roman order.
The progress of the tribes was from Gaulish barbarism to
Roman manners; and only when the Roman spirit found
itself too weak to assimilate the Asiatic Provinces and
allowed the Greek spirit free play, did the tribes turn
towards Greek civilisation (see Sections 13, 14).

After 160 the strength of the Pontic kingdom appears
to have grown greater.   Mithridates III Philopator Philadelphos Euergetes (169-121), son of Mithridates II, brother
of Pharnaces I (190-169), father of Mithridates the Great
(121-63),[1] had a glorious and successful reign.   He aided

---

[1] I follow Th. Reinach, against the older opinion, in spite of some
serious difficulties in his view (acknowledged fully by himself).   He
has also remodelled the whole Mithridatic genealogy, and reduced
the number of kings.

Attalus II in 154 against Prusias, became an ally of Rome, and sent troops to their aid in the Third Punic War, and again during the rebellion in Asia, 131-129.

In 129 Great Phrygia was granted to Mithridates III by Manius Aquillius; and though the Senate did not confirm the Consul's acts, yet Mithridates seems to have ruled Phrygia till his death in 121. But it seems impossible that he could rule Phrygia, unless he possessed the ascendancy in Galatia.[1] Yet Van Gelder's suggestion that between 160 and 130 Galatia lost its independence and passed under the Pontic domination, is improbable and unnecessary. The existence of two opposite parties in Galatia, one favouring the civilised Pergamenian and afterwards the Roman alliance, and one the barbaric and Pontic connection, furnishes a sufficient explanation. At this period the Pontic party was triumphant. But the ascendancy of Pontus, by which Galatia was now surrounded east and west, was likely soon to arouse the jealous and independent spirit of the Gauls. Rome, too, was on the watch against any Asiatic state that was growing more powerful than its neighbours.

Two measures of Rome, in 126 and 121, against the Pontic rule over Phrygia are mentioned. In 126 the Senate declared the acts of Aquillius inoperative, and recognised Phrygia as a free country. That decree of the Senate remained inoperative; and in the negotiations between Mithridates the Great and the Roman officers in B.C. 88, it is assumed on both sides that Phrygia had been given by the Romans to his father Mithridates Euergetes. This unanimous assumption must be taken to represent the

---

[1] So Van Gelder, p. 277, rightly argues.

actual fact; and recently it has been confirmed by an important inscription of the Phrygian city, Lysias, quoting a Senatus-consultum of B.C. 116,[1] in which the Senate recognises as valid all the arrangements of Mithridates Euergetes, implying obviously that he had been *de facto* ruler of Phrygia till his death in 121. Then, in the troubles that ensued, the Senate interfered to regulate Phrygia, and confirmed all that the king had done in the country, but took it away from his son Mithridates the Great.

When Mithridates the Great succeeded in 121, he was a child; and his mother Laodice ruled with full power. The Romans acted on their usual principle of reducing the strength of the leading power in Asia Minor: they now took away Great Phrygia from the Pontic rule, and made it nominally free, though of course really dependent on Rome and the governor of the Province Asia. The anti-Pontic party among the Galatae at the same time recovered the ascendancy; and they fought against Mithridates in the operations that inaugurated his first war with Rome.[2]

Yet the Senate's decree of 126, though an empty form, was appealed to by Sulla in the winter of 85-84, to prove that Mithridates the Great had never possessed any right to Phrygia. Sulla was resting his argument on an inoperative decree, which had been contradicted by the course of history. Similiarly, when he went on to maintain that Phrygia had been made free and not tributary, his contention may probably have been justified by the nominal action of the Senate; but the actual fact disproved his

---

[1] *Cities and Bish. of Phrygia*, pt. II, p. 762.
[2] Appian, *Mithr.*, 11 and 17.

argument.   Phrygia, if nominally free, was treated by the Romans as subject, or at least dependent.   Phrygian contingents were enrolled in the armies that fought against Mithridates, and the Roman officers, after their defeat on the river Amneias, tried to collect a new army of Phrygians, but found them too unwarlike to be of any use.   The epitome of Livy, LXXVII, when it says that Mithridates in 88 entered Phrygia, a Province of the Roman people, may be using an expression technically too strong ; but, practically, when Mithridates crossed the Phrygian frontier, he was invading a country that was treated by the Romans as dependent upon, and part of, their Empire.

But in 88 Mithridates overran western Asia Minor down to the Aegean Sea ; and Galatia now once more passed under the Pontic ascendancy.   The only people in Asia from whom Mithridates apprehended any serious opposition were the Galatians ; and to guard against it he summoned all the chief men, to the number of sixty, to Pergamos, where he had established his court, and massacred them all except one, who escaped.[1]   Those tetrarchs who had not come to Pergamos, he killed by secret attacks. Only three tetrarchs escaped.

At this point our authorities again permit a glimpse of the divided spirit, which seems to have been a fatal weakness to the Galatians : Mithridates massacred indiscriminately his friends and his opponents among the tetrarchs.[2] There was therefore a party that favoured and one that had opposed him.

---

[1] Plutarch, *de Mul. Virt.*, 23, and Appian, *Mithr.*, 46, doubtless, are describing the same plan.   The whole families of the tetrarchs were massacred, as Mommsen says, *Rom. Hist.*, transl., ed. II, vol. IV, p. 46.

[2] Appian, *l.c.*

The result showed that the old Gaulish spirit was still strong among the Galatae. Instead of being disheartened by this blow, the nation united; the party that had favoured the Pontic cause and facilitated Mithridates's victory, evidently joined heartily in the resistance. Eumachus, who had been sent as satrap to Galatia, was expelled along with the garrisons which he had intended to station in the Galatian fortresses; and the Galatians henceforth were the hearty allies of Rome in the wars, which terminated in A.D. 66 in the complete defeat of Mithridates.

The massacre of the tetrarchs was a critical event in Galatian history. It drove the Galatae over entirely to the Roman side; and the connection lasted long, for the war was protracted. Not long after it we find the Galatian army, at least in part, armed and disciplined in the Roman style. Whereas Greek and Pergamenian civilisation had apparently failed to make much impression in Galatia, the Roman organisation exercised more influence, as is not unnatural, since the Galatae were still a western people at heart, essentially unlike the Greek and Asiatic peoples around them. As Mommsen says at a later date, "in spite of their sojourn of several hundred years in Asia Minor, a deep gulf still separated these Occidentals from the Asiatics". At the same time the massacre weakened the old tetrarchic system, partly by reducing the number of the great nobles, partly probably by convincing the nation that the division into twelve tetrarchies was a serious weakness against external attack.

In B.C. 74, at the beginning of the Third Mithridatic War, Eumachus, the Pontic general, overran Phrygia and subdued the Pisidians and Isaurians and Cilicia, as Appian says (designating [1] as Cecilia that territory which Trogus calls *Lycaonia et Cilicia* and Strabo calls the Eleventh Strategia).[2] The countries attacked by Eumachus, therefore, were the territories lying round Galatia as enlarged by the Lycaonian tetrarchy. When this tetrarchy is taken into account, the references made by Trogus and by Appian become consistent with one another, and give an outline of the fate of the entire region lying between North Galatia and Cilicia Campestris.

Thereupon, Deiotaros, one of the tetrarchs who had escaped the great massacre, attacked Eumachus and drove him out. In 73 Lucullus carried the war into Pontus, and Galatia was free henceforth from Pontic armies.

[1] So *Bell. Civ.*, V 75, see below, p. 109 note.
[2] See above, p. 64 f.

SECTION 8.

THE GALATIAN STATE.

STRABO, p. 567, gives a sketch of the Galatian organisation and government. The three tribes all spoke the same language and were of similar character. Each tribe was divided on the old Gaulish system into four cantons, called by the Greeks tetrarchies. Each tetrarchy was administered by a special chief under whom were a judge and a general and two lieutenant-generals. There was a senate of 300 members, drawn from the twelve tetrarchies, which met at a place called Drynemeton,[1] and judged cases of murder; but everything else was arranged by the tetrarchs and the judges. This constitution lasted till B.C. 64.

In time of war the disadvantage of multiplication of leaders made them sometimes, at least, entrust the conduct of operations to three chiefs, one for each tribe, as was the case in B.C. 189. In other respects also Strabo's account must not be pressed too closely as implying an unvarying, cast-iron system. But its general truth is beyond question. Strabo was a very careful writer, and abundant evidence was open to him. The meeting of the 300 representatives

---

[1] M. Perrot took *Drynemeton* as the *Oak-grove*, and placed it seven hours south-west of Ancyra, where a few oaks still grow in that treeless land. But Holder, *Altcelt. Sprachschatz*, explains *dry* as an intensive prefix, and *nemeton* as *sanctuary*.

at the holy place Drynemeton was clearly in accordance with an old Gaulish custom. It may be compared with the meeting of the representatives of the sixty-four Gallic states at Lugudunum beside the central altar : this meeting, instituted in its Roman form in B.C. 12, was "adapted to a pre-existing national institution, for 1st August, the day of the dedication of the altar (to Rome and Augustus) and of the meeting, was also the great Celtic festival of the Sungod Lug".[1]

Doubtless there was an altar at Drynemeton. The altar, as distinguished from the temple, was a feature of the Gaulish religion (and of all primitive religions).

As Livy mentions, the Gauls had no cities. They were too barbarous to found cities, or to maintain the Phrygian cities. They dwelt in villages, and in time of war they sent women and children, flocks and herds, to strongholds on hill tops.[2] The chiefs seem to have maintained rude state in castles, surrounded by their tribesmen, and exercising sway over the subject Phrygians around. The evidence of Livy (*i.e.*, of his authority Polybius) is confirmed by the facts of history and of archæological discovery (see Anderson and Crowfoot in *Journal of Hellenic Studies*, 1899, pp. 34-130).

There had been cities of the Phrygians, Ancyra, Gordium, Pessinus, Gorbeous, and others unknown to fame. But Gordium was utterly destroyed by the Gauls.[3] Pes-

[1] Rushforth, *Latin Histor. Inscrip.*, p. 48 f. ; Rhys, *Hibbert Lectures*, pp. 409, 421, 424.

[2] Livy, XXXVIII 18, 15 ; 19, 1 ; 19, 5.

[3] It disappeared from history soon after 190, having previously been a great trade centre, though not a large city. Professor A. Körte has placed it at Pebi on the Sangarios, on a site which shows no remains except of the early period.

sinus was a city of importance, but it was not Gaulish
in the same sense as Ancyra. It was not taken by
the Gauls until between 190 and 164, and even then
there seems to have been a compromise between the old
families and the Gauls. Deiotarus, B.C. 64-40, ruled the
tribe, not from Pessinus, but from the fortresses Pêion
and Bloukion. Such was the state 'of things among the
Tolistobogii.

Among the Tectosages, Ancyra, which had been a great
city in the pre-Galatic period, became a mere chief fort
among the Gauls ; and Strabo does not call it a πόλις, but
only a φρούριον, implying that it had not that municipal
organisation which was essential to a πόλις. Gorbeous,
an old Phrygian city, had also sunk to a village, and was
the residence of Castor about B.C. 50.

Among the Trocmi three forts are named, Tavium (also
called a trade-centre, ἐμπόριον, for the surrounding country),
Mithridation, and Danala.[1]

These facts show that the Gaulish conquest caused an
almost complete destruction of the civilisation and commerce
of Galatia. The archæological evidence points to the same
conclusion. As Mr. Crowfoot, who has carefully explored a
large part of Western Galatia, says : " Most of these sites
reached the height of their prosperity perhaps in early
times,[2] and only supported feeble settlements in the
Greek and Roman periods. Only on this hypothesis can

---

[1] Possibly Δάναλα is a form of the strange name which appears
also as Ἐκδαύμανα, Γλαύαμα, etc., implying an original something
like ΓδαFμαλα or ΓδαFμανα. This identification would imply that
the territory of the Trocmi extended west of the Halys to embrace
the country called " Added," see p. 64 f.

[2] On that early period Mr. Crowfoot quotes *Histor. Geogr. of Asia
Minor*, pp. 27-35.

I account for the fact that early ware still appears upon the surface." [1]

Gallic virtues and faults, which made a deep impression on Polybius from personal knowledge, and on all Greeks, were such as are natural to their origin, situation and history. They were haughty and fierce, but straightforward and truthful personally. They set high value on their personal promise and word,[2] though this was not inconsistent with stratagem and deceit in war. They were quick to resent any insult, and to avenge it even at the risk of their life.[3]

Plutarch speaks of Celts and Galatians as the noblest of barbarians, who never give way to vehement sorrow and mourning, as Egyptians, Syrians, Lydians, etc., do.[4]

Without insisting on the exact truth of the stories about the Gauls that are reported by our authorities, we note that they are all of the same tone, and that they are a safe index to the character of the people, as reflecting the impression likely to be made by the northern barbarians on the Greeks.

---

[1] *Journal of Hellenic Studies*, 1899, p. 38.

[2] Compare the story of Chiomara ; when she brought to her husband the head of her Roman captor, he said : " Woman ! Good faith is a noble thing ! " knowing that she must have broken faith before she could have slain him. Polyb., XXII 21 ; Plutarch, *de Mul. Virt.*, 22. Also the story of Camma faithful, avenging her dead husband at the cost of her own life, Plutarch, *de Mul. Virt.*, 20.

[3] Compare the story of the sixty Gaulish nobles whom Mithridates invited to Pergamos as friends and treated as inferiors, Plutarch, *de Mul. Virt.*, 23.

[4] *Cons. ad Apoll.*, 22. Here Κέλτοι evidently is used either in the generic sense of all Celtic tribes, as distinguished from Γαλάται, or as European Gauls distinguished from Galatae of Asia. The latter is more probable, and in either case it is impossible here to take Γαλάται as meaning only the Gauls of Gallia (in which sense it is often used).

It is not strange that their qualities should have impressed the Greeks so deeply : they are the qualities of an aristocracy, proud of their own individual superiority, which gives them a certain standard of personal honour—qualities that were lacking among the Greeks.

So long as the Gauls continued to be a nation of warriors, this character would persist without serious change. Such, as we saw, was probably the case with the old Phrygian conquerors : the warrior caste kept itself free from the manners of its subjects. In the time of Polybius the Galatae were as great a terror to the Greeks as ever, and one of the most striking stories illustrating the Galatian character is not earlier than B.C. 88-86.[1]

Strabo says, p. 567, the Gauls retained their original form of government until his own time, *i.e.*, until the changes introduced by Pompey, B.C. 64, who appointed three chiefs. There is, therefore, every reason to think that the Gauls continued to preserve their native character, vigour and haughty aristocratic spirit of separation from the surrounding Asian peoples unimpaired, at least until the middle of the first century ; and that the country was reduced to a state of barbarism. Art and literature had no home there. It was a country of shepherds and rude warriors, with a scanty trade carried on by the Phrygians of the few remaining towns.

And what about the conquerors ? It is impossible that they should have remained entirely unaffected by their new surroundings. Experience and travel are educative ; and the Gauls had much of both before they finally settled down in their new country as heirs to the old-standing

---

[1] See Plutarch, *Mul. Virt.*, 23 (referred to on p. 69).

Phrygian order and religious organisation. What can be discovered as to the relations between conquerors and conquered?

It would be absurd to suppose that the older race was exterminated, or expelled, or even seriously diminished in numbers. It constituted from the first the great majority of the population, amid which the Gauls settled as a conquering and aristocratic caste, not unlike the Normans among the Saxons in England about A.D. 1066. All evidence shows that the settlement took place in a comparatively peaceful way: the kings of the surrounding lands agreed and the Phrygian people quietly accepted the new situation with their usual placid resignation.

The resulting situation was probably like that which occurred in Gaul when a not dissimilar, though less peaceful, settlement occurred : the conquerors took one-third of the soil and left two-thirds to the older people.[1]

The total number of Gauls who settled in Galatia cannot have been large. The first great army which entered Asia Minor with Leonnorios and Lutarios in 278 is stated by Livy[2] to have numbered 20,000, of which one-half were armed men : the rest presumably being women and children. Others afterwards joined them ; but these seem not to have been so important. The births in the following hundred years are not likely to have much more than counterbalanced the deaths in the unceasing wars.

This small aristocratic caste, then, owned one-third of the whole country ; and the writers who describe their wars in the second century think only of the Gauls and never allude to the subject population. Fortunately, they

[1] Cæsar, *Bell. Gall.*, I 31.

[2] Livy, XXXVIII 16 (on the authority, doubtless, of Polybius).

give an unusually detailed description of the Gaulish manners and men and women, from which we can picture their condition in that century.

Evidently they did not take to agriculture or to trade. They were warriors; and, so far were they from condescending to adopt the improved tactics and weapons of the disciplined Greek armies, that they were still fighting naked[1] in B.C. 189, without order or tactics, armed with swords and long wooden or wicker shields; and Polybius, who was writing after 145, evidently considered that these customs still continued among them. Their simple plan of battle was that one fierce, terrible charge, which swept almost every Greek army before it like chaff before the wind, but which skilful opponents soon learned to elude. They offered up their captives in sacrifice to the Celtic gods.

That is true to the old Gaulish customs. Even in 216, Hannibal's Gaulish allies fought naked at Cannae.[2] Cæsar and other writers mention the Gaulish custom of sacrificing their captives (pp. 61, 133).[3]

A people of that character cannot be thought of as agriculturists. In their own land they had thought it dishonourable to cultivate the ground, as Cicero mentions;[4]

---

[1] Livy, XXXVIII 21. Not merely without armour, but actually without clothing, which they took off for battle, showing their skin, which the Greeks remarked on as white, because they never removed their clothing at any other time (whereas the Greeks were accustomed to daily naked exercise, and their skin became darker). See Grote's note on Ch. LXXIII, p. 369, vol. IX, and Xenophon, *Hell.*, III 4, 19.

[2] Livy, XXIX 46, 6.

[3] Compare Diodor., V 32, 6; Livy, XXXVIII 47, 12; Cicero, *de Rep.*, III 9, 15 and 21, *p. Font.*, 14, 31; Cæsar, *Bell. Gall.*, VI 16; Athenaeus, IV, p. 160.

[4] *De Rep.*, III 9, 15.

and they were not likely to change as a conquering race
in Asia Minor.   So far as their third of the land was
cultivated, doubtless the work was done by the subject
population.   The Gauls, as Van Gelder[1] says, were
pastoral, so far as they were anything except warriors ;
and the pastoral life, while it kept them hardy, would also
maintain their barbarism and isolation from the settled
old population : the shepherd is the natural enemy of the
agriculturist.   But, doubtless, the labour was done almost
entirely by the subject Phrygians ; and the Gauls, when
not at war, feasted in the castles of the nobles in the rude
but plentiful style described by Phylarchus.[2]

But, if the Gaulish tribes proper were so few in numbers,
how shall we account for the immense numbers who are
mentioned as composing the Galatian armies in the second
and first centuries before Christ?   We notice that such
numbers do not appear in the third century.   The Gauls,
then, are found as mercenaries in the kings' armies, or as
raiding bands.   If not regular mercenaries, they appear as
acting in conjunction with some king's army, and not as
constituting great armies of their own.

Evidently Mommsen's view is right that the Galatian
state, after Galatia was constituted a political reality about
232, contained both Gauls and Phrygians.   The old native
population was merged in the new state.

Only in this way can we account for the recorded facts.
Livy's estimate of the Galatian loss in B.C. 189 is 18,000
slain, and 40,000 captives at Mt. Olympus,[3] and 8000 slain

---

[1] *De Gallis in Graecia et Asia*, ch. V, *de Gal. moribus*, p. 193.

[2] About B.C. 215, *Athenæus*, IV, p. 150.

[3] "Numerus captivorum haud dubie quadraginta millia explevit,"
Livy, XXXVIII 23.   See p. 57.

with a great number of captives at Mt. Magaba. How can these numbers be reconciled with our indubitable information as to the small numbers of the Gauls? Evidently the captives (about whom Livy is very positive) included not merely persons of Gaulish race, but also their Phrygian servants and dependants. No doubt the Gauls had learned to make the most use of the Phrygian people, as the Dorian conquerors of Laconia did of the Helot population. Now all captives were useful as spoil; all could be sold to increase the prize-money of the victorious Romans; all were treated as equally belonging to the hostile state.

But this fact, which can hardly be doubted, shows us Galatia as a roughly unified state, containing two distinct classes of population, but with both classes driven to co-operate against an invasion, and both classes treated by the enemy without distinction as Galatae. The headlong flight of the Galatians in both battles is easily explained, when the composition of their defensive armies is taken into account. Hence, also, we understand why Aemilius Paullus spoke so strongly in the senate of the mixture among the Galatian foes.[1]

Lucullus had 30,000 Galatae in his army, as he marched from Bithynia into Pontus.[2] That contingent cannot be taken as the whole fighting force of Galatia. A considerable number must have been left in the country to guard the home population, the families and the property, from the Pontic attacks. There can hardly have been less than 60,000 fighting men in arms, when 30,000 were serving in Bithynia. That is the army of a country,

---

[1] Livy, XXXVIII 46.   [2] Plutarch *Lucullus*, 14.

and not of a small separate ruling caste within the country.

Obviously no distinction was made by external nations as to the stock from which sprang the soldiers in these armies. They are all summed up by historians as Galatae; and this term in those cases is to be taken simply as "men of Galatia," and not as "men of Gaulish blood". Galatia had been since 232 recognised as a political fact, a definitely bounded country with its own form of government; and all who belonged to the country and contributed to its strength were Galatae.

But some New Testament critics have either practically ignored this in their exposition of the "Galatian Question," or even explicitly denied it.[1] We must therefore examine more closely the use of the name Galatian Γαλάτης. It is not, of course, denied that the name often was associated by the ancients with Gaulish descent. The element in the Galatian state that gave it firmness, vigour and character was Gaulish; and people ignored and forgot about the undistinguished element.

In the fragmentary records of enfranchisement at Delphi,[2] we are struck with the number of Galatian slaves that were set free between the years 169 and 100 B.C.

---

[1] So *e.g.* Professor F. Blass, *Acta Apostolorum*, 1895, p. 176 : *Gravius autem errarunt qui Galatas Pauli intellegi voluerunt [Phrygas et] Lycaonas, quippe qui a Romanis Galatiae provinciae essent attributi; neque enim, ut mittamalia, ea re ex [Phrygibus et] Lycaonibus Galli facti erant.* It is characteristic of the haste with which North Galatian theorists decide the case, that one has almost everywhere to amend their statements in essential points (as here by inserting two words twice) before one can begin to discuss it.

[2] Best given in Collitz, *Sammlung der Gr. Dialektinschr.*, II, parts 3-5; also Wescher-Foucart *Inscr. rec. a'Delphes.*

There are more from Galatia than from any other country, except Syria and Thrace.[1] This is in itself strange, if Gauls by blood must be understood by the term *Galatae.* Those proud and untamable warriors, "the noblest of barbarians," were among the three most frequent nations in slavery! We should have imagined from the pictures sketched by Polybius, Plutarch, and others, that the Gaul would fight to the death and would pine in captivity. Moreover, the slaves that were enfranchised were those who behaved peaceably and well, and worked out their freedom by their industry.

It is quite probable that some of the captives, Phrygians by birth, whom Manlius took in 189, were among those Galatian slaves whose enfranchisement is recorded at Delphi, for many of his captives were, beyond doubt, sold in the slave markets of the Greek world.

Further, what has become of the Phrygians, the nation marked out by nature for slavery? Compared with the Galatians in the deeds of enfranchisement they are as three to eight! Yet Socrates remarks on the industry of the Phrygian slaves; and a Phrygian slave is a frequent character in the Greek drama.[2]

Further, one of these enfranchised slaves is "Sosias, by nationality Galatian, by trade a shoemaker";[3] and he was set free between B.C. 150 and 140. Another was

---

[1] Stähelin, *Gesch. der Kleinas. Galater*, p. 57, counts thirty-three Syrians, twenty-eight Thracians, ten Galatians, eight Macedonians, five Sarmatians, four Illyrians, four Cappadocians, four Armenians, three Phrygians, three Arabs, two Jews, two Lydians, etc. A few more may be identified, *e.g.*, a slave Armenios is certainly Armenian (cp. Strabo, p. 304), in W. F., 258.

[2] See "The Slaves in the Wasps," *Classical Review*, 1898, p. 335.

[3] W. F., 429.

Athenais, a skilled artisan (τεχνῖτις),[1] B.C. 140-100. We remember that the trades and handicrafts in Galatia were wholly in the hands of the subject population, while the Gaulish aristocracy had war as their only trade; and we refuse to recognise in Sosias a Gaulish noble turned shoe-maker and good at his trade, or in Athenais a Gaulish lady who had taken to a handicraft.

Another of these enfranchised slaves from Galatia was called Maiphates, a typical Anatolian and especially Phrygian name;[2] and Strabo, p. 304, mentions that it was customary for slaves to bear names characteristic of their nation.

The case is clear. These "Galatian" slaves were simply brought from Galatia and sold in the slave-market, labelled with the name of the country from which they had been brought.

It would appear that Galatia was a great seat of the slave trade. Ammianus mentions Galatae, XXII 7, 8, as having in their hands even the trade in Gothic slaves. It is a feature of the country still, which has been preserved from ancient times, that the same trades persist in special places from generation to generation. The Galatian slave trade was likely to be much stimulated in the third century B.C., when a considerable addition was made to the population and a great deal of the land was taken away from the former owners. The food supply must have become insufficient; and the slave market was the natural resource. Even in countries such as Boeotia, where ordinarily the father had no right to sell his children into slavery, it was

---

[1] Collitz, 2154.

[2] See "Phrygo-Galatian Slaves," *Classical Review*, 1898, p. 342.

allowed that he should do so in case of destitution ; while Phrygians and Galatians are mentioned as being in the regular habit of selling their children.

The Galatian customs in treating slaves may then be assumed to spring, not from Gaul, but from the Asiatic practice. One of these customs was that they marked their slaves by cuts or wounds, as Artemidorus the Lydian mentions. The word which he uses might refer to branding, but his meaning in this case is shown by the context.[1]

The same custom has been practised in the country until recently, and one sees still ex-slaves thus marked by cuts on the face, which have been prevented from closing, so as to leave scars.[2] We may then assume that this was the usual practice of central Asia Minor in general ; but the pre-eminence of the Galatian slave traders made it known to the world as a Galatian custom.

It seems clearly proved that so early as the second century B.C. the Phrygian origin of the larger half of the Galatian population was forgotten by ordinary people of the surrounding countries ; and the whole state was thought of as Galatia and its people as Galatians.

The distinction, of course, was much more clearly perceived in the country, where the aristocratic class was marked off from the masses. But even in the country a certain approximation was brought about through the influence of the common religion.

Once more, Pausanias mentions that on account of the boar having ravaged Lydia, where Attis was, the Galatians

[1] Among the Thracians noble children, and among the Galatae slaves, are marked (στίζονται), *Oneirocr.*, I 8.

[2] Mrs. Ramsay, *Everyday Life in Turkey*, p. 7.

that lived at Pessinus refrained from eating pork.[1] It is
clear that the abstinence from swine's flesh was an old
Asiatic and East Anatolian custom, found also at the
temple of Comana Pontica. The Gaulish stock was evidently weaker in Pessinus than in most places,[2] and half
of the higher priests were of the old native families. Evidently Pausanias used the word Galatian in that passage
of the entire Pessinuntine population, and not only of the
section that had Gaulish blood.

[1] VII 17, 10, Γαλατῶν οἱ Πεσσινοῦντα ἔχοντες, ὑῶν οὐχ ἁπτόμενοι.
[2] See p. 62.

SECTION 9.

THE RELIGION OF GALATIA.

FEW traces of the old Gaulish religion can be detected in Galatia. It would be difficult to mention any except the sacrifice of captives, which was practised as late as about B.C. 160, and presumably the rites at Drynemeton.[1] It is hardly probable that the Gaulish religion was wholly disused or forgotten in the last century B.C. But, certainly, almost all the references—unfortunately very few—to Galatic religion point to the rapid adoption of the ancient and impressive religion of Cybele. That was the one possession of the old Phrygian people that exercised a really great influence on the world. The Galatians may perhaps have modified to some degree the character of the Phrygian ritual by their own nature and customs, as both the Phryges and the Greeks did.[2] But we have no evidence on this point.

There were two reasons why the Gauls should adopt the religion of the conquered race.

(1) They had to govern the conquered people; and the easiest way of doing so was to use the already existing forms of rule. The priests of the great religious centres

---

[1] See p. 73.   [2] See p. 41 f.

(86)

had hitherto been dynasts and had ruled the country round ; and the Gaulish chiefs made themselves easily heirs to the immense power of the Phrygian priests by taking their place as far as possible.   At Pessinus the Gauls took only half the places in the great priestly college.   It is uncertain whether this can be taken as typical for other cases ; but probably it was not typical.   Pessinus was the greatest and most powerful of the sanctuaries ; it was not taken possession of by the Gauls until after 189, and would certainly be able to make a much better bargain with the Gauls than the lesser *hiera* could.   Probably the higher priesthoods elsewhere were almost all monopolised by Gaulish chiefs : examples on pp. 62, 88.

(2) A strange people always found it needful to adopt the gods of their new country.   Those gods were the gods of the land ; and any calamity that happened to the immigrants was naturally attributed to the wrath of the native gods, offended at the loss of their privileges : compare the story in 2 *Kings* XVII 26.   Thus Cybele was soon an object of worship to the Gaulish conquerors.

An example of the influence of the Anatolian religion on the Galatian tribes, probably as early as the second century, is found in a tale recorded by Plutarch.[1]   The wife of Sinatos, one of the most influential of the tetrarchs, was Kamma, a beautiful woman, much respected for her character and wisdom and kindliness to the subject people.[2]

---

[1] *De Mul. Virt.*, 20 ; *Amat.*, 22.

[2] ποθεινὴ τοῖς ὑπηκόοις διαφερόντως ὑπ' εὐμενείας καὶ χρηστότητος. Plutarch's authority, some earlier writer (possibly Polybius, from whom *Mul. Virt.* 22 is quoted), undoubtedly understood ὑπήκοοι as the subject Phrygian population, whom most of the Gauls treated with harshness and contempt.

She was hereditary priestess of Artemis,[1] and the magnificent attire in which she was seen in the processions and sacrifices of the goddess made her a conspicuous figure in the country.

Sinorix, another tetrarch, fell in love with her, and slew Sinatos by treachery. Then he wooed Kamma, and made a merit of having murdered Sinatos from love of her, and not from malice of heart. Her friends pressed her to accept Sinorix, who was a man of specially great influence ; and she accepted him, and invited him to complete the betrothal in presence of the goddess. When he came, she led him before the altar of Artemis. Then, taking a cup, she poured a libation, drank of the cup, and handed it to him to drink. When she saw that he had drunk, she cried out calling the goddess to witness that for this day alone had she survived Sinatos, and that now having avenged his death she was going down to join him. Then to Sinorix she added : "For you, let your folk prepare a tomb instead of a marriage". The Gaul, as the poison began to work, leaped on to his chariot, hoping to work off the effect through the rapid tossing motion ; but he soon changed from the car to a litter, and expired the same evening (presumably on the homeward road). Kamma heard of his death, and died rejoicing.

Van Gelder (p. 199) remarks that the ceremonial preceding the marriage—formal betrothal, the great crowd of people convoying the pair, the offering of vows at the altar of Artemis, the drinking of the pair from a common cup— must be Gaulish, and certainly is not Greek or Oriental. His judgment seems to be mistaken. Professor Rhys,

---

[1] πατρῷος ἱερωσύνη, Plut., *Amat.*, 22.

when consulted, says that he knows of no Celtic custom suggesting that bride and bridegroom drank of the same cup as a ceremony of marriage, or of betrothal; but that one expression[1] may possibly (though not necessarily) indicate that eating of the same dish, something like *confarreatio* in the Roman religious ceremony, was a marriage custom.

Now drinking of the common cup is to this day part of the Greek marriage ceremony;[2] and this makes it probable that the custom was not Gallic, but part of old Anatolian ritual. Plutarch's words convey the impression that Kamma made the ceremonial as priestess, that it belonged to the ritual of Artemis and was novel to Sinorix. Artemis, then, was here not a Greek name for a Gallic goddess (which would be a reasonable hypothesis at the first glance). The Artemis, whose priestess Kamma was, was the Anatolian Goddess, Ma or Bellona, in whose ritual the annual procession, the Exodos of the deity, formed an important part. In that procession Kamma, in the gorgeous robes of the goddess herself, whom she represented, would play the conspicuous part that Plutarch describes.

With regard to marriage ceremonial in the Anatolian religion, we have unfortunately no evidence. While in all probability true marriage was not in accordance with the spirit of that religion, still it is certain that the relation

---

[1] At the opening of the story of Kulhwch and Olwen, a prince wants a wife of the *same food* with himself. This may refer to a marriage ceremony of eating food together, but more probably implies a wife of rank fitting her to sit always along with him at food.

[2] The Kubarra, or assistant, who also drinks of the same cup, is thenceforward a close relation: if a man, he may not marry the bride, if the bridegroom dies: if a woman, she may not marry the groom, if the wife dies.

between man and woman was always a very important fact in it, being closely associated with the temple service and considered as a religious act; and it is probable that some common ritualistic ceremony would be performed in the temple and before the altar of the goddess by the two parties. It is also certain that a mixed cup was a feature in the Phrygian Mysteries, and that the celebrants partook of this cup.

It is quite probable, therefore, that this drinking of the cup in the Mysteries might be adapted to a sort of marriage ceremony. A similar adaptation is known in respect of another act in the Mysteries. It is well known that the celebrant initiated in the Phrygian Mysteries pronounced the formula, " I have escaped evil, I have found a better "; and that this same formula was pronounced as part of the Athenian marriage ceremony.

That some ceremony in the temple of Artemis formed an accompaniment of marriage in ancient Anatolia is indicated in one place. In the legend of St. Abercius, it is said to have been arranged that, after the return of Verus from the Parthian War, his marriage with Lucilla, daughter of Marcus Aurelius, should be celebrated in the temple of Artemis at Ephesus. As the legend, though embodying a real tradition, was not written down before about A.D. 400, it would be a plausible explanation that " this detail is suggested (to the person who gave literary form to the legend) by the Christian ceremonial of marrying in church ".[1] But the story of Kamma suggests that the author may have correctly incorporated in the legend of St. Abercius a detail taken from the pagan marriage

---

[1] So in *Expositor*, April, 1889, p. 256.

ceremonial of Asia Minor, for he wrote before paganism
was extinct in the country.[1]

The romance of Kamma carries us back to the time
when relations between the ruling Gauls and the subject
Phrygians were beginning to be less purely that of lord
and serf. Kamma was recognised by the Phrygians as
a friend, partly because of her kindliness to them, still
more because she was a priestess of their religion.

It is most unfortunate that no clue is given in the story
to her date, except that she lived and died before B.C. 86. If
the suspicion expressed above, that Polybius was Plutarch's
authority, be correct, she could not be much later than
B.C. 140. That is probable from other facts of history,
stated in Section 7. It was during the period 181-160 that
the moderating and civilising influence was strongest; and
this influence was thereafter weakened. Kamma represents the progressive and milder type among the Gauls.
However that may be, the second century is the period to
which, doubtless, the incident belongs.

The tale points, beyond doubt, to the inference that
participation in the common religion led to a gradual approximation between the Gauls and the Phrygians of
Galatia. This is in itself probable : a common religion
was the uniting bond in every society or association in
ancient time.

Again, Deiotaros was devoted to divination and augury,
and guided his life by them. According to Cicero, who had

---

[1] Abbé Duchesne places the composition of the Abercius legend
much later than I do. His arguments seem to be wholly founded on
misapprehension, as Prof. A. Zahn, *Forsch. zur Gesch. des N. T. Kanons*,
V, p. 62 *n*, has recognised : see *Cities and Bish. of Phrygia*, II, pp. 709
ff, 723 ff.

seen a good deal of him, and conversed with him on this subject, comparing their augural principles, he never did anything important without taking the omens. He often turned back from a journey, even after several days' progress, when an unfavourable omen occurred ; and he won Cicero's heart by declaring that the favourable omens which accompanied him, as he went to join Pompey before the battle of Pharsalos, had come true, for they had led him to defend the senate and freedom and constitutional government, and the glory of this conduct outweighed in his estimation the loss of territory by which Cæsar had punished him.

The augury which he followed, and which had once saved his life, was very different from the Roman principles of interpretation. It drew omens from almost all birds, whereas the Romans paid regard only to a few ; it interpreted their flight and direction in different ways, sometimes drawing a conclusion exactly the opposite of the Romans.[1]

Deiotaros's augury was not of Gaulish origin. It was that of Cilicians, Pamphylians, Phrygians, Pisidians, Lycians.[2] It was the system of which an Ephesian fragment has been preserved.[3] The Great Goddess of Asia Minor made Phrygian birds fly and had taught her priests to interpret the signs. Pausanias (X 21) mentions that the Gauls did not practice augury (yet see Diodorus, V 31, 3).

---

[1] *Cicero de Div.*, I 15, 26 f. ; II 8, 20 ; 36, 76 f. ; 37, 78, composed in B.C. 44.

[2] *Cicero de Div.*, I 15, 26, compare *De Legibus*, II 13, 33.

[3] In the collections of Hicks, *Brit. Mus.*, 678 ; Roberts, 144 ; Roehl, 499 ; Cauer, 478 ; Bechtel, 145 ; see Bouché-Leclercq, *Hist. de la Divin.*, I, p. 140 f.

Aelian mentions that, when a plague of locusts afflicts the country, the Galatians of Asia offer prayers and perform rites invoking certain birds,[1] which come and destroy the locusts. Aelian does not vouch for the truth of this, but it is the truest thing in his book. I have seen the locust bird often during the plague that ended in 1882.[2] It is a singularly beautiful bird of bright and variegated plumage, about the size of a starling, I should think, which follows and preys on the armies of locusts, and is never seen at any other time in the country. That the inhabitants would pary for the birds and invoke them with rites, as soon as the locusts appeared, may be regarded as certain. Doubtless they do so to the present day.

This custom is attributed to the Galatians by Aelian, but it was obviously not a Gaulish custom, but a native Anatolian practice, which the immigrant Gauls adopted. The persistence of ancient feeling about locusts is noteworthy in the horror with which the idea of eating them is still regarded in Anatolia, whereas the Arab tribes eat them with relish. The same contrast between the natives of Phrygia or of Pontus and the Arabs struck St. Jerome in the fourth century.[3] This, incidentally, proves how keen was his observation as he travelled through the country, and confirms his other statements about the people.

In the inscriptions of the Roman period no allusion is made to any religion except that of the old Phrygian gods and that of the Emperors. It is possible, even probable,

---

[1] Aelian, *De Nat. Anim.*, XVII 19 : read ἔστιν ὧν according to Valckenaer's certain emendation.

[2] On the facts and the superstitions connected with locusts in Asia Minor see my *Impressions of Turkey*, p. 274 ff.

[3] Jerome, *Adv. Jovin.*, II 7.

that the Koinon of Galatians, by which the imperial religion was maintained, was the successor of the old meeting at Drynemeton, and thus concentrated in itself the relics of Gaulish feeling and cultus ; but the officials mentioned do not differ from the ordinary type in the provincial associations.

The inscriptions (all of Roman time) alluding to the religion of private individuals are quite undistinguishable from the ordinary Phrygian votive inscriptions, except that the personal names are often recognisably Celtic. The chief collection of inscriptions from the country districts, distinguished from the city of Ancyra, is that of J. G. C. Anderson in *Journal of Hellenic Studies*, 1899.

SECTION 10.

GALATIA AS A ROMAN CLIENT STATE.

AT the pacification and re-organisation of the East in
B.C. 64, Galatia was placed by Pompey under the rule of
three chiefs, Deiotaros, Brogitaros, and a third unknown,
retaining the old triple division according to the three
tribes, Tolistobogii, Trocmi, and Tectosages, but discarding the subdivision into tetrarchies. The ruling tetrarchic
families had been reduced to three at the great massacre.
Moreover, the Romans always liked to have some single
head in each district with whom they might conveniently
communicate; and it was against their policy to raise up
a single king in whose hands the whole power of the
Galatian state should be concentrated. But the ambition
of the leading Gauls had led to at least one previous
attempt at monarchy; and the same cause is discernible
in the following period, until from B.C. 44 onwards there
was a single king of Galatia.

Pompey did not restore to Galatia the whole of the
Lycaonian tetrarchy;[1] but apparently he did permanently
attach to it the northern part of the tetrarchy, including
the country immediately to the west of Lake Tatta, but
not (if Ptolemy may be followed) including Savatra. This

[1] See below, p. 106.

district retained the name of the " Added Land,"[1] and is so described by Ptolemy in the second century after Christ.   In this way the " Added Land " came to be smaller than the old tetrarchy, which Pliny describes (see p. 64 f.).

It may seem a poor return to the Galatae for their services in the Mithridatic Wars, to deprive them of the best part of the tetrarchy; but there may have been compensation given them, as for example, we know that Deiotaros received Armenia Minor from Pompey, and Brogitaros got Mithridation (which previously had belonged to Pontus).

The tetrarchies now disappeared finally from the political geography of Asia Minor; and, when Pliny speaks of the Lycaonian Tetrarchy given to Galatia, he must be quoting the name from an authority speaking of the period before the Mithridatic Wars.   The name might last, as other historical names lasted.[2]   The term tetrarchy now lost its meaning.   There were three chiefs, one for each tribe, and each was called a tetrarch; so that the term tetrarchy could henceforth denote only the territory of a tetrarch, *i.e.*, of a whole tribe.   As there is no trace of such usage, probably the tetrarchies ceased to be a political fact in 64.

This corroborates our previous conclusion that the Lycaonian Tetrarchy was attached to Galatia during the second century.

The history of North Galatia during the period 64-40

---

[1] προσειλημμένη (χώρα).

[2] Pontus Polemoniacus lasted as a name in inscriptions long after it ceased in A.D. 63 to be a political reality.   Lycaonia Antiochiana ceased to be a real division in A.D. 72, but an inscription dating later than A.D. 166 uses the name.   Ptolemy employs both these names,

has its centre in the ambition, prudence and craft of
Deiotaros. He had been appointed by Pompey chief
and tetrarch of the Tolistobogii, as Brogitaros was of the
Trocmi, and an unknown person [1] of the Tectosages. In
reward for his services to Rome, Pompey also added to
Deiotaros's realm Gazelonitis and part of Armenia Minor.[2]
Thus the dominions of Deiotaros lay both to east and to
west of the other two Galatian chiefs, and were much more
extensive. His influence was strengthened by his being
far more distinguished than the other two chiefs ; and
he augmented it by marrying two of his daughters to
Brogitaros [3] and to Kastor, son of the chief of the
Tectosages. He had succeeded his father [Dum]norix as
one of the four Tolistobogian tetrarchs. He was, apparently, among the three tetrarchs who escaped the massacre
by Mithridates about 87. He served Sulla, 87-84, Murena,
84-82, Servilius Isauricus, 78-76, Lucullus, 74-66, Pompey,
66-64, Bibulus, 51, and Cicero, 50 ; and he was honourably
mentioned by all of them.

Deiotaros was a remarkable man, and evidently had
strongly impressed Cicero, who saw a good deal of him
in his Cicilian pro-consulate 51-50. He perceived that the
best career for a king in Galatia lay in faithful adherence to
the Roman cause ; and he earned frequent commendation

[1] He was father of Kastor and Domnilaos, see below, p. 100.
Now, Bepolitanus was one of the chiefs who escaped the Mithridatic
massacre, Plutarch, *de Mul. Virt.*, 46. Only three escaped.

[2] As Pompey's acts were confirmed by the Senate in 59, this
kingdom is often said to have been given by the Senate. Gazelonitis
lay immediately east of the Halys in its lower course.

[3] Cicero, *de Harusp. Resp.*, 13, 29, which cannot be taken in the
sense advocated by Monsieur Th. Reinach, *Rev. Numism.*, 1891, p.
384 note.

from the Senate by his zeal. He led his troops, thirty
cohorts, 12,000 men, armed in Roman style, in Cicero's
army. He discussed topics of comparative religion and
ritual with Cicero. He appreciated and imitated the
Roman discipline and arms;[1] and, undoubtedly, he
carried his imitation into other departments than war.
The Gauls had always despised agriculture, and eaten the
bread cultivated by others;[2] but Deiotaros managed his
estates well, practising agriculture as well as pasturage—
a great merit in the Roman eyes.

Naturally in 48 he joined Pompey against Cæsar.
Pompey was actual master in the East; and loomed far
greater in the Galatian view than Cæsar. Deiotaros led
his own troops to Epirus, though he was now very old,[3]
and had to be lifted on to his horse. We need not credit
Deiotaros with any motives of gratitude to Pompey: he
was too ambitious to have room for the kindlier and
weaker emotion. He was ready immediately afterwards
to co-operate with Cæsar's lieutenant Calvinus, and with
Cæsar himself. It was for the Romans to settle their own
affairs: he acted along with the nearest officer or the
strongest.

Pompey had not given the three Galatian chiefs the
title of king, but only of tetrarch, though he had made
Deiotaros king of Lesser Armenia. In 58 P. Clodius
passed a law through the comitia tributa, granting the

---

[1] He had two legions for several years before B.C. 48. But he
suffered severely at Nikopolis, and brought only one legion to Cæsar
in 47.

[2] See above, p. 78.

[3] Plutarch, *Crass.*, 17, calls him in B.C. 54 a very old man, πάνυ
γηραιόν.

higher title to Deiotaros and Brogitaros. Cicero says that
the Senate had often declared Deiotaros worthy of the
kingly title ; but Brogitaros had merely bought it from
Clodius without desert. At the same time Brogitaros
induced Clodius to pass a law ejecting the high priest of
Pessinus and putting Brogitaros in his place. As Pessinus
was in the realm of Deiotaros, this was an interference
with his rights, and caused enmity between him and the
usurping priest. Within the course of the next year or
two, Deiotaros ejected his son-in-law Brogitaros, and recovered possession of Pessinus.[1]

Cicero's words might perhaps imply that the rightful high
priest, ejected by Brogitaros and restored by Deiotaros,
belonged to the old native priestly family ; but it is far
from probable that Cicero knew anything of such delicate
distinctions, and his words cannot be pressed.

Brogitaros died, or was killed perhaps by Deiotaros,
some time between 56 and 51 ; for in 47 we learn that
Deiotaros had seized several years ago the country of the
Trocmi, thus reducing the number of chiefs from three to
two.

It is probable that some shadow of the old common
council and festival at Drynemeton still existed at this
period. Something like common determination and plan
among all the tribes is clearly shown during the Mithridatic Wars and again in the Roman Civil War, for the
contingent sent to aid Pompey was evidently fixed at
300 cavalry from each tribe. Deiotaros, as chief of two
tribes, led 600 horsemen. Kastor and Domnilaos led 300 :
they were therefore joint chiefs of the Tectosages.

---

[1] Cicero, *p. Sest.*, 26, *de Harusp. Resp.*, 13, 28 f.

Now we observe that Kastor's seat was Gorbeous, whereas Ancyra was indubitably always the capital of the Tectosages. The inference seems clear that Kastor Saokondaros (of Gorbeous) and Domnilaos [1] (of Ancyra) were the two sons of the Tectosagan tetrarch appointed by Pompey in 64, and hence they jointly commanded the troops of their tribe.

Further, as Deiotaros was ruler of almost all Galatia in 47, he evidently seized the land of Domnilaos in the end of 48, presumably because Domnilaos was killed at Pharsalos. Deiotaros was then actively aiding Calvinus, Cæsar's lieutenant, on the eve of a serious war ; and his usurpation was easily pardoned. Thus in 47, Deiotaros and his son-in-law Kastor were the sole remaining Galatian chiefs. The latter had only a small territory and ·inferior title, whereas Deiotaros and his son, who was also called Deiotaros, had both been honoured with the title king by the Senate. Kastor seems to have felt his position dangerous, and he employed his son Kastor to bring an accusation in Rome against Deiotaros for attempting to poison Cæsar. Thus a bitter enmity arose between Deiotaros and his son-in-law, which had lasted for some time before 45.

In 47 Deiotaros appeared as a suppliant before Cæsar on the Pontic frontier. He brought a legion with him to the impending Pontic War ; and Cæsar restored his royal robes,[2] and used his services in the war. Other claimants

---

[1] Called Domnekleios, Strab., p. 543, if the two are rightly identified by Niese, *Rhein. Mus.*, 1883, p. 567 ff., and Th. Reinach, *Rev. Numism.*, 1891, p. 380 ff.

[2] Cæsar recognised only tetrarchs in Galatia, but acknowledged Deiotaros's title as king of Armenia (this had been granted by the Senate in his consulship, when it had confirmed Pompey's acts in the East).

were contesting his rights : possibly Brogitaros had left sons, certainly Domnilaos had two sons, Adiatorix and Dyteutos. Cæsar postponed consideration of some of these questions to a more convenient opportunity ; but punished Deiotaros by giving part of his Armenian kingdom to Ariobarzanes of Cappadocia, and the whole of his Trocmian tetrarchy to Mithridates of Pergamos, Cæsar's active and able supporter. The mother of Mithridates was Adobogiona of the Trocmian tetrarchs, daughter of another Deiotaros and sister of Brogitaros. His father was believed to be really Mithridates the Great, though a citizen of Pergamos was husband of Adobogiona.

In 45 the younger Kastor was in Rome prosecuting the case against his grandfather Deiotaros ; and Cicero defended the latter. Cæsar again postponed his decision ; and nothing was settled when he died. Immediately on hearing of Cæsar's murder in 44 B.C., Deiotaros seized all his former realm. He captured Gorbeous, and put to death his own daughter and her husband Kastor Saokondaros. The elder Kastor was still living in 45, when Cicero was pleading the case in Rome ; but Deiotaros took advantage of the disorder ensuing on Cæsar's death, to push his own claim to all three tetrarchies. A bribe to Antony and his wife Fulvia ensured him in the enjoyment of his power until his death in B.C. 41. Thus the number of Galatian chiefs was reduced to one.

In order to ensure the peaceable succession of one of his sons, Deiotaros is said by Plutarch to have put all the rest to death. But, in spite of his care, Antony conferred the kingdom of Galatia with the eastern part of Paphlagonia on Kastor in 40. Perhaps his son Deiotaros died before him or shortly after.

The monarchic system must have tended to weaken the

tribal feeling and the old free Gaulish character. The monarch in the maintenance of his authority was apt to introduce the administrative devices of more advanced nations. Deiotaros, who armed and trained his soldiers in Roman style, was fully alive to the advantages of "civilised" methods. But the monarchical system lasted barely twenty years ; and no serious and permanent effect on national feeling could have been produced before Galatia became a Roman Province in B.C. 25, for the tribal system continued in full force under the Empire.

The preceding and following Sections show how largely Galatia now bulked in the Roman mind. As in the second century the eastern question was summed up in the word "Asia," so now the Central Asia Minor problem was summed up in the word "Galatia". In each case, when a regular Province was constituted, the new name was given to it.

Note.—ADDITIONAL AUTHORITIES (see p. 52).

Th. Reinach in *Revue Numismatique* (1891), p. 378 ff.

Niese in *Rheinisches Museum* (1883), p. 583 ff.

SECTION 11.

ORIGIN OF THE PROVINCE GALATIA.

THE Roman range of authority and action in any foreign land constituted a *Provincia, i.e.,* a sphere of duty.[1] In the early part of the first century B.C. Asia Minor contained two *Provinciae,* Asia and Cilicia, the latter being the Roman term for a great, ill-defined, half-subdued agglomeration of lands, comprising parts of Cilicia, Pamphylia and other regions. In 80 we begin to get a conception of the range of this new Provincia, in which the Roman interests in southern and south-eastern Asia Minor were contained. Dolabella and his proquaestor Verres governed it (80-79); and Cicero's speech against the latter gives some conception of the range of his authority, including parts of Lycia, Milyas, Phrygia, Pamphylia and Pisidia, as well as Cilicia.[2] Servilius Isauricus succeeded and governed Cilicia 78-75. The first and most pressing duty of the Provincia was to put down the pirates of Isauria or Cilicia Tracheia.

[1] The word provincia had originally no territorial implication: the decision of law-cases between cives and strangers was the provincia of one of the praetors.

[2] *Verr.,* II I 38, 95, where the word *totam* is rhetorical: it is to be connected with all the preceding list of names (and not simply with *Phrygian*); Verres plagued all Lycia, Pamphylia, Phrygia, etc. No stress can be laid on it as proving that entire Phrygia was under Dolabella; it is a stroke of rhetoric.

Servilius did so to some extent, and was the first Roman officer to lead an army across Mount Taurus. For the efficient conduct of operations it was necessary to have the countries on both sides of Taurus under his command, and in fact part of Phrygia as well as Pamphylia, Lycia, etc., obeyed him.

Asia had been sufficiently and finally regulated by Sulla in B.C. 85-84; but the new Province Cilicia was open to continual variation according as the frontier interests of Rome varied, and for many years the history of Roman conquest and foreign policy in the East was practically identical with the Cilician sphere of duty.

To understand the subject before us, we must bear in mind that there were three classes of States in Asia Minor: (1) Countries incorporated in the Empire, in which law was administered by a Roman governor; (2) Countries connected with Rome by an agreement or alliance the terms of which were expressed in a treaty, *i.e.*, client-states, according to the usual and convenient expression, among which the chief were Galatia and Cappadocia; (3) States in no formal and recognised relations with Rome, especially Pontus and the Isaurian pirates.

The first two classes were included in the conception of the Roman world,[1] the third were its enemies.[2]

Strabo on p. 671 describes the intention [3] of the Romans in setting up these subject kings. He is speaking of Cilicia Tracheia, but he expresses the Roman theory as

---

[1] See *Christ Born in Bethlehem*, p. 117 ff.

[2] No international law was recognised then, except in so far as it was expressed in a formal treaty.

[3] This paragraph is taken verbatim from *Christ Born in Bethlehem*, p. 122.

it was applied generally. Some of the subject countries were specially difficult to govern, either on account of the unruly character of the inhabitants, or because the natural features of the land lent themselves readily to brigandage and piracy. As these countries must be either administered by Roman governors or ruled by kings, it was considered that kings would more efficiently control their restless subjects, being permanently on the spot and having soldiers always at command. But the history of the following century shows how, step by step and district by district, these countries were incorporated in the adjacent Roman Provinces, as a certain degree of discipline and civilisation was imparted to the population by the kings, who built cities and introduced the Græco-Roman customs and education.

The Eastern frontier policy of Rome at this time was expressed in the Cilician sphere of duty or Provincia. Every change in the relations of Rome to its enemies in Asia Minor implied a change in the bounds of that Provincia. Every officer sent to regulate the foreign policy, *i.e.*, the relations with the enemies of Rome, was officially governor of Cilicia.

Lycaonia had been divided between the two chief client-states, Galatia and Cappadocia ;[1] but when these states were fighting for existence against Pontus, their authority was necessarily relaxed in Lycaonia. From 80 to 75 we see that it was connected with Cilicia, and doubtless the same arrangement lasted until the end of the Mithridatic Wars, though in practice temporary conquests by the enemy, *e.g.*, by Eumachos in 74, might interfere with the connection for a time.

[1] See p. 64 f.

Pisidic Phrygia[1] (including Pisidian Antioch) certainly was added. Philomelium and most of Phrygian Paroreios, with Iconium and the west of Lycaonia, formed the Lycaonian Dioecesis,[2] as part of the Cilician Province.

Now as to the fate of Lycaonia when the readjustment of *Provinciae* occurred after the Mithridatic Wars : in B.C. 64 Pompey gave the eastern part of the former Eleventh Strategia to Cappadocia. This part extended from Kastabala to Kybistra, and the frontier lay a little to the west of Kybistra, for Cicero marching from near Iconium on 2nd September, B.C. 51, was on the frontier between Lycaonia and Cappadocia on 18th September, and reached Kybistra on 19th or 20th September.[3] This would not be possible if the frontier extended to the neighbourhood of Derbe, as it probably did in the original Strategia. Moreover, Derbe and Laranda were under the administration of Antipater, who afterwards entertained Cicero during his Anatolian journeys. Antipater was under the authority of the Roman governor of Cilicia ;[4] and therefore this part of Lycaonia must have been under the Cilician *Provincia* or sphere of duty.

[1] Pisidic Phrygia, *Polyb.*, XXII 5, 14 (where it is misunderstood by most modern writers), is practically identical with Galatic Phrygia, a later name meaning the part of Phrygia included in the Province Galatia. It was the part of Phrygia towards Pisidia (Strab., pp. 557, 569, 577, Ptolemy, V 5, 4). See *Cities and Bish. of Phrygia*, I, p. 316.

[2] Cicero, *Alt.*, V 21, 9, more fully defined in Pliny, *Nat. Hist.*, V 25, as *Lycaonia in Asiaticam iurisdictionem versa*, and distinguished from the three Phrygian Dioeceses by Cicero, *Fam.*, XIII 67. The boundary between the Phrygian and Lycaonian Dioeceses lay between the Lakes of Ak-Sheher (XL Martyrs) and Eber Göl.

[3] He started from Iconium on 29th August, but returned to it on the following day. Schmidt, *Briefwechsel des Cicero*, pp. 80 f., 397.

[4] Cicero, *Fam.*, XIII 73.

Justin defines the territory added to Cappadocia in 129 (*i.e.*, the Eleventh Strategia in its former condition) as " Lycaonia and Cilicia " (*i.e.*, part of the two countries) ; but Appian describes it in 64 as " part of Cilicia, *viz.*, Kastabala and other cities " ; [1] we now see the reason of this difference.

Evidently Phrygia Paroreios continued as before, with its chief city Philomelium, to form part of the Cilician Province, for the same reason of convenience as before under Servilius Isauricus.

It is strange that Kybistra and along with it perhaps the pass leading down to the Cilician Gates was permitted to remain part of Cappadocia, for it was regularly traversed by the Cilician governor when he crossed into Campestris Cilicia ; but Cicero calls it Cappadocian, though he had his army encamped there. The Cappadocian king was apparently found so submissive that his nominal rule over Kybistra was no inconvenience.

From 56 to 50 three Dioeceses of Asia, Laodiceia or Cibyra, Apameia, and Synnada, were attached to the Cilician Province.[2] The reason was evidently convenience. The governor, landing at Ephesus, could conveniently hold the assizes in those three cities, as he went along the great highway to the East, which passed through them as well as through Philomelium and Iconium. This arrangement shows the paramount importance of the Province. Cilicia was governed by consular, while Asia was usually administered by prætorian officers at this time.

It was the governor of Cilicia, not the governor of Asia, who was brought into close relations with Galatia during

[1] Justin, XXXVII 1 : he merely epitomises Pompeius Trogus, and the spirit evaporates in an epitome. Appian, *Mithr.*, 105.

[2] They were Asian, demonstrably, 62-56 and 49-46.

this period, as we see from Cicero's language about Deio-taros.

When the Civil War broke out, the importance of the Cilician Provincia was at an end. Asia, as being nearer the seat of war, resumed its ancient importance. There was no leisure to think of foreign relations for many years. The bounds of Rome in these regions shrank. Lands which had been enrolled in a province were even given over to dependent or client princes, implying that the over-burdened empire was no longer fit to maintain order in these outlying districts.

In these circumstances the three Phrygian Dioeceses, Laodiceia, Apameia, and Synnada, were restored to Asia ;[1] and this arrangement continued in force from 50 onwards. But the Philomelian Dioecesis was, as before, attached to Cilicia along with the intermediate regions, Lycaonia and Pisidic Phrygia. Thus, about 46 to 44, Cicero was beg-ging the officials of Cilicia, Philippus and Gallus, to attend to the affairs of his friend Egnatius, which his agent L. Oppius at Philomelium found difficulty in managing.[2] The Philomelian assizes are called *forum Lycaonium* by Cicero, and Pliny mentions that part of Lycaonia was in the same *conventus* with Philomelium.[3]

The troubled period of the Civil Wars seems to have

[1] Cicero, *Fam.*, XIII 67, says pointedly that the three Asiatic Dioeceses were thus shifted about, showing that the Philomelian or Lycaonian Dioecesis was treated separately.

[2] Cicero, *Fam.*, XIII 43, 44, 73, 74. At the same time Cicero wrote to Appuleius, proquæstor in Asia, asking him to attend to Egnatius's affairs in that province, which were managed by his slave Anchialos, *Fam.*, XIII 45.

[3] Cicero, *Att.*, V 21, 9. *Lycaonia . . . cum qua conveniunt Philomeli-enses*, Pliny, *Hist. Nat.*, V 25.

stirred up Antipater of Derbe to shake off the Roman
authority ; already under Philippus he had been on bad
relations with his superior, and that governor had taken
his children as hostages for his good conduct.[1] Cicero
wrote to Philippus interceding on behalf of Antipater, who
had formerly entertained him in some of his progresses
through the Cilician Province, 51-50. Afterwards matters
became worse, and Antipater became an open enemy of
Rome, which Strabo expresses when he calls him a brigand.

In B.C. 40, when Antony came to regulate the eastern
half of the empire, which had been placed under his care,
he gave to Amyntas, secretary of the late Deiotaros, a
new kingdom, comprising Pisidic Phrygia and Pisidia
generally. Great part of Pisidia was still practically independent, so that Amyntas's duty really was to preserve
order in this mountainous and disturbed region. Pisidian
Antioch must have been his capital, and from this time
onwards that city began to be important in the eastern
Roman world. Amyntas, like the other client kings of
this period, was a sort of chief constable for Rome ; a
Roman army could not be spared for this district, and the
king was free to construct an army of his own, and keep
the country quiet as best he could.

A similar kingdom was at the same time constructed
further east. Part of Lycaonia and Isauria and Cilicia
Tracheia [2] was entrusted to Polemon of Laodiceia, an able
man, who henceforth played an important part in the

---

[1] Perhaps the children of Antipater were permanently retained as
hostages by the provincial government ; but Philippus seems to have
had them in his power after he left his province, Cicero, *Fam.*, XIII
74.

[2] Appian, *Bell. Civ.*, V 75 ; cp. Strabo, pp. 569, 577.

eastern Roman world.   Polemon was entrusted on the
Cilician frontier with the same task as Amyntas on the
Phrygian frontier.   Iconium was probably Polemon's capital.[1]   How much of Cilicia Tracheia was given to Polemon
is uncertain, and probably was uncertain even to Antony
and to Polemon.   The country had only been very im-
perfectly subdued ; many of the tribes had never seen a
Roman soldier or official, and were completely ignorant of
Roman ways.   Polemon evidently was left to do the best
he could in his difficult and ill-defined realm.

Both these kingdoms are mere scraps out of the vast
Cilician Province.   Rome had abandoned for the time her
duties in this region ; the Cilician Province shrank into
insignificance ; and new kings were permitted to rule parts
even of Campestris Cilicia.

Polemon had an interesting and remarkable career, the
vicissitudes of which throw light on the confused state of
inner Asia Minor at this time.   He was the son of Zeno,
a rhetorician of Laodiceia, the great Phrygian city on the
Lycus, who had led the successful resistance to the Parthian inroad in B.C. 40.   In reward for Zeno's services on
this occasion his son was promoted successively to the
kingdoms of Cilicia Tracheia and of Pontus, Armenia,
and Bosphorus.   Though he did not, like Amyntas and
Deiotaros of Paphlagonia, desert his first patron Antony
before Actium, he was taken into favour by Augustus, and
passed a long and successful life in the Roman alliance.
He married Pythodoris, a rich lady of Tralles in Lydia,
whose mother was Antonia, daughter of the triumvir.
Thus the Roman rank and the name of Antonius was

---

[1] Strabo, p. 568.

bequeathed to the sons of Polemon, though he was only a Greek ; and his daughter, Tryphaina, played a part in Pauline semi-historical legend.[1]

These and other kings, such as Herod in Samaria and Idumaea, Kastor in Galatia, had all to pay a fixed tribute.

In 36 there was a fresh shuffle of the cards and the kings. Kastor died, and his Galatian realm was given to Amyntas, while his Paphlagonian dominions were left to his brother Deiotaros. Amyntas retained his Phrygo-Pisidian sovereignty ; and, if his enlarged realm was to be easily manageable, evidently either part of the province Asia, or else Iconium and the old Lycaonian Tetrarchy, must be given to him, so that Galatia might be joined to Pisidia. The latter course was taken, and Polemon lost Iconium and Lycaonia. At the same time his Cilician dominion was transferred to Cleopatra, and he was made king of Pontus, to which was added Armenia Minor in 35 as a reward for his services in the Parthian War.

A great Asiatic kingdom was now constructed for Antony's favoured Cleopatra ;[2] and a Cleopatran era was instituted of which the year 1 was reckoned to end on 31st August, B.C. 36. These changes were therefore made during the earlier months of that year.

The kingdoms of Amyntas and Polemon could be justified as attempts to provide a substitute for Roman rule amid its present difficulties. Antony did not desire to occupy his soldiers on the east in case of trouble from his western rival, Augustus. But the kingdom of Cleopatra was merely the result of Antony's infatuation.

Amyntas did not neglect the arts of peace. He had

---

[1] See the *Church in the Roman Empire,* ch. XVI.

[2] See Kromayer in *Hermes,* 1894, p. 574 f.

vast flocks of sheep in the great plains that extend between Iconium, North Galatia and Lake Tatta.

Preparations for the final struggle between Antony and Augustus interfered with the progress of affairs on the plateau of Asia Minor. Amyntas and Polemon both served at Actium under their lord, Antony. But both were pardoned and confirmed in their power by Augustus, who doubtless recognised their ability and their readiness to serve him as well as they had served Antony. Augustus even gave to Amyntas the country of Cilicia Tracheia, which Cleopatra had held since 36.

Amyntas was now entrusted with the whole task of maintaining order on the south side of the plateau, which at first, 39-36, had been shared with Polemon. He was to keep the peace among the mountaineers of Taurus, who were accustomed to raid the more fertile lands north of the mountains. Pamphylia had been added in 36 to his dominions, so that he had the mountains between his hands and was able to attack from either side. He vigorously set about his task of introducing the Roman peace into the mountains by the Roman method of war, and overcame Antipater, the lord of Derbe and Laranda, who seems to have set up as an opposition prince.

He was, however, killed in B.C. 25 during a war with the Homonades, a powerful tribe who inhabited the mountains west of Isaura, around lake Trogitis (Seidi-Sheher-lake).

Augustus, thereupon, resolved to take into the Empire great part of Amyntas's kingdom, as being now sufficiently inured to Roman methods. He despatched Lollius (to whom afterwards Horace addressed the eighth Ode of his Fourth Book) to organise the new Province, which included all the northern and western part of the kingdom.

SECTION 12.

HISTORY OF THE PROVINCE GALATIA, B.C. 25—A.D. 50.

THE history of the Province Galatia is a difficult and complicated subject; and the variation in its bounds is very puzzling. It took the place which the Cilician Province had filled under the later Republic: the growth of the Roman power on this side was now concentrated in the Galatic province. The relations of the Empire to the client-states of Pontus, Paphlagonia and Cilicia Tracheia was part of the Galatic sphere of duty. As those states were successively raised to the Roman standard of peace and order through the exertions, the personal presence and the ever-ready armies of their kings, they were one by one taken into the Empire by being incorporated in the Province Galatia. The history of that Province for almost a century is "the history of Roman policy in its gradual advance towards the Euphrates frontier, a long slow process, in which the Roman genius was exerted to the utmost to influence and impress, to educate and discipline, the population of the various countries taken into the Province Galatia".[1] The foundation of the Galatian Churches is an episode in the history of the Province; and he that would understand the "Galatian Question" aright must look at it from that point of view.

[1] Hastings, *Dict. of the Bible*, II 86.

8

(113)

The complicacy of the history of this Province between
B.C. 25 and A.D. 72 is a proof of its importance in the
Roman policy.   It resembles in that respect the history
of Cilicia Provincia between B.C. 80 and 50.   But in A.D.
72 the importance of Galatia ceased ; and Cappadocia took
its place as the centre of Roman frontier policy.   Cappadocia had been a Roman Province since A.D. 17 ; but
it was prematurely incorporated before it was ready for
strict Roman organisation, and it was placed only under a
procurator, who seems to have left the native organisation
undisturbed, and was probably chiefly concerned to see that
the proper taxes were paid.

In A.D. 72 Cappadocia was created a consular Province
with an army ; and the Galatic Province sank again into
comparative insignificance, being included in a joint Province with Cappadocia until about A.D. 106, and thereafter
separated from it.

It is somewhat remarkable that during the century of
its political importance, the Galatic Province never contained an army.   Its formation was due to the defeat of
the Roman agent, King Amyntas, by the Homonades
(see p. 112) ; and Lollius, the first governor, must have
taken with him a body of troops to inaugurate the
provincial system.   But the Homonades were left for a
number of years unpunished, and the Pisidian mountaineers to the west were far from orderly and peaceable, their
raids constituting a permanent danger.   When at last an
army was needed, the Syrian army was employed ; and an
imperial legate was sent on a special mission to operate
with the troops of the Province Syria-Cilicia, though the
Homonades were far distant from the frontier of that
Province, divided from it by the realm of Archelaos, and

pressing hard on the Galatian frontier. An official specially charged with this duty had to be sent, as his absence
outside of the territory of Syria-Cilicia was required for a
considerable time ; but his work was strictly part of the
Syrian *Provincia* or sphere of duty, as he was leading the
troops of that Province. He was therefore in the strict
and legal Roman sense *Legatus Augusti Pro Praetore Provinciae Syriae et Ciliciae.*[1] His name was P. Sulpicius
Quirinius ; and the date of his command is approximately
given by the simultaneous operations conducted on the
Galatian side, where a series of garrisons (*Coloniae*) connected by military roads with the military capital, Antioch
in Pisidian Phrygia, were established by Cornutus Aquila
in B.C. 6.

Otherwise Galatia was administered without a standing
army, though of course a few soldiers were needed there
for the ordinary purposes of order and government. The
police-system of the Empire was one of its weakest sides,
so that soldiers were needed for police and for revenue-
officers and on the great imperial estates ; also to act as
escort and ministers of the higher Roman officials, and so
on. It is true that that vast Empire was administered and
guarded with an astonishingly small army ; but, considering
that Galatia was so new as a Province and so close to
foreign and dangerous tribes, we can hardly understand
how it was left for nearly a century dependent on the

---

[1] This has been pointed out in *Christ Born in Bethlehem*, ch. XI ;
and only a blindness to the real inner nature of the Roman provincial system could suggest a doubt whether such a special mission
was consistent with Roman usage, or whether such a special officer
would be styled *Legatus Syriae Provinciae ;* those who doubt the
second point are forgetting the Roman sense of Provincia, and
taking it in our territorial sense.

distant Syrian army in the event of any disturbance, internal
or external, unless we take into account the character of the
population and their loyalty.

The Gaulish tribes were certainly enthusiastically loyal.
The long wars side by side with Rome against Mithridates
had cemented a permanent feeling of friendship, the most
striking proof of which is that Augustus could take one of
Deiotaros's Roman-armed Galatian legions and turn it into
a Roman legion, calling it XXII Deiotariana.   Other
causes described in Section 13 contributed to bind them
closely to Rome, and separate them from the Asiatic and
Greek races around them.

The non-Gaulish peoples in the rest of the Province were
kept loyal and orderly by two causes.   In the first place,
the peace and comparatively good government of the
Empire made such a welcome change from the almost
ceaseless wars of the period B.C. 334-31, with the oppres-
sion and rapacity accompanying them, that the rule of
Augustus and his successors was welcomed as a direct gift
from heaven to wretched war-worn men.   In the second
place, the temper of the Asia Minor peoples was essentially
quiet and obedient ; [1] and from the beginning of history to
the present day it has always been an easy task to maintain
peace and order among them.   The people are always
capable of being roused to fanaticism ; but it requires a
strong stimulus to excite them ; and, where the government prevents such a stimulus being applied, and maintains
anything like justice, the population remains marvellously
quiet and submissive.

In these circumstances Galatia could safely be left without a standing army.

[1] See section 4 f.

The importance attached at first in the imperial policy to the Galatic Province appears from a series of facts, small indeed in themselves, but attesting the continued attention paid to it by the Emperors. In the obscurity that envelops this region, it is remarkable how many such small details have become known to us.

The conquered Homonades were incorporated in the Province,[1] and the effort to pacify the southern frontier is probably connected with the foundation of the Colonia Caesareia Antiochia[2] and Colonia Julia Felix Gemina Lustra, with four others towards the western side of the Pisidian frontier. This brought a considerable Latin-speaking population to Antioch and Lystra, and the municipal government in both cities was remodelled after the Roman fashion. Duoviri, Quæstors and Aediles took the place of Strategoi or Archontes; lictors marched in front of these Roman magistrates; *decuriones* were substituted for the *Boule;* the language used in the municipal deeds was Latin (as we see in the inscriptions); the law administered among the *cives Romani* in the Colonies was Roman; the personal names became in large proportion Roman.[3] If we had as many names of Lystran and Antiochian as we have of Corinthian converts, we should doubtless find quite as large a proportion of Roman names in the two Galatian as in the Grecian Colonia.[4]

This event was a marked step in the Romanisation of

---

[1] See C. I. L., III 6799, in their territory, dedicated to Afrinus, governor of Galatia under Claudius.

[2] It may possibly have been founded earlier, being called Caesareia while the others are called Augusta; but, if so, it is likely to have been strengthened at this time.

[3] See section 19.

[4] See Hastings' *Dict. of the Bible,* I, p. 480.

Southern Galatia.   Neither of these two cities had previously ranked among the greater cities of Asia Minor ; and Lystra, in fact, had been an utterly insignificant place. Now Antioch was a Latin city, and its citizens had Latin rights.   Considering what dignity and practical advantages lay in the Roman or Latin citizenship, the presence in Antioch of so large a proportion of *cives* gave it a position in the land that nothing else could have conferred upon it.   Moreover, it was the military centre of the provincial frontier defence on the south ; and it was all the more important because there was no army in the Province, and the defence lay with the burghers of the Coloniae.

The two Coloniae were connected by a "royal road," an imperial highway, which is mentioned in the *Acts of Paul and Thekla*, and which in an administrative point of view must have been a most important road, until the thorough pacification of Pisidia, and the incorporation in the Empire of the whole mountainous country between the Provinces Galatia and Cilicia in A.D. 72, did away with the need for frontier defence.   Then Lystra sank back into comparative insignificance, and the use of Latin declined, as we see in the later inscriptions.

It is important to observe that the dignity and rank of these cities depended, entirely in the case of Lystra, and mainly in the case of Antioch, on their Roman character. Apart from that they were of little or no consequence. With that they were more honourable than their neighbours.   No one who has taken any interest in the history of Asia Minor at this period will doubt that the Roman feeling was strong in these cities.   The mutual rivalry of the cities in the East is familiar to every student.   They wrangled for precedence, until even the Emperor was appealed to for a decision ; they invented titles of honour for themselves to outshine their rivals and appropriated the titles invented by their rivals. In Asia, Smyrna, Ephesus and Pergamos vied with one another, in Bithynia, Nikomedia and Nicaea, in Cilicia, Tarsus and Anazarbos. In Macedonia a trace of the rivalry between Philippi and Amphipolis is visible in Acts XVI 12.[1] So in South Galatia it may be taken as certain that there was keen rivalry between the chief cities. Antioch and Lystra, strong in their Roman rank, could congratulate themselves on outshining Iconium, the old capital. See § LIII.

Yet in face of these facts, which are familiar to all who have studied the actual history of Asia Minor, it has been seriously maintained by some Biblical critics in the last year or two that about A.D. 50, the natural and hardly avoidable address for an audience in these two cities would have been "Phrygians" and "Lycaonians". To see the relation of these national names to the existing situation in South Galatia, we must observe the implication.

We must observe that a non-Roman people, and an individual who is not a Roman or Latin citizen, could belong to the empire only by virtue of belonging to a Province. The status of each non-Roman person in the Empire was that of a " provincial " ; and he was designated as a member of the Roman Empire, not by his nation, but by his Province. His nation was a non-Roman idea ; so long as a person is described as a Phrygian or a Lycaonian, he is thereby described as outside of the Empire. In the Roman theory, the foreigner, the enemy, and the slave, are related ideas. If the Roman citizen can

---

[1] *St. Paul the Trav.*, p. 206.

get a foreigner into his power, the latter thereby at once becomes a slave : the foreigner has no rights and is merely regarded as an enemy, except in so far as by a special treaty Rome has guaranteed certain rights to all members of his nation. The slave was designated by his national name as Phryx or Lycao or Syrus : so was a horse. But the Roman soldier was designated by his home in the Empire, *i.e.*, either his Province, or his city as one of the units composing the Province : only the marines, *classiarii*, who were originally slaves, were regularly designated after the servile fashion.[1]

When an audience of Antiochians and Lystrans was addressed by a courteous orator, he would certainly not address those citizens of the Coloniae by the servile designation as Phrygians or Lycaonians. If he sought to please them, he would designate them either as *Galatae*, *i.e.*, members of the Roman Empire as being members of the Province Galatia, or as *Coloni*, citizens of Roman *Coloniae*, which would be an even more honorific term. An inscription [2] of one of the Pisidian *Coloniae*, Comama, opens with the address, in Latin and in Greek, " To the Coloni," implying the pride of that obscure town in the designation. Much more would Antioch and her sister Lystra [3] demand some such Roman address, instead of the national designation, Phrygians and Lycaonians, which ruled them out as non-Roman and foreign and barbarian : a Lycaonian, in

[1] Mommsen has discussed the subject with his usual logical precision and wide knowledge from several points of view. See his papers in *Hermes*, 1884, p. 33 ff, and in *Festgabe für G. Beseler*, p. 255 ff. Also Mitteis, *Reichsrecht und Volksrecht*, p. 358 ff.

[2] See *American Journal of Archaeology*, 1888, p. 264.

[3] See section 21.

the Roman view, was either an enemy outside, or a slave inside, the Empire.

In B.C. 5 great part of Paphlagonia was taken into the Galatic Province. Paphlagonia, which was in close alliance with Galatia during part at least of the second century B.C., was conquered by Mithridates and Nikomedes of Bithynia about B.C. 110; and the conquerors divided it. Pompey, in the settlement of 64, retained the partition, and apparently gave the western half to Pylaimenes, the eastern to Attalos.

The connection of Paphlagonia with Galatia is shown by the facts that part (probably the western) was called " the country of Gaizatorix,"[1] and that the eastern with its capital Gangra was governed by Kastor 40-36, and then by his brother Deiotaros Philadelphos[2] until B.C. 5, when it passed to the Romans.

The relation of Paphlagonia to Galatia is similar to that of northern and western Lycaonia, as we saw in Sections 8, 10. In each case the strong Galatian state tended to swallow up the weaker state on its frontier.

In B.C. 2 an addition on the north-eastern frontier was made to Galatia.[3] There was there a small state carved out of Pontus, which Antony or Augustus had granted to a Gaul of tetrarchic family named Ateporix ; it comprised a village called Karana, formerly subject to Zela, which was now formed into a city by concentrating there the people of the surrounding territory. This was now taken into the

---

[1] Strabo, p. 562.

[2] So M. Theod. Reinach, *Rev. Numism.*, 1891, p. 395. Deiotaros married Adobogiona (perhaps daughter of Mithridates and granddaughter of the older Adobogiona, p. 101).

[3] Date : see *Rev. Études Grecques*, 1894, p. 251.

Empire, and Karana was re-named Sebastopolis in honour of its new rank.

Along with this accession came the more important territory of Amasia, formerly the capital of the Pontic kingdom; apparently it was for some reason taken away from King Polemon, to whom it had been given in B.C. 36. Gazelonitis (except its sea-board) was also probably annexed now to the Galatic Province, which thus comprised a considerable part of Pontus.

Tiberius, as is well known, made a point of preserving Augustus's arrangement with the least possible change; but Galatia attracted some attention. In Pisidia, south-east from Antioch, was a tribe named Orondeis, whose former tribal organisation was now changed into the city organisation of the ordinary Græco-Roman type : [1] in other words, a city was founded, and part of the tribe was concentrated in it after the fashion of Greek municipalities. This city, of course, was enlarged from one of the tribal villages. The name of the village had been Pappa or Papa: it now became Tiberiopolis; but the old name returned, first alongside of, and after a time instead of, the new title.

In 34-35 the territory of Comana Pontica, one of the greatest priestly centres in Asia Minor, was annexed to the Empire. It had been ruled by a Gaul, Dyteutos (grandson of Domnilaos), about whom Strabo tells a romantic tale. His elder brother had been condemned to death along with his father Adiatorix for massacring the Romans resident in Heracleia Pontica. Dyteutos claimed to be the elder : the real elder would not permit Dyteutos to take

---

[1] This was a characteristic process in the imperial period. The tribal organisation was much less developed and "civilised" than the city.

his place. Thus arose a contest between the brothers, each claiming to die for the other. Dyteutos survived, and was made by Augustus high priest of Comana, an office which he held at least till A.D. 19. He or perhaps his son probably died in 34-35, and Tiberius annexed the territory.

Claudius gave his name to five Galatic cities, Claudio-Seleuceia in Pisidia, Claudio-Derbe and Claud-Iconium [1] in Lycaonia, Germanicopolis-Gangra and Neoclaudiopolis-Andrapa in Paphlagonia. These honorary names were, doubtless, connected with some new arrangements introduced into the respective districts. Derbe was the frontier city from 41 onwards, and a station for customs on goods entering the Province. [2]

Nero in 63 annexed the country called Pontus Polemoniacus, incorporating it in the Province Galatia. Pontus consisted of three parts: (1) The coast on each side of Amisos, in the province Bithynia-Pontus: (2) The kingdom of Polemon II, grandson of Polemon and the noble Queen Pythodoris, called for a century afterwards Pontus Polemoniacus; (3) The Galatic territory of Pontus, called Pontus Galaticus, a name which lasted even after Pontus Polemoniacus was incorporated in the Galatian Province.

This sketch brings out the real sterling strength of the Galatic element in central Asia Minor. Not merely their narrower old Galatia, but most of the surrounding countries, were under Celtic rule before they came into the Roman Empire. These facts in their entirety show how pre-eminently the Galatic realm must have occupied the Roman attention. All others but the Galatae were an Asiatic

---

[1] This act is misrepresented by some Biblical critics as the establishment of a Roman Colonia Iconium, see p. 218.

[2] λιμήν Steph. Byz. See section 22.

mob: the Galatae were men, chiefs, kings and rulers. Only Polemon was excepted, and Polemon was closely connected with the Antonian family.

The fate of Tracheiotis or Cilicia Tracheia was closely connected with the Galatic sphere of duty. When the Province was created, Tracheiotis was given to Archelaos, King of Cappadocia; and Strabo says that the same extent of Tracheiotic territory was ruled by Cleopatra, by Amyntas, and by Archelaos. Archelaos was degraded and died soon after in A.D. 17; but even before that, about A.D. 11, owing to his imbecility, Augustus took two districts, Kennatis and Lalassis, from him, and gave them to Ajax, son of Teucer, of an ancient priestly dynastic family.

In 17 Archelaos II was allowed by Tiberius to rule part of his father's Cilician kingdom, while Cappadocia was made a Procuratorial Province. The rest of Tracheiotis, including Olba, Lalassis and Kennatis, was given to M. Antonius Polemon in 17 or soon after. Ajax, who struck coins in his fifth year under Tiberius, had probably died; and Polemon, Asiatic dynast and Roman citizen, son of Polemon I of Pontus, descended from Antony the Triumvir, ruled and coined money for eleven years or more.

In 35 Archelaos instituted a census and valuation after the Roman fashion (doubtless acting under Roman orders, like Herod in Palestine B.C. 8-6), which provoked a rebellion among his subjects the Kietai.[1] As Polemon is not men-

---

[1] Only part of Ketis or Kietis was ruled by Archelaos, evidently the northern part with its centre at Hiera-polis Koropissos (see *Cities and Bishoprics of Phrygia*, p. 11 note). The southern part had its centre at Olba, the city of Polemon. On the census see *Christ Born at Bethlehem*, ch. 8.

tioned, he was probably dead, and perhaps Archelaos had succeeded to his power.[1]

In 37 Antiochus IV of Commagene was granted part of Tracheiotis by Caligula ; and, though he seems soon to have been disgraced, Claudius in 41 restored and enlarged his Tracheiotic realm. The government of the two Cappadocian kings seems to have been feeble ; and a more energetic ruler was needed. Part of Lycaonia, *viz.*, Laranda and the territory around, was given to Antiochus, who was reckoned as king " of the Lycaonians ".

Laranda had hitherto been part of the Roman Province, and supplied soldiers to the Roman legions.[2] But, though a Lycaonian city, it is the true centre for the administration of Tracheiotis, because from it radiate the roads that lead across Tracheiotis to the coast ;[3] and, apparently, the necessity for assigning it to the king of Tracheiotis was now recognised. Coins with legend *ΛΥΚΑΟΝΩΝ* were struck by Antiochus, evidently at Laranda. Derbe now became the frontier city of Roman territory and a customs station ; and its new importance was marked with the title Claudio-Derbe.

Antiochus proved a vigorous ruler. He founded in Tracheiotis a large number of cities, two named Claudiopolis a Germanicopolis, an Eirenopolis, two named Antiocheia, an Iotapa after his queen ; and his reign marks an important step in the spread of Græco-Roman civilisation in that wild and mountainous region.[4] So successful was he, that

[1] There is, however, no certain proof that Archelaos was king of the whole of the wide Ketian or Kietian territory in 36.

[2] C. I. L., III 2709, 2818, with Mommsen's commentary on p. 281.

[3] *Historical Geogr. of Asia Minor*, p. 361.

[4] *Revue Numismatique*, 1894, p. 169 f.

Vespasian recognised Tracheiotis as fit for incorporation in the Empire, and Antiochus was degraded in A.D. 72.

Note.—NORTH GALATIAN THEORISTS ON POLEMON. We have said, p. 4, that the North Galatian Theory rests only on want of knowledge of the facts of Asia Minor in the time of Paul ; thus, *e.g.*, in the latest edition of Meyer-Sieffert, 1899, p. 8, we find the assertion that Polemon's territory had by that time come under Roman ownership (Polemon's *Gebiet unter röm. Herrschaft gekommen war*). In truth, by far the greater part of Polemon's first kingdom was still governed by king Antiochus, and practically the whole of his second kingdom was still ruled by his grandson Polemon II.

I have been blamed for unreasonably expecting theologians to be familiar with all the most recent historical investigations ; but it may surely be expected that they will refrain from repeating historical blunders and founding their theories of Pauline history on those false premises. There are a dozen works about Polemon, from Waddington's *Mélanges de Numismatique*, II, p. 109 ff., onwards, any of which would be sufficient to show the erroneousness of Meyer-Sieffert's statement. There remain many serious controversies about the various persons, Polemon I, M. Antonius Polemon, Polemon II, on which we cannot enter. We have given the views which seem established as the most probable; and Mr. G. F. Hill will soon publish a detailed argument demonstrating independently the view advocated here and in Hastings' *Dict. of the Bible*, art. *Galatia.*

It would be an endless task to correct every historical misstatement about Asia Minor made by the North Galatian Theorists. But it goes beyond the bounds of ordinary mistakes such as we wink at in theologians with a fixed prejudice, when Meyer-Sieffert, p. 11 *note*, state that Strabo wrote before the Roman Province Galatia was constituted, and Dion Cassius wrote after it had been dissolved. Did Meyer-Sieffert fancy that Galatia was constituted in 25 A.D., or did they forget when Strabo wrote? Galatia was constituted about forty years before Strabo composed his history. Galatia was much smaller when Dion wrote, but even then it was a huge Province.

SECTION 13.

CIVILISATION OF GALATIA UNDER THE ROMAN EMPIRE.

IN our sketch of the history of the Province Galatia, we have reached the period when Paul and Barnabas entered it. We must now state the evidence showing the character of the southern and northern parts of the Province respectively.

It is, of course, not open to dispute that Paul founded churches in four cities of South Galatia, *viz.*, Antioch, Iconium, Derbe and Lystra. The only point in dispute is whether Paul founded also another set of churches in North Galatia. The South Galatian theory is that no churches were founded by Paul in North Galatia ; and that when he speaks of the churches of Galatia, he means the four churches in the south of the Province Galatia. The North Galatian theory is that Paul also founded churches in North Galatia, and that, when he speaks of his churches of Galatia, he means only the churches of North Galatia, and excludes the four South Galatian cities.

The opinion that Paul included in his " churches of Galatia " both those of South and others of North Galatia is not held by any ; and is, in fact, barred by the conditions of the question.[1]   On this we need not enter.

[1] In his admirable *Einleitung*, 1897, Prof. Th. Zahn finds in the Churches of Galatia a certain North-Galatian part, but only second-

To the scholar who studies the society of the eastern Roman provinces, North Galatia stands apart and isolated from the cities of the southern part of the Province. Reserving South Galatia for the final Sections, we now gather together all that is known about society and civilisation in Imperial North Galatia.

We saw in the sketch of its history, the failure of Greek civilisation to establish itself there, and the strength of the reaction towards the Celtic national character. It has never proved easy to eliminate the national genius of a Celtic race; and the Celtic element in North Galatia, though numerically inferior, was immeasurably superior in practical strength to the older Phrygian element.

A convincing proof of the essential contrast in character between Galatia and the Græco-Asiatic Provinces that bordered on it, lies in the societies of Hellenes which formed a feature in all of them. These Hellenes were really Hellenised people of the province, and not as a rule Greeks by blood or descent; and in many provinces the Hellenes were formed into associations, meeting in the worship of the Emperors. In Asia and in Bithynia the Association of Hellenes was the Provincial Association, the Koinon of the cities of the province. The titles, "the Hellenes in (the Province) Asia," "the Koinon of the Hellenes in Asia," are precisely equivalent to "the Koinon of Asia," and the head of "the Hellenes in Asia" was the Asiarch [1] or high

ary and unimportant: to him the important and determining element lies in the four South-Galatian Churches. In proportion as that North-Galatian element is insignificant, it withdraws itself from consideration, and the self-contradictoriness of the view escapes notice.

[1] We do not enter on controversies as to the powers, etc., of the Asiarch.

priest of the Province. Similarly the Koinon of the
Hellenes in Bithynia was simply the Koinon of Bithynia,
the assembly of representatives of the cities of Bithynia,
of which the head and president was the Bithynarch. This
is very clearly put by Dion Cassius, LI 20, where he says
that " Augustus permitted the non-citizens, *Xenoi*, (according them the title Hellenes) to erect temples to him,
those of Asia at Pergamos, and those of Bithynia at
Nikomedeia ".

But in Galatia the Koinon of the Province, or the Koinon
of Galatians,[1] was distinct and separate from the Association
of the Hellenes.   The Koinon was apparently organised
on the basis of the three tribes [2] (though details are quite
unknown), and its president was the Galatarch.   The
Association of Hellenes had as its president the Helladarch;
and was doubtless formed of representatives from the *poleis*,
the cities so far as they had adopted the Greek fashion,
sent either by the cities officially or by special societies in
the cities.   There is no evidence as to the date when the
Association of Hellenes in Galatia was formed ; but none
of the inscriptions mentioning it are earlier than about
A.D. 150, whereas the Koinon of Galatians was organised by
Augustus.

As to the organisation and law of household and family

---

[1] τὸ Κοινὸν Γαλατῶν in first century inscriptions, C. I. G., 4039, *Cities
and Bish. of Phr.*, pt. II, p. 648, no. 558 : τὸ Κοινὸν τῶν Γαλατῶν in C. I.
G., 4016, 4017 (third or late second century): Κοινὸν Γαλατίας on coins
of Trajan.

[2] ἔθνη : in C. I. G., 4039, the only authority of much consequence,
"the three tribes" and "the two tribes" are often mentioned : "the
two tribes" apparently held a joint meeting at Pessinus, while "the
three tribes" met on certain festivals in Ancyra.   The Trocmi were
far less civilised than the "two tribes".

in Galatia under the Romans, the two leading modern authorities have pronounced a decisive judgment.

Professor Mitteis, speaking of the slow and imperfect adoption of Hellenic civilisation in inner Asia Minor, says that "the Galatians especially constituted a distinct and exclusive stock of the population" through the preservation of its language at least in the early imperial period,[1] and the continuance of Celtic customs.

Mommsen points out that, though the Phrygian religion was adopted by the Galatians, "nevertheless, even in the Roman Province of Galatia, the internal organisation was predominantly Celtic. The fact that even under Pius, A.D. 138-161, the strict paternal power foreign to Hellenic law subsisted in Galatia is a proof of this from the sphere of private law."

The last sentence refers to the evidence of the Roman lawyer Gaius, I 55, who, speaking of the characteristic Roman custom that the father had absolute power over his children (even to life and death), says that there are hardly any others among whom this right exists, with the one exception of the Galatians, quoting from a rescript of Hadrian the recognition of this Galatian custom. Cæsar[2] mentions the same custom as ruling among the tribes of Gaul.

Such power of a father over his children was repugnant to the Greeks; and its existence in Galatia shows how fundamentally un-Hellenic was the social system of that country even in the second century after Christ.

---

[1] He means the first two centuries, and leaves the question as to the authority of Jerome (see p. 155), to be discussed by others, *Reichsrecht und Volksrecht,* p. 23.

[2] *Bell. Gall.,* VI 19 (false reference in Mitteis, p. 24 note).

Here the questions may be asked by those who have
not specially studied the Roman provincial system, whether
the Galatian law would be made uniform throughout the
Province, and whether the Roman law would not be introduced in the Province in place of the old native law. Neither
would be done : both were contrary to the Roman system.
Each district was administered according to its private law
and hereditary usage (as is pointed out in the beginning
of Section 17). Violent or sudden changes in society were
shunned by Roman policy.

The old custom that the chiefs and leading men feasted
the tribesmen, which flourished from the beginning of the
Galatian state,[1] was still practised in the reign of Tiberius.
The public gifts and donations of leading Gauls about A.D.
10-30 are recorded in a fragmentary inscription. Such
inscriptions are common also in Asia ; and a comparison
of Asian and Galatian inscriptions shows the difference of
manners in the two Provinces. The chief Galatian enter-
tainment is a banquet to the people : the gifts of almost
every donor begin with a public feast ; sometimes it is
stated that the feast was given to the two tribes at Pessinus,
sometimes to the three tribes (meeting, of course, in Ancyra),
generally a " public feast " alone[2] is given.

After the feasts are often mentioned shows of gladiators
and combats of wild beasts (*venationes*) after the Roman
fashion ; these were not much to the Greek taste, and were
not very popular in the Province Asia, nor very common
there : inscriptions show that gladiators were sometimes
shown in the great Asian cities, but were far less popular
and common than games of the Greek style.

---

[1] See above, p. 79.   [2] δημοθοινία.

Thereafter, distributions of oil are mentioned. These were after the Greek fashion, and are the commonest form of public liberality in Asian inscriptions; but the lavish use of oil was universal in the Mediterranean lands, and does not prove much for Galatian imitation of Greek customs.

The characteristic point lies in the games that were given. These were almost always of the Roman and bloody type. An athletic contest is mentioned only once. Chariot races and horse races were commoner, but these were by that time as characteristic of Rome as of Greece. What was aimed at by the Galatian donors was clearly Circensian games of the Roman style. Bull-fights, which were said to be of Thessalian origin, but were regarded as un-Hellenic and barbaric by the true Greeks, are several times mentioned. The least Hellenic among Greek sports is the one which the Galatians patronised, for it was more after the Roman sanguinary style.[1]

Hecatombs also are often mentioned among the gifts. These were undoubtedly great sacrifices in the Imperial religion practised by the Koinon of the Galatians. Hecatombs were no longer a Greek custom, and are hardly mentioned in the inscriptions of the thoroughly Hellenised cities. Probably these Galatian hecatombs are a mild and civilised representative of the Celtic and early Galatian custom of human sacrifices on a gigantic scale (see p. 78).

Thus under Tiberius, the spectacular side of society, the shows under the patronage of the Koinon, are mainly of Celtic or of Roman, not of Greek style. And later inscriptions of the Pessinuntine State are similar.

In the tribal organisation lay the essence of the Celtic

---

[1] M. Perrot well states this, *de Galatia Prov. Rom.*, p. 85.

character as it worked itself out in practical society.   Where
the Celtic people has created any organisation, it gives to
it the tribal character.   The Celtic Church, as it temporarily
ruled in Northern England and Scotland, rises to one's
mind (in the brilliant sketch, for example, of J. R. Green).
Its strength and its weakness lay in the loose, but free, tribal
system.

The Romans did not attempt to destroy the tribal system
in Galatia.   Not merely were they always unwilling to
force sudden and violent changes on the subject peoples ;
they also saw that the tribal system was the antithesis of
Hellenism, and they were not at first eager to make Hellenism absolutely supreme in Asia.   There were only two
alternatives in the last days of the free Galatian state : it
must either be Celtic, or it must yield to the pressure of the
Greek ocean that surrounded it on three sides.

In other Provinces of the Roman State the fiction was
usually maintained that there was only one "tribe" or
"nation".[1]   Even in provinces which were composed of
many distinct nations, such as Asia,[2] the official form admitted only one "nation," *viz.*, the Roman idea, the Province:
in other words, the "nation" officially was the Province.
"The Nation Asia" (ἡ Ἀσία τὸ ἔθνος) was the technical
Greek form translating the Latin *Asia Provincia*.[3]   But in
Galatia the old Three Tribes or Nations—τὰ τρία ἔθνη—
continued to be the Roman official form.

---

[1] ἔθνος.   An exception in Bithynia-Pontus, where the double
nationality was officially recognised in the constitution and in the
technical Roman name of the Province.

[2] Mysians, Lydians, Greeks, Carians, Phrygians, Solymi in Cibyra,
etc.

[3] Dion Cassius, LIV 30.

The theory has been stated that this form was applied to the whole Province, and that the Koinon of the Galatians, *i.e.*, the Three Tribes meeting in a Diet or Common Council, was as wide as the Province.   This would imply that the other divisions of the Province were by a fiction represented as enrolled in one or other of the Three Tribes.   A trace of this is perhaps preserved in an inscription of Apollonia, dated A.D. 57,[1] implying that that city was of the Trocmi. Another indication may be found in the dedication at Apollonia of a copy of the great inscription of Ancyra, commonly called the *Monumentum Ancyranum*.   The Galatian Koinon, which dedicated the one at Ancyra, may be presumed to have dedicated the other also.   But this theory is too uncertain to be taken as evidence.[2]   It is enough that in North Galatia the Three Ethnê were recognised and left undisturbed in the Provincial organisation.

As Mommsen says, in North Galatia, as a part of the Province, at the beginning, " in public relations there were still only the three old communities, the Tribes, who perhaps appended to their names those of the three chief places, Ancyra, Pessinus and Tavium, but were essentially nothing but the well-known Gallic cantons ".   In process of time the pressure of Hellenism became too strong, while the vigour of the Roman system died out, and Galatia was Hellenised.   But the process was slow.

The two systems, Celtic and Greek, stand contrasted in their characteristic forms, the Tribe and the City or *Polis*. As the Greek system established itself, Galatia became,

---

[1] *Studia Biblica*, IV 54.

[2] If for a time Rome tried to make the Galatian tribal Koinon co-extensive with the Province, the attempt apparently failed, as the Romanising effort weakened,

like other Hellenised Provinces, a body of Cities ; and the
progress of that system can be traced by the appearance
of *Poleis.*

It is quite consistent with the Tribal system that a Tribe
should have a town-centre. The town, however, was not
organised as a *polis*, it was simply the centre of the Tribe.
Many examples might be quoted from Gaul of the growth
of town-centres in each tribe, and the growth of organised
municipal institutions in the centres.[1]

A similar process, only making Greek *poleis* instead of
Roman *municipia*, went on among the three Tribes in
North Galatia. They had as their centres the three towns,
Pessinus for the Tolistobogii, Ancyra for the Tectosages,
Tavium for the Trocmi. But these were not at first termed
cities (πόλεις). The Tribe was the essential idea, and the
town was the Tribal centre.

The strict and proper title of the town mentioned first
the nation, next the tribe, last the town, *e.g.* :—

> Galatae, Tolistobogii, Pessinuntii.
> Galatae, Trocmi, Taviani.

In each case there were varieties ; and in each the simple
Greek designation as Pessinuntines, Tavians, was gradually
introduced. The difference is not a slight one. The Greek
title makes the city the essential idea, and speaks only of
inhabitants of the city : the Galatian title makes the town
a part of the Tribe, and lays the chief stress on the Tribe.

The evolution from the idea of the town as tribal centre
to the Greek conception of the city is best shown in the

---

[1] See Mommsen, " Provinces of the Roman Empire " (*Röm. Gesch.*,
V), ch. III. ; Hirschfeld, *Gallische Studien* ; Kuhn, *Verfassung des Röm.
Reichs.* Rushforth, *Latin Historical Inscr.*, pp. 13-18, gives briefly
and clearly some typical examples.

gradual change of legends on the coins struck at the three tribal centres, as stated fully in the following paragraphs. Those who have not studied the subject as a whole in the various parts of Asia Minor for its own sake and apart from theological theories and prepossessions, will hardly appreciate the unique character of Galatian titles and the indubitable proof that is thereby given of the peculiar and distinct constitution and system existing in North Galatia. Probably some of the German champions of the North Galatian Theory will meet us with the question what the titles of Galatian cities have to do with the Biblical question. But it is on the ground of a title that they have now elected to rest their own Theory: the most recent form of the argument by which they demonstrate the impossibility of the South Galatian Theory is simply that they cannot believe that Paul (Roman citizen as he was) could apply the title " Galatae " in the sense of " Men of the Province Galatia " to the inhabitants of four South Galatian cities.[1] They give no arguments : they quote no analogous cases : they simply state a bare negative on their own authority, yet no sign appears that they have specially studied the use and implication of political titles amid the contending forces that were then causing the development of society in central Asia Minor. Every thinking man knows how delicate is the innuendo that often lies in political titles, and how much they often change in connotation amid the pressure of social forces. But the North Galatian theorist,

---

[1] See, *e.g.*, Schürer in *Theol. Littztg.*, 1893, p. 507, Blass in his larger edition of *Acts*, p. 176. [More recently Meyer-Sieffert admit the proof (given in reply to Schürer and Blass in *Studia Biblica*, IV) that Galatae could mean "people of the Province," and try to argue, reasonably and fairly, that Paul would not use it so.]

who looks on the history of Asia Minor as a mine from which he may extract some confirmation of his prejudice, has firmly made up his mind beforehand that the word "Galatae" could never have any other than the single and simple meaning, "men who are Gauls by blood and descent". We who begin by studying Asia Minor before we decide about the meaning of the titles used there, know that it would be as absurd to argue that the word "Français" now could not be used in addressing an audience of Breton and Norman towns, as that the word "Galatae" could not be used in A.D. 54 in addressing an audience of South Galatian cities.

The study of the titles chosen by North Galatian towns and impressed on their coins is of real importance in estimating the character of the social forces working in Asia Minor when Paul wrote his Epistle. History had developed rapidly in the 332 years since the Gauls entered that country; but yet the Celtic tribal feeling was still dominant for a full century later than Paul, and that feeling was the negative of Hellenism.

In the typical titles "*Galatae, Trocmi, Taviani,*" etc., the meaning of the three elements must be noticed, in order to appreciate the meaning of the variation. "Trocmi," indicates the tribe. "Taviani" indicates the tribal centre, where the coinage and other administrative powers in the tribe are situated. But "Galatae" is not a mere assertion of Gaulish or Celtic origin: it expresses a living political fact. The tribal character, as shown in the second element, "Trocmi," fully satisfied Celtic pride. The first element, "Galatae," is the Roman imperial element: it embodies the idea of Roman unity, *i.e.*, the Provincia of which the Trocmi gloried in forming a part.

That such is the force of the element "Galatae" in the typical title is proved by the common substitution for it of the "Imperial" adjective "*Sebaste*" or "*Sebasteni*". When a tribe called itself "Imperial" or "Augustan,"[1] that sufficiently recognised the Roman unity, and it did not then use the provincial title Galatae.

It must be emphatically stated, as the foundation of true conceptions on this subject, that the "Province" is the embodiment of Roman unity among all members of the Empire who were not actually *cives Romani*. The ideal which the Empire slowly worked out was the recognition of all members of the Empire as *cives* about A.D. 212. The word *Provincia* then lost its old force, and denoted thenceforward only what it now denotes, a division for administrative purposes of the homogeneous Empire.

The coinage of Pessinus, on the most probable dating, began shortly before 100 B.C., evidently connected with the temple and arranged by the priestly hierarchy. In the early Roman period the same kind of coinage persisted, with legends :—

> Mother of the Gods,
> Mother of the Pessinuntines,
> The Ilean Goddess of the Pessinuntines.

Under Claudius, 41-54, the style develops ; sometimes,

> Of the Mother of the Pessinuntines under Afrinus,

adding the recognition of the Roman provincial governor. Sometimes the Goddess is represented only by her image with,

> Of the Pessinuntines under Afrinus.

This style is quite that of the ordinary Asian Græco-Roman cities, and marks clearly the growth of Occiden-

---

[1] Sebastos was the Greek for Augustus.

talism. But it disappears again, and under Nero, 54-68, Poppaea is mentioned instead of the Goddess, with ΠE or $\Pi E\Sigma$ added, marking an increase of the Roman element and weakening of the Greek.

But after this the Celtic tone increases;[1] and for the first time the tribal system becomes fully dominant in the old Phrygian city in the legend :—

> Of the Galatae Tolistobogii Pessinuntines ;

and this continued in regular use till 160-170, when the simple Greek form began :—

> Of the Pessinuntines :

and became universal after 170.

The only two official inscriptions[2] of Pessinus are erected by the " Senate and people of the Sebasteni Tolistobogii Pessinuntines ". Both belong to the second century. They mention a course of office that is hardly of the fully Hellenised type, speaking of agoranomoi and astynomoi and eirenarchs and public feasts[3] and distributions of corn, but not of archons or strategoi and the usual career in the Asian cities. The tone is on the whole at least as much Roman as Greek.

The ancient Phrygian city of Ancyra had declined to be a mere fortress under the Gauls.[4] Though it was the capital of the Roman Province, its coins did not bear the name Ancyra during the first century, but have the legends of Romanised Celtic character :—

> Of the Augustan Tectosages,
> Σεβαστηνῶν Τεκτοσάγων.

---

[1] Hitherto it was weak in Pessinus, see pp. 55, 62, 73 f.
[2] C. I. G., 4085 ; *Athen. Mittheilungen*, 1897, p. 44 (Körte).
[3] See p. 132.   [4] See p. 74.

Koinon of the Galatians,

Κοινὸν Γαλατῶν.

Under Vespasian, 69-79, and Nerva, 96-98, coins with the full name and title of the Roman governor, and the name of Ancyra half-hidden in monogram, were struck ; similar coins under Titus, 79-81, are mentioned, with *KO · ΓΑΔ ·* in place of the city name ; and under Trajan, 98-117, similar coins with the Roman governor and the full title Κοινὸν Γαλατίας, but without the city name, were struck.

Under Pius, 138-161, the fully developed Greek fashion—

Of the Metropolis Ancyra,

was introduced and permanently fixed.

In inscriptions composed in name of the city, a similar practice was observed. Those of the later second and third centuries are in the name of Metropolis Ancyra ; but in the early second century the title runs (C. I. G., 4011) :—

Metropolis of Galatia Imperial Tectosagan Ancyra,

ἡ μητρόπολις τῆς Γαλατίας Σεβαστὴ Τεκτοσάγων Ἄγκυρα ;

earlier still the form—

Senate and People of the Imperial Tectosages,

ἡ βουλὴ καὶ ὁ δῆμος Σεβαστηνῶν Τεκτοσάγων.

At Tavium the legend—

Of the Imperial Trocmi,

was regular in the first century, and under Pius. Coins are very rare from 100 to 200. Then under Severus and Caracalla they are numerous with—

Of the Imperial Trocmi Tavians,

Σεβαστηνῶν Τρόκμων Ταουιανῶν,

and also the pure Greek style *Ταουιανῶν.* Later coins hardly occur.

In the first century B.C. rare coins reading *Ταουίων* occur,

of the pure Greek style. These point to some isolated
Greek influence at work in Eastern Galatia ; and we remember that Græco-Pontic influence was strong in Galatia
for a time, and would be strongest in Tavium.

These facts show how long the tribal idea continued
dominant in Galatia. Only after the Greek style of title
for the city had become the regular official form, are we
justified in saying that the Greek manners and customs
were dominant in the cities : *i.e.*, at Ancyra about 150,
at Pessinus about 165, at Tavium about 205. Naturally
there was a Hellenised element in the cities from an early
period, but it became the dominant element about that
time.

If such are the dates in the three great cities, what must
we say about the rustic districts and the villages, which are
found as cities and bishoprics in the fourth century, but
whose very names are sometimes unknown in the second
century ? It is certainly quite unjustifiable to speak of
Greek manners, Greek civilisation, Greek ways of thinking
among them about A.D. 50.

As to the constitution of the Galatian cities, Ancyra and
Pessinus are the only two about which any evidence has
been preserved. They are the two that were earliest
Hellenised ; and the inscriptions which give evidence are
almost all of the late Hellenising period.

Three characteristics are at once evident :—

1. The strong dissimilarity in almost every respect to
the Hellenised cities of the Province Asia. Archons,
Agoranomoi and Agonothetai are almost the only Greek
titles that occur, probably the Agoranomoi are Roman
aediles (p. 143), while the Agonothetai were presidents of
Circensian games (p. 133), not of Greek sports.

2. The resemblance in many points to the Hellenised cities of Bithynia-Pontus and the Euxine coasts, *e.g.*, Astynomoi, Politographoi.[1]

These facts show that, as might have been expected, the Galatian cities were in far closer relations with the cities of Bithynia-Pontus than of Asia. We notice in corroboration of this that the resident strangers mentioned in Galatian inscriptions are two from Nikomedeia, C. I. G., 4077, *Bull. Corr. Hell.*, VII, p. 27 ; two from Sinope, *Journ. Hell. Stud.*, 1899, p. 58 ; one from Byzantium, Mordtmann, *Marm. Ancyr.*, p. 22 ; but none from Asia. See p. 154.

3. Roman facts and analogies, so rare in the Province Asia, are very numerous in Ancyra. Even the *comitium*[2] is mentioned there. Each town tribe[3] met separately and passed its own decrees, like the Vici in Colonia Antiocheia : the Phylarch of the town tribe was an important official, corresponding to the Roman *magister vici*. The title " Son of the Phyle " takes the place of the Asian compliment, " Son of the City ".

Eirenarchs, who occur everywhere in Asia as in Galatia, were responsible more to the Roman officers than to the city administration. There is an extraordinarily large proportion of Latin inscriptions and of Latin names among the people. Hence the *agoranomoi*, who are so often mentioned, are more likely to be in reality Roman aediles than strictly Greek magistrates (as they were in Asia).

The chief results may now be summed up as follows.

---

[1] No Astynomoi are mentioned in Asia, and only once the noun Politographia (in a Latin inscription of Nakoleia, C. I. L., III 6998).

[2] C. I. G., 4019 read ἐν Κομετίῳ.

[3] φυλή, not ἔθνος.

The Gauls of Galatia were brought in contact chiefly with three classes : the Phrygian inhabitants of Galatia, the Hellenised peoples of Asia Minor, and the Romans. They learned much from all of them.

From the Phrygians they adopted their religion, adding to it certain Celtic elements. Further, they coalesced with them into a single people. The amalgamation became much more thorough after Galatia ceased to be a sovereign power, and became a mere Province of the Roman Empire. The governing Romans treated all Galatians as practically equal; and valued most those who were most useful to them. The privileges of the Gaulish aristocracy could not be long maintained under a foreign government, except in so far as they were supported either by wealth and landed property[1] or by natural ability. The domination of the aristocratic caste came to an end when Galatia became a Roman Province, and with it the broad line of separation was rapidly obliterated.

From the Hellenes of Asia Minor they adopted a second language,[2] along with many educated customs and arts. The Oecumenical Association of athletes and Dionysiac artists, known also widely over the eastern provinces, began to appear in Ancyra and Pessinus in the second century ; and along with it appeared the Society of Hellenes of Galatia ; and more attention was then paid to the Greek style of games. But the Hellenes whom they took as models and teachers were not of Pergamenian Asia but of the Black Sea coasts.

From the Romans they learned most of the arts and devices of administration. Their cities adopted the Greek

[1] See p. 145 f.   [2] See section 14.

name *polis*,[1] but they were Roman more than Greek in type ; and the name πόλις was used only because they had Greek as their official language. If they have more resemblance to the Pontic than the Asian cities, we must remember that the Pontic cities were more Roman in type than the Asian cities, where Hellenism was so old and deep-rooted.

Under all these foreign elements, however, there lay a fundamental substratum of true Celtic tribal character in the family, the society, and the town centre, as Mommsen and Mitteis have recognised.[2] It is not until about A.D. 160 that it becomes justifiable to speak of Ancyra and Pessinus as, in the strictest sense, cities of the Græco-Roman type : and the change occurred even later in Tavium. Before that time these towns were rather Galatic-Roman tribal centres, using Greek as the official language. That character was, of course, quite consistent with a high degree of splendour and magnificence : there were great towns both in European Gallia[3] and in Asiatic Galatia.

We should be glad to know more about the actual condition of those tribal centres ; but more exploration is needed in order to furnish evidence. Clearly, so long as there were only single tribal centres, the other places known by name in the territory could only be villages. But when the Greek city idea was adopted about A.D. 150-200, the more important villages had the opportunity open to them of developing into cities.

M. Perrot points out one interesting fact about North Galatia, which is characteristic of a country containing a

---

[1] It appears thrice in C. I. G., 4039 (v. Perrot, *Expl. Arch. de la Gal.*, p. 261 f.), A.D. 15-37, alongside of the more common Three Nations.

[2] See quotations on p. 131. [3] Called Galatia in Greek.

conquering aristocracy [1]—wealth and power fell to a great extent into the hands of a few leading nobles. He traces the signs of this during the first fifty years of the Roman Province. Later than that the subject passes beyond our limits.

[1] A similar state of things once existed in the most "civilised" part of Phrygia, the part most open to conquest: see *Cities and Bish. of Phrygia*, II, p. 419 f. The Tetrapyrgiai of the Phrygian nobles corresponded to the castles of the Galatian chiefs.

Note.—Van Gelder is mistaken, p. 202, in taking Pliny, *Nat. Hist.*, VII 10, 56, as showing that a Galatian boy did not speak Celtic. The boy was born in Asia, and the marvel lay in the fact that he so closely resembled a boy born in Gaul, when the two were *diversarum gentium.* The more diverse the races, the greater the wonder and the consequent price of the pair. In 1882, writing home from southern Cappadocia, and wondering at the beautiful fair complexions of many boys among the Christian families (lost as they grew to manhood), I said they were like children in our own country (though Pliny's story was not then in my mind).

SECTION 14.

LANGUAGE AND LETTERS IN NORTH GALATIA.

IT has been shown that the Gaulish tribes, when they entered the land which took from them the name Galatia, found there a much more numerous population amid which they settled as a ruling aristocracy, and thus formed a distinct country and government, recognised by the surrounding governments as one of the powers among whom Asia Minor was divided.

At first the two sections, which composed the population of this new country, Galatia, spoke two separate languages. The aristocracy spoke a Celtic tongue. Of the populace, presumably some few could speak Greek, but Phrygian was the sole tongue generally known, and even those who knew Greek must also have spoken Phrygian. There seems to be no reasonable doubt on these points, though no actual evidence remains on the subject.

The problem is to determine what was the fate of these languages. It is certain that at last Greek came to be the one sole language used in Galatia ; but the dates at which Celtic and Phrygian ceased to be spoken are unknown, and form the subject of the present investigation.

The subject has been briefly discussed by a distinguished French scholar and traveller, M. Georges Perrot. But he has not taken into account all the conditions of the problem,

(147)

and subsequent exploration has added considerably to the scanty stock of evidence available to him. As his authority and arguments have convinced many recent scholars— though Mommsen unhesitatingly and decisively rejects them—it will be best to begin by briefly stating his reasons, and showing why they must be pronounced inadequate to support his conclusion, that before the time of Christ the Celtic language had ceased to be spoken in Galatia, and Greek had become the sole language of the country.

It will be observed that he leaves out of sight one factor. He does not take into consideration the Phrygian language. He speaks as if the struggle had been only between Greek and Celtic.

The omission is due to that singular prepossession in the minds of almost all scholars—except Mommsen—who have touched this subject : they all speak and reason as if Galatia had been inhabited by Gauls only. If occasionally some one, like Lightfoot, p. 9, refers to the Phrygian element in the population, he forthwith dismisses it again from his thought and his argument. Mommsen alone declares positively and emphatically that the Galatian people must be regarded as a mixed race, in which the tone and spirit was given by the Gaulish element.

Though it cannot be proved, yet we must regard it as probable, that the Celtic language became the common tongue of the mixed race. The impressionable Phrygian population, devoid of energy, yielding readily to the force of circumstances, accepted the language of the conquerors,[1] just as of old that older race which had been conquered by

---

[1] But perhaps on the southern frontier near Kinna Phrygian was still spoken in the Roman time : one example of the Phrygian formula (see below) occurs there, *Journ. of Hell. Stud.*, 1899, p. 119, no. 117.

the Phryges adopted the speech of their rulers. The Phrygians of Galatia, though far more numerous, contributed much less to the prominent characteristics of the mixed race: they gave their religion and their manual labour in some of the simpler and more fundamental arts of life.

Thus M. Perrot's first assumption may be accepted as probably correct. In the century before Christ the battle of tongues in Galatia was between Celtic and Greek.

His next argument is founded on the supposed fact that the ancient Lydian and Phrygian languages had died out before the time of Strabo, about A.D. 19, so that "in the whole country from the Sangarios to the sea nothing but Greek was spoken". That supposition is incorrect. Strabo, XIII 4, 17, is quoted as the authority; but Strabo's words do not imply that. Strabo does not mention the Phrygian language: he says that the Lydian language had ceased to be spoken in Lydia and was used only in Cibyra, a city in the south-west corner of Phrygia, which contained a Lydian colony.

Epigraphic discovery has now proved that the Phrygian language was known in various parts of central and eastern Phrygia at least as late as the third century after Christ. Some of the Phrygian inscriptions of the Roman period were published before M. Perrot wrote, but had not yet been identified as Phrygian.[1] Their number has now been much increased. One is bilingual, a Greek and Phrygian epitaph. Two are longer, untranslated documents. The rest contain only a concluding formula in Phrygian, while

---

[1] See *Phrygian Inscr. of the Roman Period* in *Zeitschrift f. Vergleich. Sprachforsch.*, 1887, p. 381 ff. Literature of the subject quoted by Anderson, *Journ. of Hell. Stud.*, 1899 (second half).

the body of the inscription is in Greek: the Phrygian formula is a curse on the violator of the grave, and there seems to have been an idea that this appeal to Divine power was more efficacious in the old religious speech. The formula varies so much as to show that it was expressed in a living language, and was not merely a repetition of an ancient hieratic form of words.

Moreover, the exceeding badness of the Greek in some inscriptions found in Phrygia proves that they were written by persons who were almost utterly ignorant of the language. They were composed by uneducated rustics, who had only a smattering of Greek, and who ordinarily spoke in another tongue.[1]

In fact, it is no longer a matter of doubt that the native languages of Phrygia, Pisidia, Lycia, Lycaonia, Cappadocia,[2] etc., persisted in common use far longer than was believed. It was only in the cities that Greek was much used, while the rustic population continued to speak their own native languages.

Thus, in place of the argument that, since Phrygian had been forgotten in Phrygia before A.D. 19, Celtic probably had been forgotten in Galatia, we must substitute the exact opposite. Since Phrygian was still spoken in Phrygia in the third century after Christ or later, Celtic might be expected to persist in Galatia at least as long, inasmuch as Galatia was distinctly less open to Hellenic influence than Phrygia, and the Galatian people had much stronger national pride than the Phrygians.

[1] *Cities and Bish. of Phrygia*, I, p. 131.

[2] See Mommsen, *Röm. Gesch.*, V, pp. 92, 315. On Pisidian, the present writer's *Inscriptions en Langue Pisidienne* in *Revue des Univ. du Midi*, 1895, p. 353 ff. On Lycaonian, *Acts* XIV 11.

Again, it was argued that no Galatian inscriptions in the Celtic language remain, and therefore the Celtic language could not have been spoken in Galatia.

This argument would serve equally well to prove that Greek was spoken universally in Isauria, Lycaonia, Cappadocia, Pontus, etc. Strabo says that in Cibyra four languages were spoken in his time; yet not a trace of any tongue except Greek occurs in the inscriptions of Cibyra. Are we to conclude that Strabo was wrong, and that only Greek was known there?

In truth, that line of argument is founded on a misconception as to the facts of society in Asia Minor, and has no force. Fashion was powerful. It was thought rude, barbarous and uncultured to use any language but Greek. All persons that had even a smattering of Greek aired their knowledge of the educated speech. Moreover, it is highly probable that nobody who was ignorant of Greek was able to write: those who got any education at all learned Greek, and hardly anybody in Asia Minor wrote in any language except Greek. The thirty or forty late Phrygian inscriptions mentioned above are the only exception, and they have mostly a special character.

The dearth of Celtic inscriptions in Galatia only shows that Celtic was not the educated speech of the country—a fact which we know independently. Few inscriptions in Galatia are older than the second century after Christ; the epigraphic evidence tends to prove that the mass of the people were only beginning in that century to think of engraving epitaphs on the tombs of their dead.

As to the natural probabilities of the case, there is no doubt that the Roman influence was on the side of Greek.

While Rome favoured the Galatic spirit in many respects, it never seems to have admitted the Celtic tongue in official matters. Greek, the language of education, found full official recognition, and Rome made no attempt to force Latin on the eastern Provinces; but it admitted no third language. Those who wished to make full use of the opportunities of the Empire must speak either Latin or Greek. All whose knowledge was confined to some other tongue were barbarians and outsiders. The civilisation that Rome sought to impress on the East was Græco-Roman; and the constitution of the Roman Province would naturally exert a powerful influence in forcing a knowledge of Greek upon all that sought honours and official employment, if they did not know it beforehand.

Even under the kings Deiotaros and Amyntas, before the Province was constituted, Greek must have been much used in diplomacy and foreign affairs. Greek at that time filled a place like what French filled no long time ago in Europe, as the international and diplomatic tongue. But Greek was more than that: it was the speech of education and of all educated men (like Latin in the Middle Ages): it was the language in whose literature almost all scientific and artistic knowledge was locked up. No Galatian could play a part in the extra-Galatian world without Greek. There is no doubt that Cicero and Deiotaros [1] conversed in Greek. Coins struck in Galatia bore Greek legends; coins with Celtic legends could never have found international currency in Asia Minor at that time, as any numismatist will testify. In many such ways Greek was a necessity in Galatia.

[1] See p. 92.

But those facts do not prove that the Celtic language was unknown : they prove nothing as regards the speech of the uneducated mass of the population, and they prove nothing about home and family intercourse. They only show that Greek must have been familiar to the few : they do not show that it was used by the many. The strong Celtic tinge in certain respects, which indubitably coloured the Galatian State, could hardly have maintained itself so long amid the just and even tenor of Roman imperial rule, without a national language to support it.

We have more than this general presumption to trust to. There is distinct evidence to prove that Celtic was still spoken during the second century in Galatia. Both Mommsen and Mitteis [1] are fully convinced by the evidence on this point.

About the middle of the second century after Christ Pausanias [2] speaks of a native, non-Greek language, actually spoken in Galatia : " the shrub which the Ionians and the rest of the Greeks call *kokkos*, and which the Galatians above Phrygia call in their native tongue *hus* ". This native tongue can only be Celtic. It is not possible here to plead that Pausanius is speaking on the authority of some old book, and passing off borrowed information about the past as his own true knowledge about the present. A few pages before he mentions a fact which he had learned in that way regarding the cavalry of the Gaulish invaders, and there he puts it in a different way : " this organisation they called *trimarkisia* in their own tongue ".[3]   Moreover,

---

[1] Mommsen, *Röm. Gesch.*, V, p. 314 ; Mitteis, *Reichsrecht*, etc., p. 24.

[2] X 36, 1 : Frazer's translation is quoted : his note endorses this obvious interpretation.

[3] X 19, 11.

his statement about the Galatians of Pessinus [1] is couched in a form suggesting personal knowledge ; and he had been in the sanctuary of Zeus at Ancyra, I 4, 5.

A trace pointing to the persistence of the Celtic language in Galatia about the middle of the second century after Christ, is found in Lucian.[2] When the false prophet Alexander was in repute at Abonouteichos on the Pontic coast, persons came to visit him from the countries round, Bithynia, Galatia,[3] and Thrace. Occasionally questions were propounded to him by barbarians in the Syrian or the Celtic language : in such cases he had to wait until he could find some visitor able to interpret the question to him, and occasionally a considerable interval elapsed between the propounding of the question and the issuing of the reply, if a translator was not readily found. It is not necessary to understand that all questions in Celtic had to wait long for an interpreter : it was probably easier to find an interpreter in Celtic than in Syriac. But even if it were sometimes the case that Celtic interpreters were difficult to find, that would only prove that some of the Galatic visitors could not speak Celtic, while others could. But that might happen naturally. Most of those who came from Galatia, especially at first, would be traders and travellers, classes of persons who must have picked up in a rough way a good deal of education. The language of trade was, beyond all question, Greek throughout those regions ; and those who were engaged in trade (many, of course, hereditarily), would be likely to be the most thoroughly Hellenised of the

---

[1] Quoted on p. 85.

[2] *Alexander Pseudomantis*, 51. The attempt to explain away this evidence, *Revue Celtique*, I, p. 179 ff, is a failure.

[3] Pontic intercourse, see p. 143.

Galatians. Thus, there might be cases when an interpreter of a Celtic question was not readily found among Galatian merchants at Abonouteichos.

Such seems the natural explanation. The propounders of questions in Syrian or Celtic are called " barbarians " by Lucian ; but that does not prove them to have been from regions outside the Roman Empire. Any one who spoke any language but Greek (or Latin) was called by the Greeks a barbarian ; so, *e.g.*, the people of Malta are called by Luke, although Malta had belonged to Rome for about 270 years when Luke visited it. Probably some of the questions were propounded in barbarian tongues merely for the pur- pose of testing Alexander's skill, for the tendency to test even that in which one believes lies deep in human nature. Hence we need not suppose that those who put questions in Celtic were all ignorant of Greek.

Again, in the fourth century the witness of Jerome is emphatic—the Galatians spoke the universal language of the East, Greek, but they also spoke a dialect slightly varying from that used in Gaul by the Treveri. This clear testimony by a man who had travelled in Galatia and among the Treveri cannot be twisted and perverted (as Lucian and Pausanias are by some writers). There is therefore only one method : when testimony is dead against you, you can always refuse to believe it. And so Jerome is set aside, without any reason given that can stand a moment's investigation.

But the old plain and simple method of disbelieving all that contradicts one's prepossessions is now becoming discredited as belonging to the Dark Age of modern scholarship. The one argument which used to be counted sufficient—that Jerome was a Christian, and that anything stated in a Christian work is suspicious—is now no longer implicitly accepted.

Mitteis pronounces no decision on this point: it is not necessary for his purpose.   Mommsen accepts Jerome's testimony, and justifies it by solid reasons; and the voice of healthy historical criticism will assuredly be on his side.

That the Galatian people was bilingual for centuries is an interesting, but well-ascertained fact.   Compare the Welsh in modern times after many centuries of English rule.

Now, as to the date when Greek spread most among them, the evidence is far from satisfactory.

Almost the only evidence comes from the reception of Greek names in Galatia.   Already in the third and second centuries Gauls with Greek names occur: Apatourios B.C. 223, Lysimachus 217, Paidopolites 180.   At that time the Gauls were serving as mercenaries in various camps, and their leaders must have found it convenient to use Greek names.   Probably Apatourios and Lysimachus had two names, Celtic and Greek, according to a widespread custom in districts where a smattering of Greek was spread: it was convenient to have a Greek name amid Greek surroundings, and a native name amid the surroundings of home. But no evidence exists, and in fact Galatia is almost the only country of that kind in which no explicit proof of the use of alternative or double names has been found (though in all probability they were used).

This use of Greek names, beginning so early, taken in conjunction with intermarriages, might have been expected to have spread very widely in the second and first centuries. But, as we saw on p. 66, the tendency to adopt Greek ways was checked, and a strong reaction of the Gaulish spirit occurred in the second century. The anti-Hellenic tendency was strengthened by the Mithridatic Wars (in which Hellenism rallied to the Oriental king against Rome and the Galatian tribes), and by the subsequent Romanisation of Galatia under Deiotaros. The almost exclusive use of Celtic names in the ruling families, B.C. 90-40, proves that the national feeling was still strong against Hellenisation. Many names are known in the three tetrarchic dynasties, and almost all are Celtic. There is, however, one notable exception.

Amyntas bears a Greek, especially a Macedonian name. At this time the great Galatic families seem to have used Gaulish names almost exclusively.[1] Was Amyntas, then, a Greek?[2] This is highly improbable, because it would have been difficult for a Greek to govern the Galatian aristocracy, and Augustus was too politic to offend a strong national feeling. Moreover, Dion Cassius calls him Amyntas the Galatian.[3]

Now, it is probable that Amyntas did not belong to one of the great ruling families. He had been secretary to Deiotaros, and his selection for that office implies that he had not merely natural ability, but also considerable education; and the educated classes always tended to use Greek names. Very probably Amyntas had a Celtic name also; but in his relations with his South Galatian subjects and with foreign nations he would use the name which marked him as of the educated class.

---

[1] Kastor is an exception (yet Holder gives Castoriacum as a Celtic city).

[2] Van Gelder, p. 200, thinks he was a Greek.

[3] Dion, L 13, 8, 'Αμύντας ὁ Γαλάτης. Compare Plutarch, *Amat.* 22, τῷ Γαλάτῃ simply, when speaking of the Tetrarch Sinorix.

Similarly, of the four envoys sent by Deiotaros to Rome in B.C. 45 three bear Greek names;[1] it is, however, not certain that all were Gauls; the king might have found some convenient tools among the Greeks. His physician, Pheidippos, was of course a Greek.

M. Perrot, in a lucid survey of the evidence, fixes on the year A.D. 10 as about the decisive turn in the tide of naming.[2] Henceforward Celtic names are exceptional, and Greek or Latin names are customary. On this quite correct result two remarks are to be made.

In the first place, the disuse of Celtic names was not so complete as it is said by some writers to have been. In Ancyra, the centre of Galatian civilisation, they might be expected to disappear most rapidly; but even there we find in M. Perrot's inscriptions of the second century the following names, certainly or probably Celtic:[3] 133 Epona, 123 [Kau?]aros, Borianus, Mamus, Barbillus, An[. . .]natus; and in a rural district, 151 Masclus.[4] In the only rustic part of Galatia where inscriptions have been found in appreciable number, the following Celtic names occur (all probably second century A.D. or later): Vastex, Barbollas, Meliginna, Zmerton, Leitognaos, Dobedon. A short inscription of Laodiceia Combusta[5] (third or fourth century), with the names Kat[t]oios and Droumamaris, probably shows a Celtic family in that Lycaonian or Galatic city. These specimens out of a larger number known will

---

[1] Van Gelder, p. 200, says that all the names are Greek; but Blesamios is obviously Celtic.

[2] Perrot, *de Gal. Prov. Rom.*, p. 78, 89 f.

[3] Evidence in Holder *passim*.

[4] Anderson in *Journal of Hellenic Studies*, 1899, p. 81 ff.

[5] *Athen. Mittheil.*, 1888, p. 266.

suffice: they are taken from the first two sources that suggested themselves.

Secondly, it is hardly correct to say as some do, that native names lingered far longer than the native languages in Asia Minor. That is true where a language dies out in presence of the speech of a more energetic section of the population (as Phrygian did in Galatia): in such cases, as M. Perrot says, *on sait que les noms propres survivent en général aux noms communs, qu'ils restent comme le dernier vestige d'une langue sortie de l'usage.* This rule is perhaps true in a sense in Asia Minor, but it is far from expressing the whole truth. It is also true, and a more vital point in the present question, that proper names began to be disused, and Greek names came into wide use, centuries before the native language disappeared. The very persons who inscribed Phrygian formulæ on their graves[1] bore Greek, not Phrygian names.

The disappearance of names not Greek or Roman in Asia Minor is too large a topic for our pages: it is only part of a much wider subject. The fact is that at this period and throughout the Empire, the old national names were everywhere discouraged by the prevailing tone of society, which was Græco-Roman in the East, and Roman in the West. It was generally esteemed barbarous, rustic, the mark of a mere clown, to bear a native name: as the comic poet of an older time said: "It is a shame for a woman to have a Phrygian name".[2] The aristocratic feeling of the old Gaulish families made them cling for a time to the hereditary names; but the fashionable tone was too strong for them.

[1] See p. 149 f.   [2] See p. 30.

In the dearth of inscriptions—itself a proof of illiteracy
—authorities for Galatian names are so few that the argument resting on them is feeble ; but so far as it goes it is
that the early Roman period was the time when Celtic
names passed out of fashion ; and the change heralded a
marked increase in the use of the Greek language.

As to any literary interests in Galạtia, not a sign is
quoted earlier than the fourth century.   Galatia like Cappadocia is a blank in literature ; and those are the two
countries in which fewest cities (in the strict Greek sense)
existed.[1]

The evidence is overwhelming.   About A.D. 50 Galatia
was essentially un-Hellenic.[2] Roman ideas were there superinduced directly on a Galatian system, which had passed
through no intermediate stage of transformation to the
Hellenic type.   It was only through the gradual slow
spread under Roman rule of a uniform Græco-Roman
civilisation over the East that Galatia began during the
second century after Christ to assume a veneer of Hellenism in its later form.

Road-building in North Galatia seems to have begun
under Vespasian, when Galatia was united to Cappadocia
as a frontier and military Province.   The only Roman
colony was probably founded by Domitian.   It was during
the first century one of the least civilised corners of the
Empire, remote, difficult of access, with little trade, lying
apart from the world, with a strongly marked character of
its own.   As Mommsen with his unerring historic instinct
long ago recognised, it had become a Celtic island amid the

---

[1] See p. 135 f; *Strabo*, p. 537, says there were only two cities in
Cappadocia.

[2] On the talk about evidence to the contrary, see p. 173.

waves of the Oriental races, and remained so in its internal organisation even in the Roman Imperial period.[1] . . . In spite of their sojourn of several hundred years in Asia Minor, a deep gulf still separated these Occidentals from the Asiatics (among whom the Greeks of Asia Minor must for some purposes[2] be counted). The strong mutual dislike that kept the Asiatic Greeks and the Galatians apart is evident from the time of Mithridates onwards: at that time Galatians and Romans faced and conquered the Græco-Asiatic reaction.

The dislike of the Asiatic for the northern barbarians may be paralleled at the present day by the hatred of the Turkish inhabitants of the same country for the Circassian immigrants, who resemble in many respects the picture that is drawn for us of the Gauls, free, proud, rapacious, unruly, a terror to their more peaceful and submissive neighbours. Every traveller in Asia Minor, who has come to know anything of the feelings and life of the people even in the most superficial way, learns that the Mohammedan Turk hates the Mohammedan Circassians far more than he dislikes his Christian neighbours; and his hatred is rooted in fear. So the Gauls were hated in ancient Asia Minor.

This hatred lasted late; and one observes its effects, in the fourth century, in the jealousy and contempt expressed for the Galatians by the Cappadocians. Thus Basil, *Epist.* 207, 1, speaks with marked innuendo of Sabellius the

---

[1] Colonia Julia Augusta Felix Germa was not founded by Augustus (see Mommsen's commentary on his colonies in *Monumentum Ancyr.*, p. 120): Domitian named it after his beloved Julia Augusta, see *Revue Numismatique*, 1894, p. 170.

[2] In certain ways, of course, Greeks are Occidental as contrasted with Asiatics.

Lydian and Marcellus the Galatian. Gregory of Nyssa, *Epist.* 20, mentions that the garden Vanota, where he writes, was called by a Galatian name, but deserved a name more in accordance with its beauty than a mere Galatian word. And the heretic Eunomios complained, as of an insult, that Basil had called him a Galatian, whereas he was a Cappadocian of Oltiseris.[1]

In view of these facts every one who considers how closely the writings of Paul and the other Apostles (so far as we know) keep to actual life, how vivid and realistic are their pictures of the Churches which they address—every such scholar must expect that, in a letter written by Paul to a group of North Galatian churches, there should be found touches which bring before us the special character and position of these churches. He must expect that the address would throw light on, and receive illustration from, the peculiar position of the Galatians, so distinct and apart from the type and tone of all the surrounding races, whether Greek or Anatolian.

This expectation is not realised. On the contrary, there are only three points in the Epistle that have ever been alleged as signs of Gallic character.

One is the stock joke, that the Galatian Christians changed their form of belief, and the French are a fickle people. It is surprising that such a sane and clear-headed scholar as Lightfoot should have repeated this from his predecessors. In truth, he was here misled by his own historic instinct : he felt that, if the North Galatian theory was true, there must be traces of Celtic character in the Epistle, and as he would not abandon the theory he must find the traces.

[1] Greg. Nyss. *contra Eunomium*, pp. 259, 281.

The sufficient and only reply is to quote Luther's arguments that the Galatians must have been a Germanic race, because the Germans are fickle. As a matter of fact, Paul nowhere calls the Galatians fickle, or implies that their change of faith was caused by fickleness : see p. 255.

The second is that among the sins against which Paul warns his Galatian correspondents are "drunkenness and revellings," "strife and vainglory," and that he charges them with niggardliness in giving alms : it is said that these are characteristic vices of the Celtic character. They are only too characteristic of most nations and most Churches. On their nature in Galatia, see p. 450 ff, 458 f.

The third is that the Celtic people were superstitious and "given over to ritual observances," and Deiotaros was characterised by "extravagant devotion to augury : the Gauls in Galatia would find the external rites of the worship of Cybele attractive from their analogy to their own Druidic ritual," though "the mystic element in the Phrygian worship awoke no corresponding echo in the Gaul". Hence, it is argued, the Galatians were likely to fly from Pauline to Judaistic Christianity.

One can only marvel at this pedantic analysis of Galatian character. It is hardly worth while to point out that the best authorities consider Druidism a very late fact in Gallic history, and that scholars who study Galatia observe that not a trace of Druidic religion can be discovered there. The superstition of the Galatians amounts to this, that they had adopted the religion of Asia Minor !

The truth is that, though North Galatia had a peculiar and strongly marked character, not the slightest reference to its special character can be found in the Epistle. Yet the Epistle is full of references to the circumstances and

everyday surroundings of the persons addressed—full even
to a degree beyond Paul's custom.

Note.—It may be here added that, in the article *Galatia*
in Hastings' *Dictionary of the Bible*, I have gone too far in
admitting Hellenic influence in North Galatia, being over-
anxious not to colour favourably to my own theory an
account which ought to be strictly impartial. But in that
article the term "Graecised city," applied to Ancyra, is
intended to indicate "Greek-speaking," and not "Hellenised".

SECTION 15.

THE INFLUENCE OF CHRISTIANITY IN NORTH GALATIA.

AT what time and from what direction Christianity was introduced into North Galatia is uncertain. I hope shortly to discuss the subject of "the Diffusion of Christianity in Asia Minor" in a special work. Here only the salient features in the evangelisation of North Galatia can be stated. It probably began either from Bithynia or from the Province Asia, and not from the side of Syria.

The new religion was introduced in all probability at an early date : doubtless Ancyra had been evangelised during the first century (possibly even Pessinus). But there can be no reasonable doubt that the process began in the great provincial centre, Ancyra, just as in Asia it began at Ephesus, and in Achaia at Corinth. The tribal constitution of the country made Ancyra the necessary centre for at least its own tribe ; and the backward state of the country districts must have long been a decided bar to the progress of the new religion.

Ancyra and the Bithynian city Juliopolis (which was attached to Galatia about 297) are the only Galatian bishoprics mentioned earlier than 325 : they alone appear at the Ancyran Council held about 314. The Ancyran Church [1] is first mentioned about A.D. 192 as having been

---

[1] ἡ κατὰ τόπον ἐκκλησία, the local Church (on the phrase see *Cities and Bish. of Phrygia*, I, p. 272 f, no. 192).

(165)

affected by Montanism, but saved by the writer of an anti-
Montanist treatise quoted by Eusebius.   There was a great
persecution at Ancyra under Diocletian, and some of the
martyrs who suffered there were doubtless brought from
other towns of the Province for trial before the governor
resident in Antioch.   Thus, *e.g.*, we find that at Juliopolis
in the sixth century the martyrs Plato, Heuretos and
Gemellos were peculiarly venerated at Juliopolis.   Of
these Plato is known to have suffered at Ancyra on 22nd
July probably under Diocletian,[1] and hence probably he
was brought up from Juliopolis for trial at the metropolis,
but continued to be specially remembered in his own city.
The *Acta* of Theodotus, a work of high authority, contains
an interesting account of Diocletian's persecution, which
the writer seems perhaps to have regarded as the first that
occurred there.

Ancyra and Juliopolis, then, are the two points in
Galatia or on its borders where Christianity can be traced
earliest.   Now these are two of the points on the short
road from Nikomedia to Ancyra and the east—the line
which afterwards became famous and important as the
"Pilgrim's Road".[2]   As we have seen,[3] Galatia was in
specially close relations with Bithynia and Pontus; and the
extraordinary strength of Christianity in that Province at
the very beginning of the second century is attested by the
famous despatch of Pliny.   Bithynian Christianity would
spread through Juliopolis to Ancyra in the natural course
of communication.

The epigraphic evidence about Christianity in Galatia

---

[1] I can find nothing about the other two.

[2] *Histor. Geogr. of Asia Minor*, pp. 197, 240.

[3] See above, pp. 143, 154.

will be treated more thoroughly in the proposed treatise on the diffusion of that religion in Asia Minor. Here we will say only that the early Christian inscriptions found in the " Added Land," west of Lake Tatta, are due beyond doubt to the influence radiating from Iconium ; and that in the rest of North Galatia no early Christian inscriptions occur with the exception of three or four at Pessinus, which however are more probably of the fourth than the third century.

On the other hand, there is in North Galatia an unusually large number of late Christian inscriptions in proportion to the epigraphic total.

Now the want of early Christian inscriptions in a district constitutes no proof that Christianity was not known there in early time. But the contrast between the large number of third century Christian inscriptions in Phrygia [1] and the lack of them in Galatia is remarkable ; and certainly suggests that the new religion had nothing like the same hold on Galatia at that time as on Phrygia. Mr. J. G. C. Anderson expresses himself even more strongly as to the inference to be drawn from the epigraphic facts in *Journal of Hellenic Studies,* 1899 (second part).

The evidence as to the number of Jews in Galatia has been much misrepresented by the North Galatian critics. For example, an inscription found beside Dorylaion in the Province Asia is quoted as a proof of the presence of Jews in Galatia ; [2] and a decree of Augustus addressed to the Koinon of the Province Asia, a copy of which was ordered to be kept in the Augusteum at Argyre, is similarly quoted

[1] *Cities and Bish.* of *Phrygia,* Ch. XII, XVII.

[2] Schürer, *das Jüd. Volk im Zeitalter J. C.,* 2nd Edition, I, p. 690. It shows a seven-branched candlestick and the name Ἠσαΰος.

as granting privileges to the Jews of Ancyra.[1]   With such geography anything can be proved.   In the latter case the conjectural alteration of the MSS. to read Ancyra would not help the North Galatian Theorists ; for it would then be necessary to understand that the Asian Ancyra was meant.   Waddington boldly reads Pergamos for Argyre, on the ground that there was only one Augusteum in Asia when the decree was issued (which is indubitable).   Mommsen, while recognising that an Asian city is meant, does not propose any solution for the unintelligible Argyre.

A few late Galatian inscriptions, belonging to the fourth and fifth centuries, mention persons with Jewish names : at Eudoxias Jacob the Deacon [2] and Esther, at Tavium Daniel, Joannes, etc., elsewhere Joannes, Sanbatos, Thadeus, etc. ; but all are probably late, and may be Christian (or Jewish Christian).

At Pessinus an inscription mentioning a person Matatas, C. I. G., 4088, is regarded as Jewish by Lightfoot ; and similarly several in which the name Akilas or Akylas is used.   We may fairly treat Matatas as a Jewish name, Mattathias ; or, as the copy is bad, we might venture perhaps to change it to Mata[i]as, *i.e.*, Matthaias ; but, even if that be the true reading, since the wife of Mataias was named Kyrilla, he was more probably a Christian [3] than a Jew (unless he was Jewish-Christian).   Akilas seems to have

---

[1] Schürer, *op. cit.*, I, p. 690, Lightfoot, p. 11, Josephus, *Ant. Jud.*, XVI 6, 2.

[2] μνῆμα εἰερω[ἰάτου δ]ειάκωνος Εἰακὼβ [Μυρι]κηνοῦ.

[3] Kyrilla, though sometimes pagan, favours Christian origin : hence the other alteration Ma[i]atas is less probable.   With Mataias compare Mathas in a Christian inscription, *Cities and Bish. of Phrygia*, II, p. 562.

been a Phrygian name ;[1] but I think Lightfoot may be right in regarding it as one favoured by Jews : we find Jacob the son of Achilles at Oxyrhynchos in Egypt,[2] and Akilas was probably regarded as equivalent to Achilles.

Further, at Pessinus, there occurs an inscription mentioning the strange names Annonios, Eremaste, Paith[o]s, Momaion, Deidôs ;[3] M. Perrot suggests that Annonios may be the Hebrew Ananias, which seems very probable.

A rather bold speculation, which has been advanced on the strength of some Phrygian inscriptions,[4] treats a noble family settled in Akmonia and in Ancyra, bearing the name Julius Severus, as Jewish. Members of this and of some allied families boast themselves as " descendants of kings and tetrarchs ". The usual interpretation treats these as Galatian kings and tetrarchs : but, according to the theory just mentioned, they would be Jewish kings and tetrarchs, probably of the Herod family. But the speculation has too slender foundations to be treated as more than an interesting hypothesis at present ; and it is ridiculed by Prof. E. Schurer in his review of the book [5] as merely a groundless fancy.

The Jews of North Galatia were immigrants not direct from the East, but either from South Galatia or from Asia or from Bithynia. No settlements of Jews are known to have been made in North Galatia by the Greek kings, whereas large bodies of Jews were settled in the cities along the great line of communication through Lycaonia and Southern

---

[1] *Histor. Geogr. of Asia Minor*, p. 226.
[2] Grenfell and Hunt, I, p. 97.
[3] C. I. G., 4087 ; Perrot, *Explor. Arch.*, No. 105.
[4] *Cities and Bish. of Phrygia*, II, pp. 648 ff, 673.
[5] *Theolog. Literaturztg*, 1898.

Phrygia by the Seleucid kings. Thus North Galatian Jewish settlements are later and sporadic. Lightfoot recognises this secondary origin of the North Galatian Jews.

The relation of North Galatia to the rest of the Roman world was changed in the end of the third century, when Diocletian about 285 made Nicomedia, the Bithynian metropolis, one of the four capitals of the Roman world. The road system of Asia Minor had hitherto been planned with a view to communication with the one imperial centre, Rome ; and North Galatia was then on a by-path. Henceforth, communication began to run towards Nicomedia ; and North Galatia was in an important position. The change was intensified when Constantinople was made the one great capital of the Roman world. The road system was practically the same in the East for both those centres.

Ancyra now lay on the greatest of roads. All communication of Syria, Cilicia, Cappadocia and Armenia with the Imperial capital passed through it. The development of North Galatia now proceeded with great rapidity. It became one of the most important regions in the Eastern Empire. Bishops of Ancyra played a great part in many Church questions from 312 onwards : and the metropolitan Bishop of Ancyra ranked second only to Caesareia in the Patriarchate of Constantinople.[1]

The ecclesiastical system of North Galatia was still very backward even in the fourth century ; and its cities, which had been slowly growing during the third century out of villages, had not as a rule bishops of their own. This is made clear by a comparison of the ecclesiastical system of

---

[1] The order of precedence was gradually becoming fixed even during the fourth century ; but was not strictly determined before the sixth century.

the provinces of the south, where civilisation and cities had been developed rapidly owing to their favourable position on the former lines of communication. But during the fifth and following centuries the number of Galatian cities and bishops grew rapidly, and was more than doubled. In the same time the known bishops of Lycaonia increased only from fifteen to seventeen.

The failure of its bishop in a Council does not prove that a city was not then a bishopric. But it was far easier for North Galatian bishops to attend the fourth century Councils of Ancyra, Nicaea and Constantinople than for the Lycaonian and Pisidian bishops. Yet the ecclesiastical system of Lycaonia and Pisidia was nearly complete at those Councils, while that of Galatia was only in an embryo form. See pp. 213, 221.

Even the praises given so cordially to the Galatians by the rhetoricians of the fourth century—quoted so frequently as proofs of the thorough Hellenisation of Galatia—are really proofs that the Hellenic character was of quite recent growth in the country.

Themistius[1] speaks of the Galatians as acute and clever, and more docile than the thorough Hellenes : he evidently contrasts the Galatians as beginners in the higher Hellenic education with the thorough Greeks of Syrian Antioch and other cities where Greek learning was long settled. He also contrasts the cities of Galatia with Antioch as smaller and unable to vie with it.

---

[1] *Or.* XXIII *Soph.*, p. 299 Petavius, καὶ οὐ λέγω τὸ ἄστυ τοῦ Ἀντιόχου οὐδὲ ὅσοις ἐκεῖ συνέμιξα ἀνδράσι τὰ ἐμὰ φορτία μαστεύουσι καὶ περιποιου-μένοις, οὐδὲ ὅσοις ἐν Γαλατίᾳ τῇ Ἑλληνίδι· καὶ αἱ μὲν πόλεις, οὐχ οὕτω μεγάλαι οὐδ᾽ οἷαι τῇ μεγίστῃ ἀμφισβητεῖν· οἱ δὲ ἄνδρες ἴστε ὅτι ὀξεῖς καὶ ἀγχίνοι, καὶ εὐμαθέστεροι τῶν ἄγαν Ἑλλήνων.

Libanius frequently in his letters mentions his Galatian pupils, and like Themistius praises their diligence and ability. They were good pupils, and therefore favourites with a good teacher. But the majority of them evidently belonged to Ancyra, as might be shown by a comparison of the references which he makes to them : in fact, with him the word "Galatian" often seems really to mean "Ancyran". Occasionally pupils who were not of Ancyra are mentioned, as *e.g.*, in *Epist.* 1333. But on the whole Ancyra stands for him as representing Galatia.

The only other city of Galatia which he mentions[1] is Tabia, *Epist.* 1000. Wolff, in his edition, interprets that letter as referring to Tabioi, an Italian city mentioned by Stephanus ; but more probably it is the Galatian Tabium or Tavium that is meant. In that letter, which is addressed to Paeoninus, he recommends Phalerius, who is going to settle in the city as a teacher. Probably, Libanius had been asked to recommend a teacher, and sends Phalerius. The impression which the letter makes is that Tabia was now for the first time aspiring to have its own higher school of rhetoric. One thinks of the new High School founded at Como about A.D. 102-106, and the teacher recommended by Tacitus.[2]

The general impression conveyed by Themistius and Libanius is similar to the idea conveyed about Spain, Gaul and Africa by writers of the first and second centuries. The higher education was new in the country, and

---

[1] He mentions many second or third rate cities outside of Galatia, as Sinope, Rhossos, Tyana, Cucusos, Cyrrhos, Berytos, Apameia, Berrhoia, Emesa, Elousa, Bostra, Doliche, Petra, Tyros, etc.

[2] Pliny, *Epist.* IV 13. Compare the official *Grammaticus Latinus* at Magallum in Spain, C. I. L., II 2892.

was pursued with peculiar intensity by fresh and ardent pupils, who formed a delightful contrast to the rather *blasé* Greeks in the experience of their professorial instructors.

Thus the civilisation and high position which is associated with North Galatia belongs specially to the Christian period. Ancyra the great was the Christian Ancyra.[1] We are apt to forget how late most of the proofs of its civilisation are. An example of this forgetfulness occurs in some criticisms which have been made on certain statements in *The Church in the Roman Empire* similar to the preceding paragraphs. It is necessary to reply to those criticisms here, as they are likely to be repeated.

Mr. W. T. Arnold[2] says : " I suspect that Professor Ramsay has overstated the Celticism and barbarism of Galatia. I think it probable that these adaptable Celts were Hellenised early. The term Gallogræcia, compared with Themistius's (p. 360) Γαλατία τῇ Ἑλληνίδι,[3] is significant. There is plenty of evidence as to the early splendour of Ancyra (Ἄγκυρα τερπνὴ παμφαεστάτη πόλις), and the facts collected by Perrot could easily be added to."

The early splendour of Ancyra was emphasised by me as much as by Mr. Arnold : the words of the book which he reviews were : " Ancyra was the capital of the province, because it was a city of great power and wealth (beyond Iconium or Antioch)," and it is stated that it contained " a Greek-speaking population to which St. Paul could address himself ". But a city might be splendid without

---

[1] The results obtained in an intended work on " The Diffusion of Christianity in Asia Minor" must be assumed here.

[2] *English Historical Review*, 1895, p. 554.

[3] Differently accented in *E. H. R.*

being of the Greek type in civilisation and spirit.   Mr.
Arnold proves the early Hellenisation of Galatia from
Themistius, but Themistius belongs to the fourth century ;
and I have repeatedly [1] emphasised the rapid fourth century
development of the country.

Moreover, the quotation apparently is misunderstood by
my critic (as is clear when the context is read) : it does
not mean, as he takes it, " Galatia which is Hellenic,"
but in mere pedantic distinction " Galatia in the Greek
world as distinguished from Galatia in the far West " (*i.e.*,
Gallia).[2]   So also *Gallogræcia* does not mean, as he seems
to think, " Græcised Gaul " ; it was a Roman word adopted
by the Greeks in some rare instances,[3] and merely distinguished the Grecian from Transalpine Gallia.   Probably
Gallogræci was the first formation, and from it was derived
Gallogræcia.   It is grecised Hellenogalatai, Diodorus, V
32, 5.

Mr. Arnold's other quotation dates from the ninth century.

Such is the evidence by which he supports his opinion
that Galatia was Hellenised much earlier than I represent.
His vague allusion to other facts that might be quoted
implies only that he believes them to exist, but has not
got them ready.   We must assume that he quoted what
he thought telling proofs of his view.   The proofs that he
does quote entirely confirm my statements as to the late-
ness of Galatian civilisation.

[1] First in *Histor. Geogr. of Asia Minor*, pp. 74 ff, 199 ff, and often
since.

[2] " Galatia the Greek (not Galatia the Celtic) " is probably the exact
thought.   Themistius speaks of Keltoi on p. 349 Pet., meaning apparently the European Gauls.

[3] *Galli*, *Gallia*, and *Græcia* are all Roman terms, never used by
Greeks except as borrowed from Latin.

SECTION 16.

LATER HISTORY OF THE PROVINCE GALATIA.

THE end of the reign of Nero marks a crisis in the history of the Province Galatia.   Hitherto it occupied, as we have seen, a position of exceptional importance in the growth of the Roman East ; and every stage in its history was one of increase in size and strengthening of the Roman character. But from the accession of Vespasian onwards its history was one of continual decline, of waning size and diminishing importance.

It was probably in A.D. 74 that Vespasian merged Galatia and Cappadocia in a single Province.   That step was due to the growing importance of Cappadocia, hitherto so little regarded by Rome ; and the weight of the joint government lay in the eastern part, where legions were stationed and the problems of administration were more pressing.   At the same time Vespasian detached from Galatia almost the whole of Pisidia in the strict sense (as distinguished from Pisidian Phrygia).   That mountain country, once so dangerous and unruly, and always troublesome to administer owing to slowness of communication in the higher and rougher parts of the Taurus mountains, was formed into a Province along with Lycia and Pamphylia.[1]   It was practi-

[1] *Cities and Bish. of Phrygia*, I, p. 308.

cally convenient to embrace these neighbouring districts
under one administration.   Pisidian Phrygia, *i.e.*, Apollonia
and Antioch and the territory connected with them, still
formed part of Galatia.

The vast double Province of Galatia and Cappadocia
continued about thirty years.   It was not considered as a
single Province, but as a combination of two separate
Provinces ; and official usage designated it in the plural
as *Provinciae.*

It was probably in 106, or soon after, that Trajan
again separated the two parts of the double Province,
making Cappadocia (with Lesser Armenia) one of the great
Consular Provinces of the Empire, charged with the defence
of the Euphrates frontier, while Galatia was a Praetorian
command, no longer charged with any foreign relations, as
it was now surrounded on every side by other Provinces.[1]
The vigour and energy of Romanising policy seems to
have died out from it.   It was now more straggling and
loose in its parts than ever.   At the same time the old
national feeling in the parts began to revive.   Hadrian, the
following Emperor, seems to have recognised in his general
policy that it was not expedient to disregard so completely
as the earlier Roman organisation had done the national
lines of demarcation, by attempting to force the Roman
provincial unity on diverse races and peoples.   In the
first energy of Roman Imperial policy, the attempt had
not seemed hopeless ; but experience showed that the causes
of diversity were too deep seated.

The history of Iconium, classed politically for centuries
to Lycaonia, yet always regarding itself as Phrygian and

[1] Cilicia Tracheia was made a Province in 72, whether by itself or
united with some other is uncertain.

non-Lycaonian, shows how ineradicable the feeling was: see Section 20.

The fact that in one case the plural form, *Provinciae*, is applied to the Galatic Province in its later form under Hadrian, may be regarded as a sign of this growing sense of diversity in the parts.

The Province Galatia was still further diminished in size at some time about A.D. 137, when there was formed the Triple Eparchy, consisting of Cilicia, Isauria (so Cilicia Tracheia was henceforth designated) and Lycaonia. The form of name which is always used, "the Three Eparchiae," indicates the new character of Roman policy. Three distinct Greek territories were grouped under one governor for convenience. But they were not really unified. They remained distinct even in some administrative respects: *e.g.*, the Koinon of the Lycaones was instituted for the Lycaonian cities.

That part of Lycaonia which had hitherto belonged to Galatia was not all taken from it and included in the new Lycaonia ; but it is not possible to determine exactly the bounds, for Ptolemy is self-contradictory and untrustworthy. He excludes Iconium from Galatia in its new form ; and if Iconium be excluded, much more must Lystra, Derbe and Pisidian Antioch be excluded ;[1] yet in another place he includes Lystra and Antioch in Galatia, though elsewhere he puts Antioch in the Province Pamphylia.

Again he assigns Isaura to the Province Galatia, but inscriptions prove that Hadrian or Pius placed it in the Triple Eparchy. We have therefore no confidence as to the limits ; but assuredly Derbe was in Lycaonia, while

[1] Such is the view stated in the *Church in the Rom. Empire*, p. 111.

12

probably Iconium, Antioch, and perhaps Lystra, were in Galatia.

About 295 Diocletian divided the Province Galatia into two parts. The Province had always the appearance of two territories loosely joined ; that was caused by its origin from two distinct kingdoms conferred on Amyntas. Diocletian resolved the unity into its two component halves once more. One part was now called the Province Pisidia, and included Iconium, possibly also Lystra, parts of Asian Phrygia,[1] all Pisidian Phrygia, and the northern parts of Pisidia proper. The other was called Galatia, and included the " Added Land," and a strip of Bithynian territory with the city of Juliopolis : it was nearly coextensive with the Galatia of King Deiotaros.

On this system Lycaonia was divided between the Provinces Pisidia, Galatia and Isauria ; and the classification of the Bishops present at the Council of Nicæa in 325 shows that arrangement. Thus a triple partition of Lycaonia, similar to the old one, p. 65, was brought about ; and the recurrence of the old division shows that it was founded on nature.

But in 372 a new Province Lycaonia was formed by taking parts from the Provinces Galatia, Isauria and Pisidia. The " Added Land " was now restored to Lycaonia ; and so the Bishopric Glavama or Ekdaumana, which had been reckoned to Galatia at the Nicene Council, henceforth appears as a Lycaonian see.

It was perhaps at this time that, in compensation for the loss of the " Added Land," there was added to Galatia a part of Asian Phrygia, with the Bishoprics Amorion, Trok-

---

[1] Especially the whole *Dioecesis Lycaonia* of Cicero's time, p. 106.

nades and Orkistos. Orkistos belonged to the Province
Phrygia in 331, when it petitioned Constantine through
the Vicarius of the Asian Dioecesis ; and it is hardly possible that Amorion could have been added to Galatia
until Orkistos was also transferred. Hence the old
Phrygian city Amorion was henceforward in official documents styled a city of Galatia.

At some date between 386 and 395 Galatia was divided
into two Provinces, Prima and Secunda, with Ancyra and
Pessinus as their respective capitals. The division marks
the growing importance of Galatia in the Eastern Empire ;
and this was still more emphatically shown when Justinian
elevated the governor of Galatia Prima to the rank of a
Comes.

Finally in the early part of the eighth century a third
Province Galatia was formed by taking some Bishoprics
out of Secunda and others from Phrygia and Pisidia : the
metropolis of this new Province was Amorion.

The details as to these charges are minutely stated and
proved in the *Historical Geography of Asia Minor*.

SECTION 17.

THE CITIES AND THE PEOPLES OF SOUTH GALATIA.

WE have pointed out that all attempts to find in the Epistle to the Galatians the characteristic features of the North Galatian society and life have failed.

Further, there are in the Epistle many references to the circumstances of family life, of education, of inheritance, etc.[1] They all imply a settled order of the Græco-Asiatic type as existing among the Galatians. Those references would be misleading and barely intelligible to a people among whom Roman civilisation was superinduced directly on Celtic customs. They have their proper effect only among cities in which there existed a Greek form of law and society, as modified in some details to suit the Asiatic subjects of the Greek kings.

We turn now to the cities of South Galatia, in order to see whether the law which is appealed to in the Epistle is likely to have been the law that existed among them.

They are to be compared with the Asian cities on the great highway from Ephesus to the East, and must in fact be classed with the general body of Hellenised cities in Asia Minor generally. The whole of those cities were characterised by a uniform type of society, and, to a great

---

[1] See especially the summary in § xxxv.

(180)

extent, of law. They were mostly cities which the Greek kings had founded or remodelled, with the intention of making them centres of Greek feeling and manners and civilisation in an Oriental land. In founding them the kings took as models rather the Greek colonies of the coast, Smyrna, Ephesus, Miletus, etc., than the cities of Greece proper. They planted in the new cities not the pure Hellenism of Athens and Greece proper, but Hellenic institutions as they were adapted to an Oriental country. Greece had conquered the East under the leadership of Alexander the Great; but, in conquering, it modified itself and assimilated some Oriental elements.

Those Græco-Anatolian cities had now passed under the Roman rule. But the Romans did not attempt or desire to eradicate the Greek manners, or to substitute Roman law for Greek, just as they were not hostile to Greek literature or the Greek language. They left the constitution of the Greek and Græco-Anatolian cities practically unaltered. They allowed the Greek language to be on an equality with Latin. Society, manners and law were hardly affected by the Roman conquest. The Romans were skilful administrators, and knew that it would be folly to begin their rule by trying to destroy an existing civilisation and to force Roman ways and language on a Grecised people. In the barbarian western lands, which were taken into the Empire, Roman manners and language were quickly established, because the only civilisation which the barbarians saw was Roman. But, in the East, Greek civilisation was nearest and most impressive ; and Rome found in it an ally rather than an opponent.

In process of time Roman institutions were to some degree adopted in the Græco-Anatolian cities ; but that process had hardly begun in the time of Paul, and need not here be touched. Only in the Roman colonies, which were planted in a few cities of Southern Galatia, were there bodies of Roman citizens, speaking Latin, practising Roman ways, electing magistrates with Roman titles, judged according to Roman law.[1] These colonies were intended by their founder, Augustus, chiefly as garrisons to defend the Province against attack from the lawless mountaineers of Taurus, but also, probably, in part as models and centres of a more Romanised system, from which the surrounding cities might learn. But, as time passed, the Latin colonies in Southern Galatia were much more affected by Greek models than the Greek cities by Roman. The manners and society of even Colonia Antiocheia in the time of Paul, though superficially Roman, were beyond doubt in many ways fundamentally Hellenistic. The Roman character was an exotic which would not take root in the East; and all that Rome could do was to strengthen there the Greek civilisation, modifying it with some Roman elements. With Greek civilisation necessarily went the Greek language.

Such was the class of cities in which, according to the South Galatian theory, the "Churches of Galatia" were planted.

In the preceding Sections, we have traced the ultimate decay of the Province Galatia as a part of the Roman Imperial policy. But the fact that the policy of imposing a Roman unity on the Province was finally abandoned should not blind us to the power with which it was at first urged on by the young Empire. Deeper causes, which were not observed in the first flush of enthusiasm felt by

[1] See p. 204 ff.

the Eastern Provinces for the new Empire, came in time
to the surface, and necessitated some modification of the
Imperial policy. But Paul's work lay in the early time ;
and it ought not to be studied in the light of later circumstances.

The truth must once more be repeated that, in order to
conceive the position of Central Asia Minor in the time of
Paul, we must above all bear in mind the vigour and energy
of the Roman administration in the country. The Roman
idea, *i.e.*, the Province Galatia as a fact of politics and
government, was being impressed with all Rome's organising skill on the minds of the people : and the people, so
far as they were not Celtic by descent, were of the easy
tempered, easily governed type that we have described.

The Empire was popular in the highest degree as the
giver of peace and prosperity. People were glad to belong
to it, and they belonged to it only in virtue of being members of a Province, and entitled to be addressed by a Roman
official under the name " *Galatæ* " (except a few, who were
actually " Roman citizens "). Acquaintance with the more
educated persons that came from the West implanted aspirations after education ; and education could only be Græco-
Roman. The fundamental fact in central Asia Minor at
that time was this : to be educated, to be progressive, to
think, to learn, was to be Romanised and Hellenised.
To be a Phrygian, was to be rude, ignorant, unintelligent,
slavish.

Until that is firmly fixed in one's mind, it is impossible to understand the position of the new religion in the
country, or to properly appreciate Paul's attitude towards
the "Galatians ".

The history of the South Galatian cities is closely connected with the great line of communication along which Roman administration travelled. There were, in fact, at least two alternative roads; but their object was the same, *viz.*, to maintain communication by land between the Ægean coast (especially Ephesus) and the East (especially Syria and Cilicia). One road led through Derbe, Iconium and Antioch, the other kept a little further north; but both passed right across Lycaonia and Southern Phrygia. A messenger hurrying from Cilicia to Ephesus and Rome would take the northern road;[1] but those who wished to trade or to stop by the way would prefer the southern.

Under the Greek kings of the Seleucid dynasty, who ruled most of the southern half of Asia Minor, that line of communication had been the prime necessity in the maintenance of their power. It was an imperial highway in the fullest sense. In the confused time after B.C. 189, little imperial need for such a highway existed. But after 80 the great Province Cilicia was built up along the highway,[2] embracing all the districts that were most conveniently administered as the Roman governor travelled along it. When the pirates were most dangerous, all communication between Rome and the Province of Syria must have passed along that land route. As soon as the Provinces were reorganised after the civil wars, B.C. 49-31, the route became one of the greatest arteries of the Empire, probably more important than any other outside of Italy.

---

[1] By the Gates, Loulon, Hyde, Tyriaion, Metropolis, and then over the higher parts (Acts XIX 1), through Tralla and Teira. Trade from Cappadocia also necessarily took the northern road by Savatra, Tyriaion, Metropolis, then south through Lower Phrygia by Apameia and Laodiceia.

[2] See section 11.

Further, throughout the Greek and Roman period, the two roads formed a great trade-route. Not merely brisk traffic existed among the many great cities on or near the line of communication ; there was also much through traffic from inner Asia. Strabo mentions, *e.g.*, that a kind of red earth from Cappadocia, which in early time had been brought to Greece by way of Sinope and thence by ship, was in later time carried along the trade-route to Ephesus.

Such a situation was most favourable for the spread of Greek civilisation. Trade was mainly conducted on Greek lines and in the Greek tongue. Wherever trade went, there the Greek spirit, the use of Greek names and forms and language went. Only the cities, indeed, were affected thereby ; and the rustic districts and population continued to be simply Anatolian in type.

The mere statement of the general situation in South Galatia shows how complete was the contrast between it and North Galatia.

The only peoples in South Galatia with whom we are immediately concerned in the present study are the Phrygians and the Lycaonians. The Phrygians have been already described in Sections 3-5.

The Lycaonians are probably the representatives of the unmixed old race which had been conquered by the immigrant Phryges about the tenth century B.C. The strength of the conquering Phryges was sufficient to carry them as far as Iconium ; but at that point it was exhausted, and could go no further. The religion of Lycaonia, and the general character of the people, are not likely to have differed much from the description given in Sections 3-5. See Section 20.

The native tongue was spoken in Lycaonia, alongside of

Greek, the educated speech. Probably it had once been spoken all over Great Phrygia before that country was subdued by the Phryges. As to the character and affinities of the Lycaonian language nothing is known; but probably the inscriptions in "Hittite" symbols found near Tyriaion and Kybistra and elsewhere in Asia Minor will ultimately throw some light on it.

The country of Lycaonia consists mainly of a vast dead level plain; but the last outer hills and slopes of the Taurus mountains also belong to it. In the centre of the plain rises Kara-Dagh, in a gently sloping rounded glen of which are the striking ruins of a Christian city, called the Thousand-and-One-Churches (Bin-Bir-Kilise) from the twenty or thirty ruined churches that give a unique character to the site, as a holy city and a place of pilgrimage—the latter character being also proved by a number of *graffiti*. At one time I was disposed to regard this as the site of Derbe; but it seems rather to be the site of Barata. In that case, the sanctity of the site would be due to St. John in the Well, a hermit who lived ten years in one of the deep wells or cisterns, which furnish the only drinking water in the plains north and east of Kara-Dagh.[1] This hermit, who had come forth from Kybistra into the treeless, waterless plains, was buried by a man of Barata (who was summoned for the purpose by an angel).[2]

North-east from Kara-Dagh a line of sharp conical hills stretches across the level plain to Karadja-Dagh, which overhangs the town of Kara-Bunar, "Black-Fountain". The most remarkable of these cones is one about two miles south-

---

[1] Until one reaches Sultan-Khan, where there is a strong flowing stream.

[2] *Histor. Geogr. of Asia Minor*, p. 337.

east of Kara-Bunar, most obviously an extinct volcano. Few places in the world show such marked signs of volcanic action as this. The soil consists for miles of black cinders, which look like the remains from a fire of yesterday. To the ancients such a place must have seemed a home of divine subterranean power ; and here probably " Holy Hyde," the frontier city of Lycaonia towards Cappadocia and Galatia, is to be sought. Karadja-Dagh in that case would mark the boundary of Lycaonia on the north-east. North of it begins the " Added Land " of Galatia, east of it the country of Cappadocia.

On the north-west Strabo reckons Laodiceia Combusta, twenty-seven miles north of Iconium, as the frontier ; but many extended Lycaonia further west into Phrygia to include also Tyriaion, and the Romans included even Philomelion in the Lycaonian Dioecesis (which was part of the great Province Cilicia from 80 to some time after 45).[1]

On the west the broad belt of hilly country which stretches north and south about six miles from Iconium contained the frontier between Pisidia and Lycaonia : but from 372 onwards all that country was attached to Lycaonia.

The most southern city of Lycaonia, and in some respects the most important, was Laranda, which lies in a corner of the Lycaonian plain, stretching deep into the outer foot-hills of Taurus. As the centre from which radiate a series of roads across Taurus through Cilicia Tracheia to the southern sea,[2] it had been attached to the kingdom made

---

[1] See above, p. 106 ff. Philomelion was transferred to Asia either by Antony or more probably by Augustus. Tyriaion is reckoned to Galatia by Pliny (if Τεταῖον, Τετράδιον, Τετάριον, are corruptions of Τυριαῖον), but by Strabo apparently to Asia.

[2] See above, p. 125.

up of Tracheiotis and Commagene, which was conferred on Antiochus IV by Caligula in A.D. 37, and confirmed to him by Claudius in 41. Previously, as part of Amyntas's former realm, it had been included in the province Galatia.

These explanations, together with the sketch of political history in sections 7, 10-12, and 15, will render the following account of Iconium, Derbe and Lystra more distinct.

SECTION 18.

THE JEWS IN SOUTH GALATIA.

ONE influence on the development of the South Galatian cities must be dwelt upon as specially important in the religious point of view. That is the power of the Jewish settlers.

The Greek foundations in that region were almost wholly of Seleucid origin. In the west and west-central parts of Phrygia there were many Greek cities of Pergamenian origin, but not in the east. Lycaonia had never been a practically effective part of the Pergamenian realm ; and Pisidian Phrygia was actually declared free by the Romans in 189.[1] Those same regions had to be most strenuously maintained and strengthened as the backbone of the Seleucid dominion in Asia Minor.

The Jews were a class of settlers or colonists [2] especially favoured by the Seleucid kings. Seleucus Nicator granted them the citizenship and equal rights with Macedonians and Greeks, both in his capital (Syrian Antioch) and in his new founded cities generally. In those cities, of course, Macedonians and Greeks constituted a species of aristo-

---

[1] Strabo, p. 577 : what he says about Antioch may be applied to the whole region. In 190 it was one of the districts whose fate was doubtful ; see Polybius, XXII 5, 14.

[2] κάτοικοι.

cracy, with rights of governing superior to those of the
rude old native population in the Seleucid garrison cities.
Seleucus, therefore, placed the Jews among the "most
favoured colonists" in all his new foundations.

That does not mean that new Jews might at any time
go to settle with such rights in any of these Seleucid cities.
Greek cities did not permit strangers to come and settle as
citizens : strangers ranked only as "resident aliens,"[1] enjoy-
ing merely some rights of commerce and personal safety.
But citizenship was jealously guarded, and only in special
cases by a special act of the city was a resident alien permitted to acquire it.

What Seleucus Nicator did was to introduce bodies of
Jews into his cities generally, granting to these settlers the
highest class of rights in the city where they were planted.

No privileges would have satisfied Jewish settlers, unless
they guarded their religious customs and peculiarities.
This Seleucus was careful to do. A striking example, as
Josephus[2] mentions, was connected with those distributions
of oil wholly or partly at state expense, which were among
the privileges of citizens in Greek cities : Jews would not
use oil made by Gentiles, and Seleucus ordered that his
Jewish settlers should receive an equivalent in money.
That right was confirmed to them by his successors, and
the Greeks in Syrian Antioch vainly attempted to have it
abolished by the Romans about A.D. 68.

The whole body of privileges guaranteed to the Jewish
settlers in the Seleucid colonies seems to be referred to in
an Apameian inscription as "the law of the Jews".[3]   It

----

[1] μέτοικοι, πάροικοι.   [2] *Ant. Jud.*, XII 3, 1, § 119.
[3] *Cities and Bish. of Phrygia*, II, p. 668, and No. 399 *bis*.

included some provision for the proper safe-guarding of Jewish graves. Some others may be recovered by observing the difficulties which the dislike and jealousy of their Greek fellow-citizens tended to throw in their way subsequently.

The right of safe and unimpeded passage from city to city in their pilgrimages to Jerusalem was peculiarly important: detention for even a day or two might frustrate the object of their journey.

They also desired the right of sending large sums of money to Jerusalem. The cities regarded this as a spoliation of their land for the benefit of a foreign land; and resented the conduct of settlers who made money and then exported it. Moreover, it might seriously disturb the financial equilibrium of the state to remit quantities of bullion out of the country.

Such and many other rights were guaranteed by Seleucus Nicator to his Jewish colonists, and confirmed by his successors. Antiochus the Great, who about B.C. 210-200 sent 2000 Jewish families from Babylonia to strengthen his power in the cities of Lydia and Phrygia, was specially emphatic in guaranteeing their rights as well as in granting them lands; and he speaks of the strong liking which his predecessors had entertained for the Jewish settlers.

This exceptionally favoured position explains why the Seleucid monarchs, who were hated in Palestine as the abomination, found their Jewish colonists loyal and devoted. These colonists had nothing to depend on except the royal support and favour. They were naturally not beloved by the ancient Phrygian and Lycaonian population, whose lands and position had been to a large extent seized by the Seleucid settlers, and they were not popular with their fellow-settlers, who, like the Greeks in all time, hated their Jewish rivals in trade and in the royal favour.

That the Jewish colonists acquired great power in Lycaonia and southern Phrygia generally cannot reasonably be doubted. The circumstances of the time, with brisk intercourse and a large volume of trade, suited the peculiar Jewish instinct for finance and the management of large business operations; and their favourable position in the great garrison cities along the trade-routes, with special rights even beyond their fellow-citizens, enabled them to take full advantage of their opportunities.

Almost the only direct evidence that is preserved to us on the subject is found in the Acts: the Jews are represented there as exercising great influence on the magistrates in Antioch, Iconium and Lystra.

The natural probabilities of the case entirely confirm the accounts in Acts. The Jews must have been rich; and the rich are always powerful, whether they be popular or unpopular. But, beyond this, evidence derived from epigraphy or history hardly exists, because it is difficult to distinguish the Greeks from the Jews in that country. The Greek language was, of course, indispensable, and became universal among them. All Jews bore Greek (or in later times Roman) names; and it is only in rare cases that Jewish families can be identified. Recent discoveries have made possible a beginning in this subject; and, if exploration be continued, there is good prospect of making progress in it. But as yet the attempt to work the evidence of inscriptions into a sketch of the Jewish position in Southern Galatia and Phrygia[1] is too speculative to be used here;

---

[1] *Cities and Bish. of Phrygia*, II, pp. 647 ff, 667 ff.

and it is not necessary for the study of the Epistle to enter on the subject. It may, however, be said in a word, that the Jews are likely to have exercised greater political power among the Anatolian people, with their yielding and easily moulded minds, than in any other part of the Roman world; and future discovery will probably prove this, confirming in part the rather bold inference already made from the inscriptions.

Prosperity was not the atmosphere most conducive to strict religious purity among the Jews; and the Phrygian Jews were no exception. In many respects there was a considerable relaxation of religious practice among them, as is shown in detail elsewhere.[1] Paul could confidently appeal to the knowledge of his Gentile converts that the Jews did not fulfil the law.

But it was not merely in material power and prosperity that the large Jewish element affected the history of Phrygia. It also exercised a strong influence on thought and religion. That is clearly shown in Acts. In Antioch there were many devout proselytes; and the synagogue was crowded with a Gentile audience, XIII 44. The lofty purity of the Jewish faith had a powerful attraction for a people like the Phrygians.[2] There was a strong inclination to Judaism in the Phrygian and Galatian cities before Paul entered the country. Many of his converts had certainly been attracted to the synagogue first, and to Paul afterwards. The first attraction, overpowered for a time by the second, was always liable to revive.

Moreover, there was a natural preference for the more Semitic form of Christianity. This is a very important

---

[1] *Cities and Bish. of Phrygia, loc. cit. : cp.* Acts XIX 13.

[2] Compare on p. 449 the picture of them quoted from Sozomen.

13

fact. There is no reason to think that the hatred, which always seems to exist between Jews and Greeks, was equally strong between Jews and Phrygians or Lycaonians. That hatred is partly the result of racial antipathy, and partly due to the keen competition between rivals in trade and in methods of trading. Many modern stories are current in the country as to the varying methods of Jew and Greek ; and though these are usually comic and exaggerated, they point to a deep-seated difference of mental attitude and nature. No one who has come in contact with the humble Greeks and Jews of the country wonders at the strong dislike between them : education, of course, tends to smooth away strong diversities and to produce at least a superficial similarity, and creates new habits of mind and interest that are much the same in different races.

But the case was different between Jews and Phrygians. There was, of course, at the beginning a natural dislike among the dispossessed Phrygian population for the new-comers settled among them ; but it was not likely to survive through generations, without some permanent cause to keep it alive. Just as there was no lasting hatred of the Greek settlers, but rather admiration and imitation, so it is not probable that the Phrygians were repelled long by the Jews.

There was no strong racial antipathy between them. The Phrygian or the Lycaonian was much more Oriental in type than the Greek. Habit and surroundings fostered in them the character that is least like the Western barbarian and most like the Asiatic. As you gaze on the gorgeously dressed Lycaonian king who is represented on the ancient rock-sculpture at Ibriz in the act of worshipping the simple rustic God, the giver of corn and wine, you recognise an almost typical Semite; and the peasant who acts as your guide wears the same style and shape of dress as the husbandman god (except the modern fez), and is in many cases strikingly like him in type. The type which the Anatolian plateau develops is markedly Asiatic ; and there is no natural antipathy between it and the Semite. So in modern times the Jew has been on far more friendly terms with the Turkish peasantry than he has been with the Greeks, and better treated before Turkish law than before the law and government of most European countries.

Again, there was little of the keen commercial rivalry between Phrygian and Jew that there was between Greek and Jew : the Anatolian nature has always been far too easy going and easy tempered.

At the present day, almost exactly the same problem is presented in the country as in the centuries immediately before and after Christ. The so-called Osmanli Turk shows fundamentally the old Anatolian type: though the gravity and restraint and dignity of Mohammedanism in common life have been substituted for the enthusiastic licence of the old Phrygian ritual—with a certain corresponding change in the character of the men. The Greek of the coast lands is essentially of the old Greek type, with certain slight changes caused by Christianity.

There is no better preparation for understanding on their historical side the Epistle to the Galatians, who represent the type of the Anatolian plateau, and the Epistles to the Colossians and Ephesians, who represent the Greek of the coast lands, than a study of the two contrasted modern types.

Asia Minor is the Debatable Land, in which Orientalism

and Occidentalism have often striven for mastery. Under
the early Roman Empire, and again at the present day, a
vigorous Occidentalism is striving, apparently with every
prospect of success, to subdue the plateau. The ground-
stock on the plateau is not antipathetic to Western organisation and order, though it is strongly antipathetic to the
Western barbarian. But it is far more sympathetic to
Orientalism ; and whenever it seems to have assimilated
Occidental thoughts and ways, it tends to remould them
to an Oriental form. The deep-lying Orientalism always
recurs. The Western conqueror triumphs, and before he is
aware, when he turns his back for a moment, his results
have melted into the old type. See p. 449.

Such was Paul's experience. Such is his complaint.
" You are removing so rapidly " (he writes to them) back
to the old type, "you are turning back again to the old
rudiments " (I 6, IV 9). His words are exactly the same
that unconsciously the historical student finds himself employing about the people in other relations.

Such was the experience of every century in the Christian
time. Every heresy in Anatolia recurred to a more Oriental and specially Judaistic type ; and at last Phrygia and
Galatia reverted to Semitic Mohammedanism. In some
parts of Asia Minor a larger proportion of the population
preserved their Christian faith ; but in Phrygia there were
hardly more than four or five scattered remnants in small
villages who remained true to Christianity throughout the
Turkish government. There are Zille, a village beside
Iconium, Bermenda beside Philomelion, Khonas close to
Colossae, and a small body in Apollonia-Sozopolis : these
preserve an unbroken Christian tradition. But it is doubtful if Phrygia can show a fifth.

SECTION 19.

PISIDIAN ANTIOCH.

ON a hill about one and a half miles east from the modern town of Yalowatch, on the outermost slopes of the lofty massive ridge of Sultan-Dagh, the backbone of Phrygia, was an ancient sanctuary of the Phrygian religion, which was the ruling priestly centre for the whole uplands north-east from the Limnai, and for the plain of the Anthios, which flows into the southern basin of the Limnai, the great double lake now called Hoiran-Geul and Egerdir-Geul. On the upper waters of the Anthios stood that ancient sanctuary, from whence the Phrygian priests, interpreting the Divine will, ruled the country and the rude Phrygian population around. Antioch is about 3600 feet above sea-level, Yalowatch 3460, the Limnai 3030.

Strabo describes the geographical features of the country on the side flanks of Sultan-Dagh. He had seen it as he travelled westwards along the great trade route through Tyriaion and Philomelion ; and the enormous mass of that long ridge impressed his memory and is well described by the phrase which he uses, " a backbone of mountains ".[1] He errs, however, in saying that it stretched from east to west : it really stretches south-east to north-west. This

---

[1] Strabo, p. 577, ὀρεινήν τινα ῥάχιν. On his route compare *Cities and Bish. of Phrygia*, I, pp. 86, 170 ; II, p. 398.

error was not unnatural in a traveller whose route was from east to west, and who did not properly realise how much his course turned towards the north at Philomelion in order to get round the end of the mighty mountain.

Strabo saw only the great plain on the north-east side of the mountain backbone, the long level stretch of Phrygia Paroreios. He was told that on the opposite side of the ridge lay Antioch in another plain; and he pictured to himself the plain which Antioch commanded as similar to the plain that he saw before him. But in this also he was not strictly correct: the country that stretches in front of Antioch, as one looks down towards the Limnai, is of far rougher character, rolling uplands backed by mountains.

The ancient name of that Phrygian sanctuary is unknown. A new era began in its history when a Greek garrison city was planted there on the lands of the temple.

Antioch was called by the Romans a Pisidian city; and in Latin usage the name Pisidia was applied almost in a political sense to the country in which Augustus founded his *Coloniae* for defence against the Pisidian mountaineers.[1] So in later times Antioch became the capital of the Province Pisidia.

But the old national idea and the geographical view agreed that Antioch was a Phrygian city, in the district called Pisidian or Pisidic Phrygia, bordering on Pisidia proper.[2] Strabo puts this quite clearly; and in an epigram found in the city, it is called Mygdonian, *i.e.*, Phrygian, for Mygdon was one of the old Phrygian heroes mentioned in

---

[1] *Monum. Ancyr.*, V 36; Pliny, V 94.
[2] See p. 106.

the Iliad.[1] The first line of the epigram,[2] which has not
been properly understood, is to be read thus :—

τόνδε σε Μυγδονίη Διονύσιον 'Αν[τιόχεια].

The accompanying prose inscription states that the metropolis Antioch honoured with a statue Aur. Dionysios, a
centurion charged with the oversight of the region which
had its centre in Antioch. In the mutilated epigram the
city addresses him : "Thee, Dionysios standing here (in
marble), Phrygian Antioch (has exalted in honour)".

Antioch was founded by one of the Seleucid kings who
ruled Syria and the southern half of Asia Minor. Of the
date and circumstances nothing is recorded ; but the strong
and important position is likely to have attracted the attention of the first monarch Seleucus Nicator, B.C. 301-280.
This may probably have been one of the sixteen Antiochs
which he founded and named after his father.

The population of the new city consisted, doubtless, partly
of the old people, who may have probably constituted one
or more of its tribes,[3] and partly of settlers planted here by
the founder. The settlers must have constituted several of
the city tribes ; but nothing is recorded as to their former
homes, or as to the names and number of the tribes. The
refoundation as a Roman *Colonia* has obliterated the
memory of the Greek city.

Analogy may make us confident that the most honoured
tribe was called Antiochis, and probably contained Mace-

[1] See pp. 20, 27. A reference to Mygdonia Antiocheia Nisibis is
impossible.

[2] Sterrett, *Epigr. Journey*, No. 93 (but keep the reading on the
stone ῥεγεωνάριον).

[3] All these Greek cities in Phrygia were divided into tribes, φυλαί.

donian settlers only : [1] so at Laodiceia there was a tribe
Laodikis, and at Carian Antioch a tribe Antiochis.

It is practically certain that part of the new settlers
were Jews : see Section 18. The Jews of Antioch may
very probably have formed one of the city tribes.

Another tribe may have taken a name from the Phrygian
cultus in the city, and contained the old population.

While the city Antioch was thus a thoroughly Hellenised
city, Greek-speaking, organised in the regular Hellenistic
style, and administering by its own elected magistrates the
usual style of Hellenistic Seleucid law, the country round
continued its Phrygian course of life, hardly affected by
the Greek city, divided according to villages on the Anatolian system,[2] and probably for a long time speaking only
Phrygian. A great series of inscriptions, belonging to the
middle of the third century after Christ, shows that this
country, within a few miles of Antioch to the north-west
and subject to its authority, still preserved much of the old
Phrygian religious organisation, uniting under the patronage
of the Great Artemis in a society, whose enigmatic name
probably means " the friends of the secret sign," a sort of
body of freemasons recognising one another by a sign.[3]
There seems even then to have been little relation between
these rustics or *pagani* and the men of the city ; all the
" friends " (hundreds in number) are designated by their
village, with the exception of one solitary Antiochian.

---

[1] If Seleucus was the founder, another tribe doubtless was called
Seleucis.

[2] See p. 39 f.

[3] τέκμωρ : ξένοι τεκμόρειοι. On these religious societies see *Cities
and Bish. of Phrygia*, I, p. 96 f, II, pp. 359, 630, f ; the inscriptions in
Sterrett, *Wolfe Expedition;* also *Histor. Geogr. of Asia Minor*, p. 411 ff.

It is important to observe that those un-Hellenised *pagani* were still really Pagans in the third century. Christianity had here hardly affected the rustic population, and was confined to the educated citizens.

Antioch boasted itself as a colony from Magnesia on the Maeander. The meaning of this statement is uncertain. It was fashionable in the Hellenised Phrygian cities to have foundation legends involving some Greek connection; but these are as a rule far from trustworthy. In this case, however, the assertion of Strabo lends strength to the story; and possibly a body of settlers from Magnesia may have been brought by the Seleucid founder; if so, they would probably form one of the city tribes, which might bear a name suggestive of the origin.[1] Certainly the story of the Magnesian colony was current in the city, as appears from an epigram found in Rome, which has been much mis-represented by editors. The writer of this epigram calls himself a Magnesian of Phrygia. Clearly he must mean Antioch, for he speaks of the Anthian Plain, *i.e.*, the valley of the Anthios, mentioned on coins of the city and in Pliny.

Μάγνης ἐκ Φρυγίης· Σκυθίη δέ με παρθένος Αἴπη
ἔτρεφ᾽ ἐλαιηρῶι μ᾽ Ἀνθίωι ἐν πεδίωι,
παλίσκιον λιπόντα Μαγνήτων πόλιν.[2]

" I am a Magnesian from Phrygia; and an unwedded damsel, devoted to the service of the Scythian goddess, nurtured me in the olive-bearing plain of the Anthios,

[1] If the story relates to a mythic foundation in prehistoric times, it may be dismissed as an invention.

[2] Kaibel, *Inscr. Graec. Ital.*, No. 933, reads Μανθίωι in l. 2. παρθένος ἁγνή has been conjectured, probably rightly, but Kaibel rejects it because he has not found Scythia as a woman's name (a meaningless reason). He takes Magnes as a personal name, and gets no sense from this remarkable inscription.

me who have left the deep-shaded city of the Magnetes."
It is uncertain whether the epigram was longer.

The Anatolian custom described on p. 40 is here alluded
to.　Evidently the epithet Parthenos was given to the
goddess in this district : she was the Great Goddess Artemis of the Limnai, into which the river Anthius flows ; and
she was succeeded there in Christian times by the Virgin
Theotokos.　The epithet Parthenos in the cultus of Anatolia
had not the sense which we attribute to the word " virgin " :
it merely indicated that the goddess and her devotees were
not bound by the rite of marriage.　She is termed
" Scythian," as the Artemis whose seat was in the Tauric
Chersonese (the Crimea) ; she was also called Tauro or
Tauropolos.[1]

The character which this epigram reveals in the Antiochian
cultus is exactly what belonged everywhere to the native
religion of Phrygia ; but it is important to have an express
confirmation of it.

In the exoteric view, as shown in inscriptions, the Great
God in Antioch was Men Askainos,[2] who was usually
expressed in Greek form as the " Very Manifest God
Dionysos," and in Latin as Aesculapius.　These identifications with Western deities express one or other of the
many sides in the complete Phrygian idea of the God, as
the giver of wine and corn, the king, the healer, and so on.
The simple translation of the Phrygian name, *viz.*, Men in
Greek and Luna in Latin, was also used in the inscriptions.[3]

---

[1] Artemis Tauropolos at Metropolis, not far away.

[2] Such is Waddington's highly probable correction of Strabo's
reading Arkaios.

[3] C. I. L., III 6829, Sterrett, *Epigr. Journ.*, No. 135. These are really
mistranslations : the Phrygian Men or Manes was not the Moon,
Cities and Bish. of Phrygia, II, p. 626.

The goddess is never mentioned in inscriptions of the Hellenised city, where the Phrygian element remained more mystic and esoteric, as is stated on p. 42. But in inscriptions of the less Hellenised neighbourhood, she alone is named, and the male god is not made so prominent.

The first event known in the history of Antioch belongs to the year 189, when the Romans made it a free city, destroying the Seleucid power, but not subjecting the city to the rule of the Pergamenian king Eumenes. Possibly, their jealousy made them unwilling [1] to trust him with that strong fortress and the command of one of the two great Eastern routes.

From 189 to the formation of the Province of Cilicia in 80, nothing is known as to the fate of Antioch. Sheltered behind the mountains, it was protected as well as possible against the storms of that troubled time. Presumably it remained a free city for that whole century, a city governing itself by its own elected magistrates in the midst of a Phrygian land, governing itself after the Greek fashion, and called a Greek city, but by no means a city of Greeks. Its story during that century would be an interesting one ; but we must wait for further exploration and excavation.

In 39 Antioch and the rest of Pisidian Phrygia was made into a kingdom and given to Amyntas ; and in 25 it came back into Roman possession as part of the Province Galatia.

At some time before B.C. 6 Augustus planted a *Colonia*— apparently chiefly, or entirely, of veterans of the Legion V Alauda—in Antioch, which now received a new constitution and a new name, as Colonia Caesareia Antiocheia. The

---

[1] See above, p. 61.

population of the old Greek city still continued to dwell in it ; but they now ranked only as dwellers (*incolae*) alongside of the privileged *Coloni.*

Instead of tribes, the *Colonia* was divided into *Vici*, as a Roman city. The modern town of Yalowatch is divided into twelve quarters, and Professor Sterrett conjectures, ingeniously and probably, that the division is an inheritance from antiquity.[1] It may be added that the supposed twelve *Vici* were probably a Romanisation of the older twelve Greek city tribes.

The names of only six *Vici* are known, *Tuscus, Cermalus, Aedilicius, Patricius,*[2] *Velabrus, Salutaris.* The last of these is probably an acknowledgment of the old Phrygian cultus in Antioch, for the national God was now commonly called Aesculapius. The other names show a strongly marked Roman character.

Certain rights, summed up as *Jus Italicum*, were granted to the *Colonia*, which consisted mainly of veterans of the Fifth Legion Alauda. Those rights—which included freedom from direct taxation, freedom of constitutional government, and the right to hold and convey land according to Roman custom—of course, belonged in full only to the *coloni*, and not to the *incolae*, the old inhabitants, who still constituted the vast majority of the population. Only persons who possessed as individuals the Roman citizenship could rank as *Coloni*, and possess the full rights pertaining to that position.

No evidence remains on which to found an account of the precise position and rights of the non-Roman population of Antioch. We must for the present remain in ignorance,

---

[1] Turkish *mahale* translates *vicus.*

[2] PATRICVS in Sterrett's copy.

and hope for increase of knowledge through exploration and excavation. But some general principles are certain.

In a general way, the non-Roman members of the Province were in a state, so to say, of pupilage and training for the high position of Roman citizens. The goal of the Empire was universal citizenship among freemen; but for the time this was still distant, and the path of advancement was open only to the few. In a *Colonia*, the non-Roman population was indubitably in a much more favourable position as regards Roman rights than in the mere Greek cities. They had a certain secondary class of rights (including, most probably, freedom from direct taxes); and the path towards the full position of a *civis Romanus* was easier for them.

This favoured and honourable position belonged to those Greek *incolae* in virtue of the Roman Colonial rank of their city. As members of the Roman Empire, *i.e.*, of the Province Galatia, they ranked above all the mere Greek cities around, except their sister colonies, among whom they were *primi inter pares*.[1] Now in view of the intense spirit of rivalry and jealousy between city and city, which was so marked a feature of Asia Minor municipal life,[2] the citizens would, of course, pride themselves especially on those features which gave them their rank: they would be good and enthusiastically loyal Roman citizens. The account of Antioch given in the *Acta* of Paul and Thekla, with its high priest and its great shows to which crowds from the other cities of Galatia came, is instructive.[3]

In view of these circumstances it is an important fact that, in Acts, the Gentiles who came to the Antiochian

---

[1] See p. 224.   [2] See below, p. 450 f.
[3] *Church in the Rom. Emp.*, p. 396 ff.

synagogue, "the believing proselytes," XIII 43, are not
called Greeks, as they are at cities of the Greek type like
Iconium, Ephesus, etc.   This name of Greek would be
unsuitable in a Roman Colonia, among men who were
proud of their rank.   That is one of the slight instances of
exactness in expression, hardly noticeable except under the
microscope, as it were, which make up the fabric of Luke's
History.

And yet the North Galatian Theorists maintain that
these Antiochians would have preferred to be called
"Phrygians" rather than "men of the Province Galatia".
A horse, or a slave, was called "Phryx," not men who
prided themselves on being some steps nearer the Roman
citizenship than their merely Greek neighbours.

The process of acquiring the Roman citizenship evidently
went on rapidly during the first century.   It appears probable that practically the entire free population had
acquired the Roman rights before the middle of the second
century, otherwise we should find more inscriptions containing names of the Greek type.   Almost every man who
is mentioned has the three names of the Roman citizen ;
and the freedmen who occur have the standing and the
three names of Roman *libertini.*   Probably, when Hadrian
made Iconium a Colonia, 117-138, Antioch was already a
body of Roman *cives.*

In the obscurity as to the exact position of the older
inhabitants in the Colonia, it is impossible to be certain as
to the law of family and inheritance among them.   Though
the Roman *Coloni,* all doubtless Western born, whom
Augustus settled there, would preserve the principles and
forms of Roman law, it is entirely improbable that the
older inhabitants, already in possession of a settled and

developed legal system, were called upon to adopt a new and strange system. It was not Roman method to destroy an existing civilisation. One who was not a Roman citizen was not even privileged to make a will of the Roman type : he must follow hereditary and national custom. In the gradual assimilation of law in the East, it would appear that Greek law proved too strongly established, and that it was not thoroughly Romanised for centuries, if at all. The influence of the general atmosphere and intercourse in Asia Minor was strong enough to Hellenise even Celtic-Roman Galatia : much more was it able to preserve in Colonia Antiocheia the existing type of Hellenic society, even though the forms of municipal government were Roman.

Even in municipal government the inscriptions show some traces of Greek forms, while in regard to social circumstances and amusements many traces of the Greek spirit are seen.

The government of Colonia Antiocheia was of the usual Roman type. The inscriptions mention Duoviri Quinquennales, Duoviri, Quæstores, Ædiles : a senate called *Ordo*, whose members were styled Decuriones : the *Ordo et Populus* concurring in the compliment to a citizen : the *Populus* signifying its will by acclamation in the theatre, and carrying its will into effect separately in each *Vicus*. There was a priesthood of Jupiter Optimus Maximus ; and perhaps a municipal High priesthood in the Imperial religion.[1]

But there are also traces of the Greek style of municipal government creeping into that Roman organisation. The

[1] Compare C. I. L., III 6820, with the *Acta* of Paul and Thekla (see the *Church in the Roman Empire*, p. 396 f.

office of *Grammateus*, so important in the Hellenistic cities of the East,[1] is mentioned as an Antiochian office between the Quæstorship and the Duumvirate. The title of *Agonotheta perpetuus* of the quinquennial games is more Greek than Latin.[2]

There can be no doubt that the ordinary language of society was Greek, and not Latin. Greek was the language of trade and of education. It was only pride in their Roman rank that led to the exclusive use of Latin in inscriptions during the first century, and its frequent use in the second century. Similarly Colonia Lystra used the Latinised form Lustra during the first century.

Two bilingual epitaphs show that the families of Roman *Coloni* found it advisable to learn Greek ; and a number of Greek inscriptions, some of persons with Greek names, some with Roman names, some actually erected by Roman citizens in honour of Roman citizens, point to the same fact. The third century inscriptions and those of late date are usually and almost exclusively Greek : even high Roman imperial officials write in Greek and are honoured in Greek. Instead of *Colonia Antiocheia*, the pure Greek style " *metropolis of the Antiochians* " became common ; and there is even a Greek inscription in which the *Boule* honours Secundus on the occasion of his having filled the office of *Strategos*, where the pure Greek terms are used in place of *Ordo* and *Duumvir*.

The games which are mentioned are of the Greek rather than the Roman bloody character : a *certamen gymnicum*, and a *certamen quinquennale talantiaeum*. But these belong to the second or even the third century.[3] The *Acta* of

---

[1] *St. Paul the Trav.*, p. 281.   [2] ἀγωνοθέτης διὰ βίου.

[3] Compare also Le Bas and Waddington, No. 1620*a*.

Paul and Thekla attest in the first century a more Roman type of sports, gladiators and combats with beasts, showing that the Roman spirit was stronger then and grew afterwards weaker.

Antioch was not merely the metropolis of all Southern Galatia. It was also, in a special sense, the centre of a *Regio*, over which a Roman centurion had certain duties.[1] That *Regio* was the Phrygian district attached to Galatia, called Pisidian Phrygia or Galatic Phrygia[2]—the former title geographical, the latter political. It is called by the Greek title χώρα, Acts XIII 49: during Paul's residence in Antioch, the entire *Regio* heard of the new faith. Antioch was a centre of evangelic influence for the whole *Regio*, just as Ephesus was for the whole Province of which it was centre, Acts XIX 10. That *Regio* is afterwards defined more precisely as the "region which was called Phrygian (geographically) and Galatic (politically)," Acts XVI 6, or, as the antithesis might be put, "Phrygian (by the Greeks) and Galatic (by the Roman government)". More briefly it is summed up as "the Phrygian region" in Acts XVIII 23, where some prefer to take Phrygia as a noun (making, however, no difference to the sense).

It is not at present possible to feel certainty whether or not Antioch remained part of the Province Galatia down to the provincial reorganisation by Diocletian about 295.[3] The Pisidian martyrs Marcus, Alphius and others under Diocletian are said to have been of the city Antioch,

---

[1] Inscription mentioned on p. 199.
[2] Opposed to *Asiana* Phrygia, Galen, vol. VI, p. 515, Kuhn.
[3] See p. 177 f.

14

belonging to the region of Galatic Phrygia : [1] the term *Regio* is important and indicates a good ultimate authority, as we have already seen.

There are several other good features in the account : the village Kalytos or Katalytos, where the martyrs were blacksmiths : the calling in of bronze-workers ($\chi a \lambda \kappa o \tau \acute{v} \pi o \iota$): perhaps the mention of Claudiopolis as a Pisidian city, a corruption of Claudioseleuceia. The account is late and corrupt : the original *Acta* probably described martyrs from several Pisidian towns, who were tried before the governor of Galatia at Antioch during a progress through his Province. If that occurred under Diocletian, it would be established that Antioch was part of Galatia under his reign ; but the Emperor's name is far from trustworthy ; that detail was incorrectly added in late versions of many *Acta ;* and in this case the probability is that it is a mere guess of a late redactor, and did not occur in the original *Acta.*

We thus conclude that the facts are as a whole true ; but the date is probably false, being later than the truth.

Ptolemy mentions Antioch both as a city of Galatia and as a city of the Province Pamphylia and district Pisidian Phrygia. That suggests the mixing up of an earlier classification to Galatia, and a later (true in his time) to Pamphylia ; but it may be a mere blunder. At least it is certain that Antioch was classed to Galatia as late as the end of Trajan's reign.

Aelian mentions a kind of partridge ($\Sigma v \rho o \pi \acute{e} \rho \delta \iota \xi$), small, very wild, black in colour, with red beak, the flesh well-

---

[1] *Menolog. Sirletianum* quoted in Acta Sanctorum, 28th Sept., p. 563 : *sub. Diocletiano Imp. in urbe Antiochiae Pisidiae ex regione Phrygiae Galaticae* (wrongly *Galaciae*) *sub praeside Magno.*

tasted, at Antioch of Pisidia : it ate stones (*Hist. Anim.,* XVI 7).

We should be glad to know in what relation the old sanctuary stood to the *Colonia.* The great estates which once belonged to the temple are not likely to have been left undisturbed by Greek kings or by the Greek autonomous government. In some similar cases there is evidence to show that part or the whole of the vast temple properties in Asia Minor had become imperial estates.[1] In the case of Antioch, it is probable that land for the *Coloni* was found, not by depriving the older population of their property, but by presenting temple lands to the *Colonia.*

This theory explains, and is confirmed by, the evidence of Strabo, who states that the temple formerly possessed much sacred land and a large body of temple slaves, but its temporal power and wealth were put down after Amyntas died. Such is the probable meaning of his expression : [2] the temple itself was not put down, for the hereditary god Men and his priests for life are often mentioned in inscriptions.

But there must have been certain property connected with the temple, the management of which was entrusted to an officer called " Curator of the Sanctuary Chest " : [3] it is highly probable that the *Colonia* was charged with the maintenance of the temple out of the revenues of the property, which once had belonged to the temple and had been presented by Augustus to the *Colonia.*

The circumstances of Antioch suggest that the temple stood in relations to the city similar to those that existed in Ephesus. The strength of the Asiatic spirit was always

---

[1] *Cities and Bish. of Phrygia,* I, p. 11.   [2] κατελύθη.

[3] *Curator Arcae Sanctuariae.*

connected with the temple ; and the temple had considerable influence even while the Romanising spirit was most
vigorous.

A festival called Apollo's Birth,[1] mentioned at Pisidian
Antioch, must certainly be understood as a festival of Men.
The story of the birth of the god was among the great
mysteries of the religion, as acted before the initiated.
The mystic ceremonies were everywhere associated with
a public festival.

No sure trace of the Jewish element can be detected in
inscriptions.   The Antiochian Jews had apparently disused
Hebrew names completely (at least in public) ; but it is not
impossible that some of the characteristic Antiochian names,
such as Anicius, Caristanius, may hide Jews of high rank.

Few Christian inscriptions at Antioch are known.   But
in the great cities, where Roman officials were numerous,
it was always expedient for the Christians to make little
public show, and to draw as little attention on themselves
as possible.[2]

One ends with the phrase " he shall have to reckon with
the might of God " ; another with " thou shalt not wrong
God " ; two others with " he shall have to reckon with God ".
These classes of inscriptions are more fully described else-
where.[3]   An epigram uses the expression $\dot{a}\theta a\nu\acute{a}\tau o\nu$ $\psi\nu\chi\hat{\eta}s$,
which seems of Christian type.[4]

Le Quien mentions as bishops of Antioch (1) Eudoxius
about 290-300, (2) Optatus, (3) Anthimos, and (4) Cyprianus.

Of these Eudoxius is probably historical, for the account
given in a Greek menology under 23rd June seems taken

---

[1] $\Gamma\epsilon\nu\acute{\epsilon}\theta\lambda\iota a$ $'A\pi\acute{o}\lambda\lambda\omega\nu os$, *Acta SS. Trophimi, etc.*, 19th Sept., p. 12.

[2] *Cities and Bish. of Phrygia*, II, p. 711.   [3] *Op. cit.*, II, ch. XII.

[4] See Sterrett, *Epigr. Journ.*, 138, 142, 143 ; C. I. G., 3980.

from a trustworthy source : in it Eustochius of Ousada (*i.e.*, Vasada), a Pagan priest, seeks baptism from Eudoxius of Antioch ; and afterwards goes to Lystra, where he has relatives ; finally he is sent for trial to Ancyra and condemned.   There is so much correct detail in the story, that a presumption is created in its favour.

But Optatus, Anthimos and Cyprianus, though accepted by Le Quien and the Bollandists (26th Sept., VII, p. 189 f), have little claim to be historical, much less to be classed to Pisidian Antioch.   The *Acta* of Justina, in which they are mentioned, is a document of poor character ; and Syrian Antioch is mentioned as the city of Justina by many authorities.

In 314 Sergianos represented Antioch at the Council of Ancyra, and in 325 Antonius at Nicæa.

A city Antioch is mentioned very often in the ancient Syrian Martyrology, but the presumption is that Syrian Antioch is meant.

Apollonia, the city most closely connected with Antioch, and like it classed to Pisidian Phrygia, is said to have had Mark, the nephew of Barnabas, as its evangelist and first bishop ; see *Acta Sanctorum*, 21st June, V, p. 58 ; and not far south of Apollonia, the church of Seleuceia is said to have had a first century origin with Artemon as first bishop (27th March).

Eighteen bishoprics of the Province Pisidia are recorded in or before the fourth century.   Six[1] more are added in later records, mostly in the mountainous and least civilised parts of Pisidia.

---

[1] Bindaion is probably only another name for Eudoxiopolis, *Cities and Bish. of Phrygia*, I, p. 326.   Le Quien distinguishes them, and makes seven late bishoprics.

SECTION 20.

ICONIUM.

THERE is a remarkable resemblance between the beautiful and impressive situation of Damascus and that of Iconium. Both cities are situated near the western end of vast level plains, which extend to the east far further than the eye can see; and mountains, rising like islands out of the level plain, give character and variety to the wide view eastwards. Within a few miles towards the west in each case rises a great hilly, even mountainous region, from which issue streams that make the immediate surroundings of both cities a perfect garden : the streams find no outlet to the sea, but are merged in the marshy lakes that lie a little way east in the open plains. Situated thus in an always green and rich garden on the edge of the wilderness, each of the two cities enjoys a permanent importance which no political changes can destroy, however much misgovernment may diminish their wealth and prosperity. Each is of immemorial antiquity. Damascus is famed as the oldest of cities. At Iconium King Nannakos or Annakos reigned before the flood ; and, as there was a prophecy that "after him came the deluge, when all must perish," his Phrygian subjects mourned for him with a sorrow that became proverbial.

The legend of Nannakos makes him a king of the Phrygians. Xenophon, who visited it during the Anabasis of Cyrus, calls it the extremest city of Phrygia. Pliny quotes it among a list of famous old Phrygian cities,[1] evidently using some Greek authority; though, where he describes the political geography of Asia Minor, he makes Iconium the capital of the Lycaonian Tetrarchy, which was added to Galatia. In Acts XIV 6 Paul and Barnabas flee from Iconium into Lycaonia, implying that it was not a city of Lycaonia. In A.D. 163, at the trial of Justin Martyr, one of his associates, a slave named Hierax, described himself as coming from Iconium of Phrygia.[2] About A.D. 250 Firmilian attended the Council of Iconium, and describes it as a city of Phrygia. It does not on its coins name the Koinon of Lycaonia. The *Vita S. Artemii* (ascribed to Joannes Damascius) mentions Iconium as the last city of Phrygia (doubtless on some older authority).[3]

This forms a very complete chain of evidence, almost entirely taken from persons who had seen the city. On the other hand persons who thought only of political connection and geography, always describe Iconium as a city of Lycaonia: so *e.g.*, Strabo, Pliny, Ptolemy, Cicero, Stephanus,[4] etc.

The contradiction is explained by the situation of Iconium in the vast Lycaonian plain, while it was the extreme point to which the Phryges had extended their conquest. It was, in perfect truth, the last Phrygian city; all beyond it to the south and east was Lycaonian. At a frontier

---

[1] Read Iconium for Conium, V 41, 145.

[2] Ruinart alters the text of the MSS.

[3] διελθὼν τοίνυν ἅπασαν τὴν Φρυγίαν καὶ πρὸς τὴν ἐσχάτην αὐτῆς πόλιν τὸ καλούμενον Ἰκόνιον καταντήσας.

[4] Yet he mentions Nannakos and his Phrygian subjects.

city, the memory of diversity in race is sometimes preserved most tenaciously, because it is kept vividly before the minds of the people. So it was in Iconium. Usually in Asia Minor boundaries between countries and races were vague and uncertain. But the boundary between Phrygia and Lycaonia was narrowly fixed at that one point. The world in general spoke of Iconium as the chief city of Lycaonia: nature and geography make it that. But the Iconians distinguished themselves from the Lycaonians and claimed to be of Phrygian stock, even in late Roman times.

The reason why the Iconians were always so clear and positive as to their Phrygian origin must have lain in something that was vividly brought before the minds of the people; and part of the cause was, beyond all doubt, difference of language. That is revealed to us in Acts XIV 6: when Paul and Barnabas fled from Iconium to its near neighbour Lystra, they crossed into Lycaonia (out of Phrygia); and the Lystran rabble spoke in the Lycaonian tongue (p. 150).

Late authorities describe Iconium as a city of Pisidia. That is due to the political arrangement according to which western Lycaonia was part of a Province Pisidia, from A.D. 295-372.[1] Iconium was a sort of secondary metropolis of Pisidia Provincia.[2] When the new Province Lycaonia was organised about 372, Iconium became its metropolis; and Amphilochius (375-circ. 400), a bishop of great vigour, made it a highly important place in ecclesiastical history.

The tendency is often seen to take some prominent name and extend it over several regions as title of a Roman political division, in defiance of strict geographical truth: so the names Asia, Galatia, Cilicia, Pisidia, were employed

---

[1] Ammianus, XIV 2, Basil, *Epist.* 8, 393, 406.

[2] μετὰ τὴν μεγίστην ἡ πρώτη, Basil, *Epist.* 8.

in a very wide way at different times, because each was strong in the Roman mind at the time.

Iconium is about 3350 feet above sea-level : it is now a railway station, and chief city of a vilayet or Turkish province.

The extraordinary vicissitudes in the history of Iconium during the last three centuries B.C. have been described in sections 7-12.

It certainly ranked as a Hellenic city, *i.e.*, a city in which Hellenic order and municipal organisation had been naturalised, and in which the official language was Greek from the end of the fourth century. Hence, like many other Hellenised Phrygian cities, it liked to connect its origin with Greek legend : it derived its name either from the image of Medusa, brought there by Perseus,[1] or from the clay images of men which Prometheus made there after the flood to replace the drowned people. The latter story shows an intention of giving to the Iconian legend of the flood a Greek appearance.[2]

Thus we see that, though it claimed to be Phrygian in contrast to Lycaonian, it also claimed to be of Greek origin ultimately. That proves it to have taken on the Greek character, with Greek forms of government and society. Its people would be called in the customary sense Hellenes, and that name is applied to them in Acts XIV 1.

The North Galatian Theorists maintain that the Iconians would have chosen to be called Phrygians (or Lycaonians) ;[3]

---

[1] εἰκών, Eustath., *ad Dionys. Per.*, 856.

[2] Steph. Byz. Compare the development of the native legend of the flood at Kelainai-Apameia, *Cities and Bish. of Phrygia*, II, pp. 415 and 671.

[3] Many of them have taken it as a city of Lycaonia.

as if persons who claimed the rank of Hellenes would have accepted that address as anything but an insult.   Ethno-logically, they were Phrygians ; but the title Hellenes implied a certain standard of education, knowledge and social elevation, inconsistent with the address " Phryges " : pp. 129, 181 f, 230 f.

During the period 37-72 the name Lycaones had a peculiarly non-Roman innuendo, for it was regularly used to designate the inhabitants of that part of Lycaonia which was outside Roman bounds, and subject to King Antiochus. On his coins the legend " *Of the Lycaonians*" is engraved. At that time the Iconian pride in their Roman connection (*i.e.*, in their belonging to the Province Galatia) was marked by the title Claud-Iconium.   That title is a real indication of political feeling.   To understand its significance, one must try to imagine Dublin assuming and boasting in public documents of the title Victorian Dublin.   What a change in Irish feeling that would indicate !

Little can be gathered from the Iconian inscriptions about the city constitution.   It was governed by Archons ; but no decrees have been found earlier than the changes introduced by Hadrian, except C. I. G., 3991, which is an honorary decree of the Demos.

Hadrian conferred on Iconium the rank of a Colonia, with the title *Aelia Hadriana Iconiensium* (see p. 123).

Doubtless this elevation gave the position and rights of Romans to the whole body of Iconian citizens.   It is doubtful whether the ordinary colonial constitution was instituted in Iconium ; but an inscription[1] might perhaps be restored as *Γ. Ἀππώνιος Κρίσπος δ[υανδρικὸς] Εἰκωνίου,*

---

[1] Sterrett, *Epigraph. Journ.*, No. 254 (not restored there).

implying that C. Aponius Crispus was *duumvir* of the Colonia. Latin was adopted as the official language ; but there is not the slightest reason to think that this was more than a superficial Romanisation. Greek still continued, beyond any doubt, to be the only speech (besides Phrygian) in actual use among the people, as the inscription of Crispus and others show. Except in two or three official decrees, the language of inscriptions was still Greek. But it was a matter of pride to employ Latin officially on coins and in decrees of the city, to mark its new Roman rank.

As to the religion of Iconium the inscriptions and authorities give very scanty information ; but there can be no reasonable doubt as to its resemblance to the general Anatolian type. The remarkable words of C. I. G., 4000, enigmatic as they are, would alone prove this :—

ἀρη[τ]ῆρες

Ἀκά[ρ]ας δήμου χάριν τῆς δεκα[μ]άζου,¹

τετρακόρης τε θεᾶς πρόπολοι καὶ Διονύσου

" priests of the four-headed, ten-breasted (deity) on behalf of the people, and servants of the many-natured goddess and of Dionysos ": *i.e.*, priest and priestess of the patron gods of the city, a goddess of the type of Ephesian Artemis, the nursing mother of all life, and her associated god, giver of wine like the Greek Dionysos.² Moreover the goddess is called in C. I. G., 3993, by many names : she is Angdistis

---

¹ Maltreated by Boeckh and Franz: though punctuation marks show the verses, they read ἀρ[χιερεῖ]ς for ἀρη[τ]ῆρες (Homeric and late epic), and place it at the beginning of a new hexameter. The following word seems to be intended for (τετρα)κά[ρ]ας perhaps (but Franz reads ['Αχ]αίας): it may be an epithet of the goddess or of the Demos (as containing four tribes).

² τετραπρόσωπος and τρικάρανος both occur in a late hymn to Selene, *Hermes*, IV, p. 64.

and Mother Bo[ri]thene[1] and Mother of the gods. She
is also the Mother Zizimene or Dindimene: Sarre in
Oesterreich. Mittheil., 1896, p. 31.

At the same time there was doubtless a certain local
variation everywhere in the Anatolian religion.   At
Iconium we are nearing the southern side of the plateau,
and the legend of Perseus (so common on the south coast
along with the kindred tale of Bellerophon) played a great
part in the city tradition.

One of the most extensive groups of early Christian
inscriptions belongs to Iconium and the country north and
north-east from it. The inscriptions have no dates. So
far as the style of lettering goes, some of them might be
assigned to the third century; but the majority belong
more probably to the fourth and even fifth centuries.

The reason why they were so numerous then probably
is that there was at that time a great development of
education among the rustic population. The pagan Græco-
Roman civilisation had its seat in the towns, and hardly
touched the country districts. It was Christianity which
spread a knowledge of Greek and a certain degree of
education among them; and, when the country people
first began to write and to use inscriptions, their names
and other signs show they were Christians.

This large group of inscriptions extends into Phrygia
Paroreios on the west, and up through the Added Land
west of Lake Tatta on the north-east. It seems beyond
doubt to mark an influence spreading from Iconium. To
describe its character would be outside of our proper subject.

In many of those inscriptions Jewish names occur;

---

[1] Reading PI for Ħ: Boritene was an epithet of the goddess Kore
at Thyatira and Attalia (a neighbouring town).

but it is uncertain how far these can be assumed to mark
Jewish-Christians. C. I. G., 9270, is in all probability
Jewish-Christian and perhaps various others. A certain
Tyrronius of Iconium, a trainer of athletes in the second
century, has been recognised as a Jew.[1] Possibly the name
Ebourenos may also be Jewish.[2]

Iconium was always the Christian metropolis, and head
of the ecclesiastical system of Lycaonia, which was as
highly developed as that of Pisidia at an early time.
Sixteen bishoprics are mentioned during the fourth century
or earlier ;[3] one appears first in 451 (Barata) ; and one in
680 (Verinopolis). The latter, previously, was probably
included in a joint bishopric with Glavama ; but, being far
north near the Galatian frontier, they shared in the growing
importance of that northern country : see p. 170 f.

Note.—Pliny mentions a city Iconium in Cilicia. That
was true in a political and Roman sense about B.C. 80-40.
It is also true that Cilicia was used by Appian, *Bell. Civ.*,
V 75, and doubtless by others in a loose way to include a
good large slice of Lycaonia ; and the first kingdom of
Polemon, which included Iconium, is called simply " part
of Cilicia," sections, 9, 10. In the late *Notitiae Episco-
patuum* and in the late Byzantine and the Armenian
writers, Cilicia extends far beyond the Cilician Gates to
include Podandos, Faustinopolis-Loulon, and even The-
basa.

[1] *Cities and Bish. of Phrygia*, II, p. 650.
[2] Sterrett, *Epigr. Journ.*, No. 192.
[3] Glavama, according to Le Quien, is first mentioned in 451 ; but
in 325 it is mentioned as a Bishopric of Galatia, to which Province
it then belonged, p. 178. Ilistra in 325, see section 21.

Pliny in that passage, V 93, was trusting to an autho-
rity who used Cilicia in that wide, loose way. But his
statement has been perverted to prove that an Iconium
in Cilicia must be distinguished as a separate city from
Iconium in Lycaonia or Phrygia : *e.g.*, the *Liber Nominum
Locorum ex Actis* (Hieronymus, ed. Migne, III 1302) says,
"*Iconium civitas celeberrima Lycaoniae : et est altera in
Cilicia*". So some moderns.

SECTION 21.

LYSTRA.

LYSTRA was situated in a pleasant valley, bordered by gently sloping hills of no great height, through which flows a small but steady stream to be lost in the open Lycaonian plain a few miles farther east. The city was planted on a small hill in the middle of the valley, on the north side of the stream, about a mile north-west of the modern village Khatyn-Serai, which is on the south side of the water. The proof of the position of Lystra is one of Professor Sterrett's many services to our knowledge of Asia Minor; but the site was divined with marvellously sure intuition by Leake in the beginning of the century. It is about 3780 feet above sea level.

In this favourable position there must always have been a settlement somewhere near Khatyn-Serai; but the history of Lystra begins with Augustus, who founded there one of the series of *Coloniae*, which he made to defend the southern frontier of Galatia. The name Lystra is probably Lycaonian, for Ilistra and Kilistra also occur in the country: the former a city and bishopric, near Laranda, the latter a village about twelve miles up the stream from Lystra, with wonderful rock-cuttings of the Christian time: both still retain the ancient names.

But it happened that the Lycaonian name had an

obvious resemblance to the Latin word *lustrum,* and a little detail shows the Latin feeling in Lystra. It called itself Lustra, not Lystra, in all its inscriptions and coins. It spelt Roman, not Greek. Greek cities like Prymnessos never used the Latin spelling Prumnessos even if they wrote in Latin;[1] but Lystran coins read COLONIA · JULIA · FELIX · GEMINA · LUSTRA.

Accordingly Lystra did not pair herself with the Greek cities of the region. She claimed to be the sister of the Roman Antioch. So we read on the basis of a statue which Lystra sent to her sister in the second century :— [2]

> The very brilliant sister Colonia of the Antiochians
> is honoured by
> the very brilliant Colonia of the Lystrans
> with the Statue of Concord.

It is an interesting point that this inscription is in Greek, proving that, amid all the local pride in Roman names and titles, the Latin language was only a delicate exotic.

Lystra lay eight or ten miles off the great trade route in a secluded glen, and would not have full opportunity of sharing in the Hellenisation of the cities along that road, like Iconium and Derbe. Only a special occasion[3] lent it temporary importance during the first century. We should expect to find that in it Greek civilisation had not been so strongly naturalised as in the two neighbouring cities. Evidence is very scanty ; but, such as it is, it tends to support that view. Lystra is the only place in which the use of the native language among at least a section of the

---

[1] C. I. L., III 7043, 7171. Lustra in C. I. L., III 6596 (*Col. Lustrensium* in last line), 6786.

[2] Sterrett, *Wolfe Expedition,* 352.　　　　　[3] See p. 114 f.

population was prominent enough to find mention in the Acts. In its inscriptions, apart from those of the Latin-speaking *coloni*, we find few signs of Greek civilisation. There is a larger proportion of Greek among the inscriptions than at Antioch, but not the same evidence of Greek character.

At the same time it should be noticed that it was among the Pagans, engaged in an act of their religion, and not among the Christian converts, that Lycaonian was spoken. There is no reason to suppose that Paul addressed himself to people that spoke only Lycaonian. The existence of Jews, and therefore of trade,[1] proves that Greek was familiar to many ; the Roman influence really fostered Greek, as we have seen ; and there is a considerable number of Roman inscriptions.

As to the Lycaonian religion in Lystra or in Derbe, no evidence exists outside of the Acts. The name of Zeus was given by the Greek-speaking population to the great god who was the most prominent figure exoterically at the sanctuary in front of the city ; but such identifications with Greek deities prove nothing as to the real character of the worship. Doubtless it was much of the same character as in Iconium. See Sections 5, 20.

There was a disposition in Lystra to believe in actual theophany, or appearance of the gods on earth in human form, as they had appeared near Tyriaion [2] to Baucis and Philemon (according to the pretty tale related by Ovid).

---

[1] *Church in Rom. Empire*, p. 69.

[2] The corruptions in Ovid, *Metam.*, VIII 719, *trineius, fineius, thineyus, cineius, chineius, tirinthius, phyneius, thyrneius*, etc., point to Tyriaius or Tyrieius, not Tyaneius (an impossible form given in the current texts).

15

That was a Phrygian story, as Ovid says;[1] but in religion Phrygia and Lycaonia meet. The Phrygian gods were often worshipped as the "manifest God": τὸν ἐπιφανέστα-τον θεόν in inscriptions.

At the *hieron* before the city, there would certainly be a college of priests, as at the other great sanctuaries of Asia Minor, and not merely a single priest of the God, though of course there was a head in the college at all such *hiera*. At Pessinus the college contained at least ten priests; at the Milyan *hieron* there were six.[2]

Lystra ceased to be a city of any consequence after the Augustan *Coloniae* lost their importance. When the mountain country was pacified, they were no longer needed as garrisons; and Lystra had not like Antioch a situation such as to make it great in all circumstances. Hence, though it was at first so important in Christian history, and though several early traditions are connected with it, yet in later Christian history it is rarely heard of. To Roman policy Lystra owed the only political importance it ever possessed: without that support, it sank again to its original insignificance.

A Lystran martyr Zoilos is mentioned in the early Syrian Martyrology on 23rd May. The story of Eustochius is connected with the city.[3] It is mentioned in the tale of Paul and Thekla. Artemas or Artemius, one of the seventy, is said to have been Bishop of Lystra. But it was not represented at Nicæa in 325; for Tiberius, whom Le Quien makes Bishop of Lystra, was really Bishop of Ilistra.

---

[1] Ovid, *Met.*, VIII 621.

[2] *Cities and Bish. of Phrygia*, I, p. 288, Aristid, *Or.*, XXIII, pp. 451, 490.

[3] See p. 213 and *Histor. Geogr. of Asia Minor*, p. 333 f.

Paulus of Lystra is mentioned at the Council of Constantinople in 381.

The only trace of its Christian history that remains is a sacred spring or Ayasma[1] close to the city, to which the Greeks of Iconium and Zille resort, and which even the Turks respect as holy. There is much need of excavation on the deserted site in order to clear up some of the details recorded in Acts about Lystra.

[1] ἁγίασμα, the usual name for Christian sacred springs.

SECTION 22.

DERBE.

THE situation of Derbe was probably at a large mound—
of the style that Strabo calls "mound of Semiramis"—
named by the Turks Gudelisin, about three miles north-
west from the village Zosta or Losta near the straightest
road from Iconium to Laranda. Professor Sterrett placed
Derbe between Zosta and Bosola (a village two miles
further east) : in both villages there are many ancient cut
stones and some inscriptions; but it seemed to me that
these had been carried, and that the true ancient site was
at the now deserted mound, where evidently an old city
once stood. The difference is not important for our
purposes.[1]

While this site is highly probable, and suits well all our
scanty information about Derbe, yet it is very desirable
that excavation should be made in order to place it beyond
doubt that Derbe was in this neighbourhood. At one
time I thought Bin-Bir-Kilise might be the site of Derbe ;
but that does not suit so well. Others have placed Derbe
at Serpek or Ambararassi, about fifteen miles west from
Kybistra ; but that seems irreconcilable with the evidence
that Derbe was a Roman provincial city, and not a part of

[1] It is about the same altitude as Iconium ; but no observation has
been made.

the kingdom of Archelaus or of Antiochus.   Another proposed position for Derbe at the modern Divle, about twelve miles south-east of Serpek—on the theory that Divle retains the ancient name Derbe or Delbeia—is equally irreconcilable with the evidence.

The only other site that seems to have any real title to consideration is Dorla, a few miles north-west from Gudelisin.   At that village, which is given on no map, and seems never to have been visited by any traveller except in 1890, there are many late inscriptions ; but we reached it only about sunset, and after hastily copying the inscriptions in the failing light, we had to hurry on our journey in the darkness.   This place requires further examination.   It is so near Gudelisin that the same reasoning applies to both nearly equally well ; and it would make no real difference to us, if hereafter Derbe had to be moved to Dorla.

In Lycaonia epigraphy has furnished hardly any information except near Iconium and Laodiceia.   Elsewhere inscriptions are very rare and insignificant.   No decrees of cities have been found.   Part of the reason for the dearth probably lies in the higher value that attaches to good stones in a region where quarries are distant : good inscribed stones were used up in the numerous stately buildings of the Seljuk Turks.

Thus the chief source from which the history of Derbe might be reconstructed fails entirely.

The form Derbe represents a native Lycaonian name as adapted to Greek pronunciation.   Stephanus mentions that Delbeia was another form of the name.   In the Bezan Codex $\Delta o \nu \beta \acute{\epsilon} \rho \iota o \varsigma$, *Doverius,* is read instead of $\Delta \epsilon \rho \beta a \hat{\iota} o \varsigma$ in Acts XX 4 ; and this is apparently a form of the ethnic,

implying that Doubera or Dovera was a way of pronouncing the Lycaonian name. It is well known that the
Greeks found the greatest difficulty in pronouncing many
native Anatolian names, in which V or W was an element,
representing it by *ου* or *β* or *ο*, or even omitting it ; the
difficulty was enhanced if the name contained also R or
L ; and an additional complication was caused by the variation of vowel sound between U and I or E characteristic
of Anatolia (as, *e.g.*, Soublaion, Seiblia, Siblia are varieties
of one name).

Hence Duvera or Duvra or Dubra are possible variations
of Derbe or Delbeia ; and the explorer asks whether
the village name Duwer (common at the present day)
may be a survival of the old Dubra : the name, however,
is said by the peasants to be a Turkish word meaning
" wall ".

From the supposed Dubra might come the ethnic Dubrios
or *Δουβέριος*.

The thick, indistinct pronunciation of the Anatolian
peasants remains a great difficulty to the explorer at the
present day, and the ear requires long practice to catch the
sounds correctly.   Hence the extraordinary misrepresentation of names by many travellers while inexperienced : the
simple Turkish name Yuvalik appears in some archæological works as Djouk-Ovarlak : in 1882 I found it impossible
after many repetitions to feel sure whether the first sound in
the monosyllabic name of a village near Kybistra was P
or K or T.   The same coarse, rough, uneducated pronunciation characterised the people of the plateau in ancient
time, and was part of the reason why there was such a
broad division between those who had learned Greek pronunciation and accent and those who had not.   The Hellene,

i.e., the educated person, was recognised by the first word he spoke.

This is one of the fundamental facts in the life of Asia Minor at the time when Paul visited it—one of the things that is brought home to us so clearly by modern facts—one that the scholar who studies the ancient history of the country must fix deep in his memory as a foundation to build upon.

Gudelisin occupies a very important position near a great road, close to the natural frontier between the two districts of which Laranda and Iconium are respectively capitals. Hence Strabo speaks of it as a point of boundary.[1] It has therefore been described in previous works[2] as the frontier city of the Province Galatia, all beyond it to the east belonging to the realm of Antiochus. That Derbe was a Roman frontier city is confirmed by the brief description which Stephanus of Byzantium gives of it. He calls it a fortress of Isauria and a customs station :[3] it was a station for customs at the frontier of the Province beside a great trade route.

Derbe was close to the Isaurian mountains, which rise boldly from the plain just behind Zosta, and hence the inaccurate expression "a fortress of Isauria". Strabo correctly says it was "on the flanks of the Isaurican region," and goes on to describe it as "adhering (like a barnacle)

---

[1] μέχρι Δέρβης, p. 535.

[2] *Church in Rom. Emp.*, p. 55; *St. Paul the Trav.*, p. 120.

[3] φρούριον Ἰσαυρίας καὶ λιμήν: many writers, taking λιμήν as a "harbour," conjectured that λίμνη was the true reading. λιμήν also meant a "market" in Paphos, Crete, Thessaly (see *Steph. Thesaurus*); the *Limenes* or customs stations of Asia are often mentioned in inscriptions. See Wilhelm in *Arch. Epigr. Mitth. Oest.*, 1897, p. 76, Rostowzew, *ib.*, 1896, p. 127.

to Cappadocia ":[1] that seems to be an allusion to the fact
that at one time it was the frontier town of the Eleventh
Strategia attached to Cappadocia : see section 7.

In the Galatic Province about A.D. 40-60 the importance
of Derbe lay mainly in its relation to the dependent
kingdom of Antiochus. Doubtless, there would arise
frontier questions calling for the decision of the Roman
governor ; and these questions would have their centre at
Derbe. Hence it probably was that the city was honoured
with the title Claudio-Derbe, which is practically equivalent
to Imperial Derbe : see p. 218. This occurred either in
41 or soon after ; and it was probably as a compensation
for the compliment to an inferior city that Iconium was
permitted a similar title Claud-Iconium by the same
Emperor.

In "Imperial Derbe" the feeling of superiority to the
non-Roman Lycaones across the frontier would be peculiarly strong, because the city was in closer relations than
other Lycaonians with them.

Derbe was detached from Galatia and included in the
Triple Eparchy[2] about A.D. 137, and struck coins naming
the Koinon of the Lycaonians. From about 295 to 372 it
was part of the Province Isauria, as Stephanus says (probably on the authority of Ammianus).[3] Thereafter it was
in the Province Lycaonia.

---

[1] ἐπιπεφυκὸς τῇ Καππαδοκίᾳ.　　　　[2] See p. 177.
　　　　　　　[3] Compare p. 178.

SECTION 23.

SUMMARY.

THE most important political and social facts to observe in the central districts of Asia Minor, when Paul entered it, are—

1. The vigour of Roman administration: it was afterwards relaxed, but the Pauline history is true to the facts of A.D. 40-60.

2. The steady spread, through natural causes, of a uniform Hellenic form of civilisation and law throughout Asia Minor, first in the cities, later in the villages and rustic districts : as a rule, the villages on the south of the plateau begin to be Hellenised only in the third century, in the north only in the fourth and fifth centuries.

3. The alliance of Roman and Greek influence in diffusing a mixed Græco-Roman system of social and political ideas.

4. The line along which this Græco-Roman influence moved : before A.D. 285 the southern route from inner Asia through Ephesus to Rome, affecting the south side of the plateau: after 285 the northern route from inner Asia through Ancyra to Constantinople, placing North Galatia in the van of progress.

5. The character and influence of the native religion and social system in Asia Minor, fundamentally the same

everywhere, everywhere opposed to the Græco-Roman civilisation.

6. The struggle between East and West, Asia and Europe, which is always going on in Asia Minor in forms that change from century to century : in the time of Paul it was mainly between the native religion and the Græco-Roman civilisation (Christianity, on the whole, being on the side of the latter).

7. The contrast of the plateau and the western coast-lands of Asia Minor, the former tending towards the European type, the latter towards the Asiatic.

8. The essential continuity of character in the people of Asia Minor from immemorial antiquity down to the present day according to the two types, plateau and west coast-lands : the people as they are now offer the best introduction to the study of the people as they were in A.D. 40-60.

HISTORICAL COMMENTARY

ON THE

EPISTLE TO THE GALATIANS.

I

THE INTRODUCTORY ADDRESS.[1]

IN any judicious system of interpretation, great stress must be laid on the introductory address of this Epistle. It should be compared with the address prefixed to the Epistle to the Romans, a letter which presents marked analogies in sentiment and topics. In each case Paul puts in his introduction the marrow of the whole letter. He says at first in a few words what he is going to say at length in the body of the letter, to repeat over and over, to emphasise from various points of view, and to drive home into the minds of his correspondents.

The important fact, upon which the whole letter turns, is that Paul had been a messenger straight from God to the Galatians. His message, as delivered originally to them, had been a message coming from God. No subsequent variation or change of message on the part of any person, himself or others, could affect that fundamental truth ; and that fact has to be made to live and burn in their minds. Hence he begins by calling himself "an

[1] In the first draft of this Commentary, reference was frequently made to Lightfoot and to Zöckler, as representatives of English and German opinion. Subsequently, a few references have been added to the latest edition of Meyer's Commentary by Professor Sieffert, 1899.

apostle, not from men, neither through man, but through Jesus Christ and God the father ".

Next he mentions those who join with him as the authors of the Epistle.   He often quotes one or two individuals as joint-senders of a letter.   Here, and here alone, he states that all the brethren who are with him are sending the letter to the Churches of Galatia.   This important point calls for special consideration in § II.

Thereafter he introduces the second leading thought of the whole Epistle—that the action and person of Christ is sufficient for salvation.   And so he adds " who gave Himself for our sins, that He might deliver us out of this present evil world ".

II

THE EPISTLE AUTHORISED BY THE CHURCH IN ANTIOCH.

WITH regard to the persons who are mentioned in a letter of Paul's as sending messages or salutations to the persons addressed, a clear distinction must be drawn between those who are mentioned at the beginning and those who are mentioned at the end.   Salutations at the end of a letter are expressive of love, good-will, sympathy and interest. Thus, hosts of well-wishers send greetings to the Romans, to the Corinthians, to the Philippians, to Timothy (along with whom must be included the Churches which he represented), etc.

But persons who join in the address prefixed to a letter are persons whose authorisation is required and conveyed in it.   They are indicated as joint-authors.   The letter (though composed by Paul) is the letter of Paul and those named with him.   These all stamp with their authority what is said in the letter. Accordingly, where Paul associates any one with himself in the prefatory superscription of his letters, it is always some person who stands in a position of authority towards those addressed.

In *Romans, Ephesians, Timothy, Titus*, Paul speaks alone. No person shares with him in the authoritative address.

It is obvious that in those cases it would be hard to find any person whose name could authoritatively have been conjoined with his own by Paul. To the Romans Aquila, perhaps, but we cannot be sure. Moreover, Aquila probably was not with Paul in Corinth when he wrote.

It belongs to that fine courtesy which was part of the fabric of St. Paul's mind, that he never omitted to recognise in the fullest degree the authority that belonged to another. When he writes to a community in the conversion and organisation of which any of his coadjutors and subordinates had played an important part, he desired to acknowledge in his address the position which that person occupied towards the young congregation. If the coadjutor was in his company and could stamp with his authority the message that has to be sent, Paul wrote in their joint name.

Thus Silas and Timothy had gone with him to Philippi and to Thessalonica in the beginning. Both the letters that were sent to the Church in Thessalonica begin " Paul and Silvanus and Timothy". Even the polite and more dignified name Silvanus is used, not the familiar Silas.

The letter to the Philippians was sent in the name of Paul and Timothy. From the omission of Silas we might confidently infer that he was not with Paul when the letter was written—an inference that accords with all other evidence.

Timothy, who rejoined Paul in Corinth shortly after he

went there (Acts XVIII 5), is associated with him in the second Epistle. Silas, who was in company with Paul and Timothy at Corinth on the second journey, is never mentioned on the third journey.[1]

Timothy was probably the leading messenger to Colossae in the beginning.[2] He joins in the letters to the Colossians and to Philemon who resided at Colossae.

But in the circular letter, written probably at the same time as *Colossians* to the other Asian Churches, Timothy is not mentioned.[3] He had not the same right to speak to them, and his name could not carry the same weight to them. Probably various coadjutors had been sent to the great Asian cities ; and just as courtesy to Timothy seemed to Paul to require his name in the address to the Colossians, so courtesy towards the Smyrnaeans and the Sardians prevented Paul from putting Timothy in a position of authority towards them.

Sosthenes was evidently a leading member of the Corinthian Church ; possibly he had formerly been a chief of the synagogue. He was in Ephesus when Paul wrote first to the Corinthians ; and the letter is from " Paul and Sosthenes the brother ". Timothy is not mentioned, because he was absent on a mission at the time.

The instances are not numerous enough to establish by themselves a rule ; but the rule is obvious and necessary from the nature of the situation, and the instances show how the rule is worked out in practice.

---

[1] Not that he had left Paul's association, but more probably that he was detached on special service.

[2] *St. Paul the Trav.*, p. 274. There is no direct evidence to that effect.

[3] *Eph.* I 1.

If other persons were this way associated by Paul with himself, no one probably will imagine that their assent was merely assumed by Paul. He, doubtless, communicated to them what he was writing ; and their name guarantees their full approval of the letter with all that it contains.

Hence we may infer :—

(1) In some or in many cases the introductory address, like the preface to a book, was the last thing composed.

(2) When a person who stood in a position of authority to a Church is not named in the opening of a letter to the Church, he was not in company with Paul at the time.

In the Epistle to the Galatians the authors are " Paul and all the brethren which are with me ".

The phrase, " all the brethren which are with me," arrests our attention. Paul wrote in some place where there was a considerable body of Christians ; and we may confidently say that that implies one or other of the cities where there were churches. The words used by Dr. Zöckler to describe the situation in which Paul wrote are so good, that we may leave it to him to express what is implied in this phrase. As he has been so prominent an adversary of the South Galatian theory, no one will be able to charge me with straining Paul's words to suit my own view. He says : " The whole body of fellow Christians who were with him at the time in ——[1] (not merely his more prominent helpers) are mentioned by St. Paul as those who join with him in greeting the Galatians. He does this in order to give the more emphasis to what he has to say to them.

---

[1] Dr. Zöckler names " Ephesus " here, without hesitation, conformably to his theory, which is the commonly received view among North Galatian critics.

He writes indeed with his own hand (VI 13), but in the name of a whole great Christian community. The warnings and exhortations which are to be addressed to the Galatians go forth from a body whose authority cannot be lightly regarded." But on VI 13 see § LX.

The Church which here addresses the Galatians, therefore, is one which was closely connected with them, whose opinion would be authoritative among them, one which could add impressiveness even to a letter of Paul's. What congregation stood in this relation to the Galatians? Not the Ephesians, nor the Corinthians, later converts, who are not mentioned in the addresses of the letters that are known to have been written among them (Rom., 1 Cor.). Only two congregations could add weight to this particular letter—Jerusalem and Antioch. The former is, for many reasons, out of the question; but Antioch is, from every point of view, specially suitable and impressive. It was the brethren at Antioch who chose out Barnabas and Saul for the work, in the course of which the Galatians were converted. To the Galatians Antioch was their Mother-Church, and it would be specially effective among the Galatians that all the brethren who were at Antioch joined in the letter.

That Antioch was the place where the letter to the Galatians was written is confirmed by another consideration. It was probably there that Paul first received the news about the Galatian defection. As is shown in *St. Paul the Traveller*, p. 189 f, Paul's movements after his second visit to Galatia were so strange, so perplexing, so entirely unforeseen and unintentional, that he is not likely to have been able to communicate with the Galatians. Not until he was, after a long period of uncertainty, ordered to remain in Corinth, had he any fixity. Among those who were with him Timothy was the most natural messenger; and Timothy, who came to him some weeks after his first entrance into Corinth, remained there long enough to take the position implied by his being named as joint-author [1] of the Second Epistle. It is therefore impossible that Timothy could have gone to Galatia and returned to Corinth with the news. Probably he sailed with Paul to Ephesus, Acts XVIII 18, went thence up to Galatia, and met Paul in Syrian Antioch with news.

The place of origin throws light on the Epistle as a whole. In the first place, if the Church of Antioch shared in it, the letter must have been publicly read and approved —either before the whole Church, or more probably before its representatives—before it was despatched. Few, I imagine, will suppose that Paul merely assumed that all who were with him agreed in his sentiments [2] without

---

[1] Not implying that he helped to compose the letter.

[2] Thus, for example, the salutation of "all the Churches" in Rom. XVI 16, means the salutation of the representatives enumerated, Acts XX 4, who were in company with Paul as he wrote. Incidentally, it may be noted that this proves that the long list of greetings in Rom. XVI was really addressed to the Roman Church, and not, according to a well-known theory, to the Church of Ephesus. It is surely by a slip that Dr. Sanday and Mr. Headlam fail to notice the meaning of this salutation, and say, "it is a habit of St. Paul to speak on behalf of the Churches as a whole," quoting, in support of this statement, Rom. XVI 4; 1 Cor. VII 17, XIV 33; 2 Cor. VIII 18, XI 28. In none of these places does Paul speak in the name of the Churches, except Rom. XVI 4, where he has the same justification, that representatives of the Churches were with him: in the other cases he merely mentions facts about "all the Churches". Further, this shows that all the delegates assembled at Corinth, disproving the view suggested in my *St. Paul*, p. 287 (abandoned in German translation).

consulting them : those who thus conceive the character of Paul differ so radically from me that discussion of the point between us would be unprofitable. Accordingly, we must understand that the history as well as the sentiment contained in this Epistle were guaranteed by the whole Church of Antioch.

In the second place, this origin explains why it is that Antioch, which was so closely associated with the evangelisation of Galatia, is not formally alluded to in the body of the letter. The Epistle is apt to produce on the modern reader a certain painful impression, as not recognising the right of Antioch to some share in the championship of freedom. Antioch had taken a very prominent and honourable part in the struggle for freedom ; yet, on the ordinary theory of origin, it is not alluded to in this letter, except to point out that every Jew in Antioch betrayed on one occasion the cause of freedom. Considering what Antioch had done for Christianity and for Paul, every one who follows the ordinary theory must, I think, feel a pang of regret in Paul's interest that he did not by some word or expression give more generous recognition to her services. In a letter, in which he speaks so much about the actual details of the struggle, he seems, on that view, to speak only of his own services, and hardly at all to allude to the services of others. But when all Antiochian Christians are associated with the Apostle as issuing this authoritative letter, we feel that the Church of Antioch is placed in the honourable position which she had earned.

It is true that Paul does not mention Antioch in writing to the Romans. But, in that Epistle, though the subject and treatment are in some respects so similar, there is not the same need or opening for mentioning Antioch, because the subject is handled in a general and philosophical way, not in the personal and individual style which rules in Galatians.

What a flood of light does this origin throw on the history of Antioch and early Christianity! It shows us the congregation of Antioch standing side by side with Paul, sharing in his views, his difficulties, and his struggles for freedom. The Jewish Christians in Antioch had all apparently become united by this time with the Gentiles in sympathy with Paul, just as Barnabas and Peter had been. This in itself is an anwer to those who [1] blame Paul entirely for the separation between Jews and Christians. The mingled conciliation (as in Acts XV 30, 31, and XVI 3, 4) and firmness of Paul gradually produced a unity of Jewish and Gentile Christians throughout Asia Minor [2] and the Antiochian district.

The mischief caused by the North Galatian theory is not merely that it produces erroneous ideas on many points, but that it shuts the eyes to many other points. Here, for example, it deprives us of all evidence in the New Testament for the feeling that existed between Paul and the Antiochian Church after the events narrated in Acts XV and Galatians II ff.

It will hardly be advanced as an argument against Antioch as the place of origin that Syria and Antioch are mentioned in the letter by name, and that Paul does not say "hither" in place of "to Antioch," II 11. In 1 Corinthians, which was written at Ephesus, he used the expression, "at Ephesus," and mentions "Asia".

[1] For example, Mr. Baring Gould's interesting *Study of St. Paul.*

[2] Reasons for this view are stated in chaps. XII, XV, XVII of my *Cities and Bishoprics of Phrygia,* on the history of the Christians and the Jews in Phrygia.

Dr. Clemen has rightly recognised the force that lies in the phrase, "all the brethren with me," and he explains it by dating the composition of Galatians immediately after Romans, when all the delegates of the Churches were with Paul.[1] It may be fully granted that this would explain quite satisfactorily the use of the phrase ; but other considerations prevent us from accepting so late a date for the letter.

III

PERSONS MENTIONED IN THE EPISTLE.

The persons mentioned by name in the Epistle are Titus, Cephas Peter, James, John and Barnabas.

Titus was evidently unknown to the Galatians. The point of Paul's reference to him turns on his nationality. He was a Greek, and this is carefully explained in II 3, so that the readers may not fail to catch the drift of the argument. Had the Galatians known Titus, had he accompanied Paul on a journey and been familiar to them, the explanation would have been unnecessary ; and in this Epistle there is not a single unnecessary word.

It is assumed that the Galatians know that Cephas and Peter were the same person ; but we cannot suppose that they were converted without learning who the Twelve Apostles were ; and, even if Paul and Barnabas had not made the Apostles known to them, the Judaising emissaries would have done so, as the whole burden of their argument was that James, Peter, etc., were superior in authority to Paul. Yet, even as regards the three, James and Cephas

---

[1] See footnote on p. 243.

and John, the point on which the argument turns—"they who were reputed to be pillars "—is made clear and explicit. Some knowledge about the Apostles is assumed; but the crucial point is expressed, and not merely assumed.

Barnabas, however, is mentioned simply by name, and it is assumed that his personality was familiar to the Galatians—"even Barnabas was carried away ". The whole point in this expression lies in Barnabas's staunch championship of Gentile rights: it presupposes a knowledge of his action and views. Paul, who even explains that James, Peter and John were the leading Apostles, assumes that Barnabas is so familiar, that his argument will be caught without any explanation. There is only one set of congregations among whom it could be assumed that Barnabas was better known than Peter and James and John. Paul was writing to the Galatians, whom Barnabas and he had converted, and among whom Barnabas had spent many months.

We must conclude that Barnabas was known to the Galatians, while Titus was unknown to them.

Now it is argued in my *St. Paul*, p. 285, that Titus was taken by Paul with him on his third journey (Acts XVIII 23). After that journey, when Titus had spent a good many weeks among the Galatians, it would not have been necessary to explain to them that he was a Greek. On the other hand, it was a telling sequel to the Epistle that Titus, who is quoted as an example to the Galatians, and who was of course one of " the brethren which are with me " and associated in the Epistle, should personally visit the Galatians along with Paul on his next journey. There is a natural connection between the prominence of Titus in Paul's mind during this Galatian crisis and the selection of him as companion among the Galatians. One might almost be prepared to find that, when Paul went on to Ephesus, Titus was left behind for a time in Galatia, confirming the churches and organising the contribution ; and that thereafter he rejoined Paul at Ephesus in time to be sent on a mission for a similar purpose to Corinth.

Now, glance for a moment at the North Galatian theory. It is certain that, according to that view, Barnabas was personally unknown to the North Galatians, while there is a considerable probability that Titus (who was with Paul in Ephesus) had accompanied him all the way from Ephesus, and was therefore known to them. The North Galatian view leaves the tone of the references an insoluble difficulty.

IV

RELATION OF PAUL TO BARNABAS.

It has often been said that Paul is very niggardly here in recognition of Barnabas's work as a champion of Gentile rights. But Paul was not writing a history for the ignorant ; he assumes throughout that the Galatians knew the services of Barnabas. The single phrase " even Barnabas " is a sufficient answer to that charge. The one word " even " recalls the whole past to the interested readers ; it places Barnabas above Peter in this respect. Peter had recognised the apostolate to the Gentiles : Peter had eaten with the Gentiles : but his dissembling, after all that, was not so extraordinary a thing as that " even Barnabas was carried away with the dissimulation " of the other Jews. That one sentence places Barnabas on a pedestal as a leading champion of the Gentiles ; and yet it does not explicitly state that ; it merely assumes the knowledge of his championship among the Galatians.

Further, where Paul speaks of his first journey, *i.e.*, his Gospel to the Galatians,[1] he uses the plural pronoun : "any Gospel other than that which *we* preached unto you " (I 8); "as *we* have said before, so say I now again " (I 9).

The Galatians caught the meaning of " we " in these cases as " Barnabas and I ". On the other hand, where the reference is to the division which had now come into existence between the Galatians and their evangelist, Barnabas is not included, and the singular pronoun is used (IV 12 ff). There was no alienation between the Galatians and Barnabas, for Barnabas had not returned to them ; and, as we shall see, it was through perversion and through real misunderstanding of Paul's conduct on his second journey that the division arose.

V

" I MARVEL."

After the introductory address—the heading of the letter, so to say—Paul usually begins the body of the letter with an expression of thanks (so Rom., 1 Cor., Phil., Col., 1 and 2 Thess., 2 Tim., Philem.), or of blessing (so 2 Cor., Eph.) —some acknowledgment of the Divine care and kindness in respect of his correspondents and himself.

In so doing he was following the customary polite form in ordinary Greek letters. In those letters, after the super-

[1] It is important to observe that when Paul speaks of the Gospel to the Galatians, he means the message which converted them, *i.e.*, on his first visit.

scription giving the names and titles of the writer and of the person or persons addressed, there was usually added some acknowledgment of the Divine power, such as : " if you are well and successful, it would be in accordance with my constant prayer to the Gods : " or " before all things I pray that you may be in health ; " but in case of haste, eagerness, excitement or anger, this conventional part of the letter was often omitted. Now " courtesy of address to all was valued by Paul as an element in the religious life ; and he advised his pupils to learn from the surrounding world everything that was worthy in it, . . . ' whatsoever is courteous, whatsoever is of fine expression, all excellence, all merit, take account of these,' wherever you find these qualities, notice them, imitate them ".[1] So here, " it is Paul's Greek environment and his Greek education that are responsible for the expressions which he uses ".[2] In all his own life and words, and in all his teaching to others, he takes up " the most gracious and polished tone of educated society " ; but as all the forms of politeness and courtesy in ordinary life had a religious tone and acknowledged the gods, he changed them so far as to give them a Christian turn (though sometimes the change might almost have been adopted by an enlightened pagan), acknowledging God in place of the gods.

The exceptions are 1 Timothy and Titus (in which he plunges at once into the important business of Church order and teaching, the cause of the letters), and the Gala-

---

[1] Deissmann, *Bibelstudien*, p. 207 ff ; Rendel Harris, *Expositor*, Sept., 1898, p. 163 ff ; *St. Paul the Trav.*, p. 149.

[2] Harris, *loc. cit.*, p. 165. So in *St. Paul the Trav.*, p. 149, " it is the educated citizen of the Roman world who speaks in these and many other sentences ".

tian letter, which differs from all others. Not merely is
there no expression of thankfulness ; Paul goes at once to
the business in hand, " I marvel that ye are so quickly
removing," and then he pronounces a curse on any one,
man or angel from heaven, who preaches to the Galatians
" any gospel other than that which we preached unto you "
—" any gospel other than that which ye received ". The
reference, of course, is to the message which converted the
Galatians, the Gospel which originally called them from
darkness to light.

The intense feeling under which Paul was labouring is
shown by the unique character of the opening, and by the
strength—one might say, the violence—of the language.
Anything that is said in this first paragraph must be understood as being of overwhelming importance. Paul here
touches the crucial point of the Galatian difficulty.

VI

"YE ARE SO QUICKLY REMOVING."

The position of these words in the opening of the letter
shows that we must lay the utmost stress on them. Paul
had evidently heard nothing of the steps by which the
Galatians had passed over to the Judaising side. We may
assume, of course, that there were steps : however rapidly,
from one point of view, it came about, time is required to
change so completely the religion of several cities so widely
separated. But Paul had heard nothing of the intermediate steps. He heard suddenly that the Galatian
Churches are crossing over to the Judaistic side. This
point requires notice.

In the case of the Corinthian Church, we can trace in
the two Epistles the development of the Judaising tendency.   In the first Epistle it hardly appears.   The difficulties and errors which are there mentioned are rather
the effect of the tone and surroundings of Hellenic paganism : lax morality, and a low conception of purity and
duty, are more obvious than the tendency to follow Judaising teachers.   There is a marked tendency in Paul's tone
to make allowance for the Judaic point of view : the writer
is quite hopeful of maintaining union and friendly relations
with the Jewish community.   We observe here much the
same stage as that on which the Galatian Churches stood
at Paul's second visit (Acts XVI 1-5) : then, also, Paul was
full of consideration for the Jews, hopeful of unity, ready
to go to the furthest possible point in conciliating them by
showing respect to their prejudices, delivering the Apostolic
Decree, and charging them to observe its prohibition of
meats offered to idols and of those indulgences which were
permitted by universal consent in pagan society.   In 1
Corinthians his instruction is to the same general effect,
though delivered with much greater insight into the practical bearing and the philosophic basis of the rules of life
which he lays down.   He had learned in the case of the
Galatian Churches what mistaken conceptions the Apostolic Decree was liable to rouse, if it were delivered to
his converts as a law for them to keep : he knew that, if
there were any opening left, the ordinary man would
understand that the Decree would be taken as a sort of
preparation for, and imperfect stage leading up to, the
whole Law.   His instructions to the Corinthians are carefully framed so as to guard against the evils which had
been experienced in Galatia ; and yet the principles and

rules which he lays down represent exactly his conception
of the truth embodied in the Apostolic Decree.[1]   The theme
in 1 Corinthians is the statement of the moral and philosophical basis on which rested the external and rather crude
rules embodied in that Decree.

On the other hand, in 2 Corinthians the old evils are
sensibly diminished, to Paul's great joy and thankfulness,
but a new evil is coming in, *viz.*, the tendency to Judaism.
This, however, is not yet so far advanced in Corinth as it
was in Galatia when Galatians was written.   It is only
beginning.   It is a suggestive fact that Romans, written
six or nine months later than 2 Corinthians, speaks of
the Judaising tendency as a danger in a stage similiar to
Galatians ; and Dr. Drescher, in a most admirable article
in *Theologische Studien und Kritiken*, 1897, p. 1 ff, remarks
that Paul, in writing to the Roman Church, with which he
had never come into personal relations, and about whose
position and difficulties he had only second-hand information,[2] was guided greatly by the circumstances of the
Corinthian congregation, in the midst of which he was
writing.[3]   Dr. Sanday and Mr. Headlam are, on the whole,
of this opinion.   Corinth, then, early in 57, was where
Galatia stood in 53.[4]

How, then, had Paul been ignorant of the steps in the

[1] See Professor W. Lock's convincing paper in *Expositor*, July,
1897, p. 65.

[2] Reports from Aquila and Priscilla would not be sufficient, though
they may perhaps have elicited the letter.   Acts XXVIII shows that
the Judaistic difficulty had not yet become serious in Rome.

[3] Similarly his Ephesian experiences influence, to some extent, the
tone of 1 Corinthians and the early part of 2 Corinthians.

[4] The dates given in *St. Paul the Trav.* are assumed, in order to
show the interval.

Galatian defection? That was natural, on the South Galatian view. The rapid and unforeseeable changes of his life after his second Galatian visit made it impossible for exchange of letters and messages to take place.[1] Even after he went to Corinth he was still looking for the expected opening in Macedonia (which he understood to be his appointed field), until the new message was given him (Acts XVIII 9).

But on the North Galatian view, Paul was resident in Ephesus for over two years after leaving Galatia, and this residence was in accordance with his previous intention (Acts XVIII 21). Those who place the composition of Galatians after Romans cannot explain Paul's ignorance, for it is as certain as anything in that far away time can be that there was almost daily communication between Ephesus and Pisidian Antioch.[2] The commoner view, which places Galatians as early as possible in the Ephesian residence, reduces the difficulty; but still leaves it unexplained why Paul's news was so sudden and so completely disastrous, why he had no preparation. Yet the tone of these opening words is inexplicable, unless the news had come like a thunderclap from a clear sky.

VII

CAUSE OF THE GALATIAN MOVEMENT.

In order to illustrate the Galatian situation, let us suppose that at the present day a race, which had been converted to Christianity by Protestant missionaries, was

---

[1] See above, p. 242.

[2] Not so frequent between Ancyra and Ephesus; but even in that case there was easy communication, see Lightfoot, p. 25.

soon afterwards visited by Roman Catholic missionaries, and that it was as a whole strongly affected by the more imposing ritual of that form of Christianity and "was quickly removing" to it. Would any one be content to explain the situation as an instance and a proof of the "fickleness" of the race, which thus went over? One who summed up the situation in that way would be at once rebuked for his superficiality, and told that he must look for some more deep-seated reason why the race was inclined to prefer the more sensuous and imposing ritual of the second form to the stern simplicity of their original Christianity.

So in the Galatian movement, we must regard it as superficial, if any one explains that movement as caused by the "fickleness" of the Galatians. A race does not change its religion through fickleness : it changes, because it believes the new form to be better or truer or more advantageous than the old. We must try to understand the reason of a notable religious movement in Galatia, and not delude ourselves by misleading and superficial talk about Galatian fickleness.

It is characteristic of the unscientific nature of the North Galatian theory that it lays such stress on the "fickleness" of the Galatians as the one great cause of their religious movement.

Now what cause does Paul regard as lying at the bottom of the Galatian movement? There is not throughout the whole Epistle a word or a sentence to suggest that he attributed it to fickleness. The verse which we are considering merely states a fact—" you are so quickly removing from him that called you in the grace of Christ unto a different Gospel "—and there is not the slightest justification for reading into it an explanation of the cause of removal. See § XLII, pp. 193 ff, 323 f, 449.

Moreover, Paul shows throughout the Epistle that he saw certain causes for the Galatian movement, and that fickleness was not one of them. The causes will become clear as we go over the ground. Here briefly it may be said that they partly lay in misconceptions into which the Galatians had fallen through false impressions and false information conveyed to them by others, and partly in the natural tendency to recur to certain religious forms to which the Galatians had been accustomed as pagans, or, as St. Paul puts it, to "turn back to the weak and beggarly rudiments," IV 9.

In fact, the whole Epistle is the explanation of the causes of removal, which it counteracts and undermines.

VIII

PAUL AS A JUDAISTIC PREACHER, I. 6-10.

We have remarked in § V. on the intense feeling shown in this paragraph. Any topic that is touched on in these verses must be taken as a point of transcendent importance in the Galatian difficulty. Why, then, does Paul lay such stress on the supposition that he[1] may begin to preach a different Gospel ? Can anything be more improbable ? Why does he waste time on such a possibility ? What part does that supposition play in the Galatian difficulty ?

We are bound to the view that the supposition here

---

[1] ἡμεῖς, Paul and his companion in preaching,. As Lightfoot says, " St. Paul seems never to use the plural when speaking of himself alone " ; yet *cp.* 2 Cor. VI 11.

introduced in this emphatic position was really a serious
element in the Galatian trouble : *i.e.*, the Galatians had
acquired the opinion that Paul had somehow been conveying a different message, a new Gospel,[1] contrary to the
Gospel which they received from him on the first visit.
This opinion, of course, had been instilled into them by
the Judaistic emissaries, who had been preaching in the
Galatian Churches since Paul's second visit. In V 11
Paul returns to the same topic. " If," he says, " I still
preach circumcision." Here there is an unmistakable
reference to an assertion made by the Judaistic preachers
that Paul himself had been preaching the Gospel of circumcision ; and it is noteworthy that here again Paul uses
an expression of the most vehement indignation, " I would
that they which unsettle you would even cut themselves
off.[2] It was this accusation of having preached an anti-
Pauline Gospel that hurt Paul and made him use such
strong language in both places where he refers to it.

But was not the accusation too absurd ? It was, however, believed by the Galatians, for otherwise Paul would
have suffered it to "pass by him as the idle wind ". Its
danger and its sting lay in the fact that the Galatians were
misled by it. Now they could not have believed it merely
on the bare, uncorroborated assertion of the Judaisers
There must have been a certain appearance of difference
in Paul's teaching on his second visit, which gave some
support to the statements and arguments of the Judaistic
teachers, and so helped to mislead the Galatians.

We turn, therefore, to the history, as recorded by Luke,
and ask whether it can explain how the Gospel which the

---

[1] So Lightfoot, and (I think) almost every one.

[2] See below, § LII.

Galatians received on the former visit could seem to them discordant with Paul's subsequent action and teaching on his second visit.   Then we see that in Acts XVI, Luke, as always, is offering us the means of understanding the Epistles. On the second journey Paul came delivering to the Galatians (Acts XVI 4) the decree of the Apostles in Jerusalem. That might fairly seem to be an acknowledgment that those Apostles were the higher officials, and he was their messenger.   He circumcised Timothy.   That might readily be understood as an acknowledgment that the higher stages of Christian life [1] were open only through obedience to the whole Law of Moses : in other words, that, as a concession to human weakness, the Gentiles were admitted by the Apostolic Decree to the lower standard of the Church on the performance of part of the Law, but that the perfecting of their position as Christians could be attained only by compliance with the whole Law.   It is clear from Galatians III 3 that this distinction between a lower and more perfect stage of Christian life was in the minds of the persons to whom Paul was writing.   However different Paul's real motive was in respect of Timothy, the view of his action suggested by the Judaistic teachers was a very plausible one, and evidently had been accepted by the Galatians.   The action, in truth, was one easy to misunderstand, and not easy to sympathise with.

Moreover, the Decree itself was quite open to this construction.   "It seemed good to lay upon you no greater burden than these necessary things"—this expression can plausibly be interpreted to imply the ellipsis, "but, if you voluntarily undertake a heavier burden, we shall praise you

---

[1] On the predisposition of the Galatians to recognise two stages, lower and higher, in religious knowledge, see § XXVII.

for your zeal in doing more than the necessary minimum."
To zealous and enthusiastic devotees, such as the Asia
Minor races were,[1] this interpretation was very seductive.
They doubtless had heard from Paul of Peter's speech
(Acts XV 10), in which he protested against putting on
them a yoke too heavy; but, under the stimulus of en-
thusiasm, they responded to the Judaists that they could
and would support that yoke, however heavy.

Moreover, the Galatians had been used to a religion in
which such ritualistic acts (τὰ στοιχεῖα τοῦ κόσμου, IV 3)
were a prominent part; and it was natural that they
should again "turn to the weak and beggarly elements".
The result of the whole series of events described in Acts
would naturally be that the Galatians were predisposed
to follow the Judaistic emissaries, and to think that Paul
on his second visit was preaching another Gospel, and
that this second Gospel was the true Gospel, as being
brought from the real Apostles, the pillars of the Church.

This misinterpretation of his conduct, with all the danger
it involved, Paul had to meet at the outset. It was fundamental; and until it was put out of the way he could make
no progress in setting the Galatians right. He meets it,
not by mere denial and disproof (which is always rather
ineffective), but by the intense and vehement outburst:
" If Silas or I, or an angel from heaven, preach to you any
Gospel other than that which Barnabas and I preached
unto you, a curse on him!"

On the South Galatian theory the language of Paul here
is quite naturally and probably explained. Now let us
compare the North Galatian view.

---

[1] See pp. 36 ff, 196.

It is quite allowed by North Galatian theorists that the foundation for the misrepresentation of Paul's teaching alluded to in I 6-10 and V 11 lay (as we also assume) in his action on his second journey.[1] Thus they are face to face with a serious difficulty. Holding that the Galatian Churches were converted on the second journey, they have to show how Paul's teaching on the third journey (Acts XVIII 23), could appear to the Galatians more Judaistic than his teaching on the second (Acts XVIII 1-5). They cannot do so, and they do not attempt it.

It does not seem permissible to think that Paul's supposed teaching in the North Galatian cities could be materially different in spirit from his action and preaching in South Galatia a few weeks or months previously. The words of Acts XVI 5 must be taken as a proof that throughout the second journey Paul charged all his hearers to observe the Apostles' Decree; and, considering the ease and frequency of communication between the various Jewish settlements in Asia Minor, the North Galatian Jews must have known from the first about Paul's action to Timothy : in fact, the intention was that they should know. It would therefore be absurd to suppose that it was only after the third journey that their Galatian pagan neighbours came to learn what Paul had been doing in South Galatia on the second journey, and to draw their conclusions therefrom.

IX

ANOTHER GOSPEL, I 6-7.

According to the Revised Version Paul here says to the Galatians, " I marvel that ye are so quickly removing from

[1] See, *e.g.*, Lightfoot's note on Gal. II 3.

him that called you in the grace of Christ unto a different gospel; which is not another *gospel:* only there are some that trouble you and would pervert the Gospel of Christ ".

According to that rendering the force of the sentence lies in the pointed antithesis between two Greek words, ἕτερον and ἄλλο : the Galatians have gone over to a gospel which is ἕτερον and not ἄλλο : this expression is taken to mean a gospel which is essentially different, and is not another gospel, *i.e.*, is not a second example of the genus gospel. But that rendering, though widely accepted, rests on a mistaken idea of the meaning of the two Greek words, when contrasted with one another.

We are forced here to enter on a technical point of grammar, *viz.*, the exact signification of these two Greek words, when their difference is brought emphatically before the reader by close juxtaposition. Those who do not care to read the grammatical discussion on this point may rest assured that, before venturing to differ from so great a scholar as Lightfoot on such a subject, the writer consulted several excellent scholars ; and that, since the view here stated as to the force of the two Greek words was first published,[1] it has been approved by several distinguished authorities as undeniable.

It is clear that Lightfoot's usually accurate and thorough sense for Greek language was here misled by a theological theory : he thought that a certain meaning was necessary, and he proceeded to find arguments in its support, declaring that ἕτερος involves a difference of kind and means " unlike," " opposite," while ἄλλος implies " one besides," " another example of the same kind ".

[1] *Expositor*, Aug., 1895, p. 115 ff, briefly repeated in *Expositor*, July, 1898, p. 20 ff.

On the contrary, the truth is precisely the opposite. When the two words are pointedly contrasted with one another, ἕτερος means "a second," "another of the same kind," "new" (*e.g.*, "a new king succeeds in regular course to the throne"), while ἄλλος implies difference of kind. It is fully acknowledged by every one, and is stated clearly in the ordinary standard lexicons, that each of the two words is susceptible of meaning "different," and that almost every sense of the one in Greek literature can be paralleled by examples in which the other is used in the same way, so that cases can be quoted in which ἄλλος means "another example of a class," or in which ἕτερος means "unlike," "opposite".

But the point is this : When ἕτερος and ἄλλος are pointedly contrasted with one another, which of the two indicates the greater degree of difference? what is the original and fundamental distinction between them? Our contention is that in such cases, ἕτερος indicates specific difference, ἄλλος generic difference—ἕτερος expresses the slighter difference between two examples of the same class, ἄλλος the broader difference between two distinct classes. Hence Professor F. Blass, in distinguishing the two words as employed in the New Testament,[1] says that ἕτερος is in place in the sense of a second division (*eine zweite Ab-theilung*). It would not be grammatically wrong, though it would be harsh and awkward, to write in Greek about a pair of things τὸ μὲν ἕτερον ἄλλο ἐστί, τὸ δὲ ἕτερον ἄλλο "the one is quite different from the other".

Some examples may be quoted. In *Iliad*, XIII 64, ὄρνεον ἄλλο means "a bird of a different class"; [2] and

---

[1] *Grammatik des N. T. Griechisch,* p. 175 f.
[2] ἀλλόφυλον as the Scholiast explains.

ἕτερον would be hardly conceivable there, as the natural interpretation would be " another bird of the same class," " a second eagle ". So in *Iliad*, XXI 22, the fish of other kinds (ἰχθύες ἄλλοι) are chased by the dolphin ; but ἰχθύες ἕτεροι would more naturally be applied to dolphins chasing one another in play.

Again, ἑτερόπλους was used to designate an insurance effected on a vessel for the outward, but not for the return voyage, but ἀλλόπλους could not possibly bear that meaning.

Mr. R. A. Neil quotes Thucydides, II 40, 2 f, where ἑτέροις indicates another class of the Athenians (*viz.*, the industrial as distinguished from the military or the statesman class), while ἄλλοις denotes other nations as distinguished from the Athenians. He also refers to Aristotle, *Politics*, II 5, p. 1263, a. 8, ἑτέρων ὄντων τῶν γεωργούντων ἄλλος ἂν εἴη τρόπος, translating " if the farming class is a distinct sub-class of the general body of citizens, then the form of communism would be quite different (from what it would be if all citizens were farmers) ".

Professor I. Bywater points out that Bonitz recognises the same distinction between ἕτερος λόγος and ἄλλος λόγος in Aristotle, *Index Aristotel*, p. 290, b. 19.

Mr. A. Souter quotes Plato, *Protag.*, 329D-330B, where ἕτερος indicates the members of a class when all are homogeneous, ἄλλος the members of a class when each differs in kind from the other. Socrates there says—if we may put the meaning in brief—" the different parts of the whole class called gold are not different from one another (οὐδὲν διαφέρει τὰ ἕτερα τῶν ἑτέρων), except in respect of size ; but the different parts of the whole class called virtue (*i.e.*, the special virtues) are quite different in character each from the others (ἕκαστον αὐτῶν ἔστιν ἄλλο, τὸ δὲ ἄλλο [1]).

Even the derivation of the two words shows clearly what is the fundamental idea in each : ἕτερος, ἕ-τερυ-ς, is a comparative degree of the pronominal stem meaning "one" or "same," while ἄλλος is connected with words in many languages which bear the sense of "other" or "different," *e.g.*, *else* in English, *alius* in Latin.

In later Greek the tendency of these two adjectives to pass into the sense of each other became steadily stronger.

In view of this grammatical investigation and the examples quoted, it is not possible within the limits of the Greek language to admit the translation as advocated by Lightfoot and many others, "a different gospel, which is not another, a second Gospel, *i.e.*, which is not a Gospel at all".[2]

This result is not likely to be disputed by any scholar ; but it is more difficult to say what is the exact meaning that Paul intended to convey. There are two alternatives ;[3] and no third seems possible.

The simplest, and perhaps the best, is that which the American revisers give in the margin, deleting the punctuation after ἄλλο : "a different gospel which is nothing else save that there are some that . . . would pervert the Gospel of Christ," in other words "another Gospel which is merely a perversion of the Gospel". This is quite good Greek.[4]

---

[1] Equivalent to τὸ μὲν ἄλλο, τὸ δὲ ἄλλο : Stallbaum quotes instances of similar omission of τὸ μέν.

[2] ἕτερον εὐαγγέλιον ὃ οὐκ εστιν ἄλλο · εἰ μή τινες κτλ.

[3] Both are clearly stated in the articles in *Expositor*, pp. 118 and 22, quoted above, p. 261.

[4] The construction οὔκ ἐστιν ἄλλο εἰ μή τινες κτλ is quite correct, and needs no quotation of examples to defend it.

It also gives a perfectly apposite and perfectly Pauline sense, and probably most scholars will prefer it.[1] Professor Blass, in a letter to the writer, strongly advocates it.

Another sense—less probable perhaps, but more vigorous and more characteristic of Paul's habit of compressing his meaning into the fewest words and sometimes straining the force of words—would be to accept the exact punctuation given by Lightfoot and the revisers. Then we should render, " I marvel that you are so quickly going over to another gospel, which is not a different gospel (from mine), except in so far as certain persons pervert the Gospel of Christ". This is equivalent to " I marvel that you are so quickly going over from the gospel as announced by me to another gospel (as announced by the older Apostles), not that it is really different from mine (for the older Apostles agree with me), except in so far as it is distorted by the emissaries who have been and still are troubling you ".

That exactly expresses Paul's position. The gospel as preached by him was a ἕτερον εὐαγγέλιον from the gospel as preached by the older Apostles, but there was no real difference between them ; they were only two practically homogeneous members of the same class. Peter and James agreed with him on every important point. But there were Jews who came as emissaries from Jerusalem, and yet preached a totally different gospel ; these are simply distorters and perverters of the Gospel.

The difficulties in the way of this second alternative, which are likely to prevent most scholars from accepting it, are these :—

First, it may be argued that by the time when Paul wrote,

[1] The last seven words are taken *verbatim* from *Expositor*, Aug., 1896, p. 118.

the original distinction between the two Greek words had been lost to such a degree that a pointed contrast between them could not have suggested itself to his mind ; that would lead to a much more detailed study of the words than has ever been made, a study which would be out of place here.

Secondly, in 2 Cor. XI 4, Paul speaks of ἕτερον εὐαγγέλιον, ἄλλον Ἰησοῦν, ἄλλο πνεῦμα, using the two adjectives as practically equivalent.

X

"SEEKING TO PLEASE MEN," I 10.

In the *Expositor*, July, 1897, p. 66, Professor W. Locke pointed out in a most illuminative paper that, "in order to comprehend many passages in Paul's letters, we must understand that certain phrases represent the substance, if not the actual words, of the taunts levelled in speech against him by his Jewish-Christian opponents " ; and, to make this clear, he prints those phrases between inverted commas.

The phrases, " persuade men," and " seek to please men " in Galatians I 10 are evidently of this nature. Paul was accused by the Judaising emissaries of trimming his words and ideas to suit the people among whom he was : it was said that in Jerusalem he Judaised, as when he concurred in the Decree : in Galatia among the Gentiles he made the Jews of no account: even when he brought the Decree at the order of the greater Apostles, he minimised and explained it away to suit the Galatians, but yet, to please the Jews, he circumcised Timothy. It was easy to distort

Paul's method of adapting himself to his audience and "becoming all things to all men," so as to make this accusation very dangerous and plausible.

He recurs later to the taunts mentioned here ; and in VI 17 he dismisses them with the words, "from henceforth let no man trouble me ". In both places his answer is the same : he appeals to the sufferings which he has endured because of his teaching. If he had sought to please men, he would not be the slave of Christ : he bears in his body the marks of the Lord Jesus, for the marks left in his body by the stones at Lystra (and probably by the lictors' rods at Antioch and Lystra, *St. Paul*, pp. 107, 304), brand him as the slave of Jesus.[1] He leaves the Galatians to judge from his life whether he has aimed at pleasing men or at serving God.

XI

TONE OF ADDRESS TO THE GALATIANS.

This opening paragraph, I 6-10, does not merely show the intense feeling that raged in Paul's mind : it is also a revelation of Galatian nature. His power of vividly presenting the situation in all its reality before his own mind made him, in the moment of writing, as fully conscious of his correspondents' nature and mind as he was of himself. Things presented themselves to him, as he wrote, in the form which would most impress his Galatian readers. It was that intense sympathetic comprehension of the nature of others that made him such a power among men. Hence, in this Epistle, you see the whole nature of the Galatian

---

[1] On the marking of slaves in Asia Minor, see p. 84.

converts spread open before you; and it is not the bold, proud, self-assertive nature of a northern race, like the Gauls, that is here revealed. Let any one who has some knowledge of the difference between Oriental nature and the nature of the "barbarians" from the north-western lands, or who has studied the ancient picture of those Gauls who swept in their small bands over Asia, trampling in the dust the multitudinous armies of great kings and populous cities, those fierce, haughty, self-respecting barbarians, keenly sensitive to insult, careless of danger or wounds, settled as an aristocratic and con-quering caste among a far more numerous race of subject Phrygians—let any such person judge for himself whether this paragraph, or the fresh start, III 1 ff, is the way to address such an audience : the tone of authority, of speak-ing from a higher platform, is exactly what a man of tact would carefully avoid. But many modern writers seem never to have considered what was the position of the Gauls in Galatia. They write as if Paul were addressing simple-minded, peaceful tribes of gentle South Sea islan-ders, whom he treats as his children. The Gauls were an aristocracy settled for nearly three centuries as nobles among plebeians, like the Normans among the Saxons in England.

But this very tone, brief and authoritative, is the effec-tive method of addressing the native races of Asia Minor. It is so now, and it was the same in ancient time, when the very word " Phrygian " was equivalent to "slave". Every traveller who mixes with the people of Anatolia learns how necessary is the " touch of authority '" mixed with frank-ness and courtesy. On this point I can only appeal to those who know ; and add the statement that the best possible illustration of the tone of this whole Epistle is the experience of the traveller.[1]

This difference of tone from all other Epistles has, of course, been noticed by every one, and is usually explained as due to anger. But Paul, even if angry, was not one of those persons who lose their temper and say injudicious things : while deeply moved, he only became more resolute and alert and watchful : the tone of this letter is misunderstood by those who fail to read in it the character of the persons to whom it is addressed. See § XXII.

XII

THE GOSPEL WHICH YE RECEIVED.

The whole paragraph becomes most clear if we understand that " the Gospel which ye received " refers definitely to the occasion and manner in which the good news was first received by the Church or the individual. Similarly the announcement of the word (ἀγγελία τοῦ λόγου) mentioned in Acts XV 36, took place on the first journey : on that journey the apostles brought the good news to Antioch and Lystra and Derbe (Acts XIII 32 ; XIV 7, 15, 21). But on the second and third journeys " strengthening " is the term employed (XVI ; compare XV 41, XVIII 23). In Acts XV 35 διδάσκοντες καὶ εὐαγγελιζόμενοι describes the two processes of teaching the converts and carrying the good news to those who had not yet heard it.

In view of this difference it is highly probable that Paul's second visit to Galatia was a brief one, in which he con-

---

[1] See above, pp. 33, 195, and *Impressions of Turkey*, p. 27 ff.

fined his attention to strengthening and instructing the converts without seeking to carry on a further process of evangelisation. That has been assumed on the authority of Acts in the reckoning of time in my *Church in the Roman Empire*, p. 85 ; and it seems to gather strength from the language of Galatians. Εὐαγγελισάμεθα and παρελάβετε refer to the single occasion when the Churches were formed, the first journey ; and the instruction given on the second journey is distinguished from it. Paul does not trouble himself to prove that the second message was consistent with the first. He merely says, " if the second message was different, a curse be upon me : you must cleave to the first, which came direct from God ".

The point, then, which Paul sets before himself is not to show that he has always been consistent in his message, but to show that the original message which he brought to the Galatians came direct from God to him. If he makes them feel that, then the other accusation of later inconsistency on his part will disappear of itself.

This method is obviously far the most telling. Even if Paul, by a lengthened proof (always difficult to grasp for those who are not very eager to grasp it), had proved that he had really been consistent, that did not show that he was right or his message divine. On the other hand, if he showed that his first message was divine, then the Galatians would from their own mind and conscience realise what was the inner nature and meaning of his conduct on the second journey.

The line of proof is, first, an autobiographical record of the facts bearing upon his original Gospel to the Galatians, and thereafter an appeal to their own knowledge that through this first Gospel they had received the Spirit.

That was the ultimate test of divine origin. Nothing could give them the Spirit and the superhuman power of the Spirit except a divine Gospel.

XIII

DATES OF THE AUTOBIOGRAPHY.

Paul in this retrospect mentions a number of events in his past life. The question has been keenly debated whether the dates which he prefixes to some of the events are intended to mark the interval between each and the preceding event, or the period that separates each from his conversion. Let us put down the facts clearly. The following events are mentioned :—

1. The conversion and call to the Gentiles (I 15, 16). This is the starting-point, and is therefore introduced by ὅτε.

2. εὐθέως, the retiring to Arabia ; καὶ πάλιν the return to Damascus (I 17). Probably it would be right to number these as 2 and 3 ; but I refrain from doing so, lest I seem to some to press the reasoning too hard. It would strengthen my argument to class them as two distinct facts.

3. ἔπειτα μετὰ τρία ἔτη, the first visit to Jerusalem, and the stay of fifteen days there (I 18, 19).

4. ἔπειτα, the retiring to Syria and Cilicia, and continuance there (I 21-24)

5. ἔπειτα διὰ δεκατεσσάρων ἐτῶν, the second visit to Jerusalem (II 1-10).[1]

---

[1] The form of II 11 ff implies that it is not a sixth item in this retrospect. There is no ἔπειτα or other similar word to introduce it. It is marked by a new ὅτε as a fresh start, parallel to I 15.

The form of this list with the repetition of ἔπειτα seems, so far as I may judge, to mark it as a compact enumeration, in which the reader is intended to hold the whole together in his mind, and to think of each as a fact in a continuing biographical series. The thought is, as it were, " In the Divine reckoning my life begins from the conversion and call to the Gentiles. In the gradual working out of that call there are the following stages ; but in thinking of my life, you must hold always in mind the epoch-making fact of the conversion ; if you would understand my life, you must refer every act in it to that primary revelation of the will of God in me ". Hence all the numbers must be interpreted with reference to the great epoch. To consider that in this biographical enumeration each new item, as it were, blots out the previous one, so that the numbers are to be reckoned as intervals that elapsed from one item to the following, is to lose the dominance of the central and epoch-making event, which is never absent from Paul's mind.

And is it not true even now ? On our conception of that one event depends our whole view of Paul's life. So far as we understand his conversion, do we understand the man. My argument in this section is the same thought which I would apply to Paul's whole life ; and, if I be granted time and opportunity, I would write his life with that thought always dominant : " You understand nothing in Paul unless you take it in its relation to his conversion ". He that fails to do that in any case fails entirely : there is but one way, and he that misses it goes wrong inevitably in his conception of Paul's work.

It was a true instinct that led the Church to take the conversion as the day of St. Paul. For other saints and martyrs their day of celebration was their *dies natalis*, the day on which they entered on their real life, their day of martyrdom. But the *dies natalis* of St. Paul, the day on which his true life began, was the day of his conversion.

We follow that instinct here, and reckon all the events in this autobiography by reference to that thought, always dominant in his mind, and which ought always to be dominant in the reader's mind—his conversion.

Further, we observe that those who take the other view of the meaning of these numbers always argue as if the list consisted of three events : (1) conversion, (2) first visit to Jerusalem, (3) second visit. But Paul, by the form of the list, marks it as containing either five or six separate items, each introduced in a similar way ; and it does violence to the form of expression which here rose naturally in Paul's mind, if it be declared that the other items are to be dropped entirely out of sight, and we are to think only of the three.

If he had intended the two estimates of time as marking the intervals between the items of his list, he would have indicated in his expression that the list contained only three items.

Again, Paul never neglected the most vigorous and incisive way of putting his thought : he neglects rhetorical verbosity, but he never neglects, he could not neglect, the effect that is given by putting facts in their most striking form. Here the numbers derive their effect on his readers' minds from their greatness ; and, if he had been able to use the number 17, he would inevitably (according to my conception of his nature) have taken the expression which enabled him to use the larger number.

In using this passage for chronological reckoning, it

must be borne in mind that Paul's words, μετὰ τρία ἔτη, etc., do not correspond to our "three years after". For example, counting from A.D. 31, μετὰ τρία ἔτη would be A.D. 33, "the third year after"; but "three years after," in our expression, would imply A.D. 34.

This rule of interpretation is regular in ancient times; the day or year which forms the starting point is reckoned in the sum. But in the modern system the starting point is not so reckoned. Thus we count that three days after Sunday means Wednesday; but the ancients reckoned that three days after Sunday implied Tuesday. Much unnecessary difficulty, and not a few unnecessary charges of inaccuracy against ancient writers, have resulted from neglect of this rule. For example, the lapse of time in the journey from Philippi to Jerusalem (Acts XX and XXI) has been generally reckoned wrongly; and it has been gravely discussed whether or not Luke intends to bring out that Paul reached Jerusalem in time for the feast of Pentecost, which was his object. This difficulty is created simply by modern inattention to the old way of reckoning.

Similarly, as to Paul's residence in Ephesus: Luke gives the time as two full years and three months (Acts XIX 8, 10), while Paul speaks of it as three years (Acts XX 31). This had been stigmatised as a discrepancy—with the complacent self-satisfaction of the hasty critic, far removed above mere vulgar accuracy; but two years and a few months was regularly spoken of as three years by the ancients, just as we call the nineteenth century anything above eighteen hundred.

But as the best example of ancient usage in regard to reckoning of time let us take the pathetic story—a stock subject with the Roman moralists—of the death of the two sons of Aemilius Paullus almost contemporaneously with his gorgeous triumph after the conquest of Macedonia.

Cicero [1] says that Paullus lost two sons in seven days. Livy [2] says that the elder son died five days before the triumph, and the younger three days after. According to our method of counting there is a contradiction between these statements. But in a matter which was so striking and so famous, we should expect that the numbers would be accurately preserved. Cicero's words would be as effective if he had said "in eight days," and the Roman had no conception of a seven days' week, which might lead him to say roughly seven days in preference to the exact number, eight. The reason for specifying an exact number in such a case is that the writer knew it to be right; yet here, two good authorities contradict each other.

But on the Roman method of counting all is quite simple, and the two accounts agree exactly. Say that the elder son died on Wednesday; then the fifth day after, to a Roman, was Sunday. On Sunday the triumph was celebrated. The third day after Sunday was Tuesday, and the younger son died on this the seventh day after his brother's death.

XIV

THE PROVINCE OF SYRIA AND CILICIA, I 21.

The expression rendered in the Revised Version, "the Regions of Syria and Cilicia," has been treated by some scholars as describing two countries; and they seek to find a discrepancy between Galatians I 21 and Acts IX 30, as if in the former it were asserted that Paul visited Syria

---

[1] Cicero, *Ad. Fam.*, IV 6, 1.   [2] Livy, XLV 40.

first and afterwards Cilicia, whereas in the Acts it is stated
that he went direct to Tarsus. Then other commentators
seek to avoid this inference, some by pointing out that on
the way to Cilicia he would remain at Syrian ports long
enough to justify him in saying that he came to Syria and
then to Cilicia, while others argue that his residence at
Antioch during the latter part of the period justifies him
in speaking of both Syria and Cilicia, without implying
that the Syrian visit was before the Cilician.

All these views start from a misconception of Paul's
language and thought. He always thinks and speaks with
his eye on the Roman divisions of the Empire, *i.e.*, the
Provinces, in accordance both with his station as a Roman
citizen and with his invariable and oft-announced principle
of accepting and obeying the existing government. Thus
he speaks of Achaia, Asia, Macedonia, Galatia, Illyricum,
using in each case the Roman names of Provinces, not the
Greek names of countries. Achaia, to the Greeks, denoted
a much smaller territory than to the Romans, and it was
only in rare cases that the Greeks used either Achaia or
Galatia in the wide Roman sense.

But the most striking example of Paul's habit of using
Roman names is τοῦ Ἰλλυρικοῦ in Romans XV 19. The
Greeks used the name Ἰλλυρίς to correspond to the Roman
Illyricum,[1] and employed Ἰλλυρικός only as an adjective.
None but a person who was absolutely Roman in his point
of view could have employed the term Ἰλλυρικόν, and he
could mean by it nothing but " Provincia Illyricum ".[2]

---

[1] So, *e.g.*, Ptolemy, IV 12, and Strabo, often.

[2] It is noteworthy that in 2 Timothy IV 10, Paul speaks of this
same Province as Dalmatia. The difference of name cannot be appealed to as pointing to different authorship of the Pastoral Epistles

The only writers in Greek that use this Græco-Latin term τὸ Ἰλλυρικόν in place of the Greek Ἰλλυρίς are the Roman historian Dion Cassius (in two passages) and the Roman citizen and conqueror Paul, who was looking forward to the Christianisation of the Roman Empire, who counted his progress by Provinces, and planted his steps in their capitals.[1]

In accordance with his usual practice, Paul here thinks and speaks of the Roman Province, which consisted of two great divisions, Syria and Cilicia ; and he designates it by the double name, like *Provincia Bithynia et Pontus.* We must accordingly read τῆς Συρίας καὶ Κιλικίας, with the common article embracing the two parts of one province, according to the original text of א. Although I do not recollect any example of the expression " *Prov. Syria et Cicilia,*" yet the analogy of Bithynia-Pontus is a sufficient defence. It was not possible here to use the simple name of the Province Syria, for if he said that he had gone into the districts of Syria, his meaning would have been mistaken. In those composite Roman Provinces it

and of the Romans; it is merely a sign of the change which was happening during Paul's lifetime. The name Illyricum (universal in early Latin writers) gradually gave place to Dalmatia (which previously was only the southern part of the Province as constituted by Augustus in A.D. 10, the northern division being Liburnia) ; and the common name from 70 onwards was Dalmatia (as Mommsen says, " *wie sie seit der Zeit der Flavier gewöhnlich heisst,*" *Röm. Gesch.,* V, c. VI, p. 184). Suetonius, guided doubtless by his authorities, calls the Province Illyricum under the earlier Emperors, but varies between Dalmatia and Illyricum under Claudius and Otho. Similarly, in the time of Nero, Paul varies, following the common usage, which was evidently swinging definitely over from the old to the new name between 57 and 67.

[1] See also § XXV.

was sometimes necessary for the sake of clearness to designate them by enumerating the parts. For example, the official name for the great provincial festival at Syrian Antioch described it as " common to Syria Cilicia Phœnice," where Phœnice, which is generally reckoned part of Syria, is distinguished from it.[1] Similarly, the governors of the united Provinces Galatia and Cappadocia, desiring on their milestones to express clearly the vast extent of their operations, recorded[2] that they had made the roads of Galatia, Cappadocia, Pontus, Pisidia, Paphlagonia, Lycaonia, and Armenia Minor.

The meaning of I 21, then, is simply that Paul spent the following period of his life in various parts of the Province Syria-Cilicia ; and it confirms the principle of interpretation laid down by Zahn that " Paul never designates any part of the Roman Empire by any other name than that of the Province to which it belonged ; and he never uses any of the old names of countries, except in so far as these had become names of Provinces " (*Einleitung in das N. T.*, p. 124).

XV

THE KLIMATA OF SYRIA AND CILICIA.

Further, the phrase τὰ κλίματα τῆς Συρίας καὶ Κιλικίας should not be understood as " the κλίμα or region of Syria and the κλίμα of Cilicia ". Κλίμα was not used to denote

---

[1] The provincial *cultus* with its ἀγὼν was κοινὸς Συρίας Κιλικίας Φοινείκης (Henzen, *Bull. dell' Inst.*, 1877, p. 109 ; Mommsen, *Res Gestae D. Aug.*, p. 173).

[2] C.I.L., III 312, 318 : even this long list is shortened, see Hastings' *Dict. Bib.*, II, p. 87, also next note.

such a great district as Syria or Cilicia ; and it is unfortunate
that both the Revised and Authorised Versions translate
it by the same term that they used for χώρα in Acts XIV
6, XVI 6, XVIII 23. Χώρα is correctly used to indicate
the great geographical divisions of a province (as in those
cases) ; and we might speak of the χώρα of Cilicia and the
χώρα of Syria, but not of the κλίμα [1] of Cilicia. The regular usage would be τὰ κλίματα Συρίας : compare, *e.g.*, κλίματα
Ἀχαίας in 2 Cor. XI 10 : four small districts in the
west of Cilicia Tracheia were called τὰ κλίματα : [2] Sinope
and Amisos are described as πρὸς τοῖς κλίμασι κείμεναι
(Justinian, *Novella* 28).

It is difficult to define the precise geographical sense
of the word κλίμα ; and, as a rule, scholars scorn to think
about the exact distinction between technical terms of
geography. It has been suggested in the writer's *Historical
Geography of Asia Minor*, p. 417, that the term should be
taken in the sense of " lands sloping back from the sea "
when applied to Sinope, Amisos, and the four Cilician
districts. In other places, however, it seems to have a
vaguer sense, merely as " territory," though possibly there
may be in some of these cases the idea of " frontier territories ".[3] In the *Acta Theodori Syceotae* [4] the κλίμα τῆς
Μνηζινῆς evidently denotes the territory belonging to the
city of Mnêzos, which proves that κλίμα denoted a com-

---

[1] In other words, Roman Cilicia in its entirety was a territory or
region (χώρα) of the province Syria-Cilicia, just as Galatic Phrygia,
Galatic Lycaonia, etc., were territories or regions composing the
Province Galatia. In Cilicia there were many *klimata*.

[2] *Histor. Geogr.*, p. 417, and table facing p. 362.

[3] Dr. Gifford sends the illustrative quotation τῶν μὲν πρὸς Φοινίκην
κεκλιμένων μερῶν καὶ τῶν ἐπὶ θαλάττῃ τόπων, Diodorus, I 17.

[4] Greek text in Joannes Theophili, Μνημεῖα Ἁγιολογικά, p. 394.

paratively small geographical division : in that passage the sense of "frontier district" is quite conceivable, as a village on the upper Siberis near the Paphlagonian frontier is there said to be ὑπὸ τὸ κλίμα τῆς Μνηζινῆς, "classed under the district whose governing centre is Mnêzos".

XVI

THE VISITS TO JERUSALEM, I 18, II 1 ff.

"Then in the third year (after the epoch-making event) I went up to Jerusalem. . . . Then, when the fourteenth year (after the epoch) had come I went up again to Jerusalem."

It would open up too wide a subject to enter on the relation between the narrative of Acts and the account given here of the two visits. It is well known that the reconciliation of this account with Acts presents great difficulties. Some suppose that Luke has omitted a visit which Paul describes, others that Paul has omitted a visit which Luke describes. The overwhelming majority of scholars are agreed that Paul here alludes to the visits described in Acts IX 26 and XV 1 ff; but among them there reigns the keenest controversy. Many hold that Gal. II 1 ff is contradictory of Acts XV, and infer that the latter is not a trustworthy account, but strongly coloured and even distorted. Others, by an elaborate argumentation, prove that the one account is perfectly consistent with the other.

We need not here enter on this large subject. It will be more useful merely to try to construct from Paul's own words the picture which he desired to place before his Galatian readers. He describes a certain historical event.

He paints it from a certain point of view. His object is to rouse a certain idea of it in his Galatian correspondents. It is admitted by all that the author of Acts paints from a different point of view and with a different object. We need not discuss the question whether the two accounts can be harmonised. The Galatians had not before them the book of Acts, and therefore could not proceed to construct a picture by comparing that account with Paul's. Some of them had certainly heard of the visits to Jerusalem before they received this letter; but Paul had been their authority at first; and now he repeats briefly to all what he had said before to some at different times.

Let us then try simply to determine what is the fair and natural interpretation of this sharp and emphatic account. For a historian it would be necessary to add details that Paul did not need for his purpose, but which Luke thought necessary for his history. Each had to omit much from his brief account. Our present purpose is not to write a history; but to study the relations between Paul and the Galatians. What did Paul find it advisable to put before them regarding these visits?

As to the elements common to the two accounts, the opening words—"I went up to Jerusalem," "I went up again to Jerusalem"—naturally suggest that Paul is giving an account of his successive visits to Jerusalem.

Apart from the desire to harmonise Luke with Paul, no one would ever have inferred from these words that Paul's intention was to give an account only of interviews with Apostles, and that he omits visits to Jerusalem on which he did not see Apostles. As we shall see immediately, false accounts of his visits to Jerusalem were current and were injuring his cause: it was declared that his object in going to Jerusalem was to get authority and commission from the original and only real Apostles. He therefore shows that on these visits he got no authority or commission from the Apostles, and that his object in going up was quite different. We should not naturally expect that he would pass in silence over one of the visits thus misrepresented, because the facts were very strongly in his favour in that case. He mentions exactly whom he saw on his first visit. He denies that he saw any other Apostle but two. If on a second visit he saw no Apostle, one would expect him to mention this.

Throughout the description of the visits, what is stated is greatly determined by the current misrepresentations. Paul is not giving a complete history of what occurred on his visits, but simply tells enough to correct false impressions or statements.

There is, however, no need to suppose that the Judaistic emissaries who had troubled and perverted the Galatians had deliberately falsified the narrative : the events of which they spoke had occurred long ago, and it is quite natural and probable that an incorrect account might have grown up among the strongly prejudiced adherents of the extreme Judaistic party in Jerusalem.

Especially, it is clear that they forgot how long an interval had elapsed between the conversion and the first visit. They spoke—and doubtlessly really thought—as if Paul had gone up to Jerusalem immediately after that epoch-making event. Hence Paul begins by denying this, *v.* 16, "immediately I conferred not with flesh and blood, neither went I to Jerusalem to them which were Apostles before me: but I went away into Arabia ; and again I returned unto Damascus".

XVII

THE FIRST VISIT TO JERUSALEM, I 18-20.

As to the first visit in the third year, there is little to say. Paul tells that he was desirous of visiting Cephas ; and he employs the word which was " used by those who go to see great and famous cities ".[1] He is careful to state quite frankly his motive, even though it slightly tells against his argument. It puts Peter on an elevation of importance and dignity, and himself on the level of the tourist who goes to see the great man. But also it makes the situation clear : he went to Jerusalem to see Peter specially, as a distinguished and great man, whom a young convert like himself regarded with peculiar respect, but not to seek authority or commission from the Apostles as an official body. He recognises fully and honourably a certain rank and weight that belonged of right to Peter in the Church ; and he desired to make acquaintance with him on that account.

The visit was short. He continued in relations with Peter fifteen days, *i.e.*, if he saw Peter for the first time on the first day of the month, his last interview with him was on the fifteenth. As his object was to see Peter, that must be taken to imply that his stay in Jerusalem was limited to that time : he repaired to Peter as soon as was convenient after his arrival, and left immediately after he last saw him. Of the other Apostles he saw only James, and the most natural explanation is that the rest were absent on various duties. It is not a natural or in itself probable inference that, though others were present in the

---

[1] Lightfoot, from Chrysostom.

city, Paul was kept apart from them by Peter, or himself avoided them. If he desired to meet Peter it would be merely irrational to avoid the others, and would be rather like a skulking criminal than a straightforward man.

Then follows the solemn oath : " Now, touching the things which I write unto you, behold, before God, I lie not " (I 20). The position of this solemn assurance at this point implies that the truth about the first visit was particularly important. But in the details that are mentioned, there is nothing that seems in itself important. In fact the account is tantalisingly empty ; it does not even assert positively that Peter taught Paul no part of his Gospel at that time. But the importance of the account lies in the preceding events. The Judaising party had given a different account of that visit. What their account was we cannot say precisely ; but clearly it slurred over the interval from the conversion, and represented the first visit as being the occasion when Paul received a commission and instructions from the body of the Apostles ; and the brief statement of years and hours and names disproved it without further words. As to learning from Peter, Paul had probably always openly affirmed—what is here tacitly implied in the phrase " to visit Cephas "—that he had gained much from Peter's knowledge and experience.

If there existed so much misapprehension—or even perhaps falsification, though we personally see no reason to think such had been practised—about the first visit, we should naturally suppose that there was also misapprehension about Paul's other visits, as if these had been frequent and had always the same object of getting instruction and the solution of difficulties from the source of authority in Jerusalem. Such had been the object of one visit, described in Acts XV : no one could deny that ; least of all would Paul deny it. The Judaisers generalised from that visit, which was recent and familiar to all. They represented to the Galatians—doubtless they really believed—that the other visits were undertaken from similar motives. Hence Paul states so carefully in each case what his motive really was. His statements are all intended to correct false conceptions.

XVIII

THE SECOND VISIT TO JERUSALEM, II 1-10.

This visit is described much more fully than the first visit. The narrative is most difficult to understand. The Galatians could understand it, because it to a considerable extent merely recalled to them what they knew already. Modern readers find it obscure, because they have no certainty as to the facts that are alluded to. Every modern commentator holds some theory as to the correspondence with Acts ; he identifies the visit described by Paul with some visit described by Luke, and reads into Paul's narrative the spirit and even the incidents of Acts. Paul's narrative is broken by the omission of words essential to strict grammatical construction. Each commentator naturally fills up the gaps according to his own theory and his conception of the events. Thus, for example, Lightfoot makes out of Paul's words a story very like the account given in Acts XV ; but most of the resemblances are inserted bodily to complete Paul's broken clauses.

It is specially necessary in this case to carry out our principle ; [1] to add nothing, to rigidly restrict ourselves to

[1] See p. 280 f.

the actual words of Paul, and to elicit from them only what fairly and certainly lies in them.   To do so, one must exercise self-restraint—one must confess that in several places want of knowledge of facts known to the Galatians leaves us in uncertainty.

The following pages are written without a fixed theory. Mr. Vernon Bartlet, in a paper now in type but unpublished, has convinced me that there is a tenable hypothesis, which in my previous discussion of the subject[1] was not taken into account: we have no assurance that Luke describes all Paul's visits to Jerusalem: he had to omit many things from his very concise history: it is perfectly conceivable that Paul and Barnabas may have been ordered by revelation to go up to Jerusalem at some point such as Acts XI 26 or elsewhere, and that Luke left this visit unmentioned (as he did the Arabian visit), because he considered it to lie outside of the thread of his historical purpose.   That is a fair theory, which at present I dare neither reject nor accept ; and therefore in the ensuing discussion there lurks no identification with any visit described by Luke.

As to the general character of Paul's narrative, we must bear always in mind that his intention is not to give a history of his visit, or to tell why he made the visit and how he carried his primary object into effect.   The narrative is introduced because of its bearing on the question now at issue in the Galatian Churches.   Paul's point in ch. I, II, lies in this, that he is the Apostle charged by God to the Gentiles, that he was accepted as such by the chief Apostles, that he gave a message direct from God to the Galatians, and that he was not commissioned or instructed by the

[1] In *Expositor*, August, 1895, p. 105 ff, also the papers in *Expositor*, March, July, 1896.

older Apostles to deliver any message to them at first, though at a later stage he was commissioned to deliver to them the Apostolic Decree.

In the account which we have now to study, the essential and fundamental fact emerges clear to every reader that in the fourteenth year from the epoch-making event[1] Paul communicated in a certain way to certain Apostles in Jerusalem the Gospel which he preaches, everywhere and always, to the Gentiles, and that they approved his Gospel. This communication was an event of the utmost importance. We must lay the utmost stress on it, as Paul evidently did. It is the essential proof of the vital harmony that existed among the four great Christian leaders. Paul tells us of the manner in which the communication was made, and the cause that brought it about, and his intention in making it, and the reception which the three chiefs gave to it. Such fulness in this brief historical retrospect is proof of the cardinal importance of the communication. The whole history of the early stages of that first great controversy in the Church lies before us in that sentence. When the sentence is rightly understood, it disproves conclusively many laboriously spun modern theories as to the dissensions between the four leaders, "the discrepancies of Petrine and Pauline tradition," and all the rest of those airy cobwebs. Those theories all depend on misconstruction and mistranslation. And many more theories will have to be abandoned for the same reason, before the essential unity and perfection of early Christian history is appreciated.

It is not our purpose, however, to touch on any of those theories; but simply to determine what Paul meant the

---

[1] The epoch, as we hold, § XIII, was his conversion.

Galatians to gather. Only we must plead against the fixed belief entertained by many that the interpretation is now certain, and that discussion is closed. The Tübingen scholars founded their theory on a false interpretation. The present dominant interpretations are all founded on a theory of identification with Luke, and differ in many details from one another. We cannot see that the now dominant theory is any more certain than the Tübingen interpretation.[1]

In fact the dominant interpretations seem to be all too much influenced by prepossessions derived from the Tübingen theories. Those theories have deservedly and rightly exercised a strong influence on all thinking minds. There was a natural and healthy tendency even among opponents (at least the best of them), not merely to assimilate the lofty and noble qualities of the Tübingen criticism, but also to adopt as much as possible of its results. In regard to this passage in Galatians, this prepossession has had unfortunate results, which will last for some time yet.

Here once more, as in many other points, our first duty is to protest against the closed door by which so many scholars try to bar our investigations. History in all departments is being rewritten in the present age. The most important, and one of the most difficult, episodes in history is the early stage in the growth of Christianity. Here of all places it is unsuitable to assume certainty, and to refuse to reconsider without prejudice dominant theories.

We, at any rate, shall try to write here without any theory in the mind on this point.

What a sentence it is that we have to study! Involved

---

[1] It is not meant that all the "Tübingen School" agreed exactly, but that there is a general agreement in character.

and perplexed, taking up one point, abandoning it, resuming it, explaining, correcting, returning on itself. Never was such a sentence penned by mortal man before or since. Never has so much been said in so few words ; and never has it been said in such defiance of ordinary construction, and yet on such a high intellectual level. The one thing on which all commentators are agreed is the terrific, awe-inspiring nature of that portentous sentence ; for though one may thrust in a period here or there, it is really one sentence that runs through the verses 1-10.

But at least the spirit of the narrative is clear. The spirit is unity, concord, hearty agreement between Paul and the great Apostles, "the acknowledged leaders". That is the impression which any one who reads the words of Paul without prepossession by Luke's accounts must derive. Paul consulted them ; they heard : they gave the right hand of fellowship to the two new Apostles to the Gentiles : they made a formal partition of the work that lay before the young Church—Barnabas and Paul to the Gentiles, the older Apostles to the Jews.

That being so, is it permissible to suppose that Paul succeeds in conveying that impression by omitting all the facts which showed disagreement between himself and the older Apostles? This question ought to be fairly faced and answered by all commentators. But certainly some of them do not face it ; they unconsciously hide it from themselves. Here on our principles we must answer "No". It is not open to us to think that Paul attained his effect by omitting what told against him. His solemn oath before God that he is telling the truth is not needed to convince us. We know that he rested on the truth for his influence on men's minds, that without the truth his moral power was lost.

19

In passing, we notice the really almost comic—were it not almost tragic—argument in Meyer-Sieffert that Paul's solemn oath, I 20, refers only to the preceding part of the narrative.[1] The apparent implication is that Paul was not so careful to tell the truth in the rest of his narrative. Hence they, and all who found their interpretation on the theory that Paul is telling of the visit which Luke describes in Acts XV, assume that Paul omits various incidents, which were not so clearly in his favour as those that he mentions.   Hence they insert in the breaks of Paul's hurried and disjointed narrative such facts as the disagreement between Paul and the Three on the question whether Titus should be circumcised : see below, p. 297.

Accordingly, our first principle in approaching Paul's narrative is this : we must be slow to interpolate in the breaks of his story facts contrary to the spirit of what he explicitly relates.

Another essential preliminary to the right interpreting of the narrative is to apprehend correctly the distinction between the tenses.   This is very subtle throughout the whole historical retrospect, I 11-II 10.   Paul distinguishes carefully between those actions which belonged to a definite point in the series of past events (*aorist*), those actions which continued for a period but are not thought of as continuing at the moment of writing (*imperfect*), and those actions which are marked as permanent and true down to the moment of writing (*present*).   This distinction is well brought out in I 15 : "And when it seemed fit (*aorist*) to God, who set me apart from my birth and called me through

---

[1] *Abschliessend nur auf das Vorige*, vv. 18, 19.   Lightfoot expresses no opinion ; but his interpretation of I 20, "I declare to you that every word I write is true," tells rather against Meyer-Sieffert.

His grace (*aorists*) to reveal His Son in me (*aorist*), so that I preach Him (*present*) among the Gentiles". When the due moment arrived, God revealed His will to Paul and called him. These are two definite acts which produced certain lasting consequences, but were themselves momentary. But the purpose and the result of the call was that Paul became, and continued until the moment of writing to be, the preacher among the Gentiles. Again in I 22: "I continued unknown (*imperfect*) by face to the churches of Judea" (this is not said to be true at the time of writing, though it lasted for many years); "and they continued to hear reports (*imperfect*) that 'our persecutor[1] is now preaching (*present*) the gospel which formerly he was attempting to destroy' (*imperfect*), and they continually expressed their (*imperfect*) admiration of God's action in my case". Such was their conduct for a number of years : the writer does not indicate that they continue now to do so (partly, such reports were no longer needed, and his conduct was no longer a cause of wonder and special attention ; partly, many in the Judæan churches were now opposed to him, and would no longer praise or admire what he was doing for the Church).

When we apply this principle to the hard passage II 1-10, several of the difficulties disappear, and some misconceptions are cleared away.

A special contrast is indicated between a *present* and an *aorist* in the following cases :—

v. 2,"I laid before them (*aorist*) the gospel which I continue preaching to the present day among the Gentiles (*present*)".

---

[1] The participle διώκων permits no inference; present and imperfect coincide in the participle. The only distinction in the participle is between aorist II 1, 7, 9, and present-imperfect.

v. 2, " To prevent the work of my whole life (*present*), or my work then (*aorist*), from being ineffectual ".

v. 10, " Only (they instructed me) to remember permanently (*present*) the poor, which I then made it my object to do (*aorist*) ".

A difficult contrast between *present* and *imperfect* occurs in *v.* 6 : " it matters not in my estimation (now or then, or at any time, *present*) by what conduct and character they were marked out before the world for their dignified and influential position (*imperfect*)."

The necessity for the *imperfect* here becomes clearer if we substitute the *present*, and observe that the change gives an inadmissible sense. " What their permanent character is matters not to me" (ὁποῖοί ποτε εἰσὶν οὐδέν μοι διαφέρει) would be a sentiment unsuitable to the argument, and hardly becoming in Paul's mouth. The sense of what he says is, " I grant that their conduct had been noble and their prominent position was deserved, but God, who respects not persons, had chosen to communicate directly with me and through me to the Gentiles ; and I could not put myself under their directions ".

Still more clear does the necessity for the imperfect become if we take the sense preferred by Lightfoot : he says, " it does not mean 'what reputation they enjoyed,' but 'what was their position, what were their advantages, *in former times*, referring to their personal intercourse with the Lord ' ".

The many aorists of this passage are clear : each of them denotes an act in the drama, which is described. They need no elucidation or comment except the following in *v.* 5 : " we resisted them then that the truth of the Gospel might continue (*aorist*) for you ". Here it may seem that the aorist expresses an action that continues to the moment of writing. That, however, is not so : the action belonged to the moment, though its result lasts down to the time of writing ; and this becomes clear if we put the proposition in another form, " we resisted them then that the truth might not by our compliance be interrupted and prevented from continuing for you ". The *aorist* is required to express " might not be interrupted," and it is therefore required to express " might continue ".

Now let us review successively the points that are clearly stated in Paul's account of the visit, remembering always that nothing is mentioned except what had a bearing on the Galatian difficulty.

In company with him were Barnabas and Titus. The mention of Barnabas as a companion is probably intended to recall past events to his readers. Barnabas was well-known to them.[1] The companionship of Titus is mentioned, because something important for Paul's purpose among the Galatians was connected with him.

In what capacity did these two go up? The expressions used imply that the two did not stand on the same footing. Barnabas and Paul are spoken of as if they were conjoined and equal : " I went up with Barnabas ". Titus was only a subordinate, " taking also Titus with us ". This word, " taking," in the three other cases[2] where it occurs in the New Testament, is applied to a private companion or minister, who is not sent forth on the mission as an envoy, but is taken by the envoys on their own authority. Here Barnabas and Paul were official messengers ; and Titus is taken with them on their own responsibility.

---

[1] See §§ III, IV.   [2] συνπαραλαβών, Acts XII 25, XV 37, 38.

The translation "taking Titus with *me*" is unjustifiable, and wrongly imputes to Paul an assumption of superiority over Barnabas.[1] The use of the participle in the singular is necessitated by the form of the sentence: "I went up with Barnabas, taking Titus". The case is precisely analogous to Acts XV 37, "Barnabas wished to take with *them* John also".[2] It would be as reasonable there to translate, "Barnabas wished to take John also with *him*," as it is here to translate "Paul took Titus also with *him*".

What is the force of "also Titus"? In this detail, too, Acts XV 37 furnishes a perfect analogy: "Barnabas wished to take with them also John". In that case there is no other possible sense than "in addition to themselves"; and so it is in this case. Titus was taken in addition to the official envoys.

The reason for the visit lay in revelation. This statement must be taken as a denial that the visit was undertaken for the reason alleged by the Judaisers, see p. 281 f. Paul says nothing as to the recipient of the revelation. A Divine revelation to one man was binding on all whom it concerned.[3] Of course the *a priori* presumption is in favour of this revelation having been made to Paul himself: but we cannot safely say more than this: a Divine revelation was made, necessitating the journey of Paul and Barnabas to Jerusalem, and the journey was not taken by Paul through desire to get instruction or commission from the Apostles.

---

[1] Meyer-Sieffert explicitly claim that Paul is here assuming his superiority to Barnabas.

[2] Galatians II 1, ἀνέβην . . . συνπαραλαβὼν καὶ Τίτον, Acts XV 37, ἐβούλετο συνπαραλαβεῖν καὶ τὸν Ἰωάννην.

[3] Acts XI 28.

Paul gives no hint as to the immediate purpose of that visit. The incidents which he relates as occurring during the visit are described as arising out of the circumstances existing in Jerusalem.

Lightfoot connects closely, " I went up by revelation and laid before them the Gospel which I preach," giving the appearance that the setting forth of Paul's Gospel had been the object of his journey. He agrees with the Authorised Version, with Tischendorf and others. But the Revised Version and the text of Westcott and Hort are right in separating the two statements by a colon—" and I went up by revelation : and I laid before them my gospel, but privately ".

Paul laid his Gospel before them (*i.e.*, those in Jerusalem), but privately, before them of repute (whom afterwards he names, Peter and James and John). " The wide assertion is forthwith limited by the second clause " (Alford). This had an important bearing on the misrepresentations of the Judaisers : he did not lay his Gospel officially before the assembly of the Apostles, but privately before the Three. It is merely unreasonable to understand with some that Paul made both a public exposition before the whole Church, and a private esoteric exposition before the Three.

The question which underlies this whole historical retrospect is whether or not Paul had sought official guidance and official authorisation from the Apostles in regard to his message to the Galatians. He maintains and asseverates that it came from God alone, and was delivered to them from God through himself. It would be absurd, and worse than absurd, that Paul should assure the Galatians that he consulted the Three privately, if he also laid it before them in public in their official assembly. We must understand

Paul to imply that he made no public consultation on this subject.

The verb used, "laid before them," is interpreted by Lightfoot as "related with a view to consulting". He quotes Acts XXV 14, "Festus laid Paul's case before the king," and remarks that there the idea of consultation is brought out very clearly by the context, *vv.* 20, 26. It is unnecessary to quote corroborative examples from other Greek literature : they are numerous.

Paul, therefore, asked the advice of the three great Apostles as to the Gospel which he proposed to preach, or was preaching, among the Gentiles. It is difficult to suppose that he asked their advice about a Gospel which he had already been preaching—that, after delivering the message from God to the Gentiles, he asked the counsel of any man about that message. When that Gospel was still hid in his own mind, when he had not yet full confidence that he fully comprehended it, he might consult the three leaders about it. After it had fixed itself in his nature as the truth of God, so that he had proclaimed it broadcast to the Gentiles, he no longer " conferred with flesh and blood ".

We are therefore placed in this dilemma : either Paul consulted the Three before he promulgated his Gospel in its fully developed form, or there is no idea of "consultation" in the verb which he here employs. The second alternative seems to me excluded. All readers must judge for themselves.

That Paul's Gospel to the Gentiles was not fully matured until shortly before the beginning of the first journey (Acts XIII 1) will be set forth more fully elsewhere. That it was fully matured when he preached in South Galatia on that journey will hardly be disputed by any unprejudiced reader.

Accordingly, we conclude Paul consulted the three leaders privately and apart, not in public council ; as friends, not as authoritative guides. What a revelation is this as to the forethought and statesmanship with which the diffusion of the Gospel through the civilised, *i.e.*, the Roman, world was planned ! We cannot here dilate further on the immense significance of that private[1] interview between the Four— the head of the Church in Jerusalem, and the Three who in succession controlled and counselled the Church in the Roman world. I hope to do so elsewhere at an early date.

Next Paul states his object. " I consulted them—but privately—to prevent my work as it continues now, or my work then, from being ineffectual."[2] Does Paul mean that he consulted them for that reason, or that he consulted them privately for that reason ? Clearly the former : he consulted them to avoid future misunderstanding, to ensure unity, in the plans and views of the Church. But he took care to do it privately, by reason of the false brethren,[3] as he explains in *v.* 4.

Now Paul diverges from the path of the proper topic. It bears on the Galatian interest that not even Titus, his companion, Greek as he was, was compelled to accept circumcision.

The question here rises, was Titus's case made the subject of an open discussion and decided in the negative ? Many commentators assume that the extreme party formally contended that Titus must submit to the rite, and that it was decided that he should not be forced to submit. This seems not to be the natural force of the passage, but rather to be

---

[1] Meyer-Sieffert's rendering is *abgesondert, privatim.*

[2] On the tenses, see p. 290 f.

[3] Meyer-Sieffert translates the clause μήπως κ.τ.λ. quite differently.

forced into it through the inclination to read into this passage as much as possible out of Acts XV.

The plain meaning of the Greek words is that the question was not formally raised, nor publicly decided : Titus was left free and unconstrained : nobody compelled him : he was let alone.

Had the question been raised formally, it would have been a test case. Titus was distinctly a person of standing in the Church; and if the Apostles had solemnly and officially decided, after the question had been formally raised and discussed, that Titus need not accept the rite, that would have practically decided the present case in Galatia. The Apostolic Decree in Acts XV did not constitute a thorough decision, for it was too general and was open to misconstruction ; [1] but the judgment about a person in the position of Titus would have been decisive, and Paul could hardly have avoided mentioning more clearly the judgment, if there had been one.

But most entirely opposed to the plain sense of the Greek is the interpretation that the question was raised ; that the extremists contended that Titus must be circumcised ; that " concession was even urged upon Paul in high quarters as a measure of prudence to disarm opposition ; " but he " did not for a moment yield to this pressure ".[2] That sense is got by bringing together statements which Paul keeps separate. And how utterly does it sacrifice the unity of feeling and thought and aim among the Four, which is the plain implication of the passage, when read without the purpose to squeeze it into conformity with Acts XV. The whole harmony and beauty of the picture is destroyed by the interpolated idea.

[1] See §§ VIII, XXVII.   [2] Quotations from Lightfoot, p. 105.

After the parenthetic remark about Titus, Paul again takes up the thread, employing the particle δέ to indicate resumption of the topic after a digression. "Now it was because of certain insinuating sham brethren, who crept into our society, without avowing their real intentions, to act the spy on our freedom, which we true Christians enjoy in Christ Jesus, in order to enslave us (*to their ritualistic acts*) : " Paul means, " It was because of them that I acted thus," but he is led on away from the grammatical form into an account of his relations with the false brethren : " to whom we did not for a moment yield by complying with their suggestions, our object being to ensure that the Gospel in its truth should continue for you to enjoy ".

The interpretation seems clear. During the stay in Jerusalem, certain brethren came about them, and observed with disapproval the relations of Paul and Barnabas to Titus, and mentioned their opinion on the subject ; but the two Apostles of the Gentiles firmly resisted them ; and, warned by this experience, Paul (with or without Barnabas [1]) laid their whole scheme of a Gospel for the Gentiles privately before the Three.

Paul's sense of right is shocked by the conduct of those brethren : his words distinctly imply that they came to visit as pretended friends, and used knowledge acquired in private social intercourse to injure Paul among others.

The result of the communication follows : " but from the recognised leaders—how distinguished soever was their character matters not to me : God accepteth not man's person ". Here once more Paul breaks the grammatical

---

[1] In this passage Barnabas, assuredly, is to be assumed as throughout united with Paul ; but the special purpose requires Paul to use the singular.

thread, and resumes with γάρ and a different grammatical construction—"the recognised leaders, I say, imparted no new instruction to me; but, on the contrary, perceiving that I *throughout my ministry* have been charged specially with the non-Jewish mission as Peter is with the Jewish —for he that worked for Peter towards the apostolate of the circumcision worked also for me towards *the mission to* the Gentiles—and perceiving *from the facts* the grace that had been given me, they, James and Cephas and John, the recognised pillars of the Church, gave pledges to me and to Barnabas of a joint scheme of work, ours towards the Gentiles, and theirs towards the Jews. One charge alone they gave us, to remember the poor, which duty as a matter of fact I then made it a special object to perform."

The final words, on account of the aorist, must on the principles laid down above, p. 290 f, be understood as "an act in the drama which then occurred". If Paul meant that he subsequently was and still continued to be zealous in that way, he would have used the present tense: the aorist denotes something that was actually part of the incidents in Jerusalem. Paul therefore was helping the poor in Jerusalem—which we may take it as certain that he did on every visit, as *e.g.*, Acts XXI.

The analogy of Ephesians IV 3[1] might lead us even further. The same verb is there used to indicate the prominent object, "giving diligence to keep the unity of the spirit in the bond of peace". Does it here indicate that charity to the poor was the main object of the visit— not merely an act in the drama, but the principal act?

Some commentators attribute a depreciatory sense to

---

[1] σπουδάζοντες τηρεῖν τὴν ἑνότητα, Eph. IV 3, ὃ καὶ ἐσπούδασα αὐτὸ τοῦτο ποιῆσαι, Gal. II 10.

δοκοῦντες, "the so-called leaders". This is not justifiable. The Greek word means " the recognised or accepted leaders". Lightfoot quotes examples of a depreciatory sense for δοκοῦντες, but in them all the depreciatory innuendo comes from the context and not from the word. To attribute such a meaning to it here is out of keeping with Paul's courteous tone to the leaders, and is also opposed to the spirit which we have recognised in this narrative (see p. 289).

XIX

LIMITS AND PURPOSE OF THE AUTOBIOGRAPHY.

This autobiographical sketch—from I 12 to near the end of II—entirely depends on I 11 : " I make known [1] to you," *i.e.*, I proceed to show you, " as touching the Gospel which was preached by me, that it is not after man ". Then follows the statement of the facts showing that the Gospel which Paul preached came to him from God originally, and, so far from having ever been suggested to him by the Apostles, had on the contrary been stated by him to them in Jerusalem, and approved by them without any reservation or addition or suggestion, except that he should remember the poor (which, as a matter of fact, it was his object then to do).

This autobiographical statement of facts falls into three parts. First, the character of his life before his conversion is briefly described, in order to bring out what an epoch it was, what a complete reversal of his previous career.

---

[1] This formula (confined to the group Rom., Cor., Gal.) "introduces some statement on which the Apostle lays special emphasis " (Lightfoot).

Secondly, he gives an outline of his movements, intended to bring out how rare and short had been his opportunities of learning from the older Apostles. When his visit to Jerusalem was very short he counts even the days. Then he contrasts these days with the years that elapsed between the first and the second visit.

The effect of the contrast between fifteen days in Jerusalem and fourteen years in Syria-Cilicia is great; and it must have been greater to the Galatians, because they had been listening to descriptions of Paul's indebtedness to the older Apostles, his frequent consultation of them, and so on. But the North Galatians insist that this telling fact—fourteen days spent in Jerusalem during the first seventeen years of his Christian life—is got by leaving out one visit to Jerusalem: in fact, that it is obtained by suppression of truth.

The outline of his movements stops, naturally and necessarily, at the point where he delivered his Gospel to the Galatians: his purpose is only to show that up to that time he had not got any message from the Apostles. He must, of course, assume that the Galatians will believe his statements of fact: he assures them with the most solemn oath that he speaks the truth. Surely, in such a case, he would not expose himself to the charge, which the Judaistic emissaries would at once bring against him, of omitting a vital fact, *viz.*, concealing a visit and thus incorrectly making a long interval between the two which he mentions.

Now, on the North Galatian theory that limiting point is on the second journey: Paul must show that he had never received any message from the Apostles to the Gentiles up to that time. According to Luke he had visited Jerusalem

three times before that time. Therefore, if Luke is trustworthy, Paul has omitted a visit. It is not wonderful that
the inference should be drawn by many scholars that Paul
must be trusted and Luke must have made some blunder.
The discrepancy is explained away by the orthodox
theologians through a very elaborate process of delicate
reconciliation ; but the very elaborateness of the process is
a proof that they have not reached the ultimate truth.
Truth is simple. A scholar and a historian should recognise
that universal principle : until he has attained perfect
simplicity, he has not attained truth, and should struggle
on towards it. As the conclusion of that elaborate reconciliation, many theological scholars deny that there is any
discrepancy ; but the plain fact that very many other
theologians—admittedly reasonable, learned, and bent on
seeking truth—see the discrepancy, is a proof that there is
one. The last proof of reason or unreason is that competent human beings agree in their estimate. If a large
number of competent witnesses agree that there is a
discrepancy, it is vain to assert that there is none.

With his usual fairness and caution, Dr. Sanday admits
that in this question the difficulties " are no doubt great,"
but in the same breath refuses to " include them among
the serious difficulties ".[1] If we define the word " serious "
as meaning " insuperable," I am quite ready to accept
the distinction.

The result is that on the North Galatian theory there
are great difficulties in reconciling Acts with Paul ; but on
the South Galatian theory these difficulties have no existence. As in the Epistle, so in Acts, when Paul delivered

---

[1] *Bampton Lectures*, p. 329.

his Gospel to the Galatians he had only visited Jerusalem twice since his conversion.[1]

Thirdly, in this autobiographical sketch Paul relates a notable incident, in which the leading older Apostle, when in the Gentile sphere, accepted the correction and rebuke of Paul on the question of the relations between Jews and Gentiles. Not merely did the older Apostles fully recognise that the Gentile mission belonged to Paul and Barnabas, but also they submitted to learn from Paul in that sphere.

This part of the autobiography constitutes a new section, and is pointedly distinguished from the outline of Paul's movements, and we shall therefore treat it under a special heading.

XX

ST. PETER IN ANTIOCH.

This third part of the autobiography is marked as a new departure. The second part began at his conversion as the epoch in his life—" but when," ὅτε δὲ εὐδόκησεν, I 15. The third part now resumes in the same way—" but when," ὅτε δὲ ἦλθεν, II 11.

While the second part is necessarily arranged chronologically in its parts, it does not follow that the third part is later than the second. The third part begins a new thought and makes a new departure, and its chronological relation to the second must be determined by other

[1] On the theory mentioned on p. 286 there had been three visits before Paul's first missionary journey, but Paul mentions here the first and second visits, and his numbers are therefore on that theory right, though he interrupts his recital before reaching the visit described in Acts XI and XII.

considerations. Those who identify the second visit in the Epistle with the third visit in Acts are perfectly justified in maintaining (as Prof. Zahn and Mr. Turner are inclined to do) that Peter's Antiochian visit took place earlier than the incident described in II 1-10.

It is possible that Peter was sent to Antioch in the interval that elapsed between Acts XI 30 and XIII 1. On another occasion Peter and John were sent to inspect and confirm a new departure, *viz.*, the extension of the Church to Samaria, Acts VIII 14. Similarly, it would be natural that Peter should be sent to inspect the new departure in Antioch shortly after the events in Acts XI 26.

Whether that was done or not we cannot say ; but Peter may have visited Antioch more than once in so many years, and the analysis in language and situation show that probably the visit here described occurred about the time of Acts XV 1. The reasons are set forth in full in *St. Paul the Traveller*, pp. 158 ff, and need not be repeated here. Nor is it necessary here to describe the incident. It stands quite isolated, and few historical inferences are clear from it.[1]

The most important part of the incident is Paul's address to Peter II 14 ff. This address turns into a general review of the relation between Gentiles and Jews in the Church. Gradually Paul diverges from the situation in Antioch, and at last finds himself in the Galatian question ; yet it is impossible to mark where he passes away from the incident in Antioch. But the address is practically an epitome of the theme which is set forth in the following chapters ; and the commentary on them is at the same

---

[1] See, *e.g.*, §§ IV, XXX.

time an explanation of the address, and must take frequent notice of it. After working through the rest of the Epistle, one turns back to II 14 ff, and finds in those verses the whole truth in embryo.

XXI

SPIRIT OF CHAPTERS III, IV.

Paul's aim now is to revivify among the Galatians the memory of their first condition, before any contradictory and confusing messages had affected them. He must touch their hearts, and make them feel for themselves the Divine word in their own souls. He reminds them, by many subtle touches, of their original experience, how the Divine message worked in them, raised them to a higher nature, made them instinct with Divine life, implanted marvellous powers in them. If he can work them up again into that frame of mind in which he had left them fresh from his first message, his immediate purpose will be gained. Thereafter, other steps would be required. But, for the moment, he must work on their nature and conscience : he must appeal to their true selves : they had known in themselves how they had begun by simple faith, and whither it had led them. Paul knew what Goethe knew when he said :—

> O ! never yet hath mortal drunk
> A draught restorative.
> That welled not from the depths of his own soul !

How utterly out of place in effecting this purpose would laborious proofs of his own rectitude and consistency be ! " Timeserver" is he ? Think of the marks of Christ, his owner, branded on his body ![1] " Preacher of the Law " is

---

[1] See below, § LXIII.

he? Then he is false to his own message, and the cross
which he " placarded " before their eyes is set aside by
him as no more needed! But they know from their own
experience what has made them Christians! If he has
been untrue to his message, he is accursed ; but let them
hold to what they have felt and known!

The letter is not logically argumentative. It is merely
futile in the critic to look in it for reasoning addressed to
the intellect, and to discuss the question whether it is or is
not intellectually convincing. Each new paragraph, each
fresh train of thought, is intended to quicken and reinvigorate
the early Christian experiences of his readers. Naturally,
we cannot fully appreciate the effect of every paragraph.
In many places we can see that Paul refers to facts in
the past relations between them and himself—facts otherwise
unknown to us, and guessed only from the brief, pregnant
words which he here uses, words full of reminiscence to
the Galatians, but sadly obscure to us. In other paragraphs
we can be sure he is referring to something which we can
hardly even guess at.

The effect of the letter depended to a great degree on
circumstances which are to us almost or quite unknown.
Here, if ever in this world, heart speaks to heart: the man
as he was appeals direct to the men as they were.

> If feeling does not prompt, in vain you strive ;
> If from the soul the language does not come
> By its own impulse, to impel the hearts
> Of hearers, with communicated power,
> In vain you strive. . . .
>   Never hope to stir the hearts of men,
> And mould the souls of many into one,
> By words which come not native from the heart.

Thus Paul reiterates his blows, and heaps appeal on

appeal and illustration on illustration, all for the one sole end. He must rekindle the flame of faith, languishing for the moment, under misapprehension, doubt as to Paul's purpose, doubt as to his character, suspicion as to the witness and work of the other Apostles. If the flame leaps up fresh and strong in their souls, it will melt all suspicions and solve all doubts. They will once more know the truth.

Such is the spirit in which we must try to interpret chapters III and IV. I cannot do it. Probably no one will ever do it completely. In some cases, I fancy, I can in a small degree catch the tone in which the words ought to be recited, if the meaning is to be brought out of them ; and by the hope to contribute something to the understanding of this, the most wonderful and enigmatical self-revelation in literature, I have been driven to publish these pages (many of which have been written long ago, and kept back from consciousness of their inadequacy).

XXII

THE ADDRESS "GALATIANS," IN III 1.

The opening three words of the chapter, " O foolish Galatians," have in Paul's mouth, if I estimate him and them correctly, a strongly pathetic effect. It is, I think, customary to say that here his anger speaks, and he sharply censures the senseless conduct of the Galatians.[1] The most

---

[1] *Scharfrügender Ausdruck* is Dr. Zöckler's expression. Lightfoot, in his edition, p. 64, evidently reckons this apostrophe among those " outbursts of indignant remonstrance," by which " the argument is interrupted every now and then. Rebuke may prevail where reason

curious development of this idea is seen in Deissman, *Bibelstudien,* p. 263 ff. After the harsh and angry tone of the earlier pages of the letter, according to Deissmann, Paul concludes, in VI 11, with a little joke, so that the Galatians, "his dear silly children" (*liebe unverständige Kinder*), may understand that his anger has not been lasting, and that it is no longer the severe schoolmaster who is addressing them : he therefore makes the jocular remark about "big letters," which are more impressive to children than the smaller letters of the secretary who wrote most of the Epistle : " When Paul spoke thus, the Galatians knew that the last traces of the seriousness of the punishing schoolmaster had vanished from his features ! "

Not anger, but pathos, on the contrary, seems to be the prominent note in this apostrophe. The authoritative tone, of course, is there ; but the feeling is that of love, sorrow, and pathos, not anger.

It is only on rare occasions that Paul addresses his hearers, as in this case, directly by the general appellation that embraces them all and sums them all up in one class.[1] But in certain states of emotion the necessity comes upon him to use this direct appeal, so that every individual shall feel that he is personally addressed. The only other cases in the Epistles of Paul are 2 Corinthians VI 11, and Philippians IV 15. Let us compare the three.

---

will be powerless." That the tone is "severe" (in Lightfoot's previous phrase) is quite true ; but to take " indignation " as its prominent note seems to be a misreading of the purpose and drift. This misconception is one of the many wrong consequences of the North Galatian view.

[1] The need for a comprehensive address, embracing all his readers, and placing them all on a level, is illustrated from another point of view in § LVI.

To show the tone of 2 Corinthians VI 11, it is only necessary to recall the intensely emotional words (*vv.* 1-10) describing Paul's life as an evangelist, and his prayer "that ye receive not the grace of God in vain," and then to read *v.* 11, "Our mouth is open unto you, O Corinthians, our heart is enlarged". He goes on to address them as his children. But though he is censuring them, it is not anger that prompts the apostrophe; deep, yearning affection dictates the direct personal appeal.

So again in Philippians IV 15. Paul's feelings are deeply moved as he recalls that Philippi was the one Church which sent and forced on him money for his pressing wants. Here again the apostrophe, "Philippians," follows upon an autobiographical passage, describing how "I can do all things in Him that strengtheneth me".

Thus in all three cases we notice the same conditions leading Paul up to the direct address. He has been for a time putting forward prominently his own work and the spirit in which he does it. Compare the words of Philippians just quoted with Galatians II 20, "I have been crucified with Christ; yet I live: and yet no longer I, but Christ liveth in me," etc., and with 2 Corinthians VI 9, 10, "as dying, and behold we live; as chastened, not killed; as poor, yet making many rich," etc. Wrought up to a high pitch of emotion in this retrospect of his life in death as a servant and minister, he turns direct on his hearers, and places them face to face with himself, "Galatians," or "Philippians," or "Corinthians". The man who reads anger into this address as its prominent characteristic is for the moment losing his comprehension of Paul's mind. Pathos is the characteristic, not indignation.

It is not exactly the same situation, but is at least

analogous, when Paul directly appeals by name to a single correspondent.   This he only does in 1 Timothy I 18, VI 20.   In the former case there is exactly the same movement of thought and emotion as in the three cases just quoted. He casts a glance over his own career as the "chief of sinners," who "obtained mercy, that in me might Jesus Christ show forth all His long-suffering, for an ensample of them which should hereafter believe on Him unto eternal life ".   Here we find the same idea, life gained through the Divine patience (though the idea of Paul's personal suffering and affliction is not made so prominent here).   Then he continues, as in the other cases, " This charge I commit unto thee, my child Timothy ".

Incidentally, we remark here that no one who trusts to his literary sense, could attribute this passage in 1 Timothy, with its deep feeling, to a forger, who put on the mask of Paul in order to gain currency for his theological ideas. If you permit your feeling for literature to guide you, you know that the friend and spiritual father of Timothy is speaking to him in these words.

The other passage in which Paul addresses Timothy by name, VI 20, is different in type.   Towards the end of a long series of instructions to Timothy about his work, Paul sums up earnestly, " O Timothy, guard that which is committed unto thee ".   Here it is the concluding sentence ; and the letter ends, as it began, with the direct address to Timothy.

But, it will be asked, Was Paul not expecting too much, when he thought that the Galatians would understand these delicate shades of feeling, which escape many modern readers ?   Are we not trying to read our own fancies into the Epistle ?   I think not.   Paul was a great orator, not

in the sense of elaborate artistic composition—as to which
he felt with Goethe, who makes his Faust sneer at mere
"expression, graceful utterance" (which the silly pupil
considered "the first and best acquirement of the orator"),
because they

> Are unrefreshing as the wind that whistles
> In autumn 'mong the dry and wrinkled leaves—

but in the sense that he knew exactly what he could count
upon in his audience. He swept over their hearts as the
musician sweeps over the strings of his instrument, knowing
exactly what music he can bring from them, and what he
must not attempt with them. Let us read the letter to
the Galatians without the misconceptions and preconceived
theories which lead most commentators astray; and let
us acquire beforehand some idea of the political and religious situation, and the character of the Galatians. Then
the meaning will strike us plainly between the eyes, and
we shall no longer talk of anger as influencing the expression
of the writer (except for the moment, and on a special point,
in I 8 f, V 12). You never understand Paul's motives or
purposes, unless you take them on the highest level possible :
when you read in them any mixture of poorer or smaller
feeling, you are merely misunderstanding Paul and losing
your grasp of him. But they who talk so much about his
indignation in Galatians are missing the real emotion that
drives him on : it is intense and overpowering love and
pity for specially beloved children.

In III 1, then, the movement of feeling in the writer's
mind forces him to apostrophise his readers in one general
address. But by what appellation could he sum up the
whole body whom he addressed in Antioch, Iconium, Derbe
and Lystra ? There was only one name common to them

all. They all belonged to the Roman province. The Churches addressed had already been summed up as "the Churches of Galatia". The one title common to the hearers was "men of (the province) Galatia," *i.e.*, Galatae.

Here we find ourselves on ground that has been disputed. Those who hold the North Galatian view have advanced three separate arguments on this point, and each demands a short consideration. They ask, in the first place, what reason there was why Paul should have sought for some common appellation for the people of the four cities : they say that, if he were addressing Antioch, Iconium, Derbe and Lystra, he might have contented himself with the superscription (in I 2), as he does in many other letters. In the second place, they say (or, at least, used to say) that the name Galatia was not applied to the country in which these four cities were situated. In the third place, even if it be admitted that the four cities were in Galatia, they maintain that their inhabitants could not be called Galatae, for none who were not Gauls by race could be called Galatae.

The first argument has already been answered, when we showed how the march of emotion brought Paul to the point where he must apostrophise his audience ; and a further answer is given in § LVI. The whole Epistle, with its intense personality and directness, demands such a direct apostrophe.

The second and third arguments demand separate consideration.

XXIII

GALATIA THE PROVINCE.

The one decisive argument that Paul's "Galatia" must be the province, and not simply the region inhabited by the Gauls, is stated by Zahn. Paul never uses wide geographical names except those of Roman provinces. This has been stated above, § XIV, where additional arguments are given to strengthen Zahn's observation:[1] not merely did Paul use the Roman provincial names, but he even used them in the Latin form, transliterating them into Greek, and in one case employing a Latin form which was avoided by Greek writers. Paul writes as a Roman and a citizen of the Empire.

Here we note that Paul is much more Roman in his tone than the Greek Luke. The latter never uses the term "Galatia," he mentions only the "Galatic territory". Now, if Paul and Luke had been speaking of North Galatia, the country of the three Gallic tribes, it is impossible to understand why they should differ as to the name. Among the immense number of references to North Galatia made by Greek and Latin writers,[2] there seems to be not a single case where any other name than Galatia is used for the country. Why should Luke alone employ everywhere a different name for the country, diverging from the universal usage of Greek and Latin writers, and also from his master Paul? No possible reason can be given. It would simply be an unintelligible freak of Luke's; he chose to differ from everybody, because—he chose to do so.

[1] See also § XXV.

[2] Most are collected in Holder's *Altceltischer Sprachschatz, s.v. Galatia.*

But, on the South Galatian view, it was almost unavoidable that he should differ from Paul as to the name of the country. The custom of naming the province varied according as one wrote from the Roman or the Greek point of view. Now it has been shown in page after page of *St. Paul the Traveller* that Luke follows the Greek popular and colloquial usage, as it was current among the more educated half of society in the cities of the Ægean land. So far as evidence goes, that class of persons never used "Galatia" to denominate the Roman Province; only persons who consciously and intentionally adopted the Roman imperial point of view did so. The Greeks generally repeated the list of regions comprised in the Province (or, at least, as many of the regions as served their immediate purpose), thus: "Galatia (*i.e.*, North Galatia), Phrygia, Lycaonia, Pisidia, Isauria, Pontus Paphlagonia:" but occasionally they employed an expression like "the Galatic Eparchy".[1] This is exactly what Luke does. Sometimes he speaks of the region or regions with which he is concerned, Pisidia, Phrygia, Lycaonia[2]; sometimes he employs the expression, "the Galatic territory".[3]

Further, take into consideration that the adjective "Galatic" is frequently applied, in inscriptions and the geographical writer Ptolemy, to countries like Pontus and Phrygia, which were included in the Province, but that this adjective is never used in a geographical way to designate by a circumlocution North Galatia;[4] and you can only

---

[1] C. I. G., 3991, A.D. 54. The custom of enumerating parts began before 80, and spread to other Provinces in the second century.

[2] Acts XIII 49, XIV 6, 24.   [3] Acts XVI 6, XVIII 23.

[4] It is naturally used in such ways as ἔργα Γαλατικὰ, deeds like those of the Galatae; πόλις Γαλατική, a Galatian city like Ancyra.

marvel that scholars could ever conceal the facts from themselves so far as to think that Luke meant "Galatic territory" to indicate North Galatia.

A modern illustration will make this clearer. An Englishman who caught the words, "At this point they entered British territory," would at once understand that a journey was described, not in Great Britain, but in Africa or Asia or America. A German, however, unless English was very well and accurately known to him, might hesitate as to the meaning. So a Greek of Paul's time would unhesitatingly understand "Galatic territory" in the sense in which the inscriptions and Ptolemy use it. A modern critic, however, who has not made himself familiar with the ancient usage in such matters, often mistakes the meaning.

It is a false translation on the part of the North Galatian theorists to take Ἀγκύρας τῆς Γαλατικῆς in Arrian, *Anab.*, II 4, 1, as "Ancyra of Galatia": it is "Galatic Ancyra distinguished from Phrygiac Ancyra (Strabo, p. 567)".

In truth, nothing except the obscurity in which Asia Minor was enveloped, combined with the general lack of interest taken by scholars in mere geographical matters—which are commonly regarded as beneath the dignity of true scholarship—made the North Galatian view ever seem tenable. And now it stands only because its supporters among "the great scholars" of Germany will not look into the facts. Their minds have long ago been made up, and there is so much to do in other directions that they cannot reconsider *choses jugées*. The appearance of Professor Zahn's *Einleitung*, with its frank acceptance of the main points in the South Galatian view,[1] will, as we may hope, produce a

---

[1] In origin German: held by Weizsäcker, Holtzmann, Clemen, etc.

change in Germany, and show that the subject cannot be pushed aside.

The great difficulty for the moment is that the North Galatian theorists have committed themselves to such sweeping statements in geography and history, in order to prove the South Galatian view impossible, that they have, as it were, burned their boats and must fight to the last, no longer for truth, but merely for victory: *es wäre wenig rühmlich, wenn die Theologen, welche mit ihren Mitteln in der Geschichte des Urchristenthums und der alten Kirche jahrzehntelang gearbeitet haben, ehe Ramsay seine Mittel auf dieselbe Gegenstände anwandte, zu allem . . . Ja sagen würden.* Take one example, which is typical of the present situation. Learning that many inscriptions designate the Province by the list of regions composing it, a distinguished German professor wrote an elaborate article, boldly asserting that the name Galatia was never rightly applied to the whole Province, and therefore drawing the inference, as final and conclusive, that Paul could not have called Antioch, Iconium, etc., "Churches of Galatia". Now this was a real danger to scholarship. Many English theologians are accustomed to regard that distinguished professor as one whom "no one would accuse of error in a field which he has made peculiarly his own ".[1] He was understood by many to have investigated the subject with the true German thoroughness so characteristic of him, and the paper was considered by many as closing the question ; if he was right, there was no more to say, and no one would even think of attributing error to him. Yet he had written

---

[1] I quote the words of a distinguished English professor writing on this topic. The inerrancy once attributed to the text has been transferred by him to the German commentators.

that bold and sweeping negative without looking into the familiar Roman treatises on geography, which must be the foundation of all reasoning on the subject; and, as soon as his attention was called to Pliny and Ptolemy, he retracted the assertion. In truth, his assertion could not be entertained for a moment; it was flatly contradicted by the fundamental authorities. Had any English scholar made it, what scorn would have been poured on English superficiality! how the moral would have been drawn that he should study German!

Even after the German professor has withdrawn his statement and confessed his error, and other prominent German adherents of the North Galatian theory have frankly acknowledged that Iconium, etc., were in "Galatia," some English theologians continue to quote the original article as authoritative.[1] If that is the case after the article has been retracted, what would be the case if no one had ventured to charge its author with error?

XXIV

GALATIANS AND GAULS.

Many modern authors have committed themselves to another equally sweeping negative—that the title *Galatae* could not be used to designate the people of Roman Galatia (being confined to those who had the blood-right[2] to it).

---

[1] See, for example, the paper of a distinguished Cambridge scholar in *Classical Review*, 1894, p. 396, a paper never retracted, and therefore presumably maintained by the learned author.

[2] *Errarunt qui Galatas Pauli intellegi voluerunt Lycaonas, quippe qui a Romanis Galatiæ provinciæ essent attributi ; neque enim, ut mittam alia, ea re ex Lycaonibus Galli facti erant* (Gal. III 1), says one of the most learned and scholarly supporters of the North Galatian view.

Before making this sweeping assertion, it is clear that the learned writers did not take the trouble to review the passages mentioning the *Galatae,* or to recall the facts.[1] No scholar outside the North Galatian ranks, would even ask for proof that, when the Romans called a Province by a definite name, they summed up the inhabitants of the Province by the ethnic derived from the name. That is an axiom from which all historical and archæological students start. It was necessary in the administration of a Province to have some designation for the whole body of Provincials : *Afri,* all the people of Africa Provincia, whatever their race ; *Baetici,* of Baetica Hispania ; *Asiani,* of Asia ; and *Galatae,* of Galatia.

A single case is sufficient.[2] Tacitus, with his love for varying expression, speaks of *dilectus per Galatiam Cappadociamque* and *Galatarum Cappadocumque auxilia.* When this was quoted as an example, the North Galatian champion replied that these troops were obviously recruited among the Gaulish tribes (as the most warlike), and not from the Province as a whole. Once more he spoke without investigating the facts, simply inventing reasons to prop up a theological theory. The evidence has been fully collected and tabulated by Mommsen,[3] and it is to the opposite

[1] See Sections 8, 9, 12, 13.

[2] Other examples are given in *Studia Biblica,* IV, p. 26 ff. Dr. Zahn says that the discussion there given *handelt hievon ausführlich und überzeugend (Einleitung,* p. 130) ; and Meyer-Sieffert add *man wird die Moglichkeit nicht bestreiten können, dass er einen für die Gemeinden von Antiochien, Iconium, Lystra und Derbe bestimmten Brief* ταῖς ἐκκλησίαις τῆς Γαλατίας *addressirem, und allenfalls auch dieselben als Galater anreden konnte,* p. 8. See also " Galatia " in Hastings' *Dict. of the Bible.*

[3] *Observat. Epigraph.,* XXXVIII, *Militum Provincialium Patriae,* p. 190 f *(Eph. Epigr.,* vol, v.), and *Hermes,* XIX 1 ff,

effect. Recruits were drawn from all parts of the Province, and (so far as the evidence reaches) in larger numbers from the parts outside of North Galatia ; there were, at least, three auxiliary cohorts styled *cohortes Paphlagonum*, but no auxiliary cohort takes its name from the North Galatians.[1]

The details of this argument are here quoted only as an example of the straits to which the North Galatian theory reduces its defenders.   They fall into error after error, when they try to support their theory from the facts of Galatian history or antiquities.

XXV

ST. PAUL'S ROMAN POINT OF VIEW.

When he uses the terms Galatia and Galatians, Paul speaks as no mere Greek spoke : he speaks as the Roman. If so, we must look to find this view ruling both in this Epistle and through his whole policy.   That principle I have attempted to illustrate throughout *St. Paul the Traveller*.   He was at once Roman, Greek, and Jew : in political geography the Roman speaks.

Elsewhere, I hope to illustrate the principle in a more special way, and to show that Paul's career cannot be properly understood, unless his Roman point of view and

---

[1] In the names of auxiliary cohorts, words like *Galatarum*, *Cilicum*, must be taken in the sense of nation, not of Province, according to Mommsen's acute distinction.   Auxiliary cohorts were in theory assumed to originate from foreign nations (as in truth they once did originate), not from Roman Provinces ; and they bore names national and non-Roman after they were recruited entirely from the Provinces.

his imperial statesmanship is fully taken into account. Throughout his life in the Provinces and in Rome "it is not the mere Jew that speaks ; it is the educated citizen of the Roman world" (*St. Paul the Trav.*, p. 149).

The use of *Galatae* in the Roman sense may be illustrated by the term Φιλιππήσιοι. The commentators on *Philippians* IV 15 do not observe that this form is not Greek, but Latin. It is the Greek representative of the Latin *Philippensis*, according to a rule familiar to archæologists : thus, *e.g.*, *Mutinensis* becomes Μουτουννήσιος. So thoroughly does Paul take the Roman view that he avoids the Greek ethnic, which was Φιλιππεύς or Φιλιππηνός. He would not address the inhabitants of a Roman colony by a Greek name, but only by the Latin name written in Greek form. See § XIV.

XXVI

FOOLISH GALATIANS.

Now that we have fixed the precise sense of the word Galatians as "men of the Roman Province Galatia," and therefore pointedly distinguished from "men of the Lycaonian, or of the Phrygian nation," the question is as to the meaning and innuendo of the address "foolish Galatians".

First, perhaps, one must notice the objection, that one ought not to lay too much stress on a mere name in an apostrophe of this kind. That is the objection of one who sits in a study and comments on the text, not of one who recognises what use the orator or the preacher can make of a name. The very rarity and unusualness of the word "Galatians" in the Pauline sense, the very fact that only

Romans or persons speaking decidedly and pointedly from the Roman point of view employed the name in that sense, made it a word that arrested the attention of the audience, conveyed a wealth of meaning to them, and placed them at a certain point of view.

Let those who do not feel the force of the word "Galatae" in Paul's mouth, imagine what difference it would make to an audience in this country whether a speaker used the word "English" or "British" as an apostrophe: it might make all the difference with some audiences between the success or failure of the speech.

The force of the name that Paul uses depends on the state of society and feeling in South Galatia at the time. The contest that was in progress there has been described elsewhere.[1] On the one side was the native and national spirit, allied with the power of the priesthood and the great temples—the spirit of Orientalism, of stagnation, of contented and happy ignorance, of deep-rooted superstition. On the other side was the desire for education, the perception that Greece and Rome stood on a higher intellectual platform than the native religion and customs, the revolt from the ignorant and enslaving native superstition. It has been pointed out that the influence of the new religion of Christ was, necessarily and inevitably, on the side of Græco-Roman education and order, and that it proved far more powerful than either Greek or Roman government in spreading the use of the Greek language (which was the chief agent in Græco-Roman culture). The "men of the Province Galatia" are, therefore, those who desire education, who have shaken off the benumbing and degrading

---

[1] See Sections 12, 14, 23; *St. Paul the Traveller*, chapter VI, etc.

influence of the native magic and superstition, who judge for themselves as to the real value of the facts of life, who lay claim to insight and *Noesis*. There is a telling innuendo in the juxtaposition ἀνόητοι Γαλάται, "you who are showing yourselves devoid of Noesis," "Galatae who fail in the first characteristic of Galatae".

The apostrophe is, in short, a concentration into two words of the sting that lies in the whole paragraph, III 1-5. Your present conduct is irrational, you are sinking back to the old level of superstition and ignorance when you think to attain perfection by the flesh, by the physical acts and works of man, after you had for a time been on the higher level of the spiritual life.

Yet, although the meaning of the Greek adjective here used is indisputable, and is universally recognised by ancient writers and commentators, the North Galatian theorists try to read into it an allusion to the fickleness and changeableness of Celtic and French peoples. Thus one of the greatest of them, after quoting Jerome's interpretation—that the Galatians are here called fools and slow of understanding—remarks : " It is scarcely necessary to say that Jerome here misses the point of St. Paul's rebuke. The Galatians were intellectually quick enough. The 'folly' with which they are charged arose not from obtuseness but from fickleness and levity; the very versatility of their intellect was their snare."[1]

It would be hard to find a more glaring case of the distortion of a naturally sound and clear judgment by a prepossession in favour of a theological theory. First, it is assumed that the Galatians were going over to a Judaistic

---

[1] Lightfoot, p. 242 (tenth edition).

form of Christianity from mere natural volatility and changeableness ; and then this Greek adjective, whose real force
is " senseless," " dully stupid," is declared to indicate folly
arising from fickleness and levity and versatility of intellect.
Where is there any, even the slightest, justification for elicit-
ing such an innuendo out of the Greek word ἀνόητος ?
Not the smallest justification exists : the adjective and its
cognate words have a diametrically opposite connotation :
they denote the stupidity that arises, not from versatility,
but from deadness and impotence of intellect.   Or is there
any ground for charging Paul with using the adjective in a
sense foreign to its real nature ?   There is none : his writing
may sometimes be open to blame for pressing too closely
the natural sense of words, but never for blindness to their
natural sense.   To charge him with using ἀνόητος to indicate the folly due to versatility or over-subtilty or levity
of intellect is to abandon all hope of interpreting him as a
rational writer of Greek.   In that case any word in his
writings may mean anything.[1]

XXVII

THE TWO STAGES III 3.

Are you so devoid of rational perception of the real value
of things, so wanting in insight and Noesis ? Having begun
in the Spirit, are ye now perfected in the flesh ?

It is implied that the Galatian Christians had been led
astray by a theory of lower and higher stages in Christianity.   In the Mysteries they were familiar from their

[1] Compare § VII.

pagan days with this idea of progress through an intermediate to a higher stage of religious life, reaching the perfect knowledge through an imperfect knowledge. They had, in perfect honesty but in utter want of true insight, been led to the idea that their former stage of Paulinism and spiritual religion was a preliminary, and that those who were strong enough should proceed to the hard but ennobling stage of works, of troublesome and difficult service with their body and their flesh.

This idea had evidently been communicated to the Galatian Churches by the Judaising emissaries. That shows that these emissaries accepted the Apostolic Decree, Acts XV, quite as much as Paul himself did, but read it in a different sense. They did not contend, as many Jews previous to the Council and the Decree had contended, that in order to become a Christian the pagan convert must accept the Mosaic Law : they did not say "except ye be circumcised after the manner of Moses, ye cannot be saved" (Acts XV). It had been decided, formally and finally, that that contention was wrong and wicked, "subverting the souls" of the pagan converts (Acts XV 24), and that such converts could be received into the Church without doing more than accept the four necessary conditions (Acts XV 29).

But the Decree readily lends itself to a quite plausible interpretation that the four conditions are a minimum, a mere concession to the weakness of those who were unfit to bear a "greater burden"; and that those who had strength to bear more should voluntarily go on to the perfect stage of bearing the whole burden.

The Galatian Churches were honestly convinced that such was the meaning of the Decree that Paul himself had brought them. They had, in the next place, easily been brought to regard him as the mere subordinate and messenger of the Apostles, and especially of the leaders among them. After these misconceptions had taken root, it was easy to lead on the Galatians to the last error—that Paul from jealousy was keeping most of them on the lower stage, that he was their " Enemy" when he told them to neglect ceremonial and stand fast in the spiritual stage,[1] while he carried on only some special favourites like Timothy to the perfect stage (Gal. V 11).

XXVIII

THE MARVELLOUS POWERS, III 2-5.

The ultimate test and the indubitable proof that the Divine power had been working through Paul among the Galatians from the beginning, and that the Spirit had been given them, lay in the marvellous powers which had been imparted to them, and which they had exhibited in action.

It is beyond question that Paul believed not merely in the superhuman powers which he himself occasionally exerted, but also in the communication of similar powers to many of his converts. He appeals to the memory of the Galatians. They know that such powers have been exercised among them.

Tell me then (he says), you who received the Spirit, does He that liberally equips you with the Spirit and plants in

---

[1] It is clear that the word "enemy" in Gal. IV 16 ought to be printed in inverted commas (if one follows modern methods of punctuation), as being the very word which was being used in Galatia about him. See the remarks in § X, XLIX, carrying out Professor Locke's idea.

you marvellous and extraordinary powers—does He, I say, do so because of the deeds of the Law or because you have been the listeners and disciples to the preaching of the Faith? I do not need to supply the answer. You yourselves know the facts (which the historian has not failed to record), and you can answer the question. You remember the lame man at Lystra, who had the faith of salvation (as the historian says, Acts XIV 9); you remember the disciples at Antioch filled with joy and with the Holy Spirit (XIII 52); you remember the signs and wonders that were done at Iconium (XIV 3),[1] and among the Gentiles in general (XV 12), and you know that Barnabas and I could do such works only where there was in you "the faith of being saved";[2] you have learned in your own case that "God has borne you witness, giving you the Holy Spirit even as He did unto us Jews, and has made no distinction between us and you, cleansing your hearts by faith" (XV 8, 9). All this you remember; and further, you know that these mighty gifts were granted you before you had heard of this new Gospel of works of the Law, and when you knew and believed in only the Gospel of Faith, which alone had been preached to you during my earlier visit.

Are you, then, so void of insight into the truth of actual facts that, after having received such powers through the faith in which you began, you now seek to attain a more perfect stage of Christian life through physical ceremonies and acts? Has it done nothing for you that the Spirit acted so powerfully on you and in you? Nothing, do I

---

[1] Assuming that this verse is Lukan: but see *St. Paul the Traveller*, p. 108. The differences of text in the Iconian episode are very great.

[2] See note, p. 333.

say? Perchance it has actually been the worse for you that you have received the Spirit and then fallen away from it.

XXIX

THE TEACHING OF PAUL.

In the following sections it is necessary to study a number of sayings and arguments in the Epistle involving the whole theology of Paul. Our purpose must be properly understood, lest it be thought that the attempt is too bold and presumptuous. The aim of these sections is not to discuss from the theological or the philosophic point of view the real meaning and nature of Paul's doctrines. Our aim is much humbler. It is simply to try to determine what thoughts and feelings and memories Paul's words roused in the Galatians, what meaning his teaching had had for them. Our purpose is historical; and we are treating a small part, yet one of the most important and most difficult parts, of the general problem, What did Christianity accomplish in the Roman world during the first century?

The materials for forming a judgment are (1) what we know about the character and the religious ideas of the peoples of Asia Minor, especially in the districts which had been least affected by Greek influence and were most purely native : [1] (2) the information given by Luke in Acts, which, however, is very slight, as it lay quite outside of his purpose to record for future generations a picture of the character and mind of Paul's converts : (3) the information given by Paul himself in his Epistle to the Galatians. In

[1] See above Sections 3-5, 9, 13.

Colossians and Ephesians we find teaching of a more advanced character, adapted to congregations of longer Christian experience and of more rapid and advanced development; but in Galatians the intention is to rouse afresh the emotions and sentiments which characterised the Galatian Churches in their first years, to appeal from their later selves to their earlier selves. Hence Paul's arguments here have to a certain extent the character of reminiscences. for they are designed to rouse memories among his readers.

XXX

THE MESSAGE TO THE GALATIANS.

Paul had set before the Galatians from the first that the spiritual life was the true and final and perfect Christianity; and the way by which they entered this spiritual life was explained by "setting forth openly before their eyes Jesus Christ crucified". This brief phrase recalled to them many memories. We, on our part, cannot fail to ask what were these memories. How was this remarkable expression made intelligible to the pagan audiences to whom Paul had appealed? Let us try to imagine to ourselves the mind of such pagans, when such an absolutely novel form of words was first presented to them; in what way was it made to convey a distinct idea to them? We are so familiar with such phrases from childhood, that we accept them as full of meaning and power, often perhaps taking them on credit rather than really understanding what they mean. But Paul was not merely expressing this idea to pagans who had never heard it, he was expressing it for the first time in the world's history; he had stepped on to a new plane in the development of thought, beyond what any of the other Apostles had reached previously.

It was certainly not by skilful philosophic exposition of an abstruse doctrine that Paul expounded his idea of life gained through the death of Christ. Nowhere else does he allude so plainly and pointedly to his method as in the sentences that form the transition from the autobiographical retrospect, which occupies most of chapter II, to the doctrinal exposition of chapter III.

Observe, too, with what art, and yet how naturally, this reminiscence of his method is introduced. The public address to Peter before the whole Antiochian Church, II 14, passes by imperceptible stages into a recital of his own experience in his conversion and the beginning of his new life.[1] The reader begins the recital, II 15, with the idea that Paul is relating what he said among the Antiochians. He ends it, II 21, feeling that Paul has drifted away from a mere narrative of the Antiochian crisis into the memory of that crisis in his own life, which was ever present to his mind. The Galatians recognised in the recital the exact form of his message and gospel to them; they saw at the same time that it was the message spoken in Antioch; and they had the assurance given at the outset of the letter that the whole Antiochian Church joined with Paul in writing to them, and endorsed this recital as a statement of the gospel which they also had heard.

Much of the effect of this paragraph, II 14-21, depends on the place whence the letter was written. The Church in Syrian Antioch is relating to the Churches in Galatia what Paul always had preached to it and had said briefly

---

[1] See § XX.

to Peter. Thus it was impressed on the Galatians that Paul's Gospel was everywhere exactly the same, always sufficient in itself for all occasions, powerful even in face of Peter, absolutely simple and perfectly complete.

No one can really understand that idea except him in whom it has been made part of his life ; and Paul explained it to the Galatians by looking back into his own life and speaking out of his own heart. As usual, we come again to what was stated above,[1] " you understand nothing in Paul unless you take it in its relation to his conversion " ; " on our conception of that one event depends our whole view of Paul's life ". It would be out of place here to study fully the historical and biographical aspect of the problems connected with the conversion ; but the terms in which Paul refers to it here, II 19, 20, compel us to try to realise the manner in which he had set it before the Galatians, if we want to get any clear conception of the effect that this and the following paragraphs produced on them.

The idea had come to Paul through revelation, *i.e.*, through direct intercourse of man with the Divine nature. In such intercourse there is involved not merely the willingness of the Divine nature to manifest itself (for that condition always exists), but also willingness and fitness of the man to become sensitive to the manifestation—a certain state of the mind and of the body is needed. The required conditions existed in Paul on several occasions ; and it is in every case interesting to observe them so far as we can.

It is evident in these words of *v.* 19, " I through law died to law," that Paul had been originally a man profoundly convinced of sin, and eager to escape from it by zealous obedience to the Law. With that strong consciousness

[1] See p. 272.

ever present in his mind, he was travelling to Damascus,
bent on annihilating the effect produced by that Impostor,
who had outraged the Law, and rightly had suffered death
as the due penalty, but had left behind Him some mis-
guided followers, who continued to outrage the Law. As
he came along "the way of the sea," and reached the crest
of the very gentle elevation which bounds the plain of
Damascus on the south,[1] the view of the scene of his coming
work produced naturally a strong effect on his highly
strung and susceptible temperament. The long journey,
day after day, with nothing to do except to count the miles
that still divided him from his goal and to think of the
work that lay before him, inevitably produced an intense
concentration of purpose, which gave the mind supreme
sovereignty over the body. This effect was accentuated
by the spare diet, inevitable in Eastern travel—diet sufficient to keep the mind alert and the body in health, but
not sufficient to enable "this muddy vesture of decay" to
"grossly close in" the soul and screen it more effectually
from perceiving the spiritual world by which we are always,
but generally unconsciously, surrounded—just sufficient to
produce an exaltation and stimulation of the faculties,
which is as far removed from the unhealthy and morbid
excitation induced by extreme over-fatigue, or by unnatural
starvation and fasting, as it is from the dulled and contented
state that results from a full and generous diet.

[1] I follow the old tradition as to the locality—a tradition which
commended itself to the judgment of Sir Charles Wilson, and which
seems to me to have every appearance of truth and unbroken continuance. The situation, however, at Kaukab, near ten or twelve
miles from Damascus, was found to be very inconvenient for pilgrims;
and the Latins therefore moved the site in modern times to a spot
close to the city, and on the east side of it, not on the south !

Few, if any, persons can have much experience of travel in such circumstances, with the sun watching them day after day in pitiless and unvarying calmness from its rising to its setting, without having their nature deeply affected, and even passing permanently into a new life and temper. But in a nature which was already so sensitive to the Divine world around it as Paul's, all the conditions were fulfilled which raised him above the ordinary limitations of humanity. It was a supreme crisis in his life, like that in the hall of the proconsul at Paphos, like that when he perceived the "faith of being saved "[1] which looked through the eyes of the lame man at Lystra. In the bright light that shone about him, he saw and heard what none of his travelling companions could see or hear. He saw as a living, Divine reality Him whom he had believed to be a dead Impostor. Paul's whole theory of life had been founded on the belief that Jesus was dead ; but when he recognised that Jesus was living, the theory crumbled into dust. If He was not dead, He was not an Impostor. He had suffered the last penalty of the Law. He had submitted to the curse pronounced on "every one that hangeth on a tree" (Gal. III 13) ; but yet He was not accursed, but living and glorified. The Law, by being satisfied, had no longer any effect upon Him : it had ceased to exist for Him when He through its operation died to it.

Vividly and deeply conscious that he was a sinner before the Law, Paul accepted the full penalty of his sin : through the operation of the Law, he died to it : he re-

---

[1] πίστιν τοῦ σωθῆναι, an untranslatable expression. It indicates that state of the will and temperament which made a person capable of being cured or saved, able to respond to the word of Paul.

ceived the curse upon him, taking to him the crucifixion of Christ. By so doing he ceased to exist for the Law, and the Law no longer existed for him : he entered on a new life. But this new life became his only through his belief in Jesus as the living God : the rest of his life was given him through his faith in the Son of God, whose voluntary death had opened to Paul this new life free from the terrors of the Law and the ever-present fear of death. Had it been possible to attain through the Law this new life, this life free from the curse pronounced by the Law against every one who failed to walk in it (Gal. III 10), Christ's death would have been useless. Paul had found for himself that the new life could not be attained by striving to obey the Law ; he knew that nothing could give it except the perfect and soul-possessing recognition that Christ had died voluntarily to show the way, and yet was still living.

The power which Paul's Gospel had over the Galatians lay in its origin out of his own experience. He was the living proof that it was true. It had given him his new life. What it did for him it could do for all.

Therein lay the sufficient answer to the mere abstract philosophical objection : how can the death of one man gain pardon for the sins of another? In reply Paul narrated the facts. That shame and curse of the Crucifixion he had embraced as his own ; he had grasped it and taken it into his own soul ; he had made it the deepest part of his own nature ; he had founded his entire consciousness and his entire mind upon it. It remade the universe for him ; it recreated his life and soul and thought and energy ; the simple fact that he stood and spoke before them was the unanswerable proof that his message was true.

We may ask, what evidence was there that what Paul said was true? What evidence was there that he was not deceiving himself, mistaking the visions of epileptic insanity (as some of my medical friends call them) for reality and truth? Such questions we may now ask, just as now we may, some of us, doubt whether he spoke the whole truth in that autobiographical sketch, Ch. I, II, to the Galatians, whether he did not pass lightly over some inconvenient facts, such as his solemn public appeal to the Apostolic Council and the message from the Council which he carried to the Galatians. But no one that saw him could ask those questions. No one that heard his voice and looked into his eyes could doubt that he spoke the truth. Therein lay his power over men. They could not but believe him. The Galatians knew that he spoke the truth.

And now at the present day I put the question, is it possible for us, if we reason straight and fairly, to believe that Paul could have acquired that power, could have so possessed his hearers with the absolute conviction that he spoke the truth about his experiences, in any other way except by speaking the truth? To speak to the hearts of others you must speak straight out of your own heart. Paul as an impostor, or even as an unconscious deceiver, is an unintelligible and irrational figment: to be conceivable he must be taken as absolutely true.

But Paul had declared in Syrian Antioch, and it was involved in the truth of his message, that the Law ceased to have any power over him, when he accepted the penalty and the shame, and died to the Law. If, therefore, he should "build up again those things which he had destroyed" (Gal. II 18), if he should begin once more to recognise the Law as existing for him, he would "prove himself a transgressor," he would sacrifice the justifying effect of his belief in Jesus, he would be bringing himself back into the former condition of vivid, intense consciousness of sin and inability to escape from the penalty, he would "make void the grace of God" (II 21), he would be experiencing in vain the Divine power (III 4). If he made the Law a power over him, Christ would profit him nothing (V 2).

The Law had produced in him that intense and overpowering consciousness of guilt and sin, which was a necessary stage in the way of salvation. But by satisfying it, he annihilated it as a power over himself.

Those who would be saved must go through the same process : first the intense consciousness of sin ; then the actual experience how belief in Christ enabled them to die with Him to the Law, and enter on the new life, which thus was opened to them. How irrational—and worse than irrational—it was thereafter to restore for themselves the power which the Law exerted over all who were under it, suffering the hopeless consciousness of guilt which it produced. Their experience of the Spirit would be vain and useless to them, it would perhaps be a positive disadvantage to them, if they now began to build up again what they had destroyed (Gal. II 4). "If ye receive circumcision, Christ will profit you nothing" (V 2), "Christ died for naught" (I 21).

XXXI

SONS OF ABRAHAM, III 6-9.

As Abraham's faith in God was counted to him for righteousness, so your faith in Jesus was counted to you. You know, then, that they who cleave to the rule of Faith, inherit Abraham's Faith, and are his sons (for he that inherits is a son).

The idea that they who follow the principle of Faith are sons of Abraham, whatever family they belonged to by nature, would certainly be understood by the Galatians as referring to the legal process called Adoption, υἱοθεσία.

Now there were at that time in the Roman Empire two kinds of Adoption, and two kinds of law regulating it : there was Adoption of the Greek type and Adoption of the Roman type.   In their origin these two types had been so similar that, for our present purposes, they might be treated as one.   Adoption had been a process devised to supply the want of a son and heir in the course of nature : a man that had no natural son might adopt a son, in order to prevent the family from coming to an end (which would entail the annihilation of the family-cultus).   Adoption was at the same time a kind of embryo Will : the adopted son became the owner of the property, and the property could pass to a person that was naturally outside of the family only through his being adopted.   The Adoption was a sort of Will-making ; and this ancient form of Will was irrevocable and public.

Such had been the original sense of the process of Adoption.   In Greek law there had been no serious change in its character.   But in Roman law it had de-

22

veloped considerably from its primitive form, and the idea of inheritance or heirship had become dissociated from the idea of sonship : a man might be adopted without any intention of making him an heir, and property might be left to a person outside of the family [1] without adopting him.

Now Paul here assumes that all they who inherit that special property of Abraham, *viz.*, Faith, must be sons of Abraham, *i.e.*, that none but a son can inherit, and that the terms " Son " and " Heir " are interchangeable. He assumes also that his readers are familiar with that principle and custom. Obviously, that principle suits Greek law much better than Roman law as it was in the centuries immediately before or after Christ. The question then arises : Can we understand that Paul is here thinking of the Roman Adoption, or must we conclude that he is speaking with reference to the Greek Adoption ?

Dr. W. E. Ball,[2] in a highly suggestive paper on the influence of Roman ideas on the theology and language of Paul, assumes, without thinking of any other possibility, that the Apostle is here thinking of Roman law ; and Halmel has attempted to prove that in his book *das römische Recht im Galaterbrief*, Essen, 1895.[3]

Mitteis,[4] *apropos* of a passage in the fifth century Syrian-Roman Lawbook, in which the interchangeableness of

---

[1] *Adoptio per testamentum*, which is mentioned by Roman historians, seems to have been a political device, and not customary in private life : so says Mitteis *Reichsrecht und Volksrecht*, p. 340, who adds that it is never mentioned in juristic sources.

[2] In the *Contemporary Review*, Aug., 1891, p. 278 ff.

[3] On it see the quotation from Mitteis in our preface.

[4] Mitteis, *Reichsrecht und Volksrecht*, p. 339 ff. The Lawbook is published in Syriac and German by Bruns and Sachau *ein römisch-syrisches Rechtsbuch des fünften Jahrhunderts*.

"Son" and "Heir" is assumed, has discussed the same question which meets us here, and has decided it on grounds which are perfectly applicable here, though, naturally, he does not notice the parallel case in Paul's letter. In several places his argument might almost be taken as a reply to Dr. W. E. Ball's paper, though in all probability he never saw it. We simply transfer his argument to our pages, changing names, slightly modifying and greatly shortening it.

It is evidently impossible that Paul should use, or the Galatians understand, any references to the Roman law of Adoption in its original and primitive form ; they could know only the developed form of that law as it was customary in ordinary life, in which the last shred of connection between sonship and heirship had disappeared. Nor is it an allowable supposition that this form of expression had persisted in language after it had ceased to exist in law. Such survivals, indeed, are possible, but in every case they must be proved by examples : now not a trace is known in Roman literature or monuments of such interchangeableness of the terms.

On the other hand the equivalence of sonship and heirship is familiar in Greek literature. The proofs are given in every hand-book and in every dictionary of Greek antiquities.[1]

In the Greek view it was a calamity both to the individual and to the State, if a citizen died without leaving an heir to carry on the family and continue the family religion : the State, which was an association of families, lost one of its members, the gods of the family lost their worship, and the

---

[1] See *e.g.*, Daremberg and Saglio, *Dictionnaire des Antiquités Gr. et Rom. s.v. Adoptio.*

dead citizen lost the rights and gifts which he was entitled to receive from the surviving family. The State, therefore, looked after the continuance of the family, if the individual citizen had neglected his duty. The only way in which a childless individual could acquire an heir was by adopting him : hence to adopt, εἰσποιεῖσθαι, and to bequeath, διατί- θεσθαι, are used as equivalent terms : childless (ἄπαις) and intestate are practically the same idea. In Roman law adoption imitated nature, and the adopted son was assimi- lated as much as possible to the son by birth. In Athens, in order to keep the property in the family, the adopted son was permitted and encouraged to marry the daughter of the deceased, thus saving the dowry which she would otherwise require.

In Asiatic countries, where some traces of succession in the female line persisted, it is highly probable that the same marriage custom prevailed, on the theory that the adopted son acquired the right of the daughter to inherit by marry- ing her. In those countries this was not felt to make any difference between the position of the son by nature and the son by adoption, for apparently both kinds of sons, ac- cording to the primitive religious law, acquired right of inheritance by marrying the heiress, their sister by nature or by adoption. The spread of Greek customs tended to discourage marriage between natural brother and sister, except in cases where something peculiarly sacred, such as the right to the throne, was concerned. How far the Athenian custom of marrying the adopted son to the heiress was a survival of a similar ancient social custom we need not here inquire.

It is true that most of the evidence ordinarily quoted to prove this Greek idea of the equivalence of sonship and heirship is distinctly older than the time of Paul ; but there is also later evidence. In fact the passage of the Roman-Syrian Lawbook of the fifth century on which Mitteis (*l. c.*) comments is an example of the way in which the forms of language in Græco-Asiatic states continued long after Paul's time to follow the ancient Greek expression that the heir is the son, that the family of the deceased lives on in the heirs, that heir and son are interchangeable terms, that "to make a will" means "to adopt a son".

Paul, therefore, is using the ordinary Greek forms. He is speaking of a religious inheritance ; and it was specially and fundamentally on religious grounds that the Greek heir and son was adopted to continue the family cultus. On the other hand, in Rome, such a proverb as *hereditas sine sacris*, "an inheritance unencumbered by any religious duties," indicating a piece of unmixed good-luck—a proverb current as early as the third century B.C.—shows how early heirship and religious succession might be divorced in Roman practice.

Paul's thought is this : the adopted heir succeeds to the religious obligations and position of the deceased. Conversely, he who succeeds to the religious position of any man is his son : there was no other form under which succession could be made, except through adoption. He who succeeds to the faith of Abraham is the son of Abraham. He could not acquire possession of Abraham's faith in any other way than as his son. "Ye know therefore that they which be of faith, the same are sons of Abraham."

Among the Jews, adoption had no importance, and hardly any existence. The perpetuity of the family, when a man died childless, was secured in another way, *viz.*, the *levirate*. Only sons by blood were esteemed in the Hebrew view :

only such sons could carry on the true succession, and be in a true sense heirs. From every point of view the thought in III 7 is abhorrent to Hebrew feeling. It is one of the passages which show how far removed Paul was from the mere Jewish way of thinking ; he differed in the theory of life, and not merely in the religious view. Quite apart from the fact that the Jews naturally abhorred the idea that the Gentiles could become sons of Abraham, the very thought that the possessing of a man's property implied sonship was unnatural to them. Paul had grown up amid the surroundings and law of Græco-Roman society ; otherwise the expression of III 7 could not come so lightly and easily from him.

Such passages as this have led some very learned Jewish scholars of my acquaintance, whose names I may not quote, to declare in conversation their conviction that the letters attributed to Paul were all forgeries, because no Jew of that age could write like that, whether he were Christian or no. So far as I may judge, they undervalue the cosmopolitan effect produced on the Jewish-Roman and Greek citizens living for generations in Greek and Roman cities, just as much as many distinguished European scholars do, when they fancy that Paul is a pure Jew, unaffected, except in the most superficial way, by Greek education.

An example of the way in which Paul adapted his exposition and his illustrations to the circumstances and education of his readers, is furnished by the form under which he explains to the Roman Christians that same idea —that the common possession of faith constitutes a relationship, analogous to that of father and sons, between Abraham and the Gentile Christians. To the Galatians he uses a metaphor drawn from Greek law : for the Romans he employs (IV 11) a different metaphor, founded on the customary usage of the word *pater*. Both in law and in common language *pater* in Rome had a very much wider sense than " father " in English : the *pater* is the chief, the lord, the master, the leader. Æneas is the *pater* of all his followers. A man may be described as the *pater* of all to whom his qualifications constitute him a guide and leader and protector. The head of a family is the lord and *pater* over children, wife and slaves.

Accordingly, whereas Paul says to the Galatians, " your possession of Abraham's property proves that you are his sons," to the Romans he says, " Abraham's possession of the same faith that you possess fits him to be your father. He possessed faith before he was circumcised, and thus is suited to be the *pater* of the faithful Gentiles : afterwards circumcision was imposed on him, like a seal affixed to a document, making him suitable to be the *pater* of faithful Jews. Thus he is the spiritual father alike of two divergent classes—believing Gentiles and believing Jews.[1]

How delicate is the change in expression ! yet it places us amid totally different surroundings.

Another example may be drawn from Rom. VIII 16. " The Spirit Himself beareth witness with our spirit that we are children of God ; and if children, then heirs." Here there is a juxtaposition of the two ideas " children " and " heirs," just as in Galatians III 7 the ideas, possession of the same property (*i.e.*, heirship) and sonship, are brought together. But in Galatians the sonship is inferred from the possession of the property, whereas in Romans the heirship is inferred from the sonship—" if children, then heirs ". This

[1] Compare Sanday and Headlam, *Romans*, p. 106.

is in strict accord with Roman law: the children must
inherit: a will that left the property away from the
children was invalid.

XXXII

Οἱ ἐκ πίστεως.

In this phrase and the opposite, οἱ ἐκ περιτομῆς, we have
two remarkable expressions, which we can trace in their
genesis, until they gradually harden almost into technical
terms and badges of two opposite parties.   In fact, that is
entirely the case with οἱ ἐκ περιτομῆς in Acts XI 2 where
a long history is concentrated in a phrase.

The following words are practically only an expansion
and re-expression, after it has passed through the medium
of my own mind, of a letter which Dr. Gifford kindly sent
in answer to my questions, reviewing the stages of the
two phrases.

The phrase ἐκ πίστεως is used only once in the Septuagint, Habakkuk II 4—"The just shall live by his faith".
Paul took this saying, connected it with Genesis XV 6—
"Abraham believed in the Lord, and he counted it to him
for righteousness"—and found in the two the proof of his
doctrine of the righteousness that is of faith—δικαιοσύνην
τὴν ἐκ πίστεως.

It is plain that Paul had used these two sayings in his
former preaching to the Galatians, for they are quoted as
familiar truths, whose origin does not need to be formally
mentioned, III 6-11.   His doctrine, therefore, must have
been explicitly set forth to them orally, and in the letter
was merely recalled to their memory : faith is the source or

root in man of righteousness and of life, which is an expression from a different point of view of the principle studied in § XXX, that the belief in Christ becomes a life-giving power, ruling the nature of him who feels it.

Comparing the language of the whole passage beginning II 15, we see that οἱ ἐκ πίστεως is an abbreviated expression equivalent to οἱ ἐκ πίστεως δικαιωθέντες; see II 16, ἵνα δικαιωθῶμεν ἐκ πίστεως Χριστοῦ καὶ οὐκ ἐξ ἔργων νόμου; III 2, ἐξ ἔργων νόμου τὸ πνεῦμα ἐλάβετε ἢ ἐξ ἀκοῆς πίστεως; III 8, ἐκ πίστεως δικαιοῖ τὰ ἔθνη ὁ θεός. Already the phrase seems to have a stereotyped form, and to imply a suppressed thought with which the readers were familiar. Paul, therefore, in his teaching to the Galatians, must already have insisted on the distinction ἐκ πίστεως and ἐξ ἔργων νόμου (or ἐκ περιτομῆς); and hence he could use such concise and pregnant language to those who already had heard, when he desired to revivify in their mind the early lessons.[1]

But in writing to the Roman Church, Paul was addressing a body of Christians who had never listened (except a few individuals) to his doctrine; and he therefore explained his meaning more fully to them. In that letter we read what was the kind of teaching which Paul in his preaching set before the Galatians, and which he assumes in his Epistle as familiar to them.[2] His Gospel was evidently exactly the same, and quite as fully thought out in Galatia in A.D. 47-48, as in Corinth in January or February A.D. 57. He had seen the truth before that early

[1] See above, p. 306.

[2] Romans is thus on a logical earlier stage than Galatians, but, the circumstances show that logical priority does not (as some scholars assume) imply chronological priority.

date. Thereafter there was no further progress or development in his Gospel, though there was undoubtedly a
great development on the practical side, as regards the
way and the accompaniments by which the Gospel was
to be spread through the Gentile world, to which he was
from the first commissioned to preach it.

In Romans I 17, Paul declares that the revelation in
man of "the righteousness of God begins from faith and
leads on to fuller faith," ἐκ πίστεως εἰς πίστιν, and he
quotes Habakkuk II 4.

It is noteworthy that he gives the last words as a formal
quotation, when writing to those who had not heard his
teaching ; but to the Galatians he uses them as a familiar
axiom.

Faith, then, is the beginning and the end of man's
part in the reception of the righteousness of God ; and
this is emphasised in III 21, 22, "apart from the Law
righteousness hath been manifested," and III 28, "a man
is justified by faith apart from the works of the Law".

Paul had always in mind the idea of his opponents that
faith was only one element in the reception of righteousness,
that "apart from the Law righteousness is not fully manifested," that "a man is justified fully by faith conjoined
with the works of the Law". Against that view Paul
always appealed to the authority "by works of Law shall
no flesh be justified" (Gal. II 16, Rom. III 20.) The
Law is a preliminary, because it exhibits so clearly to man
his own sin, and thus helps to produce that profound conviction of sin, which is a necessary step towards justification.

Another antithesis is "through faith" and "through Law"
διὰ πίστεως and διὰ νόμου (Gal. II 16, 19, Rom. III 25,
30). This seems to indicate the indispensable condition

or means for the continued operation of the cause or source. Paul's view is that Faith itself is the indispensable condition for the continued operation of itself: it is at once the cause, and the means by which the cause continues to work. It is only another way of expressing the same truth, when in V 6 he speaks of "faith working itself out through love". Love is the outward form of faith.

The exact point in dispute between Paul and the Judaising Christians must be kept in mind. Both sides were Christians. Both held that belief in Christ was indispensable to salvation, that righteousness in man could not exist without faith. But the Judaisers held that the Law and Circumcision were also indispensable to at least the fullest stage of righteousness. They were the party of believers who set the Law alongside of faith; and it would appear from Galatians II 16 that Paul represents His opponents' view as being that in the Jew righteousness came from works of Law through (*i.e.*, on condition of) faith, ἐξ ἔργων νόμου διὰ πίστεως. Hence the Judaistic part of the Christians were οἱ ἐκ περιτομῆς πιστοί, as they are called in Acts X 45. In Acts XI 2, the title is used in a still further abbreviated form οἱ ἐκ περιτομῆς: but the meaning is the same, and the idea πιστοί has to be supplied in thought.

In regard to the Gentiles the view of Paul's opponents was expressed in the form that full and complete righteousness in them comes from faith as the cause through the Law as the condition, ἐκ πίστεως διὰ νόμου.

In both cases alike Paul maintained the origin ἐκ πίστεως καὶ διὰ πίστεως. His formula agrees always with half of theirs; and when he contradicts them, he only contradicts the discrepant half of their formula. Hence we find the contradictions thus :—

	JUDAISTIC.	PAULINE.
Jews . .	ἐκ νόμου διὰ πίστεως.	ἐκ πίστεως (καὶ διὰ πίστεως).
Gentiles .	ἐκ πίστεως διὰ νόμου.	(ἐκ πίστεως καὶ) διὰ πίστεως.

Accordingly, Rom. III 30 means, God will justify both Jews and Gentiles from faith and through the continued operation of their faith, δικαιώσει περιτομὴν ἐκ πίστεως καὶ ἀκρο βυστίαν διὰ τῆς πίστεως.

Finally the motive power in the process is expressed by the dative, by grace, χάριτι (Rom. III 24, Eph. II 8), or by what is practically the same idea, the Spirit, πνεύματι (Gal. V 5).

As the distinction between an indispensable condition and a source is very fine, the use of διά and ἐκ is hard to keep apart. But it is noteworthy that we never find the party names οἱ διά, but only οἱ ἐκ περιτομῆς, οἱ ἐκ νόμου, οἱ ἐκ πίστεως. In most places ἐκ expresses the fundamental thought; and διά is used much more rarely.

In the two passages quoted from Acts the Pauline expression has crystallised into a title and the badge of a party. But in that case it is clear that the author of Acts understood the two opposing parties to be already constituted when he applies to one of them the technical term. They who hold the view that the author was a remarkably accurate describer of events must conclude that he intentionally chose the technical term in order to show that the antithesis between the two views was already clear and definite at the time of Acts XI 2.[1]

[1] *Expositor*, March, 1896, p. 198 f.

XXXIII

A MAN'S WILL, *DIATHEKE*, III 15-18.

An illustration from the ordinary facts of society, as it existed in the Galatian cities, is here stated : " I speak after the manner of men ". The will (διαθήκη) of a human being is irrevocable when once duly executed : hence the Will of God, formally pledged to Abraham, that all nations should be blessed in his seed, *i.e.*, in Christ, cannot be affected by the subsequent act of God executed centuries later, *viz.*, the giving of the Law. The inheritance of blessing comes from the original Will, and cannot be affected by the subsequent Law.

The sense of *Diatheke* in this passage has been much debated ; and many excellent scholars declare that it does not mean Will or Testament (as we have rendered it), but either denotes a Covenant, *Bund* in German (so Calvin, Beza, Flatt, Hilgenfeld, Meyer, Lightfoot), or has the more vague and general sense of Determination, *Willens-verfügung* or *Bestimmung* (so Zöckler, Philippi, Lipsius, Hofmann, Schott, Winer).[1]

The question as to the sense of the Greek word *Diatheke* in this passage must be carefully distinguished from the far more important question as to its general Biblical meaning. Here the word is used in allusion to every-day life among ordinary men. The Biblical usage is a different topic, and will be treated in the following sections. The commentators have not been sufficiently careful to keep those two questions separate from one another. That the

---

[1] Zockler's statistics.

word must in this passage be taken in the technical sense of Will is shown by the following reasons.

In the first place the *Diatheke* is proved to indicate a Will by the fact that an inheritance, κληρονομία, is determined by it, III 18.

Secondly, Paul says that he is speaking "after the manner of men," III 15. He therefore is employing the word in the sense in which it was commonly used as part of the ordinary life of the cities of the East. What this sense was there can be no doubt. The word is often found in the inscriptions, and always in the same sense which it bears in the classical Greek writers, Will or Testament.

But, if Paul is speaking about a Will, how can he say that, after it is once made, it is irrevocable? It is this difficulty that has made the commentators on this passage reject almost unanimously the sense of Will. They do not try to determine what was the nature of a Will among the Galatians, but assume that an ancient Will was pretty much of the same nature as a modern Will. Our procedure must be very different. We have to take the word *Diatheke* in its ordinary sense "after the manner of men": then we observe what is the character attributed by Paul to the Galatian Will: finally we investigate what relation the Galatian Will bears to the known classes of Will in other ancient nations, and so determine its origin.

In Hellenised Asia Minor, at the time when Paul was writing, the *Diatheke* or Will was a provision to maintain the continuity of the family with its religious obligations; and, though it included bequests of money to the State or to individuals, these bequests seem to be always regarded in the light of provisions for the honour and privileges of the testator and his family.

It is here plainly stated that when the Will has been properly executed with all legal formalities, no person can make it ineffective or add any further clause or conditions. It is not a correct explanation to say that " no person " means " no other," for the argument is that a subsequent document executed by the same person does not invalidate the former. We are confronted with a legal idea that the duly executed Will cannot be revoked by a subsequent act of the testator.

Such irrevocability was a characteristic feature of Greek law, according to which an heir outside the family must be adopted into the family ; and the adoption was the Will-making. Galatian procedure, evidently, was similar. The appointment of an heir was the adoption of a son, and was final and irrevocable. The testator, after adopting his heir, could not subsequently take away from him his share in the inheritance or impose new conditions on his succession.

That is a totally different conception of a Will from our modern ideas. We think of a Will as secret and inoperative during the life-time of the testator, as revocable by him at pleasure, and as executed by him only with a view to his own death. A Will of that kind could have no application to God, and no such analogy could have been used by Paul. But the Galatian Will, like God's Word, is irrevocable and unalterable ; it comes into operation as soon as the conditions are performed by the heir ; it is public and open.

Such also was the original Roman Will ;[1] but that kind of Will had become obsolete in Roman law. It could have been familiar to no one except a legal antiquary ; and neither Paul nor any other Provincial is likely to have

---

[1] Maine, *Ancient Law*, ch. VI.

known anything about that ancient Roman idea. In Rome a highly developed and simple form of Will, called the Prætorian Testament, had become usual; and it was secret and revocable, and took effect only after the testator's death. But Greek law retained that ancient character much longer, and in regard to Wills, Galatian law was evidently of kindred spirit to Greek law and unlike Roman, just as we found to be the case in regard to adoption and heirship, § XXXI.

The exact sense of V 15 must be observed. Paul does not say that a supplementary Will (ἐπιδιαθήκη) cannot be made; but that the new Will cannot interfere with or invalidate the old Will. Nature may necessitate changes in the details of the first Will : new children and heirs may be born, and so on. A man can even adopt a second son and heir by a subsequent Will. Then the two adopted sons jointly carry on the family in its religious and social aspect. Inheritance was not simply a claim to property, as we now regard it. Inheritance was the right to take the father's place in all his relations to the gods and the State; and two or more sons can take the father's place jointly, each being heir. But in essence the second Will must confirm the original Will, and cannot revoke or add essentially novel conditions. One example of such a supplementary Greek Will (ἐπιδιαθήκη) is known :[1] it confirms and repeats the original Will.

The Roman-Syrian Law-Book—which we have already quoted as an authority for the kind of legal ideas and customs that obtained in an Eastern Province, where a formerly prevalent Greek law had persisted under the Roman

---

[1] Grenfell, *Alexandrian Erotic Papyrus*, No. 21.

Empire—well illustrates this passage of the Epistle.[1] It actually lays down the principle that a man can never put away an adopted son, and that he cannot put away a real son without good ground. It is remarkable that the adopted son should have a stronger position than the son by birth; yet it was so. Mitteis illustrates this by a passage of Lucian,[2] where a son, who had been put away by his father, then restored to favour, and then put away a second time, complains that this second rejection is illegal, inasmuch as his restoration to favour put him on a level with an adopted son, who cannot be turned away in that fashion.

In the Gortynian procedure, this principle of the Greek law was relaxed, and the adoptive father could put away his adoptive son by a public act, declared from the stone in the market-place before the assembled citizens, but he must give him two staters as a guest-gift. Evidently the gift is a sort of substitute for the inheritance ; the adopted son had an indefeasible claim to share the property, and by a legal fiction, the testator gives him his inheritance and sends him away.

The adopted son and heir was adopted by the will and authority of the whole community, to keep up the existence of one of the families constituting the community. The father, therefore, had less power over the adopted son than over the born son ; the latter was subject to his solitary will, the former had the will of the whole community on his side.

[1] The following remarks are taken from Mitteis' *Reichsrecht und Volksrecht*, p. 213 ff., who does not notice the confirmation by Paul's words of the view which he states.

[2] Lucian, *Abdic.*, 12.

23

When διαθήκη is understood thus, the paragraph becomes full of meaning ; but this sense could hardly have existed except in a country where Greek law had been established for some considerable time.   In Asia Minor or Syria the Will could only be of the Greek or the Roman type ; there was no third type, for in no other land had a legal doctrine of Wills been elaborated.   As the Galatian Will is unlike the Roman and like the Greek, it is clear that Greek law must have been established among the people to whom Paul was writing.

To make this subject clear, we must look at the use of διαθήκη in Epistles addressed to readers among whom Greek law had never exercised much, if any, influence, and to whom the Will of the Roman type, as current in the first century, alone was likely to be known.   This requires a special chapter, and some account of the Biblical use of the term *Diatheke.*

The expression [1] in *v.* 15, "when it hath been confirmed," must also be observed.   Every Will had to be passed through the Record Office of the city.   It was not regarded in the Greek law as a purely private document, which might be kept anywhere and produced when the testator died.   It must be deposited, either in original or in a properly certified copy, in the Record Office ; and the officials there were bound to satisfy themselves that it was a properly valid document before they accepted it.   If there was an earlier will, the later must not be accepted, unless it was found not to interfere with the preceding one.

That is a Greek, not a Roman custom.   There was no such provision needed in Roman law, for the developed

---

[1] κεκυρωμένην διαθήκην.

Roman Will [1] might be revoked and changed as often as the testator chose ; and the latest Will cancelled all others.

The passing through the Record Office took the place of the primitive custom that the Will and Adoption must be made before the whole people in the public assembly.[2] " In the Record Office were preserved public documents of all kinds, as well as copies of important private documents, title-deeds, wills, records of the sale of real property, mortgages, loans, etc. Before a copy of any such deed was accepted in the office, its legality and validity were verified ; and thus the official in charge of the office played an important part in the business of the city. The existence of a certified copy of a deed in the Record Office was accepted as proof of legal right ; and this simple guarantee facilitated the borrowing of money on the security of property, besides making the transfer of property and the verification of titles very simple." [3]

In *v.* 16 Christ is called "the seed," *i.e.*, the true seed in contrast to other seed, and we note that the preference of the " true seed," and the superior right of the " true seed " to inherit, is characteristic both of Greek thought and philosophy in general, and in particular of the late Syrian law (which we take to be a survival of Seleucid law analogous to that which prevailed in South Galatia).[4] The late Roman-Syrian Law-Book, which has already been so often quoted in these pages, justifies the preference of the male

[1] See p. 366.

[2] Compare also the statements in Greek Egyptian Wills that the Will was executed ἐν ἀγυιᾶι or ἐπὶ ἀγορανόμου : see next Section.

[3] *Cities and Bish. of Phrygia*, II, p. 368 f., and authorities there quoted.

[4] See p. 374 f, 393.

descendents over the female[1] in the same degree on the ground that the former are "sought after by the laws as the true seed ".[2]   It is not to be supposed that Paul refers to that precise doctrine ; but, when he distinguishes between seed, and distinguishes one seed as *the* seed, more fully entitled to possession of the inheritance than other seed in the same line and degree of descent, he is using a kind of distinction which was customary in Greek thought centuries before and centuries after the time when he wrote.[3]

XXXIV

THE USE OF *DIATHEKE* IN THE PAULINE EPISTLES.

The Biblical idea, which is usually rendered in the English Version by the word " Covenant," is an exceptionally important one.   It does not belong to our purpose to discuss it from a theological point of view, or to describe its origin and development in the religious life of the Hebrews.   Roughly speaking, Paul took the word *Diatheke* to indicate a certain gracious act of God, in the exercise of His own absolute power, towards His chosen people, conferring certain privileges upon them on certain conditions which they are expected to fulfil in their life and conduct : His chosen people being first the Jews, and in due course all nations, whom the Jews ought to train and instruct. That original act of God may be called a Promise, or a Covenant ; but no single word expresses fully its nature

---

[1] See p. 367.

[2] *Die Gesetze suchen den reinen Samen heraus : Röm-Syrisches Rechtsbuch*, German translation p. 4.

[3] Mitteis, *Reichsrecht*, p. 326.

and character ; every name leaves much to the imagination
and thought, the knowledge and experience, of individual
men, so that each man must make his own conception of
the thing which is meant. Every word has a misleading
connotation, due to its ordinary sense " after the manner of
men " ; and that ought to be stripped off when one applies
the word to the Divine act.

The Greek word *Diatheke*, which was most widely in
use to designate that Divine act, was frequently used in
ordinary society to indicate a certain common act of legal
character, *viz.*, a Will or Testament. This connotation
was distinctly detrimental, when the Greeks attempted to
understand the Biblical idea, and to conceive in its purity
the character of the Divine act. We have to study the
action and language of Paul in the face of this difficulty.
He had to convey to his Greek-speaking converts from
Paganism as clear a conception as possible of the Divine
act ; and he was not entirely free to use whatever words he
chose, for there was already in existence a certain customary
series of terms, employed for centuries by Greek-speaking
Hebrews. The word *Diatheke*, which we have to study,
occurs nearly 300 times in the Septuagint Version of the
Old Testament, and thirty-three times in the New (chiefly
in Paul and in Hebrews).

Now the history and sense of the Greek *Diatheke* is exceedingly obscure. The *Diatheke* was a different thing at
different periods and in different parts of the Greek world.
Yet Paul in some cases is clearly trying to use the recognised ordinary sense of *Diatheke* "after the manner of men,"
in order to aid his readers to picture to themselves the
Divine *Diatheke*, as we have seen that he is doing in Galatians III 15-17. In trying to grasp his meaning we find

so little trustworthy information about the Greek usage, that we must attempt to treat the subject a little more accurately and less vaguely than the commentators. Most writers on "Covenant" discuss the theological and philosophical side very elaborately, and confine themselves to a few vague and not very accurate words about the Greek use of the word *Diatheke*.

I touch upon the subject with reluctance and diffidence. It lies beyond the special sphere of my knowledge, among the obscurest mysteries of Greek law and of theological theory; and I shall be grateful for any corrections of, or useful additions to, the statements made in the following paragraphs.

The Septuagint translators found themselves confronted with a difficult problem, when they had to select a Greek word to translate the Hebrew *berîth*. The Hebrew word, denoting primarily an agreement, private or public, among men, guaranteed and confirmed by weighty and solemn oaths on both sides, had become almost a technical term to denote the promises made, and confirmed by repetition, by God to the ancestors of the Hebrew people, especially Abraham, and, in a much less degree, Isaac and Jacob. As Professor A. B. Davidson says,[1] it "had become a religious term in the sense of a one-sided engagement on the part of God". This sense was peculiar and unique. Nothing like it was known to the Greeks, and therefore there was no Greek word to correspond to it. Accordingly, the translators were compelled to take some Greek word, which hitherto had denoted something else, and apply it to their purpose. The word selected must necessarily be

---

[1] In Hastings' *Dict. of the Bible*, I, p. 514.

encumbered by associations connected with its recognised meaning, and, therefore, must be to a certain degree un-suitable. The problem was to find the least unsuitable word.

A word which in some respects corresponded well to the sense required was *Syntheke, συνθήκη*, which brought out the binding force and legal solemnity of the idea. But it was unsuitable, because it implied pointedly that the two persons concerned in the *Syntheke* stand more or less on a footing of equality (though not necessarily on perfect equality), each joining in the act with a certain degree of power and voluntary action. But in the Biblical idea the power and the action lie entirely on one side. God gives the assur-ance, binds Himself by the promise, and initiates alone the whole agreement. The other side merely accepts the agreement, and has simply to fulfil the conditions, which are often unexpressed, for God foresees the course of events, and knows how far the future action of the chosen reci-pients will fulfil the conditions. The Biblical idea was one-sided, but *Syntheke* was two-sided essentially.

Yet the history of the Greek rendering of the Old Testament shows that *Syntheke* must have been felt to have some claim, for the later translators, Aquila, Theodotion and Symmachus, use that word in a number of cases, where the Septuagint version has *Diatheke*.[1] The reason for this change, as we shall see, lies in the gradual development of meaning and character in the ordinary use of *Diatheke*. The word, as used in the early part of the third century B.C., was a closer and better representative of the Biblical

---

[1] The Septuagint version uses *συνθήκη* in a few cases to represent other Greek words, and, in one case, 4 Kings XVII 15, one of the texts uses it to represent *berith*.

term than it was in its later development. The development was partly in the line of natural growth in Greek Will-making (and that growth seems to have been more rapid in Egypt than in Asia Minor and Syria), partly in the way of assimilation of Roman ideas on Wills.

The word ἐπαγγελία, Promise, might also have been selected. It had the advantage of expressing strongly that the action and the initiative proceeded solely from one side in free grace. But it lacked entirely the idea of bond, of solemn guarantee, of the binding force of oaths and religious sanctity, which was absolutely indispensable. It was used, for example, to indicate the public promises, made by a candidate for public office, as to what he would do when elected; there was no binding force in those promises beyond dread of the unpopularity likely to accrue, if they were not carried out at least to some extent, and they were recognised generally as the stock-in-trade of a candidate, made to be broken as far as was safe. Hence the word is very rarely used in the Old Testament, and never to represent *berith.*

In the New Testament, on the other hand, it is rather common. Paul seems to have liked it, as expressing the perfect voluntariness of the act of God.[1] It made the "Covenant" an act of God's grace, wholly undeserved by any previous conduct on the part of the recipients. Hence he even speaks of "the covenants of the promise" (Eph. II 12), *i.e.*, the solemn, binding, holy engagement of God's voluntary grace and kindness, where he requires the two Greek words, when he desires to bring out very clearly

---

[1] Paul uses διαθήκη nine times, ἐπαγγελία twenty-five times; but in Hebrews (which is more Hebraic in its form) διαθήκη occurs seventeen times, ἐπαγγελία fourteen times.

and thoroughly the two sides in the Biblical ideas, the binding force and the free grace.

It is characteristic of the change of spirit that the Old Testament uses only the word indicating binding, inexorable legal force, the New Testament prefers the word indicating free, undeserved kindness and grace.

The word *Diatheke* was fixed upon by the Septuagint translators to represent *berîth*. This resolve must have been formed at the beginning of their work. They took the word in spite of its associations with human business on the ground of its character as a whole. Now the word *Diatheke* went through a rapid course of development during the period B.C. 300 to A.D. 100 or 200; but the Septuagint translators, taking the word about B.C. 285, found it without any of the connotation derived from the changes that affected it after B.C. 300. It had such marked advantages over any other word in Greek for their purposes that their choice could hardly have been doubtful.

In the first place, the ancient *Diatheke* was a solemn and binding covenant, guaranteed by the authority of the whole people and their gods. It was originally executed verbally before the assembled people as a solemn religious act, the people being parties to it; and even in Greek-Egyptian Wills of the late third or second centuries B.C., when the *Diatheke* had become a private document, the reigning sovereigns were made parties to it, and named executors of it:[1] this was, of course, a mere form, a sort of legal fiction, substituted for the old fact that the public authority was actually a party to the *Diatheke*. The word was

---

[1] I am indebted to Messrs. Grenfell and Hunt for much information on the Wills executed by the Greek settlers in Egypt.

therefore well suited to express the binding irrevocable solemnity of the word uttered by God.

In the second place, the *Diatheke* was primarily an arrangement for the devolution of religious duties and rights, and not merely a bequeathing of money and property.[1] The heir by *Diatheke* was bound to carry on the religion of the family, just as if he had been a son by nature, and was placed there for that purpose. The term was therefore well suited to describe God's promise of a religious inheritance to His chosen people.

In the third place, the maker of the ordinary *Diatheke* had full power in his hands; and the party benefited by the *Diatheke* exercised no authority in the making of it. The latter had only to fulfil the conditions, and he succeeded to the advantages of the *Diatheke*. The act of God was of the same one-sided type.

In the fourth place, while the noun διαθήκη is confined almost exclusively to the sense of the disposition of one's property and duties by Will,[2] the verb διατίθεσθαι has a

[1] See above, p. 341.

[2] That such was the sense of διαθήκη in ordinary Greek is attested by the lexicons and by many inscriptions. The only exception where διαθήκη seems to mean an agreement, is quoted from Aristoph., *Av.* 439, but is not clear. It contains a joke founded on some unknown popular story of the ape and the woman (or his wife): the story is explained by the scholiasts in the usual Aristophanic style, but little value attaches to their evidence, which has probably no real authority, but is merely gathered out of Aristophanes's own words : it does not show why συνθήκη (which would suit the metre) is not used rather than διαθήκη. Lightfoot says there are a few other examples of διαθήκη in that sense, but he quotes none, and they are unknown to *Steph. Thesaurus;* and we must require exact quotations to support so rare a use in prose. Hatch carries further the loose language into which Lightfoot (a rare thing with him) has fallen, and speaks of the Hellenistic usage of διαθήκη as being similar to that of the Septuagint.

wider sense, and is used in the sense of " to dispose of one's property by sale," and in various other senses of the term " dispose " or " arrange " ; but in every case the one single party disposes with authority.

Finally, the central idea expressed in the word *Diatheke* fairly represented one important side of the Biblical conception. The *Diatheke* was the concrete expression of individual authority over property, and embodied the reaction against the former system of family authority. In a more primitive stage, property belonged to the family or the tribe, and the individual had no right to dispose of it : the development of Greek civilisation put ownership of property more and more into the hands of the individual. The tradition was that Solon passed the first law in Athens permitting the owner of property to bequeath it by a *Diatheke*, whereas previously the family to which the owner belonged inherited in default of children. Solon, however, gave the right of bequeathing only in default of male children, only under the form of adoption, and with the obligation that the adopted heir must marry the daughter, if there was one. Gradually the freedom of making *Diatheke* was widened, the individual became more and more master of his property, and its disposition and the claim even of his children became weaker. He was permitted to bequeath legacies to strangers without adoption ; but these legacies seem to have been at first classed as presents or gifts (δωρεαί), not as inheritances, and were restricted in various ways : [1] by common Greek custom and the feeling of society a son must inherit, and an heir was called a son.

In the cases which are most familiar to us in inscriptions

[1] Mitteis, *Reichsrecht*, p. 336, quoting Caillemer, *Annuaire de l'Assoc. des Et. Gr.*, 1870, p. 34 f.

legacies took, as a rule, the form of religious endowments intended to perpetuate the cult and the memory of the deceased; they are exactly on the same footing as gifts made by a living person to keep up the religion and the worship of his deceased child or relative;[1] and they are often stated to be by consent of the heirs.

Hence the word *Diatheke* expressed strongly the absolute authority of the disposer, who in the Biblical conception was God Himself.

Thus, even after the Greek Will had lost its original character of being open and public, immediately effective, and irrevocable, the word *Diatheke* still retained many characteristics which fitted it to be used as the rendering for *berîth*. But, certainly, the change in the character of the Greek Will tended to make the word less suitable.

To describe the steps in the development of the Greek Will would require a treatise; but some points bearing on the New Testament usage of *Diatheke* may be put together here. The new evidence gained from the many Wills of Greek settlers found in Egypt,[2] from inscriptions, and from the Roman-Syrian Law-Book[3] of the fifth century after Christ, has never been thoroughly collected and arranged.

---

[1] A good example of this is given in *Inscriptions d'Asie Mineure* in *Rev. Ét. Gr.*, 1889, p. 18.

[2] See Professor Mahaffy, *The Flinders-Petrie Papyri*, introduction, p. 35 ff.; Grenfell, *Erotic Greek Papyrus;* Grenfell and Hunt, *The Oxyrhynchus Papyri; Griech. Urkunden aus den kön. Museen, Berlin;* Kenyon, *Greek Papyri of Brit. Mus.* (contains only one very late Will); I have seen some unpublished Wills copied by Mr. A. C. Hunt, but have not access to other publications.

[3] Bruns and Sachau, *Ein Syrisch-römisches Rechtsbuch aus dem funften Jahrhundert*, 1880.

The obscurity in which the subject is involved may be gathered from the words used by such a high authority as Dr. W. E. Ball : [1] " It need hardly be said that St. Paul, in any metaphor based upon Will-making, could only refer to the Roman Will. The Romans were the inventors of the Will." He speaks on the assumption that there was no Greek system of Will-making. But, as soon as we realise that in Tarsus, in Syria, in South Galatia, and at Ephesus, Paul was in the region where Greek Wills had been a familiar fact of ordinary life before a single Roman had set foot in the Eastern land, and where Greek Wills were still customary when Paul was writing, the case assumes a different aspect.

The case is complicated by the difference of custom and law in different Greek countries, and by the way in which Roman law affected Greek law in the Eastern Provinces. For example, a Greek Will of ·A.D. 189 in Egypt is expressed entirely in the Roman style and after Roman custom,[2] and the Roman-Syrian Law-Book, while retaining many points of Greek law,[3] uses various Roman terms, and observes the rule of the Lex Falcidia, B.C. 40, that three-fourths of the testator's property is at his own disposal, but one-fourth must go to his children.[4]

In speaking of the Roman Will, we allude only to the highly-developed " Praetorian " Will, which had become practically universal in common life, and was the only

[1] See p. 368.

[2] Mommsen in *Berlin Sitzungsber*, 1894, p. 48 ff.

[3] See above p. 338.

[4] The form was that the heir inherited the whole, but was obliged to pay out of the property such legacies as the testator ordered. The Lex Falcidia restricted these legacies to three-quarters.

form of Will likely to affect the Provinces.   Now, whereas the Greek *Diatheke* came in the third century B.C. or earlier to the East with Greek settlers and soldiers and colonies, and therefore with some of the associations of its past history, the Roman Will came much later, as a fact in the law of the conquerors, and without any associations from its past history : it appeared in the East as a document which had no standing and no meaning until after the testator's death, and was revocable by him at pleasure.   Therein lay the most striking difference between the Roman will and the Greek.   I confess that several high English authorities on Greek Wills in Egypt, when consulted privately, expressed the opinion that these Wills were revocable at the testator's desire ; but they have not satisfied me that the evidence justifies that opinion earlier than the Roman time and Roman influence.

The Greek Wills in Egypt went through a rapid development.   The soldiers who settled there were separated from their family, and were sole masters of their fortune ; and therefore the family influence on the *Diatheke*, and family rights over the property of the individual, which were so powerful from long-standing feeling in the surroundings of their old home, had little force in Egypt.   Everything concurred to give the individual owner absolute right to dispose of his property as he pleased.   The development would go on continuously through the centuries, for Egypt was a battlefield for Greeks and Romans.

In the Wills in Egypt there is often contained the provision that the testator is free to alter or invalidate. Such a provision need not have been made, if Wills were acknowledged to be revocable at the testator's pleasure : he has to guard by a special provision against the customary presumption that the *Diatheke* is irrevocable. The step from the formal insertion of this provision to the assumption that the provision is to be presumed in every case, might probably be easily made as time passed ; but whether the step was made before Roman influence came in to facilitate it, seems not to be proved. The only second Will known seems to repeat and confirm the first (see p. 352).

Again, in a Will dated in the year B.C. 123 [1] the testator leaves all his property away from his two sons, except two beds : all the rest he bequeaths to his second wife. That looks like " cutting off the son with a bed," a merely formal recognition of his right to a share : we remember that in Greek law the owner and father could disinherit his son, but at first, and probably for a long time or even permanently, the act of disinheritance must be performed by the father publicly, during his lifetime, and for good reasons.[2] Even in the fifth century after Christ the principle remained in force in Syria, persisting from Seleucid custom and law, that the father could put away his son on good grounds. The heir by Will and adoption had a stronger legal position in Greek law than the son by nature, as we saw on p. 353.

On the other hand in Greek law, a daughter was not strictly an heiress. She had an indefeasible right to a dowry, and this could be greatly increased according as her father chose, but she was styled an ἐπίκληρος, not a κληρονόμος (as a son or adopted son was) ; and her dowry must not encroach seriously on the son's portion.

[1] Gizeh Papyrus, No. 10,388, communicated by Messrs. Grenfell and Hunt.

[2] Mitteis, *Reichsrecht*, p. 336.

In an unpublished Greek Will, found in Egypt,[1] of the period of Trajan, a man leaves his property to his wife for her lifetime, and thereafter to the children of his concubine, who on their part are not free to alienate it, but must leave it to their own family. This implies a much extended power of the individual over the disposal of his property for generations; but it is probably due to the influence of Roman customs and law.

Obviously, a people who had been used to think of a *Diatheke* as a private document, which could be altered by its maker as he pleased, and which was unknown to any other until the maker died, when it was unsealed and became effective, would see hardly any points of agreement between that kind of act and the Promise of God to His people. The analogy of the ordinary use of *Diatheke* "after the manner of men" would tend to confuse their ideas rather than help them to understand the nature of God's act. The only way to attain clearness would be to treat this word *Diatheke* as a technical term of the Greek Bible, unconnected with the common Will or Testament.

That is the case with the Epistle to the Romans. The word *Diatheke* occurs there twice, but only in strictly Biblical and Hebraic surroundings.

Similarly, the Epistle to the Hebrews was written to a people who knew only the Roman Will. "The Rabbinical Will was unknown before the Roman Conquest of Palestine, and was directly based upon the Roman model."[2] Under the rule of Herod in Palestine, as of Amyntas in

---

[1] Communicated by Messrs. Grenfell and Hunt: to be published in the *Oxyrhynchos Papyri*, II.

[2] Dr. Ball in *Contemp. Review*, Aug., 1891, p. 287. Compare above, p. 341 f.

Galatia,[1] the new law introduced was almost certain to be Roman, not Greek. The pleadings in Rome about the comparative validity of Herod's last Will show the Roman character : the last Will is tacitly acknowledged to be the only one valid, unless it could be shown to have been executed in a state of unsound mind.[2]

Even if the Epistle to the Hebrews had been addressed (as some think) to the Church in Rome, not to that in Jerusalem, that would only show more clearly how Roman is the atmosphere in which it moves. But the writer of the Epistle was a Jew, perhaps resident in Cæsarea, on the theory that it was written by the Church of Cæsarea to Jerusalem during Paul's imprisonment.[3]

In accordance with this the word *Diatheke* in that Epistle is generally used in a purely Biblical and Hebraic way. But in IX 15-17 the sense of *Diatheke* "after the manner of men" moves in the writer's mind, "for where a Testament, *Diatheke*, is, there must of necessity be the death of him that made it. For a *Diatheke* is of force where there hath been death ; for it doth never avail while he that made it liveth."[4] This thought leads him into a quaint and far-fetched train of reasoning, in order to show how there was a death connected with every Divine *Diatheke*. It is quite extraordinary to see how some theologians torture these words in order to escape their plain and inevitable meaning (even plainer in the Greek than in the English).

[1] See Sections 11, 13.

[2] Josephus, *Ant. Jud.*, XVII 9, 5.

[3] *Expositor*, June, 1899, p. 401 ff.

[4] So R. V. in margin and the American Revisers in text. R. V. in text puts the words as a question.

No thought of that kind can have troubled the minds of the Septuagint translators. And Paul in writing to the Galatians, does not feel it ; and he assumes that the Galatians are familiar with the ordinary human *Diatheke* as irrevocable from the moment when it was properly executed and passed through the Record Office of the city.

XXXV

GREEK LAW IN GALATIAN CITIES.

We observe that in many places [1] Paul assumes among his Galatian readers familiarity with a certain system and state of legal procedure. They are expected to catch the force of allusions to various legal facts ; and accordingly laws of that type must have existed in their cities. Further, those legal facts are not Roman, but are either distinctly Greek in character or slightly modified from the Greek type to suit the Graecised parts of Asia.

In the first place, those allusions presuppose a considerable amount of education among the Galatians. Paul does not address them as a mere set of ignorant and untutored rustics : he addresses them as persons living amid the organised administration of cities. That must be clear to every thinking man ; but especially clear is it to those who take the pains to familiarise themselves with the state of inner Asia Minor in the century after Christ, when the cities were to a certain extent civilised and Graecised, but the country districts were still purely Anatolian in customs, inhabited by a population almost wholly ignorant of Greek.

---

[1] See above, §§ XXXI, XXXIII : below, §§ XXXIX, XLI.

Yet Dr. Zöckler seriously maintains that the Epistle was addressed to the people in the districts round Pessinus. Apart from Pessinus itself, those districts were among the most sparsely populated and the rudest in the whole of Asia Minor. As regards districts of that kind, only the most resolute ignoring of all knowledge can blind men to the fact that Western manners and ideas can hardly have even begun to penetrate there so early. Even in south-western Phrygia, separated only by twenty miles of hill country from the highly civilised and Hellenised Laodiceia, but off the main route of trade, there were districts where Greek was known only in the rudest and slightest way to the mass of the population even in the second century.[1] Yet these districts were far more open to Greek influence than the remote parts round Pessinus; and Pessinus was still little affected by Greek manners,[2] whereas Laodiceia and the other cities of the Lycus valley were probably entirely Hellenised long before the time of Christ.

Secondly, among the people whom Paul addressed Roman manners had not been superimposed directly on native ways. They were familiar with Greek rather than with Roman procedure; and Paul's illustration is drawn from Greek legal expression. It is therefore obvious that, as Greek law would not be introduced after the Romans had occupied the country, there must have been a period before the Roman conquest when Greek law ruled in the Galatic territory.

Such would be the case with the country ruled by the Seleucid, or the Pergamenian, or the Bithynian kings. All of them, including even the Bithynian princes, had, beyond

---

[1] *Cities and Bishoprics of Phrygia*, I, p. 131. [2] See p. 139 f.

a doubt, established the Greek principles of society and law in their dominions : these principles, of course, were pretty much confined to the cities, and did not affect the rural population.   But in those countries it is clear from the inscriptions that, before the time of Christ, the cities possessed an organised municipal government of the Greek type, cultivated Greek manners and education and used the Greek language.

The Pontic and Cappadocian kings are more doubtful ; but, in all probability, Greek civilisation was spread very little by their influence in their dominions.   It is true that Greek was spoken at their courts to a certain (or uncertain) extent, and their coins bore Greek legends ; but hardly the slightest trace of Greek city organisation, except in the Greek colonies of the coast, can be detected dating from their time.   Amasia is called a city by Strabo (about A.D. 19), and a *polis* must be understood to have enjoyed something of a Greek organisation ; but this was probably due rather to the natural expansion of Greek manners and trade than to the intention of any king Mithridates. Similarly, in Cappadocia, Mazaka and Tyana are called cities by Strabo.

But as to Galatia Proper, the country of the Gauls, the case is practically free from doubt.   The sketch of Galatian history given in our Introduction is conclusive that, after a brief attempt to introduce Greek ways about the beginning of the second century B.C. was quenched in blood, the loose Celtic organisation and ways continued supreme in the country, and there was the strongest opposition to Greek manners and influence.   The opinion of the best historical and legal investigators has been quoted [1] that

[1] See p. 131.

North Galatia continued for centuries to be an Occidental island amid the sea of Graeco-Asiatic peoples. Especially as regards the law of family and the rights of children, we have seen that, even in the second century after Christ, Galatian custom was strongly antipathetic to Greek ideas.[1]

Further, there is strong probability—though only scanty direct evidence exists—that, as North Galatia grew in civilisation, it was not Greek, but Roman manners and organisation that were introduced. During the century B.C. the guiding spirits in the country had been first Deiotaros and then Amyntas. Deiotaros was repeatedly praised for his Roman spirit by Roman officials and the Roman Senate : he drilled and armed his troops as Roman legions : he spent much of his life fighting against Greeks and in association with Romans. Amyntas was a creature of Rome, raised from a humble position for the special purpose of fitting the country to become a Roman Province.[2] Roman amusements and Roman devices for government were far more thoroughly naturalised in North Galatia than in the Greek cities of Asia.[3]

All the evidence is that in North Galatia Roman ways had been superimposed directly on barbarian and specially Celtic manners. The religion of Galatia was indeed hardly at all Celtic; but neither was it Greek ; it was mainly old Phrygian.[4] The language was the only Greek factor that exercised any strong influence on North Galatia ; and it did so to a great extent under Roman patronage The Romans made little or no attempt to naturalise the Latin language in the East ; they acquiesced in the fact that Greek had the advantage there, and they accepted it

[1] See p. 131.　　[2] See p. 111 f.　　[3] See p. 132 f.　　[4] See p. 144.

officially.   But even the language is exceedingly unlikely
to have been much known outside of the cities in the time
of Paul, Sec. 14.

It is simply irrational to maintain that Paul would have
attempted to make religious conceptions plain and clear to
North Galatian Christians by means of Greek ideas and legal
devices : he was careful to adapt his words and illustrations
to the needs and capacities of his congregations.   His power
over his Churches lay in his sympathy with them.   The
intense wish to be among them, IV 20, enabled him to
write as if he were beside them, seeing what they saw
around them.

But the South Galatian lands had been ruled by Greek
officers and kings from 334 onwards.   For more than a
century they had been part of the Seleucid Empire, and
had been on the main route between the Seleucid capital,
Syrian Antioch, and the Lydian and Phrygian parts of that
Empire.   Then in B.C. 189 they had been transferred to
the Pergamenian kings ; and, though Pergamenian rule
seems never to have become a reality there, and part of
the country seems to have been annexed to Galatia and
part to Cappadocia during the second century B.C., yet the
position of its cities on or near one of the main thorough-
fares of Greek trade and of Jewish travel would maintain
Greek ways and civilisation among them.   See Sec. 17-22.

Only in regard to the two Roman *Coloniae*, Antioch and
Lystra, it might be maintained that their new foundation
implied a Romanisation of society.   To a certain extent
it did so ; actual Italian settlers would not abandon their
Occidental ideas of family and of inheritance.   But it by
no means follows that the Greek population of the two
Coloniae abandoned Greek ways : on the contrary the

probability will be admitted by every historical investigator that in many respects Greek customs persisted. The surrounding sea of Greek manners would maintain the Greek element in the *Coloniae,* as is shown in Sections 17 ff.

Finally, it is evident that Greek civilisation was established strongly in the South Galatian cities in the fourth century B.C., and that the form of government in the country was not Greek after B.C. 189. So far as it goes, this establishes a probability that the civilisation of those cities had more of the older Seleucid type, and was not open to the same continuous and rapid development as among the Greek mercenaries in Egypt. An older type of Greek Will is likely to have existed in Iconium and the neighbouring cities ; and we see that Paul's references to the law "after the manner of men" imply a law on the whole of rather early type.

XXXVI

THE ARGUMENT FROM SEED, III 16.

He saith not "And to seeds," as of many ; but as of one, "And to thy seed," which is Christ.

It is necessary for Paul's argument to show that all nations, and not Jews alone, have the right to share in the blessings promised to Abraham. He finds the proof in the fact that the various promises made to Abraham were made equally to his seed.[1] Now, as Lightfoot says, "with a true spiritual instinct even the Rabbinical writers saw that 'the Christ' was the true seed of Abraham : in Him the race was summed up, as it were; without Him its

---

[1] Gen. XIII 15, XVII 8.

separate existence as a peculiar people had no meaning."
In "the seed of Abraham" all nations were to be blessed
(Gen. XXVI 8).   It cannot be doubted by those who
regard the evolution of Hebraic religion and the coming of
Christ as a series of steps in the gradual working out of
the will of God, that this interpretation of the "seed of
Abraham" is justified.

But, instead of using this way of reasoning simply, Paul
seems to have been tempted to aim at the same result by
a verbal argument.   The Greek philosophers were often
led astray by an idea that mere grammatical facts and
forms contained some deep philosophical or mystical truth :
Plato's *Cratylus* is sufficient evidence of this.   Paul, therefore, argues that as the singular, "seed," is used, not the
plural, the single great descendant of Abraham is meant,
and not the many less important descendants.   If we
rightly take the meaning, this is, obviously, a mere verbal
quibble, of no argumentative force.   Paul sees clearly and
correctly the result to be aimed at, but he reaches the result
by a process of reasoning which has no more force in logic
than the poorest word-splitting of any old Greek philosopher
or Hebrew Rabbi.

The attempt which Lightfoot makes to defend the character of the reasoning from "seed" and "seeds" cannot be
pronounced successful.   It amounts practically to this
"the theological result aimed at is right" (as we fully
admit), "therefore the reasoning can hardly be wrong".

If we set aside the verbal fallacy, the argument remains
complete and correct.

> The promises were made to Abraham and to his
> seed.

> The true "seed of Abraham" is "the Christ".

" The Christ " is the whole body of true Christians.

The promises were made to all Christians.

That is to say, the promises made to Abraham are the heritage of the whole Church of Christ, the whole multitude of those who are justified by faith in Christ.

The argument is one more of the many ways in which Paul reiterates the fundamental truth that he has to drive home into the minds of the Galatians, or rather to revivify in their memory.[1] It is specially obvious here that Paul is appealing to familiar doctrines, already set forth to the Galatians, and not arguing to a circle of readers on a topic new to them.

XXXVII

FUNCTION OF THE LAW, III 19-22.

In this passage Paul guards against a possible misinterpretation of his words, which might be dangerous. It might be said that he was representing the law as being in opposition to the Promises made to Abraham and his seed. He must therefore define clearly what he conceives to be the function of the law. The same person, the one God, gave both the Promises and the Law. The Promises were to be fulfilled, not immediately, but after a long interval, not to each individual of the human " Seed of Abraham," but to and through the " the Seed," *i.e.*, the Christ. The Law is the preparation for the fulfilment of the Promises. There must be a clear and peremptory forbidding of sin, before the sin is made emphatic and beyond palliation or excuse. " The times of ignorance God might

---

[1] See § XXI.

overlook," as Paul said to the Athenians; but none who sinned against the clear Law could try to shelter themselves behind such a plea.   Moreover, the Law was necessary (as has been said, p. 336) in order that the overwhelming consciousness of sin, which is a necessary preliminary to true faith in Christ, might be produced in the minds of men.

The Law would have been contrary to the Promises if it had been intended to produce the same result as they by a new way, and therefore had rendered them unnecessary. The Promises are promises of life and salvation; and if a Law such as could produce life and salvation had been given from Mount Sinai, then this Law would really have interfered with and nullified the Promises.

But, on the contrary, the Scripture declares that the effect of the Law is to "shut up everything under the dominion of sin without means of escape" (Lightfoot), in order that men might be forced to look forward to "the Christ" as the only means of escape, the only hope of life and salvation.

It is noteworthy that Paul makes only the vague reference to "the Scripture," and does not quote a special passage.   His words are intelligible only on the supposition that they are a brief summary of a more elaborate exposition of the combined effect of several passages, which he had delivered in his earlier preaching to the Galatians.

The expression "by faith to them that believe," V 22, ἐκ πίστεως τοῖς πιστεύουσιν, is rendered very strong by the repetition.   As has been pointed out on page 347, ἐκ πίστεως must be understood as emphatically denying the opposite doctrine of the Judaising Christians—the source is ἐκ πίστεως, not ἐκ νόμου.

XXXVIII

THE MEDIATOR, III 20.

" The Law was ordained through angels by the hand of a mediator.   Now, a mediator is not of one, but God is one."

The precise meaning of the argument that lies in the words of III 20 is very difficult to catch ; and I shall not attempt to add one to the 250 or 300 interpretations that have (according to Lightfoot) been proposed for this passage. We have in § XXXVI found a case where Paul sees the right result, and yet attains it by an argument founded on the generally accepted, though mistaken, view of that period, that grammatical forms had a deep philosophical meaning (usually assigned on arbitrary and capricious grounds to suit some individual instance).   Is it not the case here also, that he aims at a right result, but reaches it by a bad process of reasoning ?

Paul is evidently emphasising a certain contrast that exists between the free grace of the Promises and the indirect character of the Law—the Law being merely a means to an end beyond itself, and not being the sufficient and ultimate gift of the grace of God.   The distinction is undeniable and of immense importance.   In this paragraph, therefore, he does not use the word *Diatheke* to indicate the "covenant" made with Abraham.   In accordance with the distinction drawn in § XXXIV, it is necessary for him to use the word " Promise," ἐπαγγελία, in order to emphasise the character of freedom and grace in the covenant made by God with Abraham and his seed.   Accordingly, the words " Promised " or " Promises " occur three times in the short paragraph (*vv.* 19, 21, 22) : the

Greek text has the verb instead of the noun in 19, where the English translation, if literal, would be "the Seed to whom it hath been promised".

The Law did not come immediately and directly from God to men. It was conveyed from God by angels; and a mediator, *viz.*, Moses, carried it down from the Mount to the Hebrew people. This method is far less gracious and kind than the direct communication from God to Abraham; and brings out the consciousness of an impassable gulf separating God from even the chosen people. The allusion to the angels seemed founded more on Rabbinical interpretation and later tradition than on the text of the Books of Moses; but the words of Stephen (Acts VII 53) and of Herod in Josephus,[1] as quoted by Lightfoot and commentators generally, seem to imply that the common belief of the time supposed the ministry of angels.

A mediator implies one who goes between two parties to an agreement, and therefore to a certain degree might seem to diminish the absolute authority and completeness of the one party in this case. Can this, then, be the sense of the last words of *v.* 20, " but God is one ". So Lightfoot thinks, and so it may be. But it seems an unsatisfactory form of expression; and I cannot avoid the suspicion that Paul here is betrayed into a mistake, and is thinking of the other and infinitely more important sense of the words, " God is one "—as in Romans III 30.—" He is one and the same God in all His acts, one God makes both the Promises and the Law." The argument would then be a fallacy, " a mediator implies (two parties), but God is one ". I may probably be wrong; but, if one speaks, one must say

[1] *Ant. Jud.*, XV 5, 3.

what one thinks. Here, while Paul aims at a great truth, he reaches it, I think, by a mistaken argument.

We have here, as recognised in the translation (repeated by Zöckler and others, and not disputed by Lightfoot, but, seemingly, recognised by him as the obvious sense), a clear and apparently undisputed example of a participle used in the sense of καί with a finite verb : " The Law was added because of transgressions, till the Seed should come to whom the Promise had been made, and it was ordained through angels etc.," where the Greek has merely the participle " being ordained ". But, distinctly, the giving of the Law by God is the first step, and the carrying into effect by means of angels is the following step. This is one of the many examples justifying the construction διῆλθον . . . κωλυθέντες in Acts XVI 6, in the sense which I have pleaded for, " they traversed . . . and were prevented." That loose usage of the participle is common in the later Greek and Latin.

XXXIX

LAW THE CHILD-GUARDIAN, III 23-25.

Before the age of Faith began, we of the Jewish race were shut up and kept under the guard of the Law, in preparation for (with a view to) the approaching revelation of Faith. Thus the Law has played the part of " a servant, responsible for our safety, and charged to keep us out of bad company," [1] until the age of Christ arrived, so that we might be made righteous by Faith. For that result could

[1] The best way of explaining Paul's meaning is to imitate closely the description of a Paidagogos given in the *Dictionary of Antiquities* (Smith), II, p. 307.

not have been attained unless special care had been taken of us during the interval. We could not safely be permitted to be free at that time, for we could not then acquire Faith, that vitalising and strengthening power, seated in our mind and working itself out in our conduct, which enables those who have seen and known Christ to be free and yet safe.

But now the age of Faith has begun, and we are set free from the guard and the directing care of the Law.

When Paul compared the Law to a *paidagogos*, he intended undoubtedly to describe it as having a good moral character, and exercising a salutary, though a strict and severe, effect on those who were placed under it. He speaks no evil of the Law; he represents it as subsidiary and inferior to Faith, but still as a wholesome provision given in God's kindness to the Jews.

Further, he chose an illustration which would make this clear to his Galatian readers; and they must, therefore, have been familiar with that characteristic Greek institution, the *paidagogos*, and considered it salutary and good. This throws some light on the social organisation in the Galatian cities, for it places us in the midst of Greek city life, as it was in the better period of Greek history. " In the free Greek cities the system of educatisn was organised as a primary care of the State. The educational system was the best side of the Greek city constitution. Literature, music and athletics are all regulated in an interesting inscription of Teos, the salaries of the teachers are fixed, and special magistrates survey and direct the conduct of teachers and pupils." [1]

In that period it would appear that the *paidagogoi* were

---

[1] Shortened from *Cities and Bish. of Phrygia*, II, p. 440.

trusted servants and faithful attendants, standing in a very close relation to the family (in which they were slaves). Their duty was not to teach any child under their charge, but simply to guard him. Among the Romans, who adopted this institution from the Greeks, the *paidagogos* gave some home instruction to the child : he was a Greek-speaking slave, who looked after the child, and taught him to use the Greek language. Though he also accompanied the child to school, yet there was not the same kindly feeling in the relationship of guardian and ward in Rome as in Greek cities during the better period. Roman *paida-gogoi* were often chosen without the slightest regard to the moral side of their teaching, and brought the child in contact with the lower side of life among vicious slaves ; among the Greeks in the later period, amid the steady degeneration of Pagan manners in the whole Roman empire, Plutarch complains that a slave, worthless for any other purpose, was used as a *paidagogos ;* and a little earlier Juvenal gives a terrible picture of the upbringing of young children, which, though exaggerated in his usual style, is still an indication of what was characteristic of ordinary pagan homes (though certainly with some, perhaps with many, brilliant exceptions).

In contrast with the care for education shown in the government of Greek cities, the Roman imperial government lavishly provided shows and exhibitions of a more or less degrading character for the population of Rome and the Provinces, while the degeneration of the provision for watching over and educating the young in the cities was the worst feature of the Roman period. This had much to do with the steady deterioration in the moral fibre of the population, and the resulting ruin of the empire.

This passage of the Epistle, therefore, places us in the midst of Greek city life as it was in the better period of Greek history. When read in relation to the provision for education in the Greek cities, the illustration which Paul selects becomes much more luminous.

But there is nothing here characteristic of North Galatia. We are placed amid the Greek-speaking population of Antioch and Iconium, where Greek ways and customs had been naturalised since Alexander had conquered the country and left behind him a long succession of Greek kings, Even in Lystra, recently founded as a military station in a more barbarous district, and off the main line of trade, the probability is that only a minority of the population were so used to education that this illustration would have appealed to them ; but I have often argued that it was among that minority that Christianity first spread.[1]

Moreover, it is an early state of Greek manners which is here presented to us. We turn to Plato for the best illustration of Paul's meaning, and not to late writers. Compare what has been said about *Diatheke*, p. 375.

That is all characteristic of South Galatia, where the chief Græcising influence was the Seleucid rule, ending in B.C. 189. Thus it was a rather early form of Greek society which maintained itself in a city like Pisidian Antioch ; and that society was likely to be kept vigorous by the constant struggle which it had to maintain against Oriental influence.

This passage throws an interesting light on Paul's conception of the Divine purpose in the world. The Disposition by God of the religious inheritance which ultimately

---

[1] *Church in Rom. Emp.* pp. 57, 146; *St. Paul the Trav.*, ch. VI.

is intended for all men, involved a gradual training of mankind in order that they might be able to accept the inheritance by fulfilling the conditions: the Disposition is first in favour of one man, then of a nation, finally of all nations. The one man at first needed no schoolmaster: he was able to respond at once to the requirements of God. But the nation, when it came to exist, was not able in itself to rise to the conditions which God demanded. It needed education and the constant watching of a careful guardian: the Law was given to watch over the young nation as it was being trained and educated in the school of life: the Law was not itself the teacher, but the *paidagogos*. Then came the age of Christ, who opened, first to the Jews and through them to all nations, the door of Faith.

No other reference to *paidogogoi* occurs in Paul's writings, except 1 Corinthians IV 15. It may perhaps be fanciful, but it seems to me as I read that passage that it is distinctly more contemptuous in tone than the allusion in Galatians III 24, 25. Moreover, it implies, apparently, that the *paidagogoi* are teachers, elementary teachers, of those whom they look after. There we have the later, the Romanised conception of the *paidagogos*, which naturally ruled in a town like Corinth that was at once a highly developed Greek city and a Roman colony.

XL

EQUALITY IN THE PERFECT CHURCH, III 26-30.

In *v.* 25 Paul changes almost unconsciously from the use of "we," as "we Jews," to the wider sense, in which it embraces also the Galatians (and all Gentiles who come to the Faith). Then he explains in *vv.* 26-30 why he ranks

25

Galatians and Jews together. " The working of the Faith
which you feel in Christ Jesus makes you sons of God, for
all who are baptised to Christ have clothed themselves with
Christ, and put His nature and person round them in becoming His people. Christ is the sum of all who believe
in Him ; He takes them all into Himself ; He admits no
distinction of nationality, or of rank, or of sex ; all are
placed on an equality and made one in Him. And if you
are part of Christ and partake His nature, then you are the
seed of Abraham (for Christ is the true seed of Abraham,
v. 16), and therefore you are heirs according to God's
promise."

Comparing this passage with Paul's writings as a whole,
we see that this obliteration of distinctions in Christ is the
end, but not the beginning, of the life in Christ. Beyond
all doubt Paul considered that, practically, to become a
part of Christ implied membership of the Church of Christ :
that was the actual fact, as the world was constituted.
But the Church was not to begin by abolishing all distinctions in social life or in nationality : that abolition would
be the result of the gradual working of Faith in the individual, and of the gradual lessening of the distance that
separated the actual state of these struggling and imperfect
congregations from the perfect realisation of their true
nature in Christ.[1]

Paul rather accepted the existing political system and
the state of society, with its distinctions and usages, except
in so far as they were positively idolatrous. He bade the
slave continue as a slave, the woman stand in the same

---

[1] The difference in tone and spirit of the Pastoral from the rest of
the Pauline Epistles is greatly due to the fact that the former are
concerned chiefly with the practical steps in an early congregation.

relation to the man as was the rule of society.   The realisation by each individual of his or her true life in Christ was
to be sought in accepting, not in rebelling against, the
present facts of life in the world : their present situation
was of small consequence in comparison with the state to
which Faith would bring them.

But the words, which Paul here uses, necessarily and
inevitably imply that the Church, as it disengages itself
from and rises above the existing state of society, and as
it remakes the facts of the world in the course of its growth,
must rise above those distinctions which have no reality in
Christ.

How far the Apostle was conscious, at the moment, of the
full meaning that lay in his words, is doubtful.   He uttered
the truth as he saw it dimly revealed to him : he was not
interested in speculation as to its future effect on society :
he lived in the present crisis.   An observant and thoughtful
citizen of Rome might perhaps have been able to see—as
the modern scholar can now look back and see—how the
diffusion of Roman civilisation and government was tending
to obliterate the distinctions of nation and race, and to
unite alien peoples in a wider patriotism.   The philosophic
mind might perhaps see—as some philosophers then actually saw; at least dimly and faintly—that the subjection of
one man as a slave to another was unnatural, and must
pass away. We can now see that, though not very clearly :
nominally we have abolished slavery, but really slavery is
far from abolished in any country.

But what is implied as to the relation of man and woman
by these words of Paul's we still cannot discern.[1] We can

---

[1] The change of form, "bond nor free, male and female," springs
from the feeling that the two cases are not precisely analogous.

indeed see with certainty, in comparing nation with nation and religion with religion, that one of the most important forces in the progress of society lies in the education which the mother conveys to her children, and that where a religion (as, for example, Mohammedanism) does not tend to raise the standard of thought and feeling, knowledge and character, among its women, no amount of excellence in abstract principles and truths will make that religion a practical power for steadily elevating the race which clings to it.   From the contemplation of such facts we may guess as to the future, but we can only guess.

In considering the history of Mohammedanism—the contrast between the earlier glories and the later impotence and stagnation of the peoples whom it first affected—the marvellously rapid educating power that it exerts on a savage race, raising it at the first moment of conversion to a distinctly higher level of spiritual and intellectual life, and yet the following acquiescence in that level or even the sinking again below it—even the least thoughtful observer must seek for some explanation of so remarkable a history and so extraordinary a contrast.   The traveller who studies a Mohammedan people in its actual state has no difficulty in finding the explanation ; he is struck with the utter want of education inside the home, and he sees that the position of the women, their utter ignorance (which is so complete that they have no subject to converse or think about except the most elementary facts of physical and family life), their general inability to entertain for themselves or to impress on their children any ideas of duty, any principles of good conduct, any desire for a higher level of life, any aspirations after any object except the most gross and vulgar, any habits of regularity, of work, of

thought and meditation.[1] He realises that a nation cannot permanently remain on a level above the level of its
women, that if it rises, under the immediate stimulus of a
great moral idea (such as Mohammedanism was to the
brutalised Arab tribes among whom it was first preached)
to a higher plane of thought and life, it cannot long maintain itself on that plane, unless its women rise to it and
kindle and foster similar ideas in the minds of succeeding
generations when young.   He will see that the progress of
the Christian nations is founded on the keeping alive of
education and thought and conscious moral purpose among
their women, and that the opening to them in the Christian
religion from the first of suitable opportunities for growing
morally and intellectually is one of the necessary and
primary conditions of national health.   He will be slow to
set in his thought any limits to the possible future development of a nation in which the women are always on the
highest level of the existing generation.

The one occasion on which Paul has touched this great
truth is in the sentence that lies now before us.   There is
no other.   In the Epistle in which his nature is most deeply
moved, he speaks with the truest prevision of what shall
come in the future of the Church.   Where he pleads most
passionately for freedom, he speaks most like the prophet,
and least like the legislator and moralist intent on what
can be achieved in the present.   See § LIV.

The remarkable expression used here is one of the many
little touches throughout this Epistle which place the reader
in the Græco-Phrygian cities of Asia Minor.   Among them

---

[1] This is merely a condensation of one main subject in the writer's
Impressions of Turkey, especially ch. II, where the thought is worked
out as the details of life came before his mind.

the position of women was unusually high and important, and they were often entrusted with offices and duties which elsewhere were denied them.[1]   Hence, the allusion to the equality of the sexes in the perfect form which the Church must ultimately attain, would not seem to the people of these Græco-Phrygian cities to be so entirely revolutionary and destructive of existing social conditions as it must have seemed to the Greeks.   The Greeks secluded respectable women, and granted education to them only at the price of shame ; but few Phrygian cities were fully Hellenised in this respect.

Moreover, the duty of obedience had to be urged on the Greeks, but what most impressed itself on Paul was the need of encouraging the Galatians to freedom ; § LIV.

Accordingly, in writing to the Corinthians, 1 ch. XI, he seems to have been so much impressed with the danger that women were already going too far in throwing off the trammels of existing social rules, that he had to inculcate on them submission and recognition of present custom as the first duty.   The same practical necessity was on him in writing to other Greek communities as in Crete or Asia : [2] the existing congregations of Asia were all in the most thoroughly Hellenised parts of the Province.

But it is beyond doubt that Paul's frequent insistence on the duty of women to comply with existing social restraints and the uniqueness of this reference to the ideal of the future tended to lead the " Orthodox " Church too far in the direction of the subjection of women.   Moreover, the

---

[1] *Church in the Roman Empire*, pp. 67 f., 161, 345, 375, 398, 403, 452-9, 480.

[2] The letters to Timothy and Titus are of course to be interpreted with reference to the people among whom they were at work.

importance of women in Phrygia stood in close relation
with the native Phrygian religion,[1] the great foe of Christianity in its earliest steps in the country,[2] and the Church
was therefore liable to be thrown to the opposite side. The
fact is certain that in Asia Minor it was usually the "heretics"
who placed women in the most honourable position, and
the "Orthodox" who least saw the true spirit of Christianity
in relation to women and their true place in society.

XLI

THE INFANT SON AND HEIR (GAL. IV 1-7).

So long as the son who has succeeded to an inheritance
is a child, he is treated in practice like a slave subject to
orders, though in theory he is the owner and master. But
the property and its child-master are directed by guardians
and stewards, until the child has reached the age named in
the *Diatheke* of his father.

Here we observe the distinctively Greek touch that the
term "heir," used by Paul, is almost convertible with
"son".[3] The same term is often used in the inscriptions
of Asia Minor and elsewhere in precisely the same way as
here to indicate "a son after he has succeeded to the
inheritance" as the representative of his father, undertaking
all the duties and obligations of his father.

A state of society is contemplated as familiar to the
Galatian Christians, in which the father by his Will ordinarily nominated a term when his infant heir was to come
of age. This does not imply that there was no age fixed

---

[1] See p. 40 f.   [2] *St. Paul the Trav.*, ch. VI.
[3] See above, § XXXI.

by law in cases where a Will had not been made; but it does seem to imply that in the circle of Paul's readers the maker of a Will was free to fix such age as he pleased. It is known that Seleucid law differed from Roman law in regard to the legal period of full age. Mitteis[1] points out that in Tyana the legal term for coming of age was different from the Roman : he ascribes this to Greek influence, but probably it is Anatolian (and South Galatian) custom.

Further, Paul clearly describes a state of society and law in which the father by his Will appoints two distinct kinds of administrators for his child, so that the infant owner is said to grow up under the rule of guardians and stewards (ἐπίτροποι and οἰκονόμοι). The former is the regular term in Greek law for the guardian of an infant, appointed by the father, or by the law in default of the father's nomination. It was also the regular translation of the Latin *tutor*.

The *oikonomos* or steward is less easily understood. A state of the law is implied in which the father by Will named both a guardian and an *oikonomos* for his infant child. Presumably the guardian (ἐπίτροπος) exercised a more complete authority over the infant than the *oikonomos*, who (as the name implies) merely regulates household and business matters for the infant. Now in Roman law that distinction was well known : an infant was under a *tutor* until he reached the age of fourteen, and thereafter under a *curator* until twenty-five. But in Roman law the *curator* could not be appointed by the Will of the father.[2]

In pure Greek Law, as for example at Athens, this

---

[1] *Reichsrecht*, p. 107.

[2] An elementary fact, stated in any manual of Roman Antiquities or Law : see *e.g.*, Ramsay's *Roman Antiquities*, p. 255; Mitteis, p. 218,

distinction seems to have been unknown ; and Paul's words have less meaning when we think of pure Greek manners. But the law and manners of the Græco-Phrygian cities (and of the Seleucid cities generally) were not pure Greek. They were Hellenistic, having the form which Greek ideas assumed, when they went forth to conquer the East and were inevitably modified in the process.

Accordingly, everything becomes clear when we look at the Syrian Law-book. The same distinction is there drawn as in Rome : a child is subject to an *Epitropos* up to fourteen, thereafter he is able to make a Will and dispose of his own property, but the practical management of the property remains in the hands of a *curator* till the ward reaches the age of twenty-five.[1] But the Syrian law differs from the Roman in permitting the father to appoint both *epitropos* and *curator* by Will. This is exactly the state of things which Paul speaks of ; and the probability is that the distinction of *epitropos* and *oikonomos* dates back to the old Seleucid law, and thus persisted both in Syria and in South Galatia. In Syria, however, as time went on, Roman law affected native custom ; and so the name *curator* was substituted for *oikonomos*.

Thus, once more we find that we are placed amid Seleucid, and therefore South Galatian, not among North-Galatian, manners and law.

---

[1] The Syriac seems to borrow the Greek term in one case, the Roman in the other (to judge from the German translation in Bruns and Sachau, *Syrisch-Römisches Rechtsbuch*, p. 5).

XLII

THE RUDIMENTS OF THE WORLD (Gal. IV 3 and 9).

As in the world of business, so it was in religion : while we Jews, the heirs and sons, were children, we were like slaves, subjected to rudimentary principles and rules of a more material and formal character. But when the proper time, contemplated by the Father in his *Diatheke*, had arrived with Christ, then we all, Jews and Gentiles, receive in actual fact the inheritance and the position of sons (which previously was only theoretically ours, as we could not as yet fulfil the conditions necessary for accepting the inheritance).

There seems to be here the same transition as in III 25 f. from "we" in the sense of Jews to "we" embracing all true Christians, Gentile alike and Jew;[1] and Paul goes on to explain his reasons and to justify the transition.

"Previously," says Paul, "when you did not know God, you were enslaved to false gods. But now, when you have come to know God, or rather when God has taken cognisance of you (for the change in your position is due entirely to His gracious action and initiative), how is it that you are turning back again to the weak and beggarly elementary rules, to which you wish to make yourselves slaves again completely, while you pay respect to sabbaths, and new moons, and annual celebrations, and sacred years, as if there were any virtue and any grace in such accidental recurrences in the order of the world. I am afraid that I have spent trouble and labour upon you in vain."

It is clearly implied that there was a marked analogy

---

[1] See § XL.

between the bondage of the Jews under the "rudiments of the world" and the bondage of the Gentiles under the load of ceremonial connected with their former idolatry. The Jewish rudiments are contemptuously summed up as "days and months and seasons and years"; and each of these terms was applicable in startlingly similar fashion to the pagan ceremonial practised in Asia Minor. A few sentences, written in another connection and still unpublished, may be here quoted : "A highly elaborate religious system reigned over the country. Superstitious devotion to an artificial system of rules, and implicit obedience to the directions of the priests (*cf.* Gal. IV 3-11), were universal among the uneducated native population. The priestly hierarchy at the great religious centres, *hiera*, expounded the will of the God to his worshippers.[1] Thus the government was a theocracy, and the whole system, with its prophets, priests, religious law, punishments inflicted by the God for infractions of the ceremonial law, warnings and threats, and the set of superstitious minutiæ, presented a remarkable and real resemblance in external type to the old Jewish ceremonial and religious rule. It is not until this is properly apprehended that Galatians IV 3-11 becomes clear and natural. Paul in that passage implies that the Judaising movement of the Christian Galatians is a recurrence to their old heathen type. After being set free from the bonds of a hard ceremonial law, they were putting themselves once more into the bonds of another ceremonial law, equally hard. In their action they were showing themselves senseless (ἀνόητοι, Gal. III 1), devoid of the educated mind that could perceive the real nature of things.

---

[1] *Cities and Bishoprics of Phrygia,* I 134 ff., 147 ff., 94 ff., etc.

There is an intentional emphasis in the juxtaposition of
ἀνόητοι with Γαλάται, for it was the more educated party,
opposed to the native superstition, that would most warmly
welcome the provincial title.　Hence the address 'senseless
Galatians,' already anticipates the longer expostulation
(IV 3-11), 'Galatians who are sinking from the educated
standard to the ignorance and superstition of the native
religion '."

Obviously the enumeration, "days and months and seasons and years," is merely a contemptuons summary of the
formalistic side of Jewish ritual ; and there is no implication that the Galatians were actually observing at the time
a sacred or Sabbatic year.　The meaning is merely "are
you about to enslave yourselves to the whole series of their
feeble and poor ceremonies ? "

XLIII

HE SENT FORTH HIS SON (GAL. IV 4).

When the preparatory stage had come to an end and the
world was ripe for the new development, God sent forth
His Son, born of a woman, born under the Law, to redeem
them which were under the Law, that we might receive the
adoption of sons.

It seems almost incredible to the outsider, who judges
evidence after the ordinary methods of historical students,
that this verse should be quoted by some scholars as proof
that Paul understood and believed Jesus to be plainly and
literally "the son of Joseph ".　Yet the opinion has been
strenuously and confidently maintained that Paul was
ignorant of any idea that Jesus, so far as concerned His birth,

was anything else except, in the strictest sense, Joseph's son. But the words which Paul here uses plainly imply the following points in his belief and in his teaching to the Galatians :—

1. Jesus existed in the fullest sense as the Son of God before He was sent forth into the world.

2. He was sent forth with a definite duty to perform, retaining the same nature and personal character in the performance of this duty that He had previously possessed. That is proved by the common use in Luke of the verb " sent forth " (ἐξαποστέλλω), and its natural sense as the despatching of a suitable messenger, qualified by his personal character and nature, for the duty to which He is sent.

3. For this duty Jesus took human form and nature : the words γενόμενον ἐκ γυναικός express simply that He became a man among men.

4. To discharge this duty, it was indispensable that Jesus should be subject to the Law, in order to show in His own case how by dying to the Law a man rises superior to it : thus His death was the purchase of men, paid in order that they might be placed in a position to avail themselves of the adoption as sons, open to them by the *Diatheke* of the Father. He could show them the way only by traversing it before them.

It is clear that the teaching, so briefly summed up in this verse, is to be understood as already familiar to the Galatians ; Paul is merely revivifying it in their memory. And, in the discourse which Luke gives as typical of Paul's teaching in Pisidian Antioch and elsewhere (Acts XIII 16-41), exactly the same teaching is set forth in very simple language—language so simple that its full meaning

hardly impresses itself on the reader until he compares it
with the Epistle.   Paul there quotes " Thou art My Son " ;
and he says " the Word of this salvation is sent forth to
us," using the same verb as in Galatians IV 4.   The
context shows that " the Word " here is not to be taken in
the mere sense of news or spoken words, ῥήματα (as Meyer-
Wendt explain) : it is used in a more mystical sense, and
it forms the transition from the simpler expression of the
Synoptics to the language used about " the Word " in the
Fourth Gospel.   That Luke employs this term in his brief
abstract of Paul's Galatian teaching, must be taken as a
proof that Paul intentionally expressed himself in mystic
language as to the relation between the Father and the
Son.   That was not a subject about which he spoke
openly.

It has often seemed to me that this was the subject about
which he " heard unspeakable words which it is not lawful
for man to utter " in the vision described in 2 Corinthians
XII 4.   Though it is vain to seek to know the contents of
a vision, which the seer pointedly refuses to speak about,
yet the mystic language which Paul uses on this subject
may justify, perhaps, a conjecture as to the subject.

The peroration of the address at Pisidian-Antioch insisted
on the marvellous and mysterious nature of God's action in
sending forth His Son: " I work a wonder in your days, a
work which you would not believe, if one should recount
it to you ".

XLIV

THE ADDRESS AT PISIDIAN ANTIOCH.[1]

It is evident from the Epistle, that Paul must have insisted orally to the Galatians on the preparatory character of the Jewish Law ; and must have shown them in his first preaching how the history of the Jews becomes intelligible only as leading onward to a further development and to a fuller stage. That is the whole burden of the address reported in brief by Luke.[2] The typical words, " the fulness of time " (τὸ πλήρωμα τοῦ χρόνου, Gal. IV 4), are echoed in the words of that address : John was fulfilling his course (ἐπλήρου τὸν δρόμον) ; the Jews fulfilled the words of the prophets by condemning Jesus (ἐπλήρωσαν κρίναντες) ; God hath fulfilled His Promise (ἐπαγγελίαν . . . ἐκπεπλήρωκεν).

Further, Paul must have previously laid special stress in addressing the Galatian Churches on the fact that the Promise made to the ancestors of the Jews cannot be performed except through the coming of Christ ; that Christ's coming is the fulfilment of the Promise ; that Christ is the true seed of Abraham ; that men cannot be placed in a position to receive the ratification of the Promise except by being identified with Christ and becoming a part of Christ ; and that in this way only do they become fully the sons and heirs who actually succeed to the inheritance.

This, which is the burden of the Epistle, is also the burden of the address : " ye could not be justified by the Law," " through (the action of) Jesus every one that hath faith is justified." [3] That idea is urged and reiterated,

---

[1] See § XLIII. This section was suggested by Mr. A. Souter.

[2] Acts XIII 16-41.

[3] διὰ τούτου, *i.e.*, Christ. This phrase is characteristically Pauline.

time after time, in the Epistle ; it is specially emphasised in the address ; the word in which it is expressed, δικαιόω, is never used in Acts except in the address; it occurs with extraordinary frequency in the Epistle and in the kindred letter to the Romans, but is rarely used elsewhere by Paul.

The address twice declares that Jesus came as the fulfil-ment of the Promise, *vv.* 23 and 32 f. It lays stress on His being of the seed of David (therefore ultimately of Abraham). It is plain what a decisive part in the con-version of Paul, and in the message to the Galatians pre-supposed in the Epistle (see § XXX), was played by his coming to realise for himself, and his declaring to others, that Jesus was not dead. In the address the same truth is insisted on at length as fundamental in the message which God has sent.

The word "inheritance" is not used in the address with the same prominence as in the Epistle ; the more explana-tory and the more Petrine[1] "remission of sins" appears instead of it. "Inheritance" is used only of the Promised Land (κατεκληρονόμησεν).

The Epistle points out how the hanging upon a tree was necessary as a step in the working out of the duty for which Christ was sent ; and the address describes how, when the Jewish leaders "had fulfilled all things that were written of Him, they took Him down from the tree". Paul never uses this expression "the tree," ξύλον, in this sense in any other Epistle. Peter uses it twice in Acts V 30 and X 39, as well as in his first Epistle II 24.

We notice, in this connexion, that Peter also uses the word "fulfil" (Acts III 18) in a way remarkably similar

[1] Acts II 38, V 31, X 43 (Petrine) : Paul in Acts XXVI 18; Col. I 14; Eph. I 7.

to that which Paul emphasised to the Galatians, and that his addresses there and in V 30 ff. are remarkably similar to Paul's Galatian address. Is not the similarity in their view the reason why Paul specially turned to Peter, and why he went to Jerusalem at first with the single intention of interviewing Peter (ἱστορῆσαι Κηφᾶν, Gal. I 18)? Finally the resemblance between their addresses at the beginning of their career finds its confirmation at the end, when Peter's Epistle is so instinct with Pauline feeling that Lightfoot believes (as every one, surely, must believe) he had read at least Rom. and Eph. Hence he inherited the care of Paul's churches and the services of Paul's coadjutors (1 Peter I 1 ; V 12, 13).

The coincidences between the Epistle and the address at Pisidian Antioch are so striking as to make each the best commentary on the other. It may be said in explanation that the topics common to them are those which are fundamental in Paul's Gospel and must appear in every address. But there is no such close resemblance between the Epistle and any other of Paul's addresses reported in Acts, and the Antiochian address stands in closer relation to this than to any other of Paul's Epistles.

XLV

PAUL'S VISITS TO GALATIA IN ACTS.

To study the Epistle properly, we must here briefly note the account given in Acts of the visits to the Galatic Province.

It is unnecessary to repeat the elaborate study of the first visit given in the *Church in the Roman Empire* and

St. Paul the Traveller. We note merely that the visit must have occupied a considerable time. No statements of time are given in Acts, but the obvious necessities in the evangelisation of four cities and a considerable region (Acts XIII 49; XIV 6), as well as the example of the time spent on later journeys, show that the estimate of twenty months, given as a minimum in those works, if it is not correct, should be increased rather than diminished.

The evangelisation of South Galatia was remarkably successful. The whole of Antioch gathered to listen, and the Word was spread throughout the whole region; a great multitude at Iconium believed; at Derbe there were many disciples, and at Lystra Paul was treated as the messenger-god Hermes. This was the beginning of Paul's work among the Gentiles on his own lines, and its brilliant success encouraged him much (Acts XIV 27; XV 3, 4, 12).

On the whole it was Gentile Churches that were founded on that occasion. Many Iconian Jews believed; but those of Antioch were offended when they saw the Gentiles trooping to hear Paul, and their opposition and pursuit of him were relentless.

It has been used as an argument against the South Galatian Theory that on this journey Luke makes no reference to the Province Galatia. But he mentions its parts—1, Pisidia, 2, the region of which Antioch was centre, 3, the region of which Derbe and Lystra were the leading (practically the only) cities—just as in many inscriptions from about A.D. 80 onwards the Province is mentioned by enumerating the regions that composed it. Such was the "custom of the country," and Luke always follows that.

The second visit to the South Galatian Churches was deliberately planned in order to "see how they fared".

We must understand that Paul was not free from apprehension lest the great conflict in Antioch and Jerusalem might have roused some similar movement in the Churches on the great highway from Syria to the Aegean Sea.

It is admitted on all hands that he visited Derbe, Lystra and Iconium on that journey. The North Galatian theorists say that Paul did not complete his intended visitation, and turned away from Iconium north-eastwards. We, on the contrary, hold that when Luke mentions the " Region which is Phrygian and Galatic," he means the part of Phrygia that belonged to the Province Galatia—that being the most pragmatically accurate designation of the region of which Antioch was the centre (already mentioned on the first journey)—Paul carried out his intention of seeing how all his Churches fared.

All " the Churches were strengthened in their [1] Faith ". When Luke, after telling the purpose of the visit, described so much more fully than usual its result,[2] must we not understand that Paul found need for strengthening them ? Luke never wastes a word in that brief History. Already some slight tendency towards error was developing, and was corrected by Paul.

On that second visit Paul loyally carried out the arrangement made in the Apostolic Decree. Though it was nominally addressed only to the Province of Syria-Cilicia, yet he treated it as of universal application. He was eager to conciliate the Jews by conceding as much as possible to their prejudices. He could not permit Gentiles

[1] This seems probably the real meaning.

[2] Contrast the second visit to Macedonia and Achaia, hit off in such brief terms, though we know that Corinth at least had been deeply moved.

to practise circumcision ; but Timothy, who was of Jewish blood, he treated as a Jew in this respect, and he took with him as companions only Jews. He spared no pains to attain unity and concord ; and the Gentile Galatians might well begin to think after his departure that the rite performed on Timothy was the symbol of admission to the honourable position of helping an Apostle.

The third visit (Acts XVIII 23) was devoted to a thorough and systematic survey of the Churches in Central Asia Minor, in order from first to last " stablishing all the disciples ". Here again our principles of interpretation (reached in previous studies of Acts) compel us to infer that the stablishing of the Galatian Christians is mentioned because it was an important fact. How well it suits the Epistle ! Paul wrote this letter to the Churches, and then at the earliest opportunity visited them and stablished all the disciples. The fight was ended, and Paul was victorious.

But according to the North Galatian theory Paul did not at this time visit South Galatia ; they leave it un-explained why Luke should say so emphatically that Paul " stablished all the disciples," if he left out the four cities and the regions in which they were situated. In fact there is no explanation ; they treat this as one of the many "gaps" in Acts, whose existence they assume at the outset.

The inevitable meaning of the words used by Luke to describe this third journey has been recognised by Dr. Hort : see above, p. 10. Asterius, bishop of Amasia, about A.D. 400, gives the same explanation of the route " through Lycaonia and the cities of Phrygia ". Those who study Asia Minor geography for its own sake must recognise the overwhelming evidence that the term " Galatic Region " (Γαλατικὴ χώρα) could not be used to

designate North Galatia, but only the territory of the enlarged Galatia : see p. 478.

Thus we see that Paul visited the South Galatian cities
three times, and finally after long efforts stablished the
Churches permanently on the Paulinistic side.

XLVI.

PAUL'S VISITS TO THE GALATIC CHURCHES.

Nowhere are the immediate personal relations between
Paul and the Galatic Christians so minutely described as
in the verses IV 12 ff. Here, therefore, is the suitable
place to collect the evidence which the Epistle affords as
to the previous connection between them. The following
points have been generally accepted as naturally following
from the words used by the Apostle. It is better to
avoid disputed points as far as possible; and therefore I
would concentrate attention chiefly on the facts on which
Lightfoot and Zöckler are agreed; for they may be
taken as specially good representatives of the general
opinion.

Paul had already visited the Galatic Churches twice,
and distinguishes between his first and his second visit,
IV 13, "I preached the Gospel to you the former time"
(marginal reading of Revised Version).

It might seem sufficient that Lightfoot and Zöckler are
agreed in this interpretation. But the point is occasionally
disputed, and therefore is treated in a *Note*, 414.

Assuming, then, from IV 13 that Paul had twice visited
Galatia before he wrote to the Churches, we ask whether
any further references occur in the Epistle to the two visits

and to the relations between him and the Galatic Christians on each occasion.

On the first visit the reception given the Apostle and his Gospel by the Galatians was extraordinarily kind, cordial, and even enthusiastic. "Ye received me as an angel of God, even as Christ Jesus." They were hardly satisfied with treating him as an ordinary human being : they regarded him as a special heaven-sent messenger. They congratulated themselves on their happy lot in that Paul had come among them (IV 15).

On the second visit the reception had not been so absolutely cordial and enthusiastic. Twice in this letter[1] he refers to the fact that he is now repeating warnings and reproofs which he had already given : "as we said before, so say I now again" (I 9): "I testify again to every man that receiveth circumcision that he is a debtor to do the whole Law" (V 3). These former warnings would not have been given unless Paul had felt they were needed. Moreover the words of IV 16, "Am I become your enemy because I tell you the truth?" must refer to free exhortation, not unmingled with reproof, during the second visit. Paul feels that there has already come into existence a feeling among the Galatians that he has been holding them back from what is best for them ; and he regards this as due to former plain speaking on his part, which can only be the language used by him during the second visit.

It is, however, also clear that, on the whole, the second visit was a successful one. "Ye were running well" (V 7) proves that ; and moreover the Epistle as a whole indubitably implies (as all interpreters are agreed) that the bad

---

[1] As Zöckler, p. 73, points out.

news which elicited the letter had come to Paul as a complete surprise. He left them running, apparently, a good race in the proper course; and the first news that he received was that disaffection and change were rapidly spreading, and that his own Churches were moving rapidly in a retrograde direction.[1]

A certain interval had elapsed between the second visit and the Epistle, so that he can contrast their conduct in his absence and in his presence.[2] The length of interval needed will be estimated variously by different persons according to their conception of the possible scope of the words " so quickly " in I 6.[3] There came emissaries (doubtless from Jerusalem ultimately) not long after Paul's second visit; and these produced a marked effect, which spread rapidly from congregation to congregation. But the change began some time before Paul heard of it; and he did not learn about it till it was well advanced.

At the same time, while Paul, during his second visit, was speaking very freely on a tendency towards Judaism which was already perceptible in the Galatic Churches, he also used words or performed acts which were taken by some persons as equivalent to an admission (1) that he regarded circumcision (implying of course, observance of

---

[1] Lightfoot, p. 25 (who puts Gal. late, and near Rom.) admits (as he was bound to do) that Paul at Ephesus was in regular correspondence with the Galatic Churches. This would be quite inconsistent with the idea that a schism had begun, and was progressing shortly after he left Galatia, for he would have learned what was going on in the Churches (see § VI, p. 254).

[2] *Doch scheint nach* Gal. IV 18 *seit des Apostel's Abreise aus Galatien immerhin einige Zeit vergangen zu sein;* Zöckler, p. 72 *ad fin.*

[3] Lightfoot's view that the interval is to be measured from the first visit seems not justifiable.

the Law as a whole) as incumbent either on Christians generally, or at least on those who were to attain a position of importance and responsibility in the Church ; (2) that he was only a messenger and subordinate of the original and leading Apostles in Jerusalem.

The former of these two misconceptions is clearly referred to in V 11, " If I still preach circumcision, why do the Judaistic party persecute me ? " and it led to the further misrepresentation that Paul was insincere in these words or acts, and used them only to curry favour with a party which was so powerful that he shrank from offending it openly (I 10).

The second misconception obviously underlies the whole argument in chapters I and II, and has already been considered in § VIII.

Probably no one will maintain that these misconceptions were caused by Paul's words and acts during his first visit. The Epistle, as a whole, from first to last, bears on its face the plain intention to bring back the Galatic Christians to their first frame of mind. " They began spiritually, they seek to complete their religious course by physical ritual." On this see § VIII.

The historical inferences from the Epistle as to Paul's relations to the Galatic Churches are, then, clear. His first visit had been one of unclouded and brilliant success, calculated to give extraordinary encouragement to the non-Jewish Christians everywhere. A new step had been taken, and it was entirely confirmed by the manifest signs of God's favour. God had supplied to them the Spirit ; He had " wrought miracles among them " ; and all this had resulted, not from their " performing any part of the Jewish ritual," but purely from " the willing hearing which comes of Faith "[1] (III 2 and 5). That was the confirmation which had defended Peter's action in the case of Cornelius : " The Spirit fell on all them which heard the word : and the champions of circumcision were amazed because that on the Gentiles also was poured out the gift of the Holy Spirit " (Acts X 44, 45).

Now at what point in the narrative of Acts does such a stage of the great question naturally fall ? Here we have a Gentile province, in the heart of Asia Minor, evangelised ; and at once the Divine Spirit, by manifest, indubitable, external signs—signs which were clearly displayed to the senses of every onlooker—is imparted to them and recognised generally as dwelling among them. It is obvious that this is the precise stage which was made known by Paul and Barnabas to the Christians of Phœnicia and Samaria, when they " declared the conversion of the Gentiles, and caused great joy to all the brethren " (Acts XV 3). It was an epoch-making step ; and, if this step in advance resulted soon afterwards in those Galatic Churches retrogressing into Judaism, the blow to Paul's gospel would have been most severe and probably fatal. The very importance of the step, the joy that it caused to the non-Hebrew Churches, made the possible defection of those Galatic Churches a crisis of the gravest character. From Acts we see what an epoch-making step was taken when the South Galatian Churches were converted. From the Epistle we gather what a serious crisis it was to Paul when the Churches of Galatia showed symptoms of schism. Why suppose that the Churches in South Galatia are not " Churches of Galatia " ? Why try to make an artificial

---

[1] This is Lightfoot's rendering. Zöckler similarly " *Aufnahme der evangelischen Predigt im Glauben* ".

separation ?   It is answered that Paul could not call his
Churches in South Galatia by the title of the " Churches
of Galatia ".   Yet it is admitted that only a few years
later Peter summed up these Churches in South Galatia
among his Churches of Galatia.   If Peter used about A.D.
64[1] the Roman system of classifying these Pauline Churches
according to the Province in which they were situated—the
invariable method of the Church in all later time—why
could not Paul classify his own Churches in that way about
53-57 ?   Whether is it more likely that Paul the Roman
would employ the Roman principle from the first, or that
Peter the Palestinian would substitute the Roman principle
for Paul's non-Roman system ?   But this is a digression.

Now, as to the second visit, we have seen that during it
there were some signs of trouble : the ideal harmony that
reigned between Paul and his Galatian converts on the
first visit was not maintained on the second.   At what
point in the narrative of Acts are the complications of
that visit most naturally to be placed ?

The answer cannot be for a moment doubtful.   In Acts
we have a picture of the Church as it passed through the
stages of this struggle ; and the second Galatian visit clearly
harmonises with the stage described as resulting from the
apostolic council.   Every feature of the second visit, shown
in the Epistle, is either expressly attested, or natural and
probable, in Paul's second journey through South Galatia
(XVI 1-5).

1. With the constant stream of communication between
Syria and the West that poured along the great route, it is
practically certain that the struggle in Antioch would rouse

[1] Our argument here is directed against scholars who admit that
date : for my own part, I think that Peter wrote about 75-80.

some echo in the South Galatian Churches. There was a considerable Jewish population in that country; it was influential, politically, socially, and, above all, as regards religion;[1] many of the pagans had long been to some degree under the influence of Jewish ideas. There were Jews in the new Churches, though the mass were converted pagans.

Moreover, it is natural that some tendency towards Judaic ceremonies should exist from beforehand among many of the converts : indeed, it was inevitable that this should be so. They had of old been influenced by the impressive character of the Jewish faith ; they heard the Gospel first in the synagogue ; and Paul's arguments were regularly drawn from the Jewish Prophets and Law. This produced a tendency, which Paul had to warn them against on his second visit ; and the man who had just come from the conflict in Jerusalem and Antioch would not be slow to warn them of the possible dangers of that tendency. The Phrygians always tended to Judaism, pp. 193 ff, 449.

2. Paul's words and acts on the second visit had created the impression that he regarded circumcision as a duty. Lightfoot fully recognises[2] that this impression was due to Paul's action at Lystra in his second journey, Acts XVI 2, and that this affords a distinct argument in favour of the South Galatian theory. He circumcised Timothy. The act was seized on by his enemies, and was certainly open to misconstruction.

3. His words and acts on that second Galatian visit had also been construed as an attempt to please men. Such,

---

[1] On this point see Sec. 18 and *Cities and Bishoprics of Phrygia,* chap. XV, The Jews in Phrygia.

[2] See his note on V 11, p. 206. See also his remarks on p. 29.

too, was sure to be the case on his journey in South Galatia, Acts XVI 1-5. It was natural that one who was loyally carrying out a compromise and going as far as possible in the hope of conciliating the Jews should thus be misunderstood. His action to Timothy was easily set in that light. The action can be defended ; but every one must feel that it is one of those acts which need defence, not one whose propriety is obvious and indisputable.

4. His conduct on the second visit further suggested that he was merely a messenger and subordinate of the apostolic leaders in Jerusalem. Similarly, on his journey in South Galatia, he actually appeared as a messenger, and "delivered them the decrees for to keep, which had been ordained of the apostles and elders that were at Jerusalem " (Acts XVI 4) : the misinterpretation referred to in the Epistle was quite natural as a corollary from that action.

5. The second visit was successful in its issue : Paul seemed to have eradicated the dangerous tendencies. That also was the case with the second journey through the Churches in South Galatia ; " the Churches were strengthened in the Faith " (Acts XVI 5). The words read as if they were an explanatory note on the Epistle to the Galatians. And that is the character of the narrative of Acts as a whole, when the South Galatian theory is applied. The facts recorded in the History fit the Epistle. The Epistle is elucidated throughout by the History.

Now, let any one attempt to do this for the North Galatian theory. It is admittedly impossible. The one authority does not fit the other. The events and emotions recorded in Acts XVI do not suit the first visit, those recorded in Acts XVIII do not suit the second visit, as these visits are alluded to in the Epistle. The North

Galatian theory ends in that pathetic conclusion, the refuge of despair, that the most striking fact about the History of Luke is " the gaps " in it. And the inevitable inference from that theory—an inference drawn by all its adherents—is that the author of that History, the intimate friend and companion of Paul, did not know the Epistles of Paul or the real facts about the Galatian Churches, or concealed his knowledge of the facts.

He who judges from Acts must expect that the South Galatian Churches would play an important part in the struggle for freedom on one side or on the other ; and that is so as the South Galatian theorists read the Epistles of Paul.

But on the North Galatian theory, the Churches whose foundation is heralded by Paul to the Phœnician and Samarian Christians as so important a step towards freedom disappear at once from history : they play no part in subsequent events, except that Paul pays a passing visit to some of them [1] in XVI 1-5 : though they lie on the main track [2] of communication by land between East and West, yet they participate in no further stage of the great struggle : their action is never referred to by Paul either as a pattern or an encouragement to his other Churches : his first-born spiritual offspring,[3] whose birth was celebrated by him as an encouragement to distant peoples, Acts XV 4, is never alluded to by him in writing

[1] It is explicitly maintained by some North Galatian theorists (and is obviously forced on any who try to work that theory into a geographical possibility) that Paul went north from Iconium, without going westwards as far as Pisidian Antioch.

[2] Except Lystra, which was ten or twelve miles off the track in a retired glen.

[3] Compare Gal. IV 19.

any of the letters that have come down to us, except once to tell what he suffered there. The place they might be expected to fill is said to be taken by a different group of Churches in the northern part of the same Province.

One further inference from the Epistle as to the relations of Paul to the Galatians remains. It is evident (as Zöckler, p. 73, rightly points out) that, when Paul was writing, the schism was not yet completed. It was only in process (I 6). The whole of Paul's appeal in the Epistle is directed to prevent a process which is going on, not to undo what has already been completed. The "little leaven is leavening the whole"; but it may be removed in time to prevent the worst and irretrievable consequences. Especially (as Zöckler emphasises) the Galatians had not yet accepted circumcision. Paul says: "If ye receive circumcision, Christ will profit you nothing" (V 2). Contrast this with IV 10, "ye are observing days and months"; and it is clear that the latter step has been taken, and the Jewish ceremonial is commonly observed, but the more serious step has not yet been made.

Note.—τὸ πρότερον. Prof. Blass[1] has recently added his weighty authority to the opposite view—*viz.*, that τὸ πρότερον here merely means "at a former time". Lightfoot's note seems to me to show beyond question the fallacy of this view, which he carefully considers and dismisses. His argument is elucidated and confirmed by the two following considerations.

(*a*) On the opposite side 1 Timothy I 13 is quoted as a case in which Paul uses τὸ πρότερον in the sense of

[1] *Grammatik des N.T. Griech*, p. 34.

"formerly". Lightfoot, however, sees what escapes his opponents—that this is not a parallel case. In 1 Timothy I 13 [1] τὸ πρότερον materially influences the meaning of the whole sentence; it means "previously, but not at the time in question"; and the sentence would not be correct if τὸ πρότερον were omitted. Thus the adverb expresses a direct and emphatic contrast between the earlier and the later time.

Now, it is impossible to understand that in Galatians IV 13 τὸ πρότερον indicates such a contrast as in 1 Timothy I 13. It would be absurd to translate "You know that it was because of bodily disease that I preached the Gospel to you at a former, but not at a later time". This would be meaningless except as distinguishing two visits.

Suppose now that Professor Blass is right, and that the verse only means, "You know that it was because of disease that I preached to you at a former time". The adverb here might be omitted, and the meaning would be as perfect and complete as it is when the adverb is expressed. Is this characteristic of Paul? Is it even permissible? For my own part I cannot admit that in this letter a single word is used in an otiose and useless way. Τὸ πρότερον must have a marked and distinct sense—all the more so because it occupies the emphatic position at the end of a clause. As Lightfoot says: "it is difficult to explain the emphasis," except by interpreting "the former of my two visits to Galatia".

---

[1] πιστόν με ἡγήσατο θέμενος εἰς διακονίαν τὸ πρότερον ὄντα βλάσφημον : "He counted me faithful, appointing me to His service, though I had previously been a blasphemer". Paul had ceased to be a blasphemer before he was appointed. If τὸ πρότερον were omitted, the meaning would be that he was appointed while still a blasphemer.

The only objection to this is that it is true Greek ; and some scholars have made up their mind that Paul and Luke were quite unable to distinguish between a comparative and a superlative.

(*b*) Again, if we take τὸ πρότερον here in the bare sense of " formerly," we must infer that Paul had preached the Gospel to the Galatic Churches only once. It would be absurd in itself, and is wholly irreconcilable with the historical narrative in Acts, that Paul should claim to have preached twice by reason of bodily illness. Here he distinctly refers to one definite occasion, one definite visit, on which sickness was the reason why it came about that he evangelised.[1] Therefore, either he had only once before " preached the Gospel" to the Galatians,[2] or he must make some distinction between the two visits, and use words referring only to one of them ; and the distinction can lie only in the adverb τὸ πρότερον. Sickness was the cause on the former occasion, but not on the second.

We know from Acts, alike on the North and the South Galatian theory, that Paul's words can only refer to the first visit, for his second visit was planned with the firm resolve and intention to preach to those Churches. Why struggle to avoid the obvious truth, that τὸ πρότερον has its plain and natural sense of " the former of two occasions ? "

---

[1] Notice the aorist εὐηγγελισάμην.

[2] Mr. Vernon Bartlett takes this view, placing the composition of Galatians at Antioch in the interval between Paul's return from Pamphylia and his visit to Jerusalem in Acts XV 3 ff. He thus avoids one difficulty ; but τὸ πρότερον remains idle and unnecessary. According to Zöckler, the same date was advocated by Calvin, and by some German scholars.

XLVII

CAUSE OF THE FIRST GALATIAN VISIT.

It was because of bodily disease, "infirmity of the flesh," that the Apostle had first preached the Gospel to the Galatians. Taking this expression by itself, we see that two explanations of it are possible :—

1. When I was in your country, but not intending to preach there, a disease caused me to change my intention and preach to you.

2. When I was not intending to enter your country, but had other plans of work, a disease caused me to change my plans, and thus led to my visiting you and preaching to you.

No third explanation seems open.

1. The first of these explanations has been adopted by all adherents of the North Galatian theory. It is perhaps not absolutely necessary for them to have recourse to it ; but as they have unanimously adopted it, we need not discuss whether the other explanation would not be open to them.

Put in this bare and severely simple form, this explanation seems awkward. It is not at first sight probable that Paul would go across a country without any thought of evangelising there, unless there were some distinct impediment. He twice crossed, evidently without preaching in it, the land ruled by King Antiochus of Commagene and Cilicia Tracheia. But that was not Roman territory, and was therefore outside of his plans ;[1] and, moreover, on both

---

[1] As Principal A. Robertson says in *Expositor*, Jan., 1899, p. 2 : " I assume that the evangelisation of the Roman world as such was an object consciously before his mind and deliberately planned ".

27

occasions he was passing on to carry out a pressing work among his own Churches (Acts XV 36, XVI 1, XVIII 23). Again, he crossed Asia without preaching in it, but his plan of preaching there had been expressly prohibited by the Spirit (Acts XVI 6).

But, it is said, when he was at Lystra or Iconium, and found that his plan of preaching in Asia was prevented, he formed a new plan of preaching in Bithynia, and, as he was going thither, while crossing North Galatia, he was detained by illness, and to this detention " the Galatians owed their knowledge of Christ ".[1]

But the road from Iconium to Bithynia never touches North Galatia. It lies in Phrygia as far as Dorylaion, and then enters Bithynia. It is marked out by nature, and by immemorial use: that is beyond dispute. If Paul formed at Lystra or Iconium the plan of preaching in Bithynia, he would not traverse North Galatia as he went to his goal.

When this undeniable fact is pointed out, the reply is that Paul was going to eastern Bithynia and Pontus—" the east parts of Bithynia and of Pontus ".[2]

But our one authority says only Bithynia, and we have no right to add Pontus and to make Paul travel to Pontus, dropping Bithynia out of notice. The obvious meaning of our one authority is that Paul, prevented from his first aim of evangelising Asia with his great and civilised cities, be-

---

[1] Lightfoot, p. 22. He, however, holds (as I have always done) that Paul traversed the Galatic region before he touched Asia or learned that he was not to preach there : see p. 478. Other supporters of the North Galatian theory, however, take the view stated in the text.

[2] *Expositor*, Dec., 1893, p. 415.

thought himself of the nearest country to it—Bithynia, with its great and civilised cities ; Nicomedia, Nicæa, Cæsarea, etc. He would never select second-rate remote places in the far corner of the Roman Empire, such as Tion, Sinope, and Amisos. There is no conceivable reason why he should traverse and neglect North Galatia in order to reach unimportant towns like those.

The course of the second missionary journey is quite too extraordinary on this supposition. First, Paul aims at Asia ; then he aims at Pontus ; then he falls ill on the way, and proceeds to evangelise North Galatia, founding there several Churches—a process which requires long time and much travel. Then he proceeds to carry out his previous intention and goes on towards Pontus ; and in doing this he finds himself κατὰ τὴν Μυσίαν. Whether we translate this "beside Mysia" or "over against Mysia," it is a plain impossibility, for the traveller going from North Galatia into "eastern Bithynia and Pontus" would be going north-east, with his back turned towards Mysia.

But it is needless to proceed, as I might, in the enumeration of the absurdities in which this hypothesis is involved.

Those who cling to the first explanation must be content to recognise here one of those "gaps" in the narrative of Luke which they so often find. They maintain that the "gaps" are numerous and puzzling, and one more added to the number will not be a serious addition.

2. On the second explanation there must have been some occasion, during Paul's travels, when he changed his plans of work under compulsion of illness. He twice changed his plans on the second journey—first when he entered Asia, and next when he was approaching Bithynia ; but in both cases the reason is distinctly assigned by Luke

as the Divine guidance and orders ; and we cannot admit, with Lightfoot,[1] that the same action is sometimes attributed to Divine command and sometimes to the pressure of external conditions ; none of his examples will bear examination (*St. Paul the Trav.*, p. 154 f.).

On the first journey, however, there was an occasion when Paul changed his plans. The scope of that journey, as originally contemplated, embraced the lands which were naturally in closest relation with Syrian Antioch, *viz.*, Cyprus and the Pamphylian coast. So long as these were the scene of work, John was a willing companion. But when Paul and Barnabas resolved to abandon Pamphylia and cross Taurus into the Galatic Province, John left them, and left the work. Luke does not state the motives of either party : he does not explain either why the two Apostles resolved to go to Pisidian Antioch, or why John refused to go. The reasons for his silence we can only conjecture ; but two causes, both of which might be combined in his mind, seem both natural and adequate ; he is little concerned with personal details, and he did not desire to dwell on an occasion when John had played a part which he probably afterwards regretted, and which deeply wounded Paul.

With regard to the situation, we may regard the following four statements as highly probable :—

1. There was no express Divine command, for we can hardly believe that John would have disobeyed it ; and, if he had disobeyed such a command, Barnabas would not afterwards have urged so strongly that John was a useful companion for a similar journey (Acts XV 37).

----

[1] On *Gal.*, p. 125.

(2) John considered the move into the Galatic Province as a change of plan, and justified his refusal by this plea. He was willing to go to Pamphylia, but not across the mountains; the former sphere of work had been contemplated from the first, the latter had not.

(3) The cause that made Paul and Barnabas change their original plan must have appeared to them strong and compelling. It was not that they simply began to consider the north side of Taurus a better field than the south side, for they had been sent forth by the Holy Spirit, and given leave of absence by the Church, with an eye to a distinct sphere of work; and mere human calculation of superior advantage would not have seemed to them a sufficient reason for changing the sphere. It was not that Pamphylia was found to be a hopeless district, because when they returned they preached there. There was some reason which made work in Pamphylia impossible at the time, but which, afterwards, on their return, was not operative.

Accordingly, we see what was the actual fact. They changed their plan, and they entered the Galatic Province; but the reason was not simple desire to evangelise there, it was some other compelling motive. Here the Epistle clears away all doubt. In it Paul clearly intimates, as his words must be interpreted, that his first visit had been caused not by a desire to preach to the Galatians, but by bodily disease. This cause satisfies all the conditions.

Thus, the way in which these two accounts mutually supplement and explain one another is a most conclusive proof of the honesty and direct simplicity of both.

Other points, as for example, that Paul's circumstances in Pamphylia were such as to bring out any weakness of the system, do not directly arise out of the Epistle, and have been sufficiently treated elsewhere.[1]

XLVIII

THE THORN IN THE FLESH.

From the Epistle we can gather something as to the nature of the disease. Lightfoot's discussion of the subject is excellent, and we adopt every one of his conclusions, except his final opinion that the disease was epilepsy, and his suggestion that "the meanness of his personal appearance (2 Cor. X 10) was perhaps due to" the permanent effects of his painful malady.

First, the disease was active during Paul's residence in Galatia, and yet it was quite compatible with long journeys. That is implied alike on the North and the South Galatian theories. The disease was active, because the Galatians saw it and did not despise the sufferer; it is implied that the Galatian Churches in general, and not some single one alone, witnessed the Apostle's condition. Yet he was able to make long journeys; on the North Galatian theory he went about between Ancyra, Tavium and Pessinus, then proceeded towards Bithynia (or, as some say, Pontus), then went through Mysia to Troas; and all these journeys must have been made very quickly, for no chronological system leaves free a long period for this work. On the South Galatian theory Paul went from Perga to Syrian Antioch, and then to Iconium, etc. These journeys need not have been performed with the speed and exertion im-

[1] *Church in Rom. Emp.*, p. 63; *St. Paul the Trav.*, p. 194 ff.

plied in the North Galatian theory, but still one of them is very long.

It follows that the disease did not take the form of one single attack of illness. It was intermittent. At one time Paul was prostrated by an attack, at another he was able for considerable exertion, both in travel and in preaching.

Second, the disease was such as to be naturally regarded by the people of Asia Minor with contempt or loathing; but, far from so regarding him, they received him as an angel of God. The verbal contrast is so pointed as to suggest that the disease was one which the people ordinarily regarded as due to the direct action and curse of God. We need not understand that it caused any loathsome external effect; but a sufferer was usually regarded as one under the Divine curse on account of some crime.

Now, the inscriptions show that one disease was regarded in Asia Minor as due to the immediate action of God. These show that, when a native of the country prayed to the god or goddess to avenge him on his enemy, he asked that his enemy should be " burnt up " with fever, " in which strength wastes away without any visible affection of a. part of the body. This kind of disease was understood to be caused by fire sent from the world of death by direct act of the god, which consumed the inner life and spirit of the sufferer." [1] A full description of an attack of fever, with its recurring paroxysms and characteristic symptoms, is given in a late curse: " May he suffer fevers, chill, torments, pallors, sweatings, heats by day and by night ".[2]

[1] See *Expository Times*, Dec., 1898, p. 110; comp. Wünsch in *Corp. Inscr. Att.*, Appendix, p. XII.

[2] Wünch, *Sethianische Verfluchungstafeln*, 1898, p. 7. These were found in Rome; but embody magic of indubitably Oriental type.

When Paul was among the Galatians, this disease was "the thing that tried them in his body"; it tested the reality of their love for him and their respect for him: it constituted a temptation to regard him as a person cursed by God. But they stood the test; they resisted the temptation; and they regarded him as a messenger come from God.

Every one who is familiar with the effect of the fevers that infest especially the south coasts of Asia Minor, but are found everywhere in the country, knows that they come in recurring attacks, which prostrate the sufferer for the time, and then, after exhausting themselves, pass off, leaving him very weak; that a common remedy familiar to all is change to the higher lands; and that, whenever any one who has once suffered has his strength taxed, physically or mentally, the old enemy prostrates him afresh, and makes him for a time incapable of any work. Apart from the weakness and ague, the most trying and painful accompaniment is severe headache.

Now, the tradition about Paul was, for some reason, far more closely concerned with his personal appearance and physical history than was the case with any other Apostle. This must undoubtedly be due to the immense personal influence that he exerted on Asia Minor, where the tradition had best chance of being preserved owing to the very early general adoption of the new religion in several parts of the country.[1] His personal appearance, his age, at conversion and at death, are recorded in Asia Minor tradition, and, as

[1] The Phrygian saint of the second century, Avircius Marcellus, travelled "with Paul in his hands"; he mentions no other Apostle or teacher in his epitaph (*Cities and Bishoprics of Phrygia*, II, p. 722).

I believe, with trustworthiness. The common opinion, current as early as the second century, was that the extreme physical pain, which he describes elsewhere as "the stake in the flesh," the accompaniment of his disease, was severe headache. Lightfoot rightly recognises that, if we give any weight at all to ancient opinion, we must follow this statement, which was current in the second century and may confidently be taken as forming part of the unbroken Asia Minor tradition.

In *St. Paul the Traveller* (p. 97 f.) an argument is founded on the remarkable analogy between the expression used by Paul himself to describe one specially prominent accompaniment of his disease—"a stake in the flesh "—and the words which rise to the lips of several persons known to me, all innocent of Pauline prepossession in describing their own experience of the headache that accompanies each recurrence of chronic malaria fever—" a red-hot bar thrust through the forehead ". In corroboration of this, we may quote the description of " a bad attack of malarial neuralgia," given by the South African author, A. Werner, on p. 236 of his collection of stories, entitled *The Captain of the Locusts*, 1899. He speaks of " the grinding, boring pain in one temple, like the dentist's drill—the phantom wedge driven in between the jaws," and describes the acuteness of the suffering, in which every minute the patient seems to have " reached the extreme point of human endurance ".

Is it possible to have more convincing analogies than this? A similar metaphor rises to the lips of quite independent persons to describe the sensation. There are perhaps some who may think it wrong procedure to imagine that Paul was really describing with what they might brand as morbid anatomical detail the exact species of pain that he suffered. I think Paul was not so different from the ordinary human being that he must describe his enemy in the flesh only by some general and vague expression. Every one who has to contend often with any special enemy of this kind, if he speaks of it at all, tends to use some phrase about it that reveals his own personal experience. Commonly he is silent about it; but if he is deeply moved, and alludes to it while he is showing his inmost soul under the stimulus of emotion, his expression lights up by a flash the physical fact.

That is the case in 2 Corinthians XII 7. There is no passage in all Paul's writings in which he is more deeply moved. There is no other passage in which he shows so much of his inner mind, or speaks so freely of his private personal experiences. He alludes, among these experiences, to his secret communing with the Divine nature; and he describes the counter-balancing evil at once an extremely painful, almost unendurable, suffering, and a serious impediment to his work. These are the two features about this enemy in the flesh, on which the human being is sure to insist. It is "a stake in the flesh,—a messenger of Satan," the enemy of the truth.

When we take this striking realistic detail in conjunction with the strong and very old tradition that Paul was in this expression describing the fever-headache, it seems to me that there is an exceedingly strong case, such as one could hardly have expected about such a matter. And this is clinched by the superstition current in Asia Minor that fever was the special weapon hurled by the gods of the underworld against criminals.

The theory that Paul's disease was epilepsy deserves a

word. Appearances are, at first sight, in its favour—the example of Julius Cæsar, Napoleon, Cromwell, all epileptics —the fact that the nervous system, when working at its highest pressure, is nearest to breaking down. But if we take epilepsy as Paul's trial, then we must accept the medical inferences from it. It follows inexorably that his visions were epileptic symptoms, no more real than the dreams of epileptic insanity. In fact, it is the visions which give probability to the theory of epilepsy: as a distinguished pathologist says to me, you will find hundreds of exact parallels to Paul's visions, if you want them : any lunatic asylum in the country will furnish them in plenty. The nerve-centres of sight and vision are close together, and naturally affected together, when the system is on the point of collapse. The temporary blindness that followed the first vision is exactly what the pathologist expects as the sequel of an epileptic vision.

The theory is seductive. But are we prepared to accept the consequences? Paul's visions have revolutionised the world. Has the modern world, with all that is best and truest in it, been built upon the dreams of epileptic insanity? Is reason the result of unreason, truth of falsity?

Moreover, we do not find that Cæsar or Napoleon attributed their greatness to their epileptic seizures. But Paul did so : he regarded his visions as the crowning glory of his life, the sole source of his knowledge and his power : he distinguished absolutely his visions from the " messenger of Satan, the stake in the flesh ". Now the latter has much less analogy to epileptic seizure. Lightfoot shows conclusively that " the stake in the flesh " must be some " physical pain of a very acute kind "; but pain is not a feature of epileptic fits. The premonitory symptoms, the *aura*, sometimes include pain ; but on the epileptic theory the visions were the *aura*, and the fit followed.

We cannot take Paul as an epileptic lunatic. The only alternative seems to be to take him as afflicted by those seizures which were regarded as the messengers of the gods of the underworld.

XLIX

SEQUENCE OF THOUGHT IN IV 12-20.

The expression in this paragraph is rather disjointed and awkward. It can be best explained on the supposition that Paul is here catching up and turning to his own purposes certain phrases used by the Galatians.

The meaning is : " I beseech you, brethren, set yourselves free, as I am, from the slavery of ritual, for I made myself as a Gentile[1] like you in order to preach to you ". He had put himself on an equality with them ; and did not, like the Judaistic preachers, claim to be on a superior level.

" You say with truth in your letter that you ' do not wrong[2] me,' but are conscious how much you owe me, even although you have to modify your attitude towards my teaching." Paul repeats the word employed by them, and dwells on the thought. " I bear you witness that you did not in the past ' wrong me ' or act unkindly to me. On the contrary, as you know well, you treated me more like ' a messenger of God,' though your inherited ways of

[1] Compare II 14.

[2] Lightfoot says of these words, " Possibly the true explanation is hidden under some unknown circumstances to which St. Paul alludes ". Paul alludes to the use of the words by the Galatians.

thought would naturally have made you regard one afflicted like me as accursed and consumed by the messenger of the underworld. You would have put at my disposal what was dearest to you, had it been possible to benefit me thereby.

"But I do not admit your explanation that you 'are not wronging me' now. You are indeed wronging me: you are troubling me (VI 17). What is the reason? Evidently you regard me as an enemy, that you treat me so. Is it because I spoke the truth to you on my second visit, and warned you of some faults among you, that you now look on me as an enemy?"

The Galatians also seem to have conveyed to Paul their sense of the extreme zeal and interest that the Judaistic missionaries had shown in their welfare, and to have used the phrase " they take a keen interest in us " (ζηλοῦσιν). Hence Paul plays upon that word, " They ' take a lively interest' in you, as you say; but they do it in no good way. In reality they desire to make you think that you are outside the pale of Jewish pride and birth and privilege in order that you may ' admire and envy' them,[1] who are within the pale. It is not true zeal for your interest that prompts their action. It is their deep-seated Jewish pride which refuses to regard you as really their brethren (whereas, as I said, I always regard you so): they will not put you on an equality with themselves (as I do): they seek to mislead you into the belief that they are a superior class by right of birth (whereas you can become as truly sons of God and sons of Abraham as they).

"I regret my absence and inability to show you face to

---

[1] He repeats the word ζηλόω in a different sense.

face my interest in you ; and I should think it good if there were always some one present with you to take such interest in you (provided it be in a good way), so that you should not be dependent on my presence for a true friend. My own children, I would I were present with you now, and speaking with the old tone of mutual affection, not in the tone you have forced on me ; for I am troubled about you."

When the last sentence is read rightly, it is seen not to spring from some special cause, which makes it impossible for him to come to the Galatians now. He is not explaining that he cannot go to see them (as some commentators imagine). He is merely regretting that he is writing far away and in an unwonted tone. The messenger who carried his letter would announce his coming visit.

Read thus, as catching up the words and excuses of the Galatians, the paragraph ceases to be disjointed, and becomes simple. But whether the Galatians' words were reported by Paul's informant, or written in a letter by the Churches, is difficult to determine (§ LIX). Only the word " enemy " was evidently reported, not written, to Paul.

L

THE ALLEGORY OF HAGAR AND SARAH (IV 21, V).

This paragraph is one of the most difficult in the whole Epistle to understand aright ; and it is the one which would probably outrage Jewish prejudice more than any other.

The children of Abraham are divided into two classes : the descendants of Sarah free, and the descendants of Hagar slave. The Jews, though Sarah's sons, are described as the offspring of Hagar, because they, like Ishmael, are descendants by nature ; the Gentile Christians are described as the offspring of Sarah, because they, like Isaac, are descendants by promise of God.

It must be at once admitted that, if this passage were to be taken simply in its relation to the preceding and following parts of the Epistle, as rising spontaneously in Paul's mind in the sequence of his own philosophic argument, it would be unnecessarily insulting and offensive to the Jews, weak as an argument, and not likely to advance his purpose of changing the current of feeling among the Galatians. But Lightfoot's interpretation of verse 21 is, " Will ye not listen to the Law ? "—explained by him thus, " Ye who vaunt your submission to the Law, listen while I read you a lesson out of the Law "—and if we follow this interpretation, we must regard the passage as arising in the free development of Paul's argument within his own mind.

The rival interpretation, adopted both in the Authorised and the Revised Version, " Do ye not hear the Law ? " *i.e.*, " Is not the Law constantly read to you ? " (comp. Acts XV 21 ; 2 Cor. III 14),[1] must therefore be preferred. This leaves it quite open to take the passage as forced on Paul from the outside, *i.e.*, as a reply to an argument either used in Galatia by his opponents (and reported to him by Timothy), or employed in a letter sent by the Churches to Paul (§ LIX).

This opposition argument must have taken the following

---

[1] I quote *verbatim* Lightfoot's exposition of this interpretation. Zöckler's interpretation, " Do ye not obey the Law ? " misses the real point of the passage. All three interpretations are grammatically possible.

form : The Jews are the true sons of Abraham, descended
by birth from Sarah, and granted to her by a special promise of God, after hope of offspring in the natural course
had ceased ; Gentile Christians cannot be regarded as in
any way on an equal footing with the true sons, unless
they comply with all the obligations imposed on the true
sons.   Further, this argument may perhaps have been
united with the anti-Pauline view (so often referred to in
the Epistle) that the Gentile Christians stood on an inferior platform, but could rise to the higher platform of
perfection (III 3), as true sons, by accepting the law and
its prescribed ritual.

It may be doubted whether the Judaic emissaries in
Galatia were prepared to go quite so far as this argument
implies in the direction of admitting Gentiles to the full
rights of sons of Abraham.   Hence it seems more probable
that this argument was actually stated in a letter by the
Churches, explaining their views and doubts.

Accordingly, the paragraph may perhaps be read best as
quoting from a letter : "Tell me, you who express to me
your desire[1] to come under the Law, do you not know
what the Law says?   Do you not hear it read regularly
in your assembly?   You argue that the Jews are the true
sons, and you are outsiders ; and on this argument you
justify your desire to come under the Law ; but this reasoning is not supported by a correct understanding of the
Scripture as contained in the Law.   Hagar, the Arabian
slave, and her son, the slave—when the allegory is properly
interpreted—belong to the same category with the present
Jerusalem and her children the Jews, all enslaved to the

---

[1] "Θέλοντες *desiring*, and not merely being willing"; ç. XII 17.
Westcott's note on Hebrews XIII 18.

Law as it was delivered from the Arabian mountain. You, as free from the Law, inheriting through the free *Diatheke* of God, are classed to the heavenly Jerusalem, your true city and your true home,[1] of which all we Christians are the children. Thus you, my brothers, are children of promise (not of mere natural, fleshly birth) like Isaac. You are persecuted by the fleshly children now, just as Isaac, the child of promise, was persecuted by the fleshly child, Ishmael of old. And, just as the slave child Ishmael was cast out and lost his inheritance, so now ——[2]. We Christians, all, Jew like me or Gentile like you, my brothers, are sons of the free woman, not of the slave woman."

Thus, as we see, Paul was not voluntarily dragging into his letter a gibe at the Jews. He was saying to the Galatians, " The view you state that the Jews are the true sons of Abraham, and that you ought to make yourselves like them, shows that you do not rightly read the Law. The passages to which you refer are to be interpreted allegorically, not verbally—by the spirit, not by the letter. Literally, the Jews are the sons of Sarah; but, in the spiritual interpretation, you are become the free woman Sarah's children, and the Jews are the sons of the slave woman."

This paragraph, perhaps, assumes as a fact of law and society that the status of the child follows the mother, not the father. The illustration would be meaningless to the Galatians, unless they regarded the son of the master of

[1] The contrast between an earthly city, Derbe or Iconium, where one is a citizen according to the world, and the heavenly city, the real city of all Christians, is implicit here. Similarly it is implicit (and disregarded by most scholars) in the epitaph of Avircius Marcellus (*Cities and Bishoprics*, II p. 724).

[2] Paul does not express the analogy fully.

the house by a slave mother as a slave. Now that was not Semitic custom, nor is it natural where polygamy is practised. In Mohammedan sacred law such a son ennobles the mother. Among the Hebrews it is evident that Dan, Asher, Ishmael, etc., who were born in that way, were not regarded as of servile station.

But among both Greeks and Romans the son follows the mother.[1] The inhuman custom prevailed that the offspring of slave-women was like that of domestic animals: they were all mere property. A similar principle probably existed both in South and North Galatia, for both Galatian and Phrygian fathers were in the habit of selling their freeborn children, and are therefore not likely to have regarded the son of a slave mother as anything but a slave.

LI

THE CONCLUSION (V 1).

Paul now sums up the argument of chapters III and IV in the brief conclusion : " It was with a view to our full freedom (and not for any new kind of slavery) that Christ has set us Christians free from the bondage of sin.[2]

[1] The rule is familiar in Roman law. As to Greece see Mitteis *Reichsrecht und Volksr.*, p. 241. At Edessa or Salonika enfranchisements occur in inscriptions of " my slave born of my maidservant," *Berlin Phil. Woch.*, May, 1899, p. 635, *Athen. Mitth.*, 1893, p. 415.

[2] The marginal reading in R.V. (preferred by the American Revisers) is undoubtedly right. Lightfoot reads : "sons of her who is free with the freedom with which Christ set us free. Stand firm, then, etc." It is difficult to sympathise with Lightfoot in discarding our text, preferred also by Tischendorf, Weiss, Zöckler, etc., and in saying that that text "is so difficult as to be almost unintelligible ".

Stand firm, then, and do not submit yourselves anew to the yoke of slavery."

The rapid variation between "we" and "you" in the passage IV 21-V 1 is full of meaning. The MSS. vary a good deal on this point ; but the preponderance of evidence is so clear that all the chief editors adopt the same text so far as that variation is concerned ; and the Authorised and Revised Versions agree with them.

At this point Paul would naturally proceed to the warnings set forth in V 13 ff. ; but he turns away for the moment to a digression, V 2-12.

LII

PERSONAL RECAPITULATION (V 2-12).

This paragraph is personal and parenthetical. The allusion to the yoke of bondage which the Galatians were about to put on themselves, leads Paul to insist once more on the terrible danger of the step and the ruinous consequences that must follow from it. The paragraph is very closely akin to III 1-6.

You know, says Paul, that your salvation comes through faith. The proof that you have faith lies—in having faith. But, if you yield to their persuasion, and suffer yourselves to be circumcised, you cease to have faith in Christ, you cease to benefit by His grace, and Christ will no longer profit you, as I protest and reiterate : in that case you put your trust in the Law, and you must trust to it alone, and be a slave to it in its entirety.[1] In itself the act of circumcision has no effect ; it is nought ; but your accept-

---

[1] On this see § LIII.

ing it now is a proof that you no longer trust to Christ, that you no longer have faith.

Lightfoot is, indubitably, right in taking the emphatic " I, I Paul,"[1] as "an indirect refutation of calumnies ". " I, I Paul, who have myself preached circumcision forsooth, who say smooth things to please men, who season my doctrine to the taste of my hearers, I tell you, etc."

Verses 7-9. How has this awful change happened, when you were running the race so excellently? Who has had such influence over you? Who has bewitched you? I marvel that you are so irrational and inconsistent with yourselves (compare III 1). You may be sure that no person who has thus prevented your progress can be a messenger of God (as you once thought that I was). It is not a strong party that has thus acted ; but if they once establish a footing among you, then, you know the proverb —*a little leaven !*

Verse 10. But Paul then goes on to express his firm confidence in the judgment and faith of the Galatians. They have been momentarily deceived, but they assuredly will not permanently entertain different views from those which they recently had. Thus the doubt and perplexity which he expressed, IV 20, the apprehension lest his work among them had been in vain, IV 11, are dissipated. He knows whom he is addressing ; he sees into their soul ; and, as he looks, his doubts about the issue disappear.

Verse 10. Punishment must follow : he that has troubled the Galatians has earned his reward, and must submit to it : he has perverted the Gospel of Christ (I 7), and will

---

[1] Ἐγὼ Παῦλος is stronger than "I, Paul "; to use ἐγώ in Greek is emphatic, but to use " I " in English is necessary, and carries no emphasis.

pay the penalty, however great and important a position he occupies in the Church. This last expression favours Lipsius' view that a single Jew of some standing had come to Galatia and caused the whole trouble.

Verse 11. Being thus carried back to the same topic as in the opening paragraph, I 6-10—the presence of the disturber—Paul glances, as in that passage, at the charge which had wounded him so deeply—*viz.*, that in his conduct to Timothy (Acts XVI 3) he had been a time-server, shifting his principles to suit his surroundings, preaching circumcision to some, though he refused it to others. As for me, he says, if I preach it, why do they still continue to persecute me? Of course, if I am preaching it, then the cross which so scandalises them, the cross which is their stumbling block, has been done away, and they have nothing to complain of in my preaching.

Does verse 10 point to punishment from man, and hint that the offender should be dealt with publicly by the Galatian Churches? Surely not. The judgment is left to the hand of God. Then in V 12 Paul recurs to this thought of the punishment awaiting the guilty party, "I wish," he says, "that those who are turning your moral constitution[1] topsy-turvy would inflict the proper penalty on themselves, and cut themselves off."

In spite of the almost complete unanimity of the recent authorities that V 12 refers to a different kind of self-inflicted injury, *viz.*, mutilation such as was practised in the worship of the Phrygian goddess, I venture to recur to the rendering of the Authorised Version.[2] I doubt

---

[1] Ἀναστατοῦντες carries a political metaphor, as Lightfoot rightly sees.

[2] So, too, the Revised Version in text.

whether even on this point—the one about which alone
Paul shows real anger—he would have yielded so completely to pure ill-temper as to say what this favourite
interpretation attributes to him.   It is true that the ancient
peoples, and many of the modern peoples in the same
regions, resort to foul language when they express anger,
in circumstances where Anglo-Saxons have recourse to
profane language.[1]   It would be mere affectation to try
to deny or conceal that, on the current interpretation, Paul
uses a piece of foul language in the ordinary style of the
enraged Oriental, who, regardless of the utter unsuitability
of the expression employed, heaps insult on his enemy,
animate or inanimate, man or brute, seeking only to be
foul and insulting, and all the better content the more
he attains this end.

There would be nothing suitable, nothing characteristic,
nothing that adds to the force of the passage, in the act
which, on the ordinary interpretation, Paul desires that
this grave Jew of high standing should perform on himself.
It was expressly forbidden by the Law of Moses.   The
scornful expression would be a pure insult, as irrational as
it is disgusting.

But the Authorised Version gives an excellent sense,

---

[1] The traveller in the East knows that the use of profane language,
objectionable as it is, constitutes a really great step in civilisation
and refinement, compared with the unutterable hatefulness of the
style of objurgation used by the angry Oriental.   The same was the
case in ancient times; and it is almost amusing to observe how,
from ignorance of this fact, the commentators treat, for example,
Catullus's objurgations against those whom he disliked as sober
testimony to their moral character.   Catullus would have said much
the same about his *petorrita*, if it broke a wheel, as he says about his
enemy, regardless of the meaninglessness of the expression.

adding distinctly to the force of the paragraph. The proper punishment for disturbing the Church was that the offender should be cut off like a useless member : and the wish is expressed that he would cut himself off. But the objection is that this sense cannot be justifiably elicited in Greek from ἀποκόπτεσθαι: the word in the middle voice is quoted only in the sense of " mutilate oneself," or " cut oneself (in mourning) *i.e.*, mourn for ".[1]

The objection has some ground, but is, I think, not conclusive. The word σκάνδαλον in V 11 suggests[2] to Paul the words of the Saviour (Mark IX 43) ἐὰν σκανδαλίσῃ σε ἡ χείρ σου, ἀπόκοψον αὐτήν.[3] He therefore continues in V 12 the thought of V 10—I wish they would cut themselves off. If he presses further than was customary the use of the middle form of the verb, he is not out of harmony with the spirit of the middle voice, and he perhaps trusted to the Galatians also recognising the reference to the Saviour's words.

But those who maintain the customary interpretation must recognise what is the character of the thought and language attributed to Paul, and should not try, with Lightfoot, to explain it away by saying that this mutilation

---

[1] In the latter sense the simple κόπτεσθαι is usual: the force of ἀπό is lost in it.

[2] The fact that the word is used in a different relation in the one case and in the other furnishes no argument against the suggestion. In V 10 the thought of the suitable punishment, severing from the Church which the offender has wronged, is in Paul's mind. In V 11 the word σκάνδαλον comes in. The juxtaposition suggests that saying of Jesus in which σκάνδαλον is in juxtaposition with cutting off.

[3] Compare V 45 (of the foot). Matt. XVIII 8 reports the same saying, but uses ἐκκόπτειν in place of ἀποκόπτειν. Paul thought of the saying in Mark's form.

"must at times have been mentioned by a Christian preacher". Certainly, he sometimes mentioned it along with other enormities in the pagan ritual ; but that does not justify him in expressing the hope and wish that a fellow-member of the Christian Church would voluntarily commit this crime upon himself. Dr. Sanday sees that the expression would be indefensible, and can only be regretted.

LIII

THE WHOLE LAW, V 2-4

It is remarkable with what emphasis Paul urges that, "if ye receive circumcision, Christ will profit you nothing. If you accept that part of the Law, you are bound to obey the entire Law. You cannot accept part, and neglect part. You cannot retain the Gospel of Faith, if you trust to part of the Law." Compare this with III 10, where he insists that a curse is pronounced against those who do not continue in *all things* that are written in the Law.

This seems to point to some idea among the Galatians that they might accept part of the Law, as being a useful help to them in their difficult path (see p. 444 f). Paul would hardly urge that they who adopt part of the Law are bound to adopt the whole Law, except in answer to a plea of the Galatians that they wished to adopt only part. They who are already bent on complete acceptance of the Law will not be deterred by an argument that, if they begin, they must go through to the end.

Probably, the Galatian idea was that it would be good for them to cut themselves off from the heathen society around them by a marked and irrevocable act, constituting an outward sign and symbol of their new profession ; and they found such a sign in the Jewish rite. They may have explained this, and added that they would not feel bound to accept the whole Judaic Law. Unless there were some such idea in their mind, it is hard to see any force in Paul's emphatic assertion that, if they begin, they must go on to the end.

Very often we conceive Paul's intention clearly only when we picture to ourselves what he is denying or replying to.

This idea in the mind of the Galatians must either have been explained to Paul in a letter, or reported to him by a messenger (§ LIX).

LIV

FREEDOM AND LOVE, V 13-15.

Verse 13 resumes the subject of verse 1.[1] " Now, as I was saying, *you* have been called to be free, but do not misunderstand the word ! Do not misuse the freedom as an opening for sensual enjoyment ! Rather serve one another through love. You desire to be slaves of the Law. Let this service to others be your slavery, and remember that for you the Law is completely fulfilled in the observance of the one principle, *Thou shalt love thy neighbour as thyself.* Whereas, if you show malignity in word or deed to your neighbour, the issue will be mutual destruction."

Very characteristic here is the recurrence to the word Freedom ; the most remarkable feature. in the whole Epistle is the prominence given to the idea of Freedom.

[1] The particle γáρ, in 13, is not to be treated as giving a reason for something said in the last verse. It indicates that the proper subject is taken up again after a digression.

An arithmetical statement will make this plain. The words ἐλεύθερος, ἐλευθερία, ἐλευθερόω, occur in this Epistle eleven times ; but in Romans they occur only seven times, in the two Corinthians eight times, and in all the rest of Paul's Epistles twice.

It is not a sufficient explanation to say that the idea was forced into prominence by the subject on which Paul has to write. The same subject is treated at far greater length in Romans, and the words occur much less frequently there in proportion to the size of the two letters. The idea of freedom is not the only form under which the struggle against Judaism can be expressed ; one might also look at it from other points of view. The prominence of the idea is something special to this Epistle.

It may be said that Paul here appeals to a specially strong feeling in the minds of his readers : that it is because they were free in heart and in aspiration that he tries to rouse this strong characteristic of theirs against the Judaistic propaganda.

That argument does injustice to Paul. From that point of view one will always misjudge him. If he simply desired to win a victory over Judaism, he might appeal to them in that way ; but he has a far wider view and aim. He does not simply select such arguments as will weigh most at the moment with his Galatian readers. He is content with no victory that does not strengthen the whole mind and character of the Galatians. As has been already pointed out, his purpose in the Epistle is not to frame an argument against Judaism : he tries to elevate and ennoble the minds of the Galatians, so that they may look at the question from a higher and truer point of view.

Therefore he does not seize on the more powerful emotions and passions of his readers, and try to harness these against Judaism. He tries to strengthen their weakness, and to make their minds harmonious and well-balanced, so that they may judge truly and wisely. If Paul calls the Galatians to freedom, and repeats the call, and presses home the idea to them, it is not because they were already specially free in mind and thought. It is because they were a people that needed to be roused to freedom—a people in whom the aspiration after freedom was dormant, and must be carefully fostered and fanned into flame.

In writing to the Churches of Asia and Achaia, he could not safely speak too much about freedom : for the Greek influence was strong among them, and an abuse of freedom degenerating into licence was the besetting weakness of the Greek race. He had to summon them to obedience to rule and law, instead of calling them to freedom. It was more important to insist on self-restraint, on abnegation, on contentment, than to stir up aspirations and longing after a new state of society.

The contrast between the insistence on rule and order to the Ephesians or the Colossians, all strongly Hellenised, and the preaching of freedom to the Phrygians and Lycaonians, still only half freed from native ritual, is very characteristic of Paul's versatile sympathy.

It is obvious how appropriate and necessary this topic was in addressing a people like the Phrygians and Lycaonians of the South Galatian Province, "just beginning to rise from the torpor of Oriental peasant life, and to appreciate the beauty of Greek thought and the splendour of Roman power".[1] Lack of the sense of individuality and freedom characterises the Oriental mind as distin-

---

[1] *St. Paul the Traveller*, p. 149.

guished from the Western. That sense was peculiarly lacking in the Phrygians, who were reckoned by the ancients as pre-eminently the nation born and intended for slaves ; but what is called the Phrygian character by the ancients was really the character of the Anatolian plateau as a whole (apart from the mountaineers of the coastward rim), simple, easy-minded, contented, good-humoured, submissive, yet capable of being roused to extreme religious enthusiasm ; a people possessing many of the fundamental virtues, but needing intermixture with a more sprightly people in order to develop into a really strong and good race. Mixture and intercourse and education had planted the seeds of higher individual development among them, but the young growth needed careful tending. All that is said in Chapter VI of *St. Paul the Traveller* on the situation in Antioch, Iconium, Derbe and Lystra at the time of Paul's first visit, and on the spirit of his work there, bears on this subject. The Epistle is a continuation of the work of the first journey.

So he leads them up towards freedom. But there is a danger. Freedom may easily be misconstrued and abused, and he points out the safeguard. It lies in Love ; and he quotes the Saviour's epitome of the whole law of human conduct.

It would add to the pointedness of this passage, if we could suppose that the Galatians had pleaded [1] as a´ sort of apology for their defection to Judaism, that they felt the need of some helper and guide as they struggled along the difficult path towards Christian perfection ; and that they found such a guide in the Law.

[1] Whether actually in a letter addressed to Paul or through the messenger who reported the situation to him : see § LIX.

Paul may actually be quoting that plea, when he says in V 21, " Tell me, ye that desire to be under the Law " ; and it may have suggested to him the explanation of the Law's true function as child-ward (§ XXXIX). He fully sympathised with the difficulty which the Galatians felt ; and he therefore shows how in practice the effect of Faith was gradually perfected in the character, with Love as the guide. It was true that the " lusts of the flesh " were strong and dangerous, yet the Galatians ought not to look to the Law to tell them what to do and what to avoid. Love will eradicate these lusts by substituting for them new and stronger motives of action. Paul has already shown in III 2 ff. that it is unreasonable to look to the Law for help in perfecting what has been begun by Faith.

A single enunciation of this so important warning, about the danger and the safeguard, was not enough. Therefore a special paragraph repeats and enlarges it (§ LV).

LV

THE SPIRITUAL LIFE, V 16-26.

"What I mean is this : if you make the Spirit your guide, you will not live the sensual life. For, in the Divine plan, the spirit and the flesh are ever in opposition within your minds ; and in so far as you walk by the Spirit you are freed from Law. You can see for yourselves what are the results of the two opposing principles. Around you in the Galatian cities you see [1] the vices that are the works of the flesh ; and they who are guilty of those vices shall

---

[1] Φανερά is in an emphatic position as first word of the sentence, and must be pressed in translation.

never be the heirs of God. I warned you against those évils, when I was last among you,[1] and I warn you now again.

" The life of the Spirit matures in love and the kindred virtues : where they rule, Law ceases. If you are of Jesus Christ, you have nailed on the cross the flesh with its passions and lust, and died to the life of sensuality. Therefore, if you make the Spirit your guide, this must be seen in your daily life. To take a special example of the general rule, if you are jealous and censorious of your neighbours, you are not living the spiritual life."

The prominent faults of South Galatian society are set before the readers in *vv.* 19-21. These are the faults that they saw everywhere round them, and these are the faults to which they were themselves liable. Paul had seen this on his second journey, and had already cautioned them. His first journey was the period of conversion, followed by organisation : on his second journey the dangers that beset the young Churches were brought painfully home to him, and he warned them against reproducing under a disguise of Christianity the faults of their age and surroundings. Now, once more he strives against them. He must strengthen their whole nature and character, and then the Judaistic evil will be corrected with their growing strength.

LVI

THE FAULTS OF THE SOUTH GALATIC CITIES.

In the list of fifteen faults, there are three groups, corresponding to three different kinds of influence likely to

---

[1] See the last paragraph of this section.

affect recent South Galatian converts from paganism. Such converts were liable to be led astray by habits and ways of thought to which they had been brought up, owing to (1) the national religion, (2) their position in a municipality, (3) the customs of society in Hellenistic cities.[1] We take each group separately.

1. Faults fostered by the old Anatolian religion. These are five : fornication, impurity, wantonness, idolatry, sorcery or magic. The first three are usually regarded by commentators as springing from the character of the individuals addressed, in whom sensual passion is assumed to have been peculiarly strong. But more probably and more naturally, Paul thinks here of the influence exerted by their old religion in patronising vice, and treating it as part of the Divine life.[2] The subject is too unpleasant to enter on. Yet to understand properly the position of the new religion in Asia Minor, one must take into consideration that the old religion had remained as a relic of a very primitive state of society ; that it consecrated as the Divine life the freedom of the beasts of the field ; that it exhibited to the celebrants in the holiest Mysteries the relations of the Divine personages, who are the emblems and representatives and guarantees of that primitive social system amid which the religion had taken form ; and that it regarded all moral restraint and rules as interference with the Divine freedom. The religion of the country was actually on a lower level

[1] The list 1 Corinthians VI 9 ff., is not exactly parallel, but near enough to be called by Steck the model after which this whole list of fifteen faults in Galatians has been forged. The contrast between them is remarkable. The Galatian list is narrowly defined : the Corinthian list ranges over the various crimes of human nature.

[2] Not so in Col. III 5 ff., where he is expressly speaking of the evil tendencies that lie in human nature and character.

than the tone of ordinary pagan society. Vice was not regarded as wrong in pagan society : it was regarded as necessary—the only evil lying in excess. But in the old religion it was inculcated as a duty ; and service at the temple for a period in the practice of vice had once, apparently, been universally required, and was still imposed as a duty on individuals through special revelation of the Divine will. This extreme was looked down upon with contempt, but without serious moral condemnation, as mere superstition, by the more educated society of the cities. Yet even in the cities it certainly was far from having lost its hold ; and to obey the Divine command and live the Divine life at the temple for a period caused no stigma on the individual, and was actually recorded publicly in votive offerings with inscriptions. See pp. 40, 201 f.

From this point of view the third fault—ἀσέλγεια—is illustrated. Lightfoot explains that it implies something openly insolent, shocking public decency. The act which was most characteristic of Phrygian religion in the eyes of the world was the public self-mutilation practised sometimes by votaries in religious frenzy (p. 38). The word ἀσέλγεια is the strongest term of its kind in Pauline usage ; and acts like that public mutilation, or those alluded to in the last words of the preceding paragraph, merit it.

It is unnecessary to say a word about the faults of idolatry and magic. The latter stood in close relation to the native religion ; and it is difficult to draw the line between religion and magic in the numerous class of inscriptions in which curses and imprecations of evil or death are invoked on personal foes and on wrong-doers.

We shall not rightly conceive the Asia Minor character,

unless we remember that the excesses of which it is capable spring from religious enthusiasm. It is peculiarly subject to religious excitement. A passage of Socrates, that careful and unprejudiced historian, is valuable here, as illustrating both the Anatolian character and the influence exerted on it by Christianity. He says, IV 28, that Phrygians exercise stronger self-restraint than other races, being less prone to anger than Scythians and Thracians,[1] and less given to pleasure than the eastern peoples, not fond of circus and theatre, and hating fornication as a monstrous crime.

These were the people that eagerly followed Novatian in refusing the sacraments to those who had after baptism been guilty of serious sin. Like Paul's Galatians, the Phrygian Novatians were eager to go to the extreme in religious matters; and like them, they tended towards Judaism,[2] and made Easter agree with the Passover. It is precisely the same tendency of mind that caused both movements: not fickleness and changeableness, but enthusiasm, intense religious feeling, the tendency to extreme severity, and the leaning towards the Oriental and the Jewish forms.[3] See p. 193 ff.

[1] Taken as representatives of the northern barbarians.

[2] Novatian himself showed no tendency to Judaism.

[3] One might trace the tendency of the Phrygians towards Judaistic practices through the intermediate period, and in other parts of Phrygia. At Colossæ Paul had to correct the inclination to "a feast-day, or a new moon, or a sabbath day" (Col. II 16), and to point out wherein lay the true circumcision (Col. II 11). In an inscription of about A.D. 200, which is probably Jewish-Christian, the name Azyma is used to indicate Easter (see *Cities and Bish. of Phrygia*, pt. II, p. 545 ff. ; and there is now more to say about this inscription from recent discovery). On the Judaic-Christian inscriptions of Phrygia, see *Cities and Bish. of Phrygia*, part II, pp. 566, 652, f., 674 f., 700.

2. Faults connected with the municipal life in the cities of Asia Minor. Every one who reads this enumeration—enmities, strife, rivalry (so Lightfoot), outbursts of wrath, caballings, factions, parties, jealousies—eight out of fifteen —must be struck with the importance attached by Paul to one special tendency to error among the Galatians.

Partly, no doubt, the Judaizing tendency would lead to division and strife, for we can well imagine that it was not universal, and that there was at least a minority that continued faithful to Paul in the Galatian Churches. But it would be a mistake to suppose that Paul was thinking of that one fact only : that would not explain the striking prominence of the idea. He is here viewing their life as a whole, and is not thinking only of the Judaistic question.

First, the rivalry of city against city was one of the most marked features of municipal life in Asia Minor. The great cities of a province wrangled for precedence, until even the Emperor had to be invoked to decide between their rival claims for the first place. They invented titles of honour for themselves so as to outshine their rivals, and appropriated the titles that their rivals had invented. So in the Province Asia, Smyrna and Pergamos vied with Ephesus ; in Bithynia Nicomedia vied with Nicæa ; in Cilicia Anazarbos vied with Tarsos ; and in Galatia we may be sure that Iconium vied with Antioch. See p. 118 f.

As Mommsen says, "the spirit of faction here at once takes possession of every association" ; and again, "the urban rivalries belong to the general character of Hellenic politics, but especially of the politics in Asia Minor." [1]

But, if that was true of the unregenerate citizens, had the

---

[1] *Provinces of the Roman Empire*, ch. VIII, vol. I, pp. 329, 357.

converts changed their nature? Surely not! The same characteristics existed in them as before. They were still citizens of Antioch or of Iconium. Throughout Paul's Epistles we see that his converts had not changed their nature, but were still liable to fall into the errors of their pre-Christian life. We may feel very certain that there were strife and wrangling and jealousy between the Antiochean Church and the Iconian Church about precedence and comparative dignity.

Second, even within the cities there was room for jealousy and strife. There was in Antioch and Lystra the great division between Roman or Latin citizens of the Colonia and the *incolæ* or native dwellers: the burning subject of inequality of rights was always close at hand. We may be sure that there were both Roman and non-Roman members of the Church. No list of Galatian Christians has come down to us; but the Colony Corinth, where Latin names form so considerable a proportion [1] of the known Christians, furnishes a pertinent illustration. In Iconium and Derbe, where no Roman element of any consequence existed, there was the other cause (not absent in the Coloniae) of difference in race—the native element, the Greek element, the Jewish element. Of these the native element was probably the weaker in the Churches, because the natives who were familiar with the Greek language usually reckoned themselves Greek: in fact the Greek element consisted mainly not of settlers from Greece, but of those Phrygian and Lycaonian families that had adopted Greek manners and education and dress. [2]

[1] Achaicus, Crispus, Fortunatus, Gaius, Lucius, Quartus, Tertius, Titius Justus. See Hastings' *Dictionary of the Bible*, I, p. 480.

[2] See pp. 129 f, 180 f, 230 f.

It is noteworthy that at Lystra those who are said to have spoken in the Lycaonian tongue were not Christians, but pagans (Acts XIV). It was among the more educated classes that Christianity spread most rapidly (*St. Paul the Trav.*, p. 133 f.).

With these causes at work, it is easily seen how caballing and jealousy should be a serious danger in the young Churches.

As Mommsen says again of Asia Minor: " Rivalries exist, as between town and town, so in every town between the several circles and the several houses ". There were no great political or patriotic interests to absorb the passions and powers of man, and so they frittered away their energies in petty jealousies and rivalries and factions.

Paul's words seem, beyond any question, written with an eye to the ordinary Græco-Asiatic city : " Let us not be vainglorious, challenging one another, envying one another, V 26 ". Vainglory and pride in petty distinctions was the leading motive in municipal life ; the challenging of one another to competition in this foolish strife was almost the largest part of their history amid the peace and prosperity of the Roman rule.

But that is not the type of the North Galatian tribes ; the Gaulish element was an aristocratic one, and such are not the faults of an aristocracy.

If the Churches were thus liable to import the old urban rivalries into their mutual relations, what was Paul's part likely to be ? Would he not impress on them the excellence of unity, the criminality of faction and jealousy ? Would he not, even in small things, avoid anything and any word likely to rouse their mutual rivalry ? Would he not class them as one body of Churches, the Churches of the Province, and appeal to them as "members of the Province Galatia". There was no other unity except that of Christian by which he could designate them. They lived in different countries, they sprang from different races. The one thing in which they were united was as members of the Empire, and their status in the Empire was as members of the Province, *i.e.*, *Galatae.*

But when I pointed out that this term *Galatae* was the only common name by which Paul could address the four Churches, some North Galatian critics replied that there was no reason why Paul should sum up the four Churches in a common name. Surely that argument misses the character of the situation ; it was urgently needful to sum them up as one body by one common name, recognised equally by all the four Churches.

The word φόνοι, introduced in most MSS. after φθόνοι, has been rightly rejected by many modern editors relying on its omission in the Vatican and Sinaitic and some less important MSS. It spoils the picture, and is merely a scribe's reminiscence of Romans I 29.

3. Faults connected with the society and manners of the Græco-Asiatic cities. These are two—drinkings, revellings.

No comment is needed. The remains of the later Greek comedy, and the paintings on Greek vases, show how characteristic and universal such revels were in the Greek cities. Komos, the Revel, was made a god, and his rites were carried on quite systematically, and yet with all the ingenuity and inventiveness of the Greek mind, which lent perpetual novelty and variety to the revellings. The Komos was the most striking feature in Greek social life. Though we are too absolutely ignorant of the Græco-Phrygian society to be able to assert that this Greek custom flourished there, yet it is highly probable that those who adopted Greek manners and civilisation adopted that characteristic feature, the Komos. It is too often the case that the vices of civilisation are the first elements in it to affect the less civilised races when brought into contact with it.

Thus the second and third classes of faults belong specially to the Hellenising section of Phrygian society, springing from the too rapid and indiscriminate assimilation of Greek ideas and Greek tone. The first class of faults was most characteristic of the less progressive section of society, the old native party. Both sections, doubtless, were represented in the young Churches : at any rate the faults were always blazoned before their eyes (p. 445, note), and the customs of society are apt to exercise a strong influence on all persons unless they are on their guard.

LVII

THE UNFORGIVING PHRYGIANS (VI 1-5).

The opening paragraph of chapter VI is occupied still with the same subject as the last two. Paul is looking quite away from the Judaic controversy. He is absorbed in the development of his own Churches and the special faults that they have to face. He saw one serious danger in that Anatolian people, easy-tempered and orderly in most things, but capable of going to any extreme in religious madness. Just as in later time, " that unpitying Phrygian sect " was apt to cry :—

> Him can no fount of fresh forgiveness lave
> Who sins, once washed by the baptismal wave—

so already Paul saw their tendency to unforgiving condem-

nation of him who had sinned, and warned them, " Brethren,
even if a man be overtaken in any trespass, restore such a
one in a spirit of meekness ". To continue the quotation :—

> She sighed,
> The infant Church! Of love she felt the tide
> Stream on her from her Lord's yet recent grave.

And so Paul's Epistle to the Galatians is an outline of
Phrygian Christian history : he saw what was the one safeguard for his young Churches, and he urges it on them, in
paragraph after paragraph—Love.

And what have the North Galatian theorists to say in
illustration of this most characteristically Phrygian passage?
Why, they are struck with the fact that a man in Corinth
had committed a grave offence; Paul's appeal to the
Corinthian brethren to punish the offender "had been
promptly and zealously responded to"; and "he had even
to interpose for the pardon of the guilty one". And therefore "the remembrance of this incident still fresh on his
mind, may be supposed to have dictated the injunction"
to the Galatians here. Because the Corinthians had been
severe, therefore the Gauls must be warned not to be
severe !

But that is not Paul's method. When he warns the
Galatians against a fault, it is not because the Corinthians
had committed it, but because the Galatians were prone to
it. If in any of his Epistles Paul is wholly absorbed in
the needs of his first audience, it is in this to the Galatians.
But so it was in all, more or less, with the exception of
Romans ; he speaks to the Church in Rome, not from
personal knowledge, nor from report of their special circumstances (as to the Colossians), but in preparation for his
own visit and from his experience in the Eastern Churches.

In the first four and a half chapters Paul is occupied specially in revivifying in the Galatians the impressions and the teaching of the first journey; from V 13 onwards he is repeating the warnings that we can imagine formed the burden of his preaching on the second journey. But everywhere he feels himself on Anatolian soil, and is speaking to a typically Anatolian, and in particular a Phrygian, people; and the best preparation for studying the adaptation of his words to his readers is to study the typical peasant of the present day, as he presents himself to the travellers that have observed him with sympathy and affection. He is called an Osmanli now—he does not call himself a Turk, and rather resents the name—but he has much of the old Phrygian character : pp. 33, 234.

LVIII

VOLUNTARY LIBERALITY TO TEACHERS (VI 6-10).

This paragraph continues the subject of the last : Paul is still engaged with the dangers to which the Galatian Churches are exposed through their proneness to certain faults. He now urges them to treat with wise liberality their religious teachers, to persevere and not to lose heart in beneficence generally, to take advantage of every opportunity of doing good to all with whom they are brought into contact, but more especially to their Christian brethren, " the members of the household of the faith ".

This is only a further exposition of what is involved in the "Whole Law for the Christian, Thou shalt love thy neighbour as thyself". That "Whole Law" was quoted in V 14; and the remaining verses have been devoted to explaining its consequences and its meaning to the Galatians in their special situation and with their special temperament.

The duty of every congregation to support liberally the ministers of the Word is mentioned, not merely to the Galatians here, but also to the Corinthians (1 Cor IX 11 ; 2 Cor. XI 7 f.), to the Philippians (IV 10 f.), to the Thessalonians (1 Thess. II 6, 9), to the Asian Churches (1 Tim. V 17, 18). Paul kept it before the attention of the Churches of all the four Provinces—Achaia, Macedonia, Asia and Galatia.

The duty was one that was quite novel in ancient society. It was something that no convert from Paganism had been accustomed to. Paul, who was never content simply to convert, but was equally watchful to organise and to build up, by subsequent care and watching, his young Churches,[1] could not safely neglect to provide for their permanent guidance when he was absent, and the frequency of his references to the subject attests the importance that he attached to it.

There was no system of instruction in the Pagan religions. The favour of the gods was gained by acts of ritual, not by moral conduct. Every prayer for help was a deliberate bargain ; the worshipper promised certain gifts to the god, on condition that the god gave the help implored. The priests had the right to certain dues, a sort of percentage, on all sacrifices and offerings, and these dues were paid in various ways. A fee had to be paid for entrance into the temples ;[2] or a part of the victim offered

---

[1] Compare Acts XIV 22 f, XV 41, XVI 5, XVIII 23, XX 2.

[2] *Mercedem pro aditu sacri,* Tertullian *Apologet.* 13, and commentators. In the Roman world generally, fees were imposed for entering the temple, for approaching the place of sacrifice, for the

went to the priest; or other methods were practised. In one way or another, the priesthoods of the Pagan gods were so lucrative in Asia Minor that they were put regularly up to the auction by the State, and knocked down for a term to the highest bidder; and various inscriptions record the exact prices paid for them in some cities.[1] But all these methods take the form of a tariff of dues upon rites which the worshipper performs for his own advantage. There were no instructors, and no voluntary contributions for their support.

Hence the duty of supporting teachers or preachers had to be continually impressed upon the attention of all Paul's converts from Paganism. The tendency to fail in it was practically universal; it was connected with a universal fact in contemporary society; perhaps it was not unconnected with a universal characteristic of human nature.

It is therefore quite unjustifiable in the North Galatian theorists to find in this precept which Paul delivered to the Galatians an indication of their Celtic nature and Celtic blood; and it is quite unfair to quote as an illustration the Gaulish tendency to raid and plunder, or the Gaulish greed for money. It would be more to the point if those theorists were to quote in illustration of this passage the parsimony

presentation of gifts or the offering of sacrifice; and the collecting of the fees was farmed out by the State. Sometimes the right to engage in worship and sacrifice without payment of fees was granted to individuals (*immunitas sacrum faciendorum, Corp. Inscr. Lat.* VI 712). A tariff of charges is published, *Corp. Inscr. Lat.* VI 820, Henzen 6113. This custom is hardly known in republican times, except that Cicero, *Leg.* II 10, 25, says *sumptu ad sacra addito deorum aditu arceamus.*

[1] See especially the great inscription of Erythræ of the second century B.C.; it has been often published, see Michel *Recueil d'Inscr. Gr.* 839.

of King Deiotaros, whose presents were considered by his friend and advocate, Cicero, to be rather mean.[1] Here we have a distinct analogy between Paul's Galatians and a great North Galatian king. But parsimony is not by any means confined to a single nation, and is at least as common and characteristic a fault in Asia generally as in the Celtic lands ; Armenians and Phœnicians and Jews are as penurious and economical as Deiotaros or any other Celt.

One of the objects that Paul had most at heart was to train his converts in voluntary liberality, as distinguished from payments levied on ritual. He saw what a powerful, educative influence such liberality exerts on the individual, and what a strong unifying influence it might exert between the scattered parts of the Church. The contribution in Antioch for the relief of the sufferers from famine in Judæa (Acts XI 29, XII 25),—the joint contribution of the " Churches of the Four Provinces " for the benefit of the poor congregation in Jerusalem, poor in comparison with the duties and opportunities open to it [2]—were devices at once of a teacher training his pupils, and of a statesman welding countries and peoples into an organic unity.[3]

There is no bond so strong to hold men together as the common performance of the same duties and acts. The

[1] Cicero *ad Fam.* IX 12, 2. I do not remember any reference to this passage in the North Galatian commentators, but should be glad to accept correction on the point.

[2] On these opportunities, especially of showing hospitality to Jewish or Jewish-Christian pilgrims, and thus promoting the sense of brotherhood among the scattered Jewish communities, see *Expositor*, June, 1899, p. 408 f.

[3] This has never been so well stated as by Rev. F. Rendal in *Expositor*, Nov. 1893, p. 321 ff. See also *St. Paul the Trav.*, pp. 287 f., 60 f.

skilful organisers of the Roman Empire, Augustus and his early ministers, devoted themselves to fabricating such bonds by uniting the parts of every Province with each other, and the separate Provinces with their common head —the Emperor—in the performance of the ritual of the universal imperial religion of " Rome and Augustus ".

A common ritual is an immense power among men.[1] Even the ritual of such a sham as the imperial religion was a great bond of unity in the empire. But Paul, while he was fashioning and elaborating the external forms of organisation that should hold together the world in its brotherhood, never made the mistake of trusting to a mere unity of ritual. He saw clearly that, strong as is the common performance of ritual among men, a stronger and more educative power was needed, the voluntary common performance of duties taken up and carried into effect by the conscious deliberate purpose of individual men and women—not of men alone (so he says to the Galatians more emphatically[2] than to any other people), for in the perfected Divine unity of the Church, as it shall be, not as it is, there can be neither bond nor free, there can be no male and female.

It is an important point that Paul requires the beneficence of the Galatians to be extended to all men, and not confined " to them that are of the household of faith," though the latter have a special claim. Every opportunity is to be seized of benefiting their Pagan neighbours. It

---

[1] Compare, *e.g.*, the power of the Greek Church in holding together within the Turkish Empire, races divided by distance, by want of communication, by diversity of blood and of language (*Church in the Rom. Emp.*, p. 467).

[2] See § XL.

would be an interesting thing for all who study the state of society in the Roman Empire to know how far this precept was carried into effect in the Pauline Churches. But evidence is at present miserably defective in regard to such practical matters. The establishment of institutions for the general benefit of orphans and exposed children was certainly common in the Early Church.[1]

LIX

WAS THERE A LETTER FROM THE GALATIANS?

The question arises, how did Paul learn what was occurring in Galatia? Obviously, the news had just reached him, when in the first excitement he wrote this Epistle. Some messenger must have brought the news. But the messenger may have merely brought letters from the Galatians, or he may have given a report of his own observations, or he may have done both. The last alternative seems most natural.

According to the theory already stated,[2] the messenger was probably Timothy, who, landing at Ephesus, had gone up to Pisidian Antioch and his own home at Lystra, and then rejoined Paul at Syrian Antioch, bringing with him grave intelligence.

But, whoever the messenger was, there is certainly a probability that he brought with him a letter, or a series of letters, from the Galatian Churches : possibly, each Church separately wrote to its founder. It is not probable that any of Paul's Churches ever allowed a messenger to go from them to him without a letter.

[1] See Lightfoot, *Colossians and Phil.*, p. 324 ; *Cities and Bish. of Phrygia*, II, p. 546.

[2] See p. 243.

Yet the first three and a half chapters do not appear to be couched in the form of a reply to a letter. These chapters refer as a whole to subjects which one can hardly fancy any of the Galatian Churches venturing to discuss with their spiritual father in the controversial way that is implied, for they are represented as dissenting from him and almost as resisting him. See p. 430.

Moreover, the usual forms of a letter, after the address which occupies the first five verses, are conspicuously absent (see § V). Paul plunges at once into a matter which we cannot imagine that any of the Galatians would venture to state directly to him, *viz.*, the charge that he had been inconsistent with himself in the teaching imparted on his two visits, and that he was a time-server. From this he is led into a historical retrospect, which gradually changes into a series of vehement appeals designed to revivify among his readers the feelings with which they had received his first preaching to them.

But, in the last two and a half chapters, after Paul has given vent to the strong and irrepressible emotions which demanded instant expression, his writing assumes a tone more like that of an ordinary letter, and he uses various expressions which perhaps take up and reply to words or explanations or questions addressed to him directly (*i.e.*, in the form of a letter) by the Galatians.

In order to test the idea that Paul's expression in this Epistle was influenced by the terms of a letter from the Galatic Churches, we must suppose for the moment that the idea is true, and bring together all that can be advanced in its favour. To do so properly would require the quick, sure, intuition of Professor Rendel Harris, who has traced with singularly delicate perception the letters to which

Paul was replying when he wrote to the Colossians and others ;[1] but it is not given to every one to " plough with his heifer ". Possible traces of a Galatian letter to Paul have been found already in §§ XXXVIII, XLIX, L, LIII, LIV.

We may confidently say that the Galatian letter or letters would take an apologetic and explanatory tone : they needed some help and some guide as they struggled along the difficult way towards Christian excellence (III 3, *cp.* § LIV) ; they wanted an outward symbol to mark them off from heathen society (§ LIII) ; in Paul's absence Jewish missionaries had taken a lively interest in their welfare (§ XLIX) ; they found help and a teacher in the Law and the ceremonies recommended by those missionaries (§ XXXVIII, to which Paul refers, " Ye that desire to be under the Law," IV 21) ; but, in spite of this movement, they retained their strong sense of duty to Paul, and they were resolved not to wrong him, even when they looked to others for help.

It has been shown that some of Paul's words should be treated as echoes of Galatian statements. He appreciates their need of some one to take interest in them when he is far away (IV 18) ; but he desires that the interest should be for their good. The project is here foreshadowed that a trusty representative should be left among them at his next visit (to which he points in IV 20). On the third journey this project was surely carried out. May we not guess that Silas was the representative? He was peculiarly

---

[1] *Expositor*, Sept.-Dec., 1898. But when he reaches the result that *Eph.* was not a circular letter, I begin to doubt : the reasons proving that it was a circular letter seem too strong to be overthrown by an argument, which is of so subjective a character.

suited to combat Judaism, as being at once Jew and Roman. He does not appear in the rest of the third journey. Yet he probably had great knowledge of Asia Minor, for he was selected to carry the Epistle of Peter to the Churches of that whole land.

Perhaps the fact that the first three and a half chapters are obviously prompted by the report of a delegate, and not by a letter of the Galatians, may seem to many to constitute a proof that the whole Epistle should be taken in the same way ; and it must be conceded that nothing in the Epistle imperatively demands that a Galatian letter lay before Paul as he wrote. The knowledge which he shows of the Galatian desires and aims may have been gained from the report of a trusty messenger like Timothy.

But, if Paul trusts here solely to the report of a messenger, we may feel sure that the messenger was one in whose knowledge, judgment, and sympathy with all parties Paul had perfect confidence. He treats the messenger's report of the catchwords of the Galatian movement as indubitably correct ; and he feels as certain on this point as if he had before him a formal statement in the Galatians' own words.

Such a messenger Timothy was.

LX

THE LARGE LETTERS (VI 11-17).

As in several other cases, Paul ends with a peculiarly direct and personal appeal to his correspondents, summing up afresh the critical points in his letter.

Habitually Paul employed a secretary, to whom he dictated his letters ; but his custom was to add a parting message with his own hand as a mark of authenticity, " the salutation of me, Paul, with mine own hand, which is the token in every Epistle" (2 Thess. III 17). He sometimes marks this concluding message as his own by the words as well as by the handwriting, as in Colossians IV 18, 1 Corinthians XVI 21. Sometimes he trusts to the handwriting alone, and we may confidently take such concluding paragraphs as Romans XVI 25-37, Ephesians IV 23-24, as the parting messages in Paul's hand, though in some cases it is difficult to detect the point of transition.

In no other case is the point where Paul takes the pen marked so emphatically as here ; and in no other case is the parting message so important. Paul returns to the primary subject after having diverged from it in his eagerness to give counsel and advice to the Galatian Churches. He adds with his own hand a brief and pointed *résumé* of the leading thoughts in the letter ; and he arrests attention and concentrates it on the *résumé* at once by the opening words: " Look you in what big letters I wrote with my own hand ".

The tense " I wrote" is an epistolary usage, especially common in Latin, but also found in Greek : the writer puts himself at the point of view of his readers, so that his own action seems to him to lie in the past, as it must be to them when they read it. Paul rarely employs this epistolary tense,[1] but here it is forced on him by the opening word " Look". He imagines himself to be standing beside his correspondents as they are reading his letter, and saying to them, " Look what big letters Paul used here "

It has been inferred by many from this sentence that

---

[1] A case in Philemon 19.

30

Paul's ordinary handwriting was very large. But if that were so, it would be unnecessary for him to say both " with my own hand" and "in big letters". Moreover, those who suppose that a trifling detail, such as the shape or size of Paul's ordinary handwriting, could find room in his mind as he wrote this letter, are mistaking his character. The size of the letters must have some important bearing on the parting message, or it would not have been mentioned. We must here look for the cause, not in any personal trait, but in some principle of ancient life and custom.

In modern times publicity for documents of importance is attained by multiplication of copies. In ancient times that method was impossible : anything that had to be brought before the notice of the public must be exposed in a prominent position before the eyes of all, engraved on some lasting material such as bronze or marble. When a document was thus exposed in public, attention was often called to some specially important point, especially at the beginning or end, by the use of larger letters.[1]

On this familiar analogy Paul calls attention to the following sentences as containing the critical topics of the letter, and being therefore in bold, striking lettering. Lightfoot, who adopts this view,[2] is probably right in taking ὑμῖν as an ethical dative, translating " how large, mark you ".

Dr. Deissmann's interpretation of the " large letters," as belonging to the region of pure comedy, has been alluded to in § XXII. It is rightly rejected by Meyer-Sieffert.

[1] Examples at Pisidian Antioch in Sterrett's *Epigr. Journey*, Nos. 97, 99, 101, 102, 108, etc. ; others are quoted by Meyer-Sieffert ; others may be found in Pompeian advertisements.

[2] He does not, however, mention the epigraphic custom, but treats the device as special to Paul.

LXI

THE PARTING MESSAGE.

What, then, are the points which are thus placarded, as it were, before the eyes of the Galatians? They may be specified in a rough list as follows :—

1. The advocates of circumcision are persons who wish "to make a pretentious display" in "external rites" (without a thought about spiritual realities).

2. Their object is to avoid persecution for the cross of Christ. There is here no thought of persecution by the Roman State : it is solely persecution by the Jews that is in the apostle's mind. The State, if it punished Christians as such, would be equally ready to punish circumcised and uncircumcised Christians. We are here carried back to a time when persecution of Christians existed only in the form of action originated by Jews, who on various pleas iuduced either imperial officials or city magistrates to interfere against their personal enemies. This takes us back to a very early stage in history : except in Palestine, such persecution was very unlikely to last much later than the decision of Gallio (Acts XVIII, 15), which constituted a precedent. In Southern Phrygia and Lycaonia, along the line of the great road between Ephesus and Syria, where Jews were specially numerous and influential, persecution of that kind was most likely to constitute a real danger.

3. The champions of circumcision, so far from being eager that the Gentile converts should keep the whole Law, were themselves far from keeping it completely ; but they desired to subject the Galatians to that rite in order that they might "gain credit with the Jews for proselytising"

successfully, and thus increasing the influence, wealth and power of the nation (VI 13).

4. Paul personally desired no credit except in the cross. He himself regarded circumcision as an external and in itself valueless ceremony. We may gather that he considered the rite to have some symbolical value for the Jews, but absolutely none for the Gentiles : to the latter it was positively hurtful in so far as it tended to withdraw their attention from the real spiritual fact, that a remaking and regeneration of man's nature was essential.

The emphasis which is several times laid on the burdensome nature of the Law, and the inability of the Jews themselves to observe its provisions and requirements, is one of the most remarkable features in the question that was being fought out within the Christian Church about A.D. 50.

Peter spoke of the Law as "a yoke which neither our fathers nor we were able to bear" (Acts XV 10). Paul assumes in this Epistle as a fundamental fact familiar to the Galatians that no person can fulfil the law entirely, but that all are liable to the curse pronounced against any one who fails in any point of the Law (III 10, compare II 14) ; and it was certainly on this impossibility that Paul's personal deep conviction of his own permanent sinful condition had rested before his conversion.[1]

The assumption that this fundamental impossibility was a familiar matter of knowledge to the Galatian Christians[2]

---

[1] See § XXX.

[2] It must be remembered that this Epistle does not move in the line of new arguments that Paul was right and the Judaisers wrong : its power rests in its being a revivification in the Galatians of their former thoughts and knowledge and experience. See § XXI.

can hardly rest only on a universal admission of such impossibility. It must rest on former teaching; and if so, the teaching must be that of the second journey, when the frank and complete admission made by Peter, and the tacit agreement of the apostolic decree in the practical truth of his admission, were set forth to the Galatians. We cannot doubt that, when Paul delivered this decree to the Galatian congregations to keep (Acts XVI 4), he explained to them fully the circumstances of its enactment, and the meaning which they should attach to it.

Sufficient attention has hardly been given by the commentators to this point. Peter's words to the Council could not have carried much weight unless they had been too obviously true for open dispute: there must have been a belief among the more reasonable Jews, even among those who were personally strict, that the Law was too burdensome for practical life.

What was the reason for this belief? It must have lain in the new circumstances of the Jews amidst the Roman Empire. A Law, which had been possible in Palestine only for the few most elevated spirits, became too obviously impossible amid the wider society of the empire, when every reasoning Jew perceived the magnificent prospects that were open to his people, if they accomodated themselves in some degree to their situation in the Roman world. Those prospects are both material and spiritual. The Jews as a race have never been blind to prospects of material success for the individual or the nation; and the peace, the order, the security of property, the ease and certainty and regularity of intercourse in the Roman world, with the consequent possibilities of trade and finance on a vast scale, opened up a dazzling prospect of wealth and power. Of old, wherever there was anything approaching to free competition, the Semitic traders of Carthage had beaten Rome in the open market; and the Romans obtained command of the Mediterranean trade only by force of arms. The Jews could now repeat the success of their Carthaginian cousins.

There were also Jews whose vision was filled entirely with the spiritual prospects of the race, the influence that it was exerting, and might in a hundredfold greater degree exercise, on thought and religion, especially among the loftier minds of the Empire. But if they were to exercise properly their legitimate influence in the Roman world, they could not carry out completely the Law with its fully developed ceremonial: they must distinguish in it between that which was spiritually real and that which was mere external and unessential ceremonial.

The question with regard to accommodation to their new situation could not be evaded by the Jews. The Sadducees answered it by perfect readiness to concede anything. The Pharisees originally assumed the impossible attitude of a firm resolve to concede nothing. Paul's position was that nothing should be conceded that was spiritually real or symbolically valuable, but that mere external and unessential ceremonial should be sacrificed ; and he held that this was the attitude of the true Pharisee (Acts XXIII 6).

LXII

THE CONCLUDING BLESSING AND DENUNCIATION (VI. 16-17).

As the letter began in a style unique with Paul, and unlike the ordinary epistolary forms, so it ends. Other letters, as a rule, end with a blessing or benediction. Here the blessing is restricted, and in the restriction a negative is implied : "and as many as shall walk by this rule, peace be on them and mercy "; then are added the more gracious words, "and on the Israel of God" (though even here there lurks a contrast to the Israel after the flesh).

But there follows a note of denunciation : "From henceforth let no man trouble me ; for I bear branded on my body the marks of Jesus ". In 1 Corinthians XVI, 21-24, where there is mingled with the blessing a curse, "if any man loveth not the Lord, let him be accursed," the more emphatic final blessing and expression of love to all comes after the curse, and swallows it up. But here after a restricted benediction, comes a denunciation, combined with a strong assertion of his authority as the servant of Christ—too emphatic to be merged and forgotten in the short blessing conveyed in the final verse.

What is the reason of this most marked characteristic ? Is it merely due to indignation (which the commentators make out to be one of the strongest features in the letter)? Was the writer so angry that even his concluding blessing is marred by a note of denunciation and self-assertion ? From V 13 onwards he has, apparently, forgotten his indignation, and has impressed on the Galatians in successive paragraphs, from various points of view, the supreme duty of love, the evil of wrath, enmity, strife. Can we suppose that immediately after this he gives the lie to his own teaching by letting his indignation again get the upper hand, and make itself felt in what are almost the last words of the letter ?

It cannot be so. This paragraph is the crowning proof that it is a mistake to read indignation as the chief feature of this letter, and that the interpretation advocated above in § XXII is 'true: though "the authoritative tone, of course, is there," yet the emotion that drives him on throughout the letter "is intense and overpowering love and pity for specially beloved children ".

But to deal with those children one must always use the note of authority. Here, as everywhere throughout the letter, one recognises, not the proud and sensitive Celtic aristocracy, but the simple, slow, easy-going, obedient, contented, good-tempered and rather stupid people of the Phrygian country, the ground-stock of the Anatolian plateau.

LXIII

THE STIGMATA OF JESUS (VI 17).

The idea that these were marks similar to those inflicted on the Saviour's body at the Crucifixion belongs to the "Dark Ages" of scholarship. The marks are those cut deep on Paul's body by the lictor's rods at Pisidian Antioch[1] and the stones at Lystra, the scars that mark him as the slave of Jesus. This custom to mark slaves by scars—produced by cuts, prevented from closing as they healed, so as to leave broad wounds—is familiar even yet to the observant traveller,[2] though since slavery was brought to an end in Turkey cases are now few, and will after a few years have ceased to exist.

The same custom existed in the country from ancient times. It was practised on the temple slaves from time

---

[1] *St. Paul the Trav.*, pp. 107, 304.

[2] Mrs. Ramsay, *Everyday Life in Turkey*, p. 7.

immemorial ;[1] and the Galatian slave owners practised it on their slaves, as Artemidorus mentions, having adopted it from their predecessors in the land.[2]

The idea suggested by Dr. Deissmann, *Bibelstudien*, p. 266 ff., that the marks of Jesus are prophylactic, guarding the bearer of them against trouble and evil, is out of keeping with the spirit of the letter and with the tone of this passage. Meyer-Sieffert's latest edition discusses and rejects that interpretation (ninth edition, 1899, p. 364).

It is not easy for us in modern times to catch and understand clearly the thought in VI 17 : yet it was to Paul perfectly natural and simple. The nineteenth century must often fail to understand fully the first. This sentence, in its emphatic position, with its impressive language and its tone of denunciation and warning, carries more meaning "than meets the ear". Obviously, it must appeal to something that lay deep in the hearts and memories of the Galatians. They knew, fully and absolutely, that Paul was the servant of Jesus, or, as he says, how deeply branded in his flesh are the marks that prove him Jesus' slave (for in ancient times the slave was far more closely bound by feeling and affection to his master than a hired servant—strange as that may seem to us). They have only to make that fact clear in their minds, and they will at once understand how completely Paul is the messenger of Jesus, how entirely the Divine message has taken possession of his nature and his whole being, how thoroughly the Gospel that he brought them in the beginning was the

[1] The evidence of Lucian, *de dea Syria*, 59, about the temple slaves at Syrian Hierapolis, may be taken as proof of a general custom.

[2] See p. 84.

Divine Word, how necessary it is for them to come back to that first Gospel.

To understand this verse you must grasp the Epistle in its entirety. You must feel that it is not a carefully framed series of sentences and paragraphs, but is an absolute unity, a single expression, a crystallisation of Paul's mind at a moment of intense feeling, or (to change the metaphor) a volcanic flood of thought poured forth in one moment and in one effort.

It was said above (p. 288 f.) that II 1-10 is really a single sentence. One might almost say that the whole Epistle is really a single sentence. You feel at the point we have now reached that the Epistle is like a living organism, so fully conscious that every part feels and vibrates to the slightest touch on any other part. It is the word of Paul ; and one remembers that, as Plato says, word is spoken thought, thought unspoken word.

But, in order to approach to understanding VI 17, we must hold together in our mind especially I 8-12, 15 f., II 19 f., IV 12-20.

LXIV

RESULT OF THE EPISTLE.

So ends this unique and marvellous letter, which embraces in its six short chapters such a variety of vehement and intense emotions as could probably not be paralleled in any other work. It lays bare and open in the most extraordinary degree the nature both of the writer and of the readers.

And this letter is pronounced by some of our friends in

Europe to be an accretion of scraps round and between bits of genuine original Pauline writing. How blind and dead to all sense of literature and to all knowledge of life and human nature must the man be who so judges—a mere pedant confined within the narrow walls and the close atmosphere of a schoolroom and a study!

To argue with such critics—happily, for the credit of modern scholarship, a hardly perceptible remnant—would be as absurd as it would have been for Paul to employ to the Galatians a series of arguments addressed to the intellect. In such cases one must see and feel. Those who cannot see and feel for themselves cannot be reached by argument. You must kindle in them life and power. Paul could do that for the Galatians. Who will do it in the present day?

What was the result of the letter to the Galatians? Was it a success or a failure?

It has been suggested by some North Galatian theorists, in explanation of the silence of the historian Luke about their supposed Churches of North Galatia, that the Epistle was a failure, that the Churches of Galatia were lost to Paulinistic Christianity, and that the painful episode was passed over lightly by a historian whose sympathies were so strongly on Paul's side.

That is the only serious and reasonable attempt to explain the silence of Luke as to the North Galatian Churches. The customary explanation, that the silence is merely one more of the strange gaps that seem to North Galatian theorists to be the most remarkable feature in the Acts, is really an appeal to unreason. Almost all the supposed gaps are the result of the North Galatian theory, directly or indirectly, and have no existence when that theory is discarded; and the rest have been shown to be due to some other misapprehension.[1] The "Gap-theory" first creates the gaps, and then infers that the historian cannot be judged according to the ordinary rules because his work is full of " gaps ". In regard to any other historian of good rank and class, the principle is admitted that an interpretation which rests on the supposition of an unintelligible gap must yield to an explanation which shows order and method and purpose ruling in the work.

But the explanation quoted above is reasonable, and calls for serious consideration. It does not, however, stand the test of careful dispassionate examination.

The confidence that Paul expresses as to the issue, V 10, is not a hasty and rash trust in his own power. It comes out at the close of a careful weighing of the situation, in which Paul looks into the hearts of his old converts, and reaches the full certainty and knowledge that he has them with him. His knowledge of human nature gives him the confidence that he expresses.

Moreover, the history of Christianity in Asia Minor during the immediately following period shows that the victory was won once and for ever. The question never again emerges. A few years later, we see what was the state of another Phrygian Church, that of Colossæ, in which Judaic influence was very strong. But it is clear that the Galatian difficulty never affected them. The Epistle to the Colossians is " specially anti-Judaistic,"[2] but there is nothing in it to suggest that they had ever thought of the Mosaic Law as binding on them, That point had been definitely settled; and the Judaistic tendency had taken another and more subtle direction. The Judaic rules and

---

[1] *St. Paul the Trav.*, *passim.*

[2] Hort, *Romans and Ephesians*, p. 192.

prohibitions did not appear to the Colossians as imperative commands of God which must be obeyed, but as philosophic principles which appealed to their intellect and reason.

But if the first Pauline Churches that were attacked had accepted and endorsed the principle that the Mosaic Law was binding on them, their example would have been a serious danger to the neighbouring Phrygian Churches of the Lycus valley, and could hardly have failed to secure at least careful attention for the view which they had accepted.

Finally, to regard this letter as unsuccessful is to despair of Paul. The letter, with its commanding and almost autocratic tone—though I feel and confess that these adjectives are too strong, and ignore the emotion, and sympathy, and love which breathe through the words and take much of the sting from them—is one that could be justified only by success. If it failed, then it deserved to fail. No man has any right to use such a tone to other men, unless it is the suitable and best tone for their good ; and the issue is the only test whether it was suitable and best. Paul's knowledge of human nature in his converts is staked on the success of the letter. See § XI.

Is it not clear, then, that Paul's appeal succeeded? The letter fulfilled its purpose of rekindling the old feelings in the Galatic Churches. Paul's confident expectation was justified. Acts completes the natural result of the Epistle. Soon after, the effect was confirmed by Paul's personal presence [1] among these Galatians : he went through Galatic Lycaonia and Galatic Phrygia in order from first to last, " stablishing all the disciples " (Acts XVIII 23), see p. 404.

---

[1] Accompanied, as I believe, by Titus : *St. Paul the Trav.*, p. 285.

The great struggle was won; the religion of the first
Roman province on the road to the West was determined
as free and non-Judaistic; and that meant that the religion
of the Roman Empire was determined.   Can we doubt
that this struggle was critical and decisive?   If Paul had
been vanquished in the first Province that he entered, and
in the first Churches that he founded, he would have been
vanquished definitely; but the first great victory made the
remaining stages easier.   It is obvious that the Church in
Corinth passed through a Judaic struggle, but that it
surmounted it far more easily.   So with the Churches of
Asia.   They were distinctively free and Pauline in character;
and it is evident that the Galatic struggle was practically
conclusive for them.

Taken in conjunction with later evidence, we can thus
make some steps towards a picture of Christian and Jewish-
Christian history in Asia Minor.   But on the North Galatian theory the issue of the Epistle remains as obscure as
the Churches to which it was addressed.   The Churches
are created to receive the Epistle.   After it is received they
vanish, and leave not a trace behind.

Note.—It was intended to add a discussion of some technical
points, especially the geographical sense of *Galaticus;* but the effects
of an accident in September, 1899, made it impossible to complete
the notes.   Some references forward to the intended notes remain
in the text.   It is said that Mr. Askwith treats the phrase τὴν Φρυγίαν
καὶ Γαλατικὴν χώραν skilfully; but I have not seen his recent book.